101 951 628 3

A **phoenix** is a mythical bird with a colourful plumage and a tail of gold and scarlet. It has up to a 1,000-year life cycle, near the end of which it builds itself a nest of twigs that then ignites; both nest and bird are reduced to ashes, from which a new, young phoenix is reborn. The new phoenix is destined to live as long as its old self.

Adapted from *The phoenix and the carpet* by E. Nesbitt,

ONE WEEK LOAN

1 0 FEB 2011

2 1 FEB 2011

D1338719

PHOENIX CITIES

SHEFFIELD HALLAM UNIVERSITY
LEARNING CENTRE
WITHDRAWN FROM STOCK

The fall and rise of great industrial cities

Anne Power, Jörg Plöger and Astrid Winkler

JOSEPH ROWNTREE
FOUNDATION

This edition published in Great Britain in 2010 by

The Policy Press
University of Bristol
Fourth Floor
Beacon House
Queen's Road
Bristol BS8 1QU
UK
t: +44 (0)117 331 4054
f: +44 (0)117 331 4093
e: tpp-info@bristol.ac.uk
www.policypress.co.uk

North American office:
The Policy Press
c/o International Specialized Books Services
920 NE 58th Avenue, Suite 300
Portland, OR 97213-3786, USA
t: +1 503 287 3093
f: +1 503 280 8832
e: info@isbs.com

© London School of Economics and Political Science 2010

British Library Cataloguing in Publication Data
A catalogue record for this book is available from the British Library.

Library of Congress Cataloging-in-Publication Data
A catalog record for this book has been requested.

ISBN 978 1 84742 683 3 paperback

The right of Anne Power, Jörg Plöger and Astrid Winkler to be identified as authors of
this work has been asserted by them in accordance with the 1988 Copyright, Designs and
Patents Act.

All rights reserved: no part of this publication may be reproduced, stored in a retrieval
system, or transmitted in any form or by any means, electronic, mechanical, photocopying,
recording, or otherwise without the prior permission of The Policy Press.

The statements and opinions contained within this publication are solely those of the
authors and not of the Joseph Rowntree Foundation, the University of Bristol or The
Policy Press. The Joseph Rowntree Foundation, the University of Bristol and The Policy
Press disclaim responsibility for any injury to persons or property resulting from any
material published in this publication.

The Policy Press works to counter discrimination on grounds
of gender, race, disability, age and sexuality.

Cover design by The Policy Press
Front cover: image kindly supplied by www.alamy.com
Printed and bound in Great Britain by The Charlesworth Group, Wakefield

Contents

List of figures, tables and boxes

Figures

Tables

Boxes

List of acronyms

ANRU	*Agence Nationale pour la Rénovation Urbaine* (National Agency for Urban Renovation)
BIG	*Bremer Investitions-Gesellschaft mbH* (Bremen Investment Agency)
CBD	central business district
CDC	community development corporation
CMSA	consolidated metropolitan statistical area
GDP	gross domestic product
GEMS	Gasworks Employment Matching Service
GVA	gross value added
HLM	*habitation à loyer modéré* (rent-controlled housing)
ISP	*Investitionssonderprogramm* (Special Investment Programme)
MSA	metropolitan statistical area
Peace III	European Union Programme for Peace and Reconciliation in Northern Ireland and the Border Region of Ireland
SCoT	*Schéma de Cohérence Térritoriale* (Framework for Regional Coherence)
UDC	urban development corporation
WiN	*Wohnen in Nachbarschaften* (Living in Neighbourhoods)
ZFU	*zone franches urbaine* (urban-free zone)
ZRU	*zone de redynamisation urbaine* (urban redynamisation zone)
ZUS	*zone urbaine sensible* (fragile urban zone)

Acknowledgements

We wish to thank the Joseph Rowntree Foundation for their generous funding of this work over three years, their encouragement and support, and their assistance with this publication. In particular, Katharine Knox has acted as constant adviser throughout this very complex project.

We must also thank the British government, the European Union, the German government, the Caisse des Dépôts and the Basque provincial government for their continuous involvement and contributions.

A particularly heavy debt is owed to the seven cities, their leaders, deliverers and reformers. Without them, we would never have carried out this study. In particular, we must thank Oliver Weigel, Massimo Bricocoli, Jörn Ehmke, Stephan Muzika, Rachid Kaddour, Sylvie Harburger, Gianfranco Presutti, Giovanni Magnano, Andrea Bocco, Elisa Rosso, Juan Alayo, Mikel Candina-Villar, Bob Kerslake, Marie-Therese McGivern and Ulrich Pfeiffer, who have all helped us throughout the three years.

We received special inputs from the Joseph Rowntree Foundation's policy advisory group. Other inputs are too numerous to mention but we are grateful to them all while accepting full responsibility for inaccuracies and mistakes.

For helping us prepare this book, our earlier reports and for organising the four international workshops, we must thank Laura Lane, Nicola Serle, Anna Tamas, Abenaa Owusu-Bempah, Olga Gora, Caroline Paskell, Catalina Turcu and Jane Dickson. Finally, and most importantly, we want to thank the Brookings Institution Metropolitan Policy Program, Washington DC, Bruce Katz, Jennifer Vey, Alan Berube and Marikka Green in particular, for collaborating closely throughout, providing exhaustive evidence on the US experience and for shedding new light on the struggle towards recovery of the weak market cities.

Copyright material

We gratefully acknowledge the permission granted to reproduce the copyright material in this book. All reasonable efforts have been made to identify the holders of copyright material and to obtain permission for their use. If we have unwittingly infringed any copyright, we apologise sincerely and would appreciate being corrected.

Sources: Figure 2.1a: http://vagabondages.cpa.free.fr/22/index.htm; Figure 2.1b: http://vagabondages. cpa.free.fr/22/index.htm; Figure 2.2: http://vagabondages.cpa.free.fr/22/index.htm; Figure 2.3: www. simplonpc.co.uk/2WhiteStar/Titanic-02.jpg; Figure 2.5: www.aukevisser.nl/supertankers/; Figure 2.10: Juan Alayo at City Reformers Group 1 at LSE, March 2006; Figure 2.11: http://libcom.org/library/20-years-since-the-great-coal-strike-of-1984-1985-dave-douglassome.htm; Figure 2.12: www.time.com/time/world/article/0,8599,1726385,00.html; Figure 2.14: Stadt Leipzig; Figure 2.15: Stadt Leipzig; Figure 3.7: www.neue-harth.de/nh/neuseenland/cospudenersee/; Figure 3.12: www.dlr.de/iss/en/desktopdefault. aspx/tabid-4410/7315_read-4019/gallery-1/gallery_read-Image.19.2051/; Figure 4.10b: www.bilbao.net/ lanekintza/; Figure 5.1: http://europa.eu/abc/maps/members/germany_en.htm; Figure 5.2: http://europa. eu/abc/maps/regions/germany/sachsen_en.htm; Figure 5.4: http://lexikon.freenet.de/images/de/0/01/ Bucket_wheel_excavator_in_Ferropolis.jpg; Figure 5.5: http://shop.alte-ansichtskarten.com; Figure 5.6: http://einestages.spiegel.de/static/entry/_wir_sind_das_volk/1618/demonstrationszug_am_leipziger_ring. html?o=position-ASCENDING&s=11&r=1&a=372&c=1; Figure 5.8: UFZ Leipzig www.ufz.de/; Figure 6.1: European Commission; Figure 6.3a/b: Bremen Atlas, 2006; Figure 6.7: Bremer Investitionsgesellschaft (BIG) (2004) Überseestadt Bremen. Projekte-Flächen-Nutzungskonzepte; Figure 7.1: http://europa.eu/abc/ maps/members/uk_en.htm; Figure 7.2: http://europa.eu/abc/maps/regions/uk/yorks_en.htm; Figure 7.3: Watts, 2004; Figure 7.6: Source: Josvig, 1968; Figure 7.7: ONS (2001); Watts (2004); Figure 7.8: www.sheffield-fm.co.uk/meersbrook_park.htm; Figure 7.9: Urban Splash, Park Hill. Photographer: Jan Chlebik, Image ID: PARK_000, ©Jan Chlebik Photography; Figure 7.10: Dabinett and Ramsden, 1993; Figure 7.11: Sheffield City Council, 2007; Figure 7.12: Kerslake, 2005; Figure 7.14: Sheffield One, 2001; Figure 7.15: ONS, 2001; Watts, 2004; Figure 7.17: www.itcyorkshire.com/image/upload/amrc per cent20facto.jpg; Figure 8.1: http://europa. eu/abc/maps/members/uk_en.htm; Figure 8.2: http://europa.eu/abc/maps/regions/uk/nthire_en.htm; Figure 8.3: www.rediscoverni.com; Figure 8.10: Boal, 2006, p 75; Figure 8.16: Belfast City Council (online); Figure 9.1: http://europa.eu/abc/maps/members/spain_en.htm; Figure 9.2: http://europa.eu/abc/maps/regions/spain/ pais_en.htm; Figure 9.5: Juan Alayo (from presentation at CRG I, March 2006); Figure 9.6: Port of Bilbao, 2005 (modified by authors); Figure 9.10: Juan Alayo (from presentation at CRG I, March 2006); Figure 9.16: Juan Alayo (from presentation at CRG I, March 2006); Figure 10.1: European Commission; Figure 10.2: http:// europa.eu/abc/maps/regions/italy/piemonte_en.htm; Figure 10.3: www.polygraphicum.de; Figure 10.4: www. jobmagazine.net/citta/torinopalazzo.jpg; Figure 10.5: www.kennell.it/schedaLINGOTTOstoria.htm; Figure 10.6: www.autoblog.it/post/4677/fiat-500-e-lauto-piu-sexy-del-mondo; Figure 10.7: www.uil.it/Cronologia. html; Figure 10.9: Officina Città Torino; Figure 10.10: www.noviconsult.it/; Figure 10.20: www.docushare.it/ mediasoft/italy/piemonte/images/torino_piemonte.jpg; Figure 11.1: http://europa.eu/abc/maps/members/ france_en.htm; Figure 11.2: http://europa.eu/abc/maps/regions/france/rhone_en.htm; Figure 11.3: http:// vagabondages.cpa.free.fr/22/index.htm; Figure 11.4: Archives Municipales de Saint Étienne; Figure 11.7: www.forez-info.com/photo/thumbnails.php?album=34; Figure 11.7: www.forez-info.com/photo/thumbnails. php?album=34; Figure 11.8: Ville de Saint-Étienne; Figure 11.11: Saint-Étienne Métropole; Figure 11.12: Alain Fayard; Figure 11.13: Foster + Partners; Figure 11.14: Saint-Étienne Métropole; Figure 13.1: http:// maps.google.co.uk (adapted); Figure 14.3: http://en.wikipedia.org/wiki/Inner_Harbor; Figure 14.5: City of Baltimore, Department of Planning; Figure 14.6: www.ci.baltimore.md.us/neighborhoods/snap/typology. html; Figure 14.8: www.trfund.com/planning/market-phila.html; Figure 14.11: http://en.wikipedia.org/wiki/ File:LouisvilleDowntownSkyline2.jpg; Figure 14.12: http://wikitravel.org/en/Image:WalnutStreetBridgeCha ttanoogaTN.jpg); Figure 14.13: http://wikitravel.org/upload/shared/3/38/Ohio-U_of_A-Polymer_Science_ Bldg.jpg; Figure 16.4: www.moneyvsdebt.com/2008/01/28/huge-kite-helps-containership-across-atlantic/; Figure 16.6: Veolia Environmental Services District Energy Network, Sheffield; Figure 16.7: www.spiegel.de/ international/business/0,1518,grossbild-959122-532917,00.html

Part One
The tale of seven cities

ONE

Introduction: what are 'weak market cities'?

Weak market cities are cities that have experienced acute loss of purpose over the last generation, going from urban industrial giants to shadows of their former glory and pre-eminence.[1] Their loss of viability and purpose in the 1970s, 1980s and 1990s has undermined national economies, threatened social stability and exposed the fragility of the earth's eco-systems.

Across Europe, for 200 years, from the mid–18th to the mid–20th century, there was unprecedented urban growth and industrial expansion, centred around areas of easily exploitable natural resources such as coal, iron and water. A tradition of craft and trade alongside other historic assets, such as location on major river systems, facilitated new inventions and rapid industrialisation in particular towns, which rapidly expanded into cities. The extraction and conversion of natural resources such as water, wood, coal, iron and other metals, led to a manufacturing economy based on machine engineering, textiles, tools, shipbuilding and many other forms of mass production. This created a huge range of domestic as well as industrial goods. These new industrial cities were at the core of the industrial revolution and dominated European economies until the late 20th century.

The concentrations of new-found wealth in cities, the emergence of new professions and a fast-growing middle class led to a parallel growth in need and inequality that forced the creation of totally new systems of local government in 19th-century industrial cities.[2] Urban growth led to major social and economic transformations, creating pressures on the environment, physical infrastructure, family life, social relations and governance that had no precedent.[3] As a result of vast internal and international movements of people as well as goods and materials, industrial cities generated forms of squalor, disease, overcrowding and social dislocation previously unknown.

The four most direct consequences for industrial cities in Europe were:

- intense concentrations of wealth in the hands of owners of property and production systems;
- a steep rise in the manufacturing labour force;
- the growth of political and social movements that shaped European and world democracy;
- an increase in public services, civic activity and the expansion of universal education, transforming citizen engagement and human potential.

On the other hand, there were four disastrous consequences of this dramatic new growth:

- significant environmental degradation of urban spaces and surrounding countryside through industrial smoke stacks, slum housing, chemical outpourings and concentrated human waste;
- depletion of the natural resources that fuelled the industrial revolution;
- economic and social upheaval that accelerated eventual industrial decline;
- large concentrations of people and buildings whose earlier functions and roles became increasingly redundant in the latter decades of the 20th century as a result of resource depletion.[4]

The production systems that drove European industrial expansion transferred to other, cheaper, and as yet, under-exploited places, and industrial cities went through a period of steep decline from which they only began to emerge at the turn of the 21st century. They now face a completely new set of challenges resulting from the legacy of the 'old economy' and the unravelling of the 'new economy' based around high-tech, service and knowledge industries. The virtual collapses in the 'free market' operations of international banking, and the latest evidence on the impact of human activity on the environment tightly constrain the scope for hard-hit cities to continue their recent progress towards recovery. We will consider these relatively recent developments and their likely impacts later in the book, after tracing the industrial and post-industrial experience of seven European cities, famed for their inventions, products and explosive, exuberant growth.

Why did cities all over the West hit such acute problems, following a period of unprecedented wealth creation and expansion? Three major changes in the international economic order accelerated the process of decline of former industrial cities:

- The *oil crisis of 1973* and the steep rise in the price of energy hit energy-intensive industries particularly hard, causing chain effects throughout industrial economies. The accumulation of pressures and costs were most serious in those industrial cities whose wealth relied on cheap, plentiful energy.
- The *opening of European markets to global trade*, a long-run consequence of modern economic expansion, created intense trade competition, both within the fast evolving European Union (EU) and globally, as former colonies and less developed economies grew, and learned to produce more cheaply the goods that these older cities had thrived on. The rapid emergence of cheap industrial production centres in the developing world, particularly in eastern Asia, undercut European industry.
- The *misuse of the environment* on which cities depend and the over-exploitation of the natural resources that drive industrial growth, such as coal, water and iron, led to losses and damage that destroyed the image of these once enviable cities, making them deeply uncompetitive.[5]

The cumulative impact of over-exuberant growth and changes in the international order eventually led to the collapse of cities across Europe and the United States.

Learning from Europe and the US

This study is the outcome of three years spent tracking the fortunes of seven cities across Europe, uncovering the actual experience of these former industrial centres and their populations as they build a new post-industrial future. The wider framework within which their decline has occurred is the subject of many other urban studies,[6] and by examining the wider economic processes as they impact on local economies, we learn that the two processes, one local at city level, the other global at an international level, are deeply interconnected. In the EU, there are over 300 cities sharing an industrial past. Even relatively non-industrial cities were eventually caught up in the processes of modern production.[7]

In a parallel study, the Brookings Institution in Washington is examining cities experiencing similar acute industrial decline, concentrated in the 'rust belt' states on the eastern seaboard and the mid-west of the US. There are around 160 older industrial cities in these 'older' regions of the US, generally referred to as the 'rust belt', but to some extent many of the more recently growing cities with industrial sectors in the 'sun belt', such as Atlanta and Dallas, also show telling signs of reaching their environmental and physical limits. The Brookings Institution has described the problem of weak market cities, or 'core cities' as they now tend to call them, in the following way:

> Metropolitan areas both in Europe and America have become characterized by population and employment decentralization and racial and economic separation. As a result, core cities must continually grapple with a series of challenges that undermine their ability to attract and retain the skilled workforce and new growth industries needed to create a better economic future. These challenges include loss of home value and equity, diminishing tax base, large-scale vacant and abandoned property, concentrated poverty, and a low-educated workforce.[8]

'Weak market cities' in the US have been renamed 'core cities' to underline the key role they can play in the future. Our findings from seven European case study cities are matched by findings from six US former industrial cities, showing the parallel experiences of decline and some contrasting outcomes.

The seven European cities included in this study are Leipzig and Bremen (Germany), Sheffield and Belfast (UK), Bilbao (Spain), Torino (Italy) and Saint-Étienne (France). The US cities we look at in parallel are: Philadelphia (PA), Pittsburgh (PA), Baltimore (MD), Louisville (KY), Chattanooga (TN) and Akron (OH). All the cities were chosen because of three characteristics:

- rapid growth and intense wealth-creation on the back of heavy industry;
- their common experience of severe job and population losses due to the decline of manufacturing;
- their inventive recovery efforts.

Two German cities were included in order to reflect the post-communist transition in eastern Europe to a west European market model; and two UK cities were included to reflect the significance of Ireland and the regional distinctiveness of the different countries of the UK. Although the study focuses on Europe, it does draw on US experience where possible. The direct experiences we recount from recovering cities can help policy makers at city, regional, national and European levels to understand how intense urban problems arise and continue, and what progress is possible in overcoming them. It will also shed some light on sharp differences with US urban policy and directions.

The study focuses on three related questions:

- What are the causes of decline in European weak market cities?
- What recovery measures are cities adopting to combat the consequences of such steep decline?
- What progress is being made as a result of these measures and what are the outstanding challenges?

We draw on ground-level experience, collected from within the seven cities, offering a cross-section of perspectives on the problems and ways of resolving them. One important way of expanding our understanding of what is really happening has been to develop practical and policy-oriented exchanges between key actors from the seven cities. These exchanges allowed city policy makers and practitioners attempting to secure urban recovery to share their experiences and to learn from the wider problems facing other cities. The exchanges included European representatives, US cities, the Brookings Institution and the Joseph Rowntree Foundation (the main funder of the project). By linking recovering ex-industrial cities from across Europe, with US counterparts, we were able to learn much about their progress and problems that otherwise would have remained buried within the lived experiences of each city. Our work draws heavily on the evidence that city reformers presented during six international exchanges, as well as during visits to the cities. The book should be relevant to city-level policy makers and practitioners, both in Europe and the US. It should help ground decisions at government and international levels on both sides of the Atlantic, and it should shed new light on sometimes dry academic debates about growth and decline.

Hotbeds of social, economic and environmental transformation

A defining characteristic of the core cities that later became weak market cities is the sheer scale of devastation wreaked by the explosion of industrial invention, unprecedented growth in production, destructive exploitation of natural assets and total transformation of social structures. Each of these four aspects of the breakthrough into modern economic, social and environmental conditions simultaneously underpinned unprecedented wealth creation and caused havoc with established patterns of development. As we look back into the history of industrial cities, we find majestic achievements built on the back of dire poverty, filth and degradation, reaching far into their still rural hinterland. They were all too soon to run out of the wealth-creating energy and labour they so readily fed on as they raced for growth.

Eventually, this tumultuous overgrowth and exploitation caused industrial power itself to decline and eventually pushed these cities into a crisis of non-viability – costs were too high; raw materials too short; labour too powerful and expensive; and the environment ransacked. One by one, country by country, industries closed, order was threatened and the poisoned land and waterways fell idle. In time, people left cities if they could, not to be replaced. It is a shocking story of human degradation and waste that still comes back to haunt us, but it is also an impressive story of attempts to rise above these problems and to create new ways of dealing with them.

The economic rationale for European industrial hotbeds had passed, so the value of the vast industrial infrastructure plummeted. The decline of the physical aspects of the cities followed on from industrial closures and the loss of economic investments. This in turn accelerated the decline in social and environmental conditions. Environmental problems and the decay of the built environment went together with economic failure because it was the loss of viable and productively conserved natural and built environments that accelerated the final demise of major manufacturing centres.

Yet the fascination of this study is that old industrial cities, wrecked by closures and loss of purpose, over a short generation, began to reinvent themselves. In city after city, new ideas were tried and new ways forward were found. Our perspective on the prospects for recovery of former industrial cities is driven both by lessons from the past and by the dual global financial and environmental crises they now face. Only by seeing these twin crises as linked will we understand the new environmental imperatives underpinning our future prosperity.[9] Three interacting elements will allow these cities to recover: their *economies*, on which jobs and population retention depend; their *social conditions*, which require a level of stability and security that vanished with their failing industries; and their *physical environments*, which were deeply scarred by the growth in wealth but which nonetheless contain invaluable recoverable assets.[10] We ignore these interactions at our peril, as the leadership in the US and China are now realising, and the United Nations (UN) first accepted at the environmental summit in Rio de Janeiro in 1999.[11]

Outline of the book

The book is divided into five parts. **Part One** describes the historic importance and industrial dominance of the cities in the 19th and 20th centuries; it details the economic and social collapse that followed from the loss of this wealth-creating power base; and it explores the ways the cities chose to forge new roles, to uncover new routes forward and to build new industries. It includes important new evidence about the small-scale neighbourhood-based efforts to tackle social disintegration, segregation and alienation, showing neighbourhood renewal, community-based organisation and skills transformation as powerful tools for change. **Part Two** provides case studies of the seven European cities. **Part Three** sets out a framework for assessing the recovery trajectories of the seven cities. **Part Four** offers a look at the US counterpart cities. **Part Five** links the fortunes of industrial cities with the resource-constrained limits of their future. It concludes with the optimistic view that these cities point to a more sustainable way forward for cities, and more generally for the planet.

The research is grounded in the lived experience of the cities, seen at close quarters in sharply contrasting settings, therefore each city's own story offers unique insight into the lessons that could be drawn, based not only on statistical evidence but also on the fine-grained realities, often missed in higher level figures. Our US evidence is similarly grounded in visits to the actual cities and the research carried out in the cities by the Brookings Metropolitan team.

The long-term prospects for the cities are tempered by caution about the frightening uncertainties, particularly around their economies, jobs, resource limits and climate change impacts. Nonetheless, through traumatic economic shocks, city leaders and innovators have pieced together new ways of doing things that have put weak market cities back on the map as asset-rich engines of a new and different kind of growth. Burgeoning cities around the globe can learn from their harsh and hard-won experience. The next chapter examines the rapid rise to dominance of the seven cities.

TWO

Industrial giants: emerging on the back of history

Introduction

To understand the challenges facing former industrial cities today, we need to grasp the essential threads of their history and role in building their countries' wealth. Their fall from a great height made their recovery all the more unlikely. The seven cities, Leipzig, Bremen, Sheffield, Belfast, Bilbao, Torino and Saint-Étienne, played an important part in their country's history even before the industrial revolution. Five of the seven cities occupied strategic crossing points on earlier international trading routes. For example, Torino was historically a major European centre, as a gateway to Italy through the Alps. It became the capital of the powerful Duchy of Savoy in the mid-16th century, and its Baroque city centre is still one of Torino's most important assets. Leipzig was located at another European crossroad and became the crossing point between eastern and western Europe for medieval trade fares. It has recreated this role today. Bremen was one of only three German city-states, a member of the powerful Hanseatic League. Bilbao was the major port for the ancient Basque nation, a great sea-faring people. And Belfast, originally a Viking port, became the vital capital city of a province of the UK that would dominate much of our modern history. The two, purely industrial cities of Sheffield and Saint-Étienne, produced pre-industrial iron-based and craft goods, becoming famous for their production at the advent of the industrial revolution. Table 2.1 summarises these diverse roles.

The seven cities played many different, intrinsically transforming industrial tasks over the period of Europe's greatest manufacturing growth in the 19th and 20th centuries. These cities came to dominate national economies as a result of their prolific output and transforming contributions for more than 150 years. They were the hubs of the new economy, the new politics and new urban forms. Their rich resources, natural harbours and trading routes, trans-continental gateways and political leadership catapulted them to the forefront of their national economies in the 19th century.

The seven cities became industrial giants, building on their strategic and productive advantages. They became internationally renowned for spawning the biggest, most powerful industries and inventing the most dramatic breakthroughs in modern production, as the world rapidly industrialised. The economic power of these cities seemed for a long time to be invincible. For example, Manufrance was founded as a simple arms workshop in Saint-Étienne in the 1880s, but soon grew into a pioneering mail order business, making guns, bicycles, sewing

Table 2.1: Historic roles

Leipzig	At the crossroads of major trading routes between Eastern and Western Europe; centre for historic international trade fairs; home to Bach and Goethe; houses one of Germany's oldest universities
Bremen	City-state and port. Member of the prosperous medieval Hanseatic League
Sheffield	Medieval metal-working district and centre for early cutlery manufacturing; close to major coalfields
Belfast	Nearest Irish port to Britain; main centre of British domination; strong links with Scotland due to short sea ferry; early linen production; shipbuilding
Bilbao	Historic port for early trans-Atlantic trade; early iron extraction; early banking centre for the trade-oriented independent Basque Country
Torino	Gateway city through Alps; capital of the princely state of Savoy from the 16th century; developed a textile industry during the 19th century, and became the first capital of a united Italy in 1861
Saint-Étienne	Medieval centre for arms manufacturing and later ribbon making; early coal and iron extraction; site of France's first coal mines; starting point for continental Europe's first railway line, built in 1827

machines and many other machine-based products that were sold nationwide and beyond (see Figures 2.1a-b). The huge factory was a symbol of Saint-Étienne's industrial pre-eminence, eventually becoming a state-owned survivor in the 1980s. Likewise, steel in Sheffield and shipbuilding in Belfast eventually fell under the wing of national governments, receiving huge subsidies as a result of their economic significance and the national threat posed by their decline. Table 2.2 underlines the scale of the industrial might of the seven cities, showing the specific manufacturing strengths of each city.

The functions, financial foundations and physical form of the cities were transformed through the demands of growth. Each city became highly specialised, developing a series of secondary services to back up and feed into high-value, high-volume industrial production.

Figures 2.1a-b: (a) The emblematic Manufrance factory, 1890s; (b) Bicycle frame and wheel assembly at the Manufrance factory

Table 2.2: Industrial giants

Leipzig	Open-cast coalmining and other extractive industries; most important railway centre in Central Europe, building on trading history, engineering and chemical industries
Bremen	Major shipping port for raw materials, industrial goods and internal shipping; important ship building and engineering centre; developed early aircraft industry and engineering
Sheffield	Became the world's major steel production centre.; specialised in cutlery manufacturing, spawning innovations, including stainless steel and silver plating techniques
Belfast	Big centre for industrial production of textiles (linen) and ships. Also strong engineering centre. Harland & Wolff, which built the *RMS Titanic*, was once the biggest shipbuilding company of the world
Bilbao	Coal carried along the coast from Asturias and iron extracted from mountainous surroundings turned Bilbao into the richest manufacturing, engineering and ship building centre of north Spain
Torino	Centre of early modern communications, e.g. typewriters. Pioneered development of electricity for production and harnessed hydropower from Alps to fuel industrial growth after losing administrative function as Italy's first capital. Also imported Fordist mass manufacturing techniques from the US so Fiat became one of the world's leading car manufacturers
Saint-Étienne	Biggest arms manufacturer in France; built the first steam trains and bicycles

Their contribution to the national wealth and prestige grew in proportion to the sheer scale of their own growth and the innovative nature of their products. Governments often directly supported their expansion through investment in infrastructure and also eventually through state ownership of industrial enterprises. However, most of the growth was internally generated, based on the rich primary materials (iron) and energy sources (coal and water) nearby. Sheffield invented silver plating and stainless steel through the most advanced metal engineering processes in the world. It became the leading producer of knives, blades, tools and cutlery. Belfast's Harland & Wolff, the world's largest shipyard around 1890, built the biggest ever ocean liner, *RMS Titanic* (see Figure 2.3). This great ship became lastingly famous for sinking on its maiden Atlantic voyage after colliding with an iceberg. Symbolically, it was too large to manoeuvre quickly enough, marking the beginning of the end of overgrown industry. Table 2.3 shows how these cities became centres of national importance and attracted investors, inventors and labourers from near and far.

Population growth and shrinkage

The large influxes of population to work in fast-developing industries showed in the steep rise in the size of the cities. Throughout the 19th and early 20th century, the population of these seven cities doubled, tripled, quadrupled. In the case of Torino, it multiplied twelvefold. However, Leipzig was the first city to begin a steady path of decline at the outset of the Second World War. The growth of Belfast and Sheffield levelled off in the inter-war years, but only began to decline in the 1970s; the population for the other cities declined from the 1970s

Table 2.3: Major national power houses of growth and invention

Leipzig	International trade fairs, expanded importance of commercial role with post-war communist-driven industrial growth; the city played an important role in the Deutsche Demokratische Republik
Bremen	One of the three city-states in post-war Germany; strategic role of the port
Sheffield	So important were steel and coal, the backbone of the UK's economy, that both were nationalised, projecting Sheffield to centre stage in the UK's political economy.
Belfast	Belfast for British governments was a capital city in a small but vital province, receiving huge investment in comparison with Scotland and Wales
Bilbao	The Basque region became the richest in Spain under Franco, in spite of Basque resistance; Bilbao was by far the richest and most powerful centre
Torino	The Agnelli Family, founders of the Fiat car manufacturer, dominated not only Torino but also the post-war Italian political scene and had huge patronage and clout; Torino became a 'one-company town'
Saint-Étienne	Saint-Étienne likewise was so important to France that its arms manufacturer was state owned and its related industries were considered of national political as well as of economic importance

Figure 2.2: Industrial giants: the Imperial Arms Factory, 1894 (Saint-Étienne)

Figure 2.3: Industrial giants: the new White Star Line *RMS Titanic* nearing completion in the largest graying dock in the world, 1912 (Belfast)

onwards, except Bilbao, which held up until the 1980s and then declined. Figure 2.4 illustrates these trends.

A close look at Figure 2.4 shows distinctive patterns of population growth and decline in different cities, with Torino growing most dramatically and ending up with a population double the size of the other cities. Leipzig grew extremely fast between 1880 and 1940. It declined steeply until the turn of the 21st century, when its fortunes began to turn. Bremen grew until 1970 and then experienced only slow decline. Bilbao meanwhile went into slow reverse only in the 1980s. Belfast, Sheffield and Saint-Étienne stagnated for decades until the oil crisis set in during the 1970s. In spite of these differences the overall pattern of rapid population growth followed by slower decline is clearly recognisable in all the cities. The population changes were largely driven by the exploding then declining economies.

Figure 2.4: Historic population development trends in the seven cities, 1350–2005

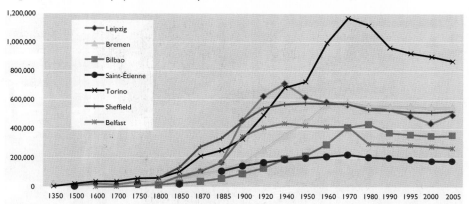

Note: Graphs start at first record of data.
Source: National and regional statistical bureaux

Decline in manufacturing

The 1970s proved a watershed for many European industries in the aftermath of high inflation, spiralling costs and loss of investor confidence, following the international oil crisis in 1973. As economic troubles bit deeper into Western economies in the late 1970s and early 1980s, they affected these cities particularly badly because their economies had become so dependent on manufacturing, even though in Bremen, Torino and Belfast, broader civic traditions, functions and responsibilities gave them a rationale beyond major industry. Cities such as Sheffield and Saint-Étienne struggled to find new roles, while Bilbao, as the most significant economic centre of the Basque region, retained a power base under the post-Franco regional settlement that ensured continuing strong support from the federal and regional governments. Leipzig, on the other hand, faced cataclysmic changes, beyond any other city in the study, with the demise of communism. Bilbao, Belfast and Leipzig all faced radical political upheavals simultaneously with their industrial problems, as they found themselves at the centre of much wider conflicts of national and international significance. While the context of each city was distinct, the pattern of industrial and post-industrial change was remarkably common to all the cities.

The decline, beginning at different times in different cities, hit all seven cities in broadly similar ways with the exception of Leipzig, where the powerful and authoritarian communist regime of the German Democratic Republic (DDR) artificially propped up failing industries until the collapse of the regime and the reunification of Germany in 1989. Torino numerically lost by far the most jobs over the critical 30 years of decline, from 1970 to 2000, but Leipzig experienced the most dramatic losses over the shortest period and in proportion was the hardest hit.

Figure 2.5: Giant shipyard, AG Weser (Bremen)

Manufacturing in 1970 still accounted for half or more of all jobs in four industrial cities: Torino, Sheffield, Saint-Étienne and Bilbao. In the other three, it was between 30% (Leipzig) and nearly 40% (Belfast). Table 2.4 and Figure 2.6 show the scale of job losses in manufacturing in each.

The proportion of manufacturing jobs lost over a 35-year period ranged between 30% to nearly 90% in Leipzig. Belfast and Sheffield did nearly as badly, losing three quarters of their industrial jobs. Certain working-class communities in the cities, traditionally supplying semi-skilled and unskilled labour to heavy

Table 2.4: Number of manufacturing jobs lost up to 2005

Cities	Period	Number of manufacturing jobs lost
Leipzig *(city)*	1989–1996	87,000
Bremen *(region: Land)*	1970–2003	55,000
Sheffield *(city)*	1971–2004	86,000
Belfast *(city)*	1973–2001	51,000
Bilbao *(metropolitan area: Gran Bilbao)*	1970–2001	56,000
Torino *(province)*	1971–2005	171,000
Saint-Étienne *(metropolitan area)*	1977–2001	29,000

Note: In all tables, charts and graphs, 'city' refers to the current administrative boundaries of the city. Where the wider metropolitan area is referred to, this is made clear.
Sources: Germany: Stat. Landesamt Sachsen; City of Leipzig; Stat. Landesamt Bremen; BAW Research Institute; UK: ONS; Nomis (2007); Sheffield City Council; NISRA; DFPNI; Spain: Eustat; Italy: ISTAT; France: INSEE; Assedic

Figure 2.6: Proportion of manufacturing job losses in each city, 1970 and 2005 (% of all manufacturing employment)

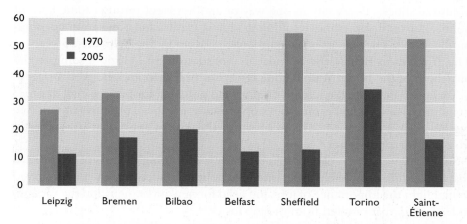

Sources: Stat. Landesamt Sachsen; City of Leipzig; Stat. Landesamt Bremen; BAW Research Institute; Eustat; INSEE; Assedic; ISTAT; ONS; Nomis (2004); Sheffield City Council; NISRA; DFP

Figure 2.7: Changes in the proportion of the city workforce in manufacturing employment, 1970–2005 (%)

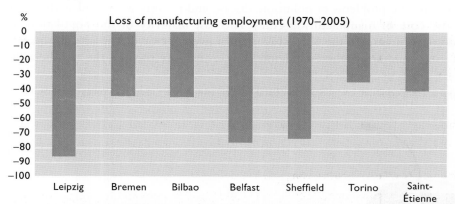

Note: All percentages are calculated from the baseline of the earliest date.
Sources: Germany: Stat. Landesamt Sachsen; City of Leipzig; Stat. Landesamt Bremen; BAW Research Institute; UK: ONS; Nomis (2007); Sheffield City Council; NISRA; DFPNI; Spain: Eustat; Italy: ISTAT; France: INSEE; Assedic

industry, were literally laid to waste in the decades of decline. Figure 2.7 shows the proportion of manufacturing jobs lost over this period, underlining the scale of change in patterns of employment as industries closed. The shift away from manufacturing led to extremely high overall unemployment levels in the cities for at least two decades following the crisis.

Over this period, the workforce moved out of manual jobs. Belfast, Leipzig and Sheffield now have the lowest shares of industrial jobs among the seven cities, with only just over 10% doing traditional industrial work; these cities have suffered the most dramatic shift away from manufacturing. In these cities, many political conflicts arose, and spilled over onto city streets, partly caused by industrial shocks. Every city in one way or another went through some kind of political turmoil, sometimes resulting in violent clashes and population uprisings on the streets. The miners' strike and police clashes in Sheffield, the 25 years of The Troubles in Belfast, the Monday demonstrations in Leipzig leading to the breaching of the Berlin Wall, Basque terrorism in Bilbao and the Red Brigades in Torino, all illustrate the intense disquiet and potential for massive civil disorder in industrial cities when economies stop growing and social pressures mount (see Figures 2.10, 2.11 and 2.12). Table 2.5 shows the type of unrest that arose directly from industrial job losses.

So serious were the problems that each city went through a crisis of confidence that for a while completely disoriented the political leadership. The unrest served to highlight the importance of jobs, the need for new investment and the vacuum in leadership that resulted from the job losses.

Inner-city decay and suburbanisation

The long industrial boom before the cities began their decline drove suburbanisation as the more affluent beneficiaries of economic success sought to escape the problems of pollution, disease and poverty associated with living in the core of manufacturing cities. The vast majority of the population of industrial cities up to the Second World War lived in crowded, insanitary squalor, creating conditions where epidemic diseases became rife and the rich became

Figure 2.8: Economic crisis: environmental burden and derelict industrial relics (Bilbao)

Figure 2.9: The vacant Harland & Wolff offices now awaiting refurbishment as part of the Titanic Quarter redevelopment (Belfast)

vulnerable, above all, to cholera in the 19th century, but also to scarlet fever, measles, tuberculosis and other contagious diseases in the 20th century. More salubrious inner suburbs were soon enveloped and decayed in turn (see Figures 2.13a–b). But the rapid expansion of trains allowed outer suburbs to spread. The exodus accelerated as industrial wealth declined, the cities decayed and wealthier people sought to protect themselves from the intractable problems of dislocation and alienation that accompanied manufacturing job losses.

Table 2.5: Unrest linked to industrial change, 1970–90

Leipzig	Centre of political protest against East German regime, which collapsed in 1989
Bremen	As city-state with power and responsibility, Bremen lost almost all its industrial jobs, had a large, poorly integrated immigrant population and lost its political consensus
Sheffield	Left-wing socialist control in the 1980s fought budgetary tightening from right-wing Thatcher government, refused to acknowledge inevitable collapse and closure of mines; the City became the headquarters of national miners' strikes and experienced intense social upheaval and disorder
Belfast	Loss of industrial and shipyard jobs intensified hostilities between communities and fuelled disorder, riots, and clashes in inner cities
Bilbao	Major strikes by dockers and other industrial workers; activities by Basque terrorist group ETA fed into social and economic problems
Torino	Strong left-wing coalition, major political unrest, subject to violent revolutionary attacks by 'Red Brigades' on centres of power; political instability and clientalism coupled with worker unrest in the face of mass redundancies; a violent anti-capitalist terrorist movement active in the city paralysed the local political system
Saint-Étienne	Communist control of the city in the late 1970s and 1980s; attempt to turn industrial clock back while industrial closures devastated local communities; extreme politics failed; city later experienced serious riots among minority ethnic youth

Figure 2.10: Job losses in manufacturing: striking workers, early 1980s (Bilbao)

Figure 2.11: Job losses in manufacturing, striking miners outside a coke plant, 1984 (Sheffield, South Yorkshire)

Figure 2.12: Belfast riots

The rapid growth of outer suburbs far beyond city boundaries further damaged the urban economy, by stripping cities of their business and professional classes, placing key decision makers in living conditions that bore little resemblance to the problems they needed to address, and leaving inner cities and city centres denuded of income as well as organisational and management skills. The populations of the wider metropolitan areas around all the cities had, by 2005, outstripped the core city population three times over. Furthermore, the cities' boundaries, along with their political and administrative structures which had been drawn at the industrial zenith of each city, in reality no longer bore any relation to their functional sizes. Over the 20th century the boundaries were breached by suburbanisation on an extraordinary scale (see Figure 2.14).

Meanwhile, another population trend was undermining the viability of the cities, taking on extreme forms in some cases – the flight of the middle classes to the suburbs. This had been going on from the turn of the 20th century as a result of appalling slum conditions in the cities' working-class neighbourhoods.

The Brookings Institution, in their parallel study, recognised this by focusing city studies on 'metropolitan' areas; this conceals the true extent of problems in core cities, however, so we use traditional and still official city boundaries.[12] Table 2.6 shows the dominance and impact of suburban growth, showing wider metropolitan areas to have at least double the population of the cities.

While the expansion of suburbs drew more stable, more ambitious and more affluent workers out of the cities, another lower-income exodus was gathering pace. A powerful public response to the urban slums that had evolved during the heyday of industrial growth was the construction of 'mass housing' estates in the 1950s–60s and 1970s. An industrial model of concrete block building to house the workers of large-scale industry first evolved in the inter-war years in Vienna to draw lower-income people away from traditional crowded neighbourhoods, often to the periphery of cities, but clearly separated from the affluent middle classes.[13] The mass housing programme, supported by all governments, quickly became a factory-based production system totally unsuited to the domestic needs of low-income families, and rapidly turned into a social nightmare.[14] The ambition to build mass estates was driven by the rapid population expansion, the multiplication of slums, the rise in wealth, the growth in factory systems and the sheer political optimism about continuing growth, following the Second World War. Over-ambitious building programmes created an over-supply of ugly concrete estates, sometimes in the core but more often at the edges of all the cities, simultaneously depleting inner areas (see Figure 2.15). These estates were modelled on the mass production methods that their giant factories had perfected.

Le Corbusier, inventor of the idea of cellular 'machine living' and 'streets in the sky', tried out his early ideas in Firminy, the neighbouring town to Saint-Étienne. His work was celebrated at the Venice Biennale (2007) and his estate near Saint-Étienne has become one of the city's new tourist attractions. But unfortunately for modern cities and housing experts, his path-breaking model did not work

Figures 2.13a-b: Inner decay: growing depopulation and abandonment of decayed inner-city areas (Leipzig)

Figure 2.14: Suburbanisation: rapidly built new developments on the urban fringe (Leipzig)

well without intensive management, high–quality materials and well–maintained environments, none of which were deliverable by fast-expanding public or social landlords. Le Corbusier's imitators quickly discovered that mass estates did not offer a 'new kind of Utopia'. Saint-Étienne, in imitation of the worker housing of Le Corbusier, built the now famous *Muraille de Chine* (Wall of China) to the south-east of the city. So unmanageable did its living conditions quickly become that it had to be demolished only 25 years after it was built.

Meanwhile, Sheffield, which strongly embraced the 'mass housing' philosophy, has demolished several of its most spectacular concrete estates, saving the most imposing one near the station as a 'historic monument' to a failed ideal. Both

Table 2.6: Population size of city and wider metropolitan area in 2005

City (2005)	Population	Wider metropolitan area (2005) estimated
Leipzig	498,000	1,000,000
Bremen	546,000	1,100,000
Sheffield	521,000	1,300,000
Belfast	269,000	650,000
Bilbao	353,000	900,000
Torino	868,000	2,200,000
Saint-Étienne	177,000	350,000

Note: Bremen is part of the official metropolitian region Bremen-Oldenburg, which had 2.37 million inhabitants in 2006.
Source: www.metropolregion-bremen-oldenburg.de

Figure 2.15: Unpopular housing estates: peripheral *grand ensemble* (Saint-Étienne)

Leipzig and Bremen are caught up in partial demolition programmes of oversized concrete blocks on over-scaled outer estates, which they are trying to salvage.

As the popularity of estates declined and their costs mounted in parallel with economic decline, their populations became poorer and social landlords were forced to let low-demand properties to low-income, often immigrant households and other marginal, rejected social groups, while indigenous lower-skilled workers were losing their jobs. Eventually, even the new and poorer influx into the mass housing estates failed to stop the population losses, such that their viability came into question.[15] Table 2.7 summarises the all but ubiquitous problems posed by the mass housing estates in the seven cities.

Possibly one of the worst political mistakes in the history of industrial cities was to build for population growth on the basis of past trends, leading to a debilitating over-supply of inadequate new homes, creating empty inner-city sites where people had moved out to new estates. Costs quickly mounted to unmanageable proportions.

The process of suburbanisation and the development of mass housing estates depleted core cities and ran in parallel to the gradual loss of wealth, the growth in unemployment and the intensification of poverty within the cities, as industry after industry declined. This made cities deeply unattractive places in which to live or to invest. The urban governance systems that had grown up around major industries no longer matched the new shape of cities and the challenge of suburbanisation. Meanwhile, the great industrial giants themselves flagged under the twin pressures of deindustrialisation coupled with depopulation.

The shock to the social structure and cohesion of cities, and the impact on the internal and wider environment of cities caused by the 20th-century

Table 2.7: Dominant problems posed by mass housing estates in the seven cities

Problem	Leipzig	Bremen	Sheffield	Belfast	Bilbao	Torino	Saint-Étienne
Located on edge of city	✓	✓	✓	✓	✓	✓	✓
Housing predominantly lower income	Mixed	✓	✓	✓	✓	✓	✓
Many newcomers and immigrants	✓	✓	✓	✓	✓	✓	✓
Poor maintenance, lack of investment	✓	✓	✓	✓	✓	✓	✓
High unemployment	✓	✓	✓	✓	✓	✓	✓
Difficult access to job market	✓	✓	✓	✓	✓	✓	✓
Over-large blocks	✓	✓	✓	Mainly houses	✓	✓	✓
Some selective demolition	✓	✓	✓	✓	✓	✓	✓
Poor quality environments	✓	✓	✓	✓	✓	✓	✓
High political priority to help	✓	✓	✓	✓	✓	✓	✓

Source: City visits (2006-08)

population exodus were both immense. Spreading population, housing, roads, services and jobs over an ever-wider expanse of territory as a way of improving urban conditions quickly became self-defeating as urban neighbourhood after urban neighbourhood, along with city centres, succumbed to a parallel process of population and job losses, thinning out core cities and progressively destroying their wider environments. Belfast was particularly hard-hit because of its 'troubles', losing over a third of its population, but Torino and Saint-Étienne also lost over 20% of their 1970 population by 2005. All the cities felt the consequences in low rates of employment, unwanted infrastructure and unpopular, low-demand homes. Figure 2.16 shows the decline in the cities' total populations, leaving them emptier and more denuded of skills, human and financial resources than before.

Ironically, the decline of these cities, led by a population exodus, began during the economic heyday of the cities, driven by wealth and overgrowth rather than impoverishment.

Neighbourhood polarisation

The knock-on effects of population decline on housing markets, neighbourhood services, schools, public transport, shops and other aspects of city life showed up most acutely in the poorest neighbourhoods where the job losses were concentrated. An intense hierarchy of more and less popular neighbourhoods emerged as poverty, joblessness and polarisation opened up a visible cleavage between the poorer and richer neighbourhoods. Traditional working-class families, now often without earned incomes and dependent on state benefits, became significantly poorer in real terms and employment rates between traditional

Figure 2.16: Population decline in the seven cities, 1970–2005 (%)

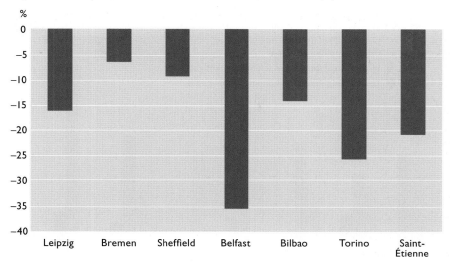

Note: Percentage decline from 1970 baseline.
Source: National and regional statistical bureaux

working-class areas and more prosperous city neighbourhoods diverged radically.[16] So controversial within cities was this rising inequality that since 2001, when the EU first collected these figures, cities have been reluctant to update the record of neighbourhood inequality.[17] We know from the neighbourhood studies we carried out as part of this study that the problems persist in acute form, as we show later in Chapter Four. Figure 2.17 shows the variation in employment rates between the neighbourhoods with the highest and the lowest levels of unemployment within cities in 2001.

Saint-Étienne showed by far the most extreme divergence in employment rates between traditional working-class and more affluent areas, a gap of 20% between the most work-poor and work-rich neighbourhoods. Belfast came next with a 16% gap, then Sheffield third, closely followed by Torino and Leipzig. The lowest differences were in the German city-state of Bremen where the gap was only 6%, reflecting much lower overall levels of inequality in Germany.[18] The two German cities had generally high unemployment but it was more evenly spread between areas, leading to lower levels of neighbourhood polarisation. The gaps in neighbourhood unemployment rates reflect the much greater economic polarisation of some cities, such as Saint-Étienne and Belfast, compared with others such as Bremen. However, everywhere the average rate of unemployment in the more traditionally working-class neighbourhoods was extremely high, ranging from between 12% and 27%.

Figure 2.17: Variation in unemployment rates between neighbourhoods in the cities, 2001 (%)

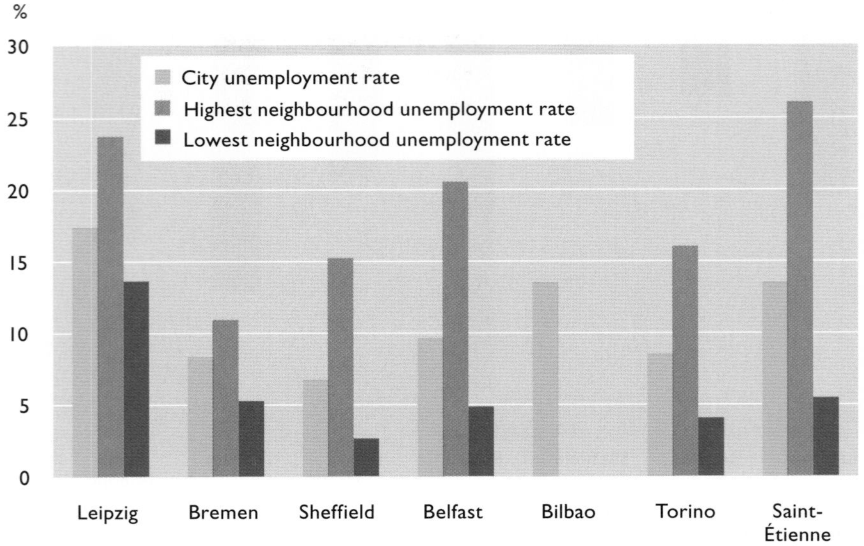

Legend:
- City unemployment rate
- Highest neighbourhood unemployment rate
- Lowest neighbourhood unemployment rate

Cities: Leipzig, Bremen, Sheffield, Belfast, Bilbao, Torino, Saint-Étienne

Note: Bilbao is not in Urban Audit; city-level data only.
Source: Urban Audit

Conclusion

Over a period of 30 years up to 2000, all the cities lost their core economic rationale, prominence and political weight. The devaluation of industrial and manual skills undermined community confidence, destroying a way of life and local culture that had been bred in miserable working conditions but had, in the end, built up a skilled industrial tradition, an elite workforce and a much more socially progressive civic governance system than had previously existed. As producer cities, they had been central to their countries' prosperity; now they were increasingly seen as liabilities, obsolete industrial 'leftovers', with an insignificant or at least unrecognised place in the new economy, based on services and 'new knowledge industries'. The skills that were needed for the new economy were more flexible, service-oriented skills. These proved hard to generate within local communities and even today many new jobs go to outsiders with a different work tradition, and with more adaptable skills, rather than to local manual workers.[19] Many low-income communities appeared stranded by a fast receding tide of job losses and service decline. The cities as a whole suffered in consequence. Civic pride was damaged along with urban landscapes. Social exclusion within the cities came to reflect a deep and multifaceted form of separation from mainstream society.[20] Civic leadership, often still embedded in the fading realities of the industrial era, lost its way. The future of former industrial cities seemed bleak and the prospects for recovery were extremely unpromising. In the next chapter we examine how the seven cities adapted to the new realities of decline, unemployment and shrinkage. We explore the measures they adopted to promote recovery and the innovations they uncovered in pursuit of a new prosperity.

THREE

A change of direction: political turmoil and a ferment of new ideas

The seven cities faced an intractable set of problems by the 1980s: declining economies, shrinking populations, loss of investment, decay and demoralisation. It was unclear how new ways out of such acute problems would emerge. The mismatch between what former industrial cities could offer and the requirements of the new economy, made starker by the obvious gaps between old industrial cities like the seven in this study and the blossoming economies of more knowledge and service-based cities, was extreme. Rapid economic changes far beyond the cities and their social impacts on the cities themselves changed the political dynamics of the cities and of whole countries. Many wider structures began to shift.

In the countries where the seven cities were, these shifts took on concrete new forms. Both Italy and France devolved considerable power to regional governments and to city mayors in the 1980s and 1990s. Spain became a democracy after 40 years of dictatorship in the late 1970s. In 1990, Germany underwent a huge political and economic transformation with the reunification of its two divided parts, making it by far the largest and most powerful country in Europe. The UK in the 1980s moved from its heavily state-run, state-subsidised and state-owned economic structures towards a radical and confrontational privatisation of many previously public forms of ownership and production.[21] The EU was expanding, and, in the late 1980s, Soviet domination of eastern Europe disintegrated, opening the door to new forms of growth and the transformation of Europe itself.

Such was the scale of the changes underway that it gave new political direction to national and local governments across Europe, throwing up new leadership in cities in the search for a new economic rationale, and new ways to fit within the changing environment. The major challenges for the seven cities were to:

- stop the haemorrhage of people and jobs
- create new functions for post-industrial cities
- attract new resources and new players
- retain the most skilled people and build new skills in an increasingly redundant workforce
- remodel the expensive infrastructure of the cities.[22]

Each city had its own turning points, driven by particular events, but the political change of direction was in every city underpinned by the clear need to do things differently. An important unifying event, such as the election of a visionary mayor, willing to break with tradition, began the turnaround in Torino and Saint-Étienne.

A sharp change in the wider political context transformed the potential of Belfast, Bilbao and Leipzig. A bold strategy to foster the new economy emerged from city and regional debates in Bremen and Bilbao. Explosive political and social pressures led to new forms of governance in Sheffield, but also in Torino and Leipzig. Cities had unique patterns of change, yet shared many common features, driven by a common sense of urgency.

This chapter captures the common patterns, while the city case studies in Part Two detail the particular events and the distinctive political and historical dynamics at work in each city.[23] Table 3.1 highlights the key turning points, city by city.

A new sense of direction

Local political leadership, where it existed, had become defensive, reactive and disoriented in the face of loss of prosperity, but a new sense of political direction emerged from the crisis and galvanised important sections of the community into forcing the pace of economic change. Civic leaders mobilised new actors to shape a response strong enough to counter the loss of viability confronting the cities. A new generation of city leaders found new ways of tackling entrenched problems. They generated new ideas and encouraged a new economic dynamism that fostered strong partnerships between local government, the private sector and grassroots community initiatives, to promote new investments and enterprises, as well as to respond to the problems of decay and decline. Below are some illustrations:

- Leipzig's students, helped by a city centre church leader, played a pivotal role in the final stages of opposition to the communist domination of eastern Europe, leading directly to the collapse of the Berlin Wall in 1989. This conspicuous shift attracted many bright and energetic young entrepreneurial leaders to the city in the 1990s.
- Sheffield became the national symbol for opposition to 'Thatcherism', privatisation and central domination by becoming the national headquarters for the 1980s miners' strikes; the local council held out longest against government spending cuts, and was the most spectacular investor in unaffordable public works, that cost the city years of near bankruptcy but dramatically attested to the urgency of Sheffield's situation. These confrontations eventually led to a totally new, partnership-based, private sector-oriented approach in the late 1990s, which turned Sheffield into an avant-garde, locally led model of city reform. (see Figure 3.1)
- Belfast's long troubled history and 30 years of sectarian conflict led to a divided, physically damaged city on a scale unlike any other in our study. But it gradually reunified its political leaders around a fraught peace process. The famous Good Friday Agreement in 1998 allowed reinvestment and regeneration to gather pace. Painstakingly, civic bodies, community leaders and public officials have pieced together new initiatives that have helped to heal the city's wounds.

Table 3.1: Key turning points in each city, showing how the cities began to recover

	Date, events, strategies, initiatives
Leipzig	• 1989: popular Monday demonstrations opposing the communist regime of East Germany based in a church in central Leipzig; collapse of the socialist regime, reunification with Western Germany • 1998: Leipzig was first Eastern German city to recognise the crisis of depopulation and develop a counter strategy at an urban workshop hosted by the city • 2000: Expert Commission on structural change in the housing market • 2001: federal *Stadtumbau Ost* programme to help Eastern German cities cope with surplus and poor quality housing, supporting demolition and renovation of empty housing • Strong political and administrative city-level leadership and organisation
Bremen	• 1991: new political coalition determined to turn decline around • 1995–2004: substantial financial aid by federal government due to massive budgetary deficit • Subsidised investment in university research to develop new technologies • Diversification of economic structure, fostering new-technology businesses • Late 1990s: city-region debates about the urban future leading to major regeneration
Sheffield	• 1997: new political leadership of city council and partnership-oriented chief executive • New direction focused on creation of dedicated public–private agencies • New Labour government offers many new funding streams to core cities • City centre regeneration • 2000: neighbourhoods strategy and Closing the Gap policy
Belfast	• 1994: peace process along with the paramilitary ceasefires • 1996: major regeneration of city centre and Laganside • 1998: Good Friday Agreement between all main political groupings at Stormont • 1999: reinstallation of Northern Ireland Assembly • Special financial aid from EU and central UK government to repair conflict damage
Bilbao	• Late 1970s: strong Basque local leadership emerges following the institution of democracy • Early 1980s: regional autonomy of Basque Country re-established • 1980s: fiscal autonomy at provincial level (Vizcaya) • Late 1980s: all layers of government working towards a Strategic Plan for the city • 1991/92: innovative regeneration agencies set up including Bilbao Ria that delivered the Guggenheim, and new bridge
Torino	• 1993: 1st directly elected mayor; renewal of political initiative • Civic bodies play leading role backed by bank foundations with major resources • 1998: urban masterplan and city-wide strategy • Torino Neighbourhoods Unit leading to participatory social and physical regeneration supported by the council • Successful bid for Winter Olympics leads to major investment and renewal • 2000: city strategic plan
Saint-Étienne	• 1983–2001: first recovery phase, emphasising economic development and employment • Late 1970s: major shift away from communist to pro-market leadership in city council • 1999: central government heavily involved; funding neighbourhood renewal programmes • 2001–present: second phase, emphasises residential appeal • 2003: partnership with wider metropolitan authorities and attempt to consolidate wider city-region

Source: City reports and visits

Figure 3.1: Sheffield's restored City Hall

- Bilbao was a major player in the re-emergence of a democratically based Basque nationalist government in the late 1970s and managed to rebuild its international reputation, symbolised in its visionary backing of the 'Silver Guggenheim' phenomenon. It fostered a diversified economy and reclaimed many of its historic industrial sites (see Figure 3.2).
- Saint-Étienne, formerly run by a beleaguered communist local council, with strong ties to the traditional communist-dominated unions, rapidly restored its city centre with a completely new emphasis from the 1990s on what the city could offer in a new world of high-tech industries. Services and residential accommodation became an alternative to its vanishing industrial tradition (see Figure 3.3).

The other cities also had particular political dynamics at work that led to new leadership and a new sense of direction. Bremen and Torino both played unique roles that reached far beyond their industrial base:

- Bremen, along with Berlin and Hamburg, had a legally autonomous government, dating from the Middle Ages, with jurisdiction over and fiscal responsibility for most functions that in the UK would be national or regional responsibilities. It was a major port of entry for central and eastern Germany. As the industrial crisis of the 1970s deepened, a broad coalition of local leaders forged a new consensus about the future, building on its existing strengths –

high-tech engineering, new sciences, advanced industrial processes and port activities. This laid the ground for later recovery and resilience (see Figure 3.4).

• Torino was home to Italy's most powerful industrial giant, the Agnelli family's Fiat car industry. It also hosts the fourth largest private banking foundation in Europe, the Compagnia di San Paolo, giving the city far reaching influence throughout Italy and Europe.[24] The foundation played a key role in the new citizen engagement that emerged as Torino elected a mayor for the first time in the early 1990s, leading to a ferment of new ideas.

Figure 3.2: Landmark turning point: Guggenheim Museum on reclaimed riverfront (Bilbao)

Figure 3.3: Restored train station and tram (Saint-Étienne)

The political changes of direction gave a sharp focus and potency to the social and economic change that was needed. Economic recovery became possible largely because the political upheavals of the 1970s and 1980s led to the emergence of a stronger, more democratic form of local government in these cities, with a new kind of leadership, more consensual and pragmatic, more open to new ways of doing things.

Figure 3.4: Science Park (Bremen)

As each city emerged from political turmoil, the new leadership centred its energy on looking forward, not back, on change rather than managed retreat, on innovation rather than the defence of old patterns. Civic leadership depended on three main sources of support:

- the mass of *citizens and civic organisations* at key turning points played a dominant role in reshaping the direction of their cities;
- *strong central and regional governments* wanted to invest to support new urban initiatives, reshape old infrastructure and encourage social programmes;
- *private companies* still owned large interests in the cities and had a major stake in their future.

By the 1990s, this combination of public, private and civic interest groups came to recognise the decline of heavy industry as inevitable and unavoidable. The different players had to work together building conciliatory, forward-thinking, multisectoral collaboration. The potential for recovery grew as new rather than old methods were adopted, building on the new sense of direction that was emerging. At the same time, more sophisticated systems and services emerged to orchestrate ever more complex machine-based enterprises. This meant that old ways of working even in surviving industries were no longer valid. Creativity, high skills and technology drove new forms of work in industry, communications, trade, finance, urban development and culture.[25] This more service-based economy, trading even more on new knowledge, new ideas and new inventions than the first industrial revolution, became known as the second industrial revolution of the 'knowledge economy', gradually modifying, sometimes supplanting the older, goods-based industrial economy.[26] Ironically, the new economy required even more energy and material throughputs than the old, because the new wealth it generated demanded more and more goods, increasingly made elsewhere.[27] These new forms of consumption and production in the second industrial revolution were going to be a large part of the eventual unravelling since 2007 of the modern international banking and trading system.[28]

The local workforce was still largely embedded in a manual tradition and even the children of former manual workers, who themselves had little direct experience of this industrial past, inherited the traditional view of work that described 'real jobs' as manual jobs.[29] Manufacturing employed only a fraction of the earlier workforce. As mechanisation led to greater productivity, job losses in the surviving industries have continued up to the present day.[30] Changing young people's attitudes to work became a central pre-occupation of city administrations, job agencies and local communities.[31] We look at the special programmes the cities developed to tackle this problem in Chapter Four, and in Chapter Sixteen return to the special challenge of alienated youth in former industrial cities. Meanwhile, we need to understand how the cities shifted from decline to recovery, from job losses to job gains, from population outflows to stabilisation.

New ways forward for core cities

If new enterprises were to be attracted and to grow, the workforce had to match the new labour demands, while the social and physical conditions had to be attractive to new investors. But the cities required large-scale public backing to attract new investment, given the decayed conditions, in order to offer a sufficient incentive to newcomers. As the service-based economy grew in advanced, highly developed countries, there was a renewed recognition by governments, private interests and civic society of the value of large old cities as centres of diverse labour markets, universities, professions, cultural assets and transport hubs. Alongside industrial restructuring, new uses quickly emerged for former industrial cities with their extensive urban conurbations and their rich if decayed central infrastructure. Weak market cities in Europe began to show signs of becoming 'core' cities once more.[32]

City councils determined that rebuilding a 'sense of place' was a prerequisite for recovery. They could only achieve this by reinvesting in central squares, civic monuments and existing urban neighbourhoods. They depended heavily on higher levels of government to make good the cities' loss of earned resources, arguing that they had long contributed to their countries' wealth, prestige and power. There was a kind of national debt to repay. But progress also relied on improving social conditions and the economic landscape, alongside physical upgrading and environmental restoration. Cities could not escape the need to act on all three fronts simultaneously. It was profoundly impressive that a similar pattern of initiatives quickly seemed to emerge in each city, driven by a common set of imperatives. The cities' recovery was premised on operating on these different fronts, with different programmes, projects, initiatives and strategies, multiplying over the two decades of recovery attempts.

The broad-based efforts of all the cities fell into three main types of action: social, economic and physical/environmental. The most common initiatives across the seven cities fitted within this broad framework of sustainability. Table 3.2 sets out the framework for action adopted by the cities, illustrating the direct ways the cities implemented these actions, and showing how comprehensive and multifaceted the efforts had to be.

Table 3.2: Framework for understanding the cities' attempts at recovery

	Focus of city effort	Types of initiative
Social	• Social inclusion and integration • Community development • Developing new skills • Improving access to the wider city • Neighbourhood and community rebuilding • Immigration and minority inclusion • Mixed income communities	• Community projects • Social programmes • Citizen participation • Social enterprises • Skills development • 'Hand-holding'/advice • Events, festivals • Youth activities • Multi-ethnic programmes
Economic	• High tech development • Innovation • Increasing competitiveness • Higher education • 'Cluster approach' to business • Business creation/start-ups • Transport linkages • Regional/intercity interaction • Service sector development	• Tourism • Cultural facilities • Retail expansion • Financial and legal services • 'Residential appeal' • University programmes • Incentives for inward investors • Finance and professional services • Lower skill services, e.g. retail, construction, call centres • Higher-skill knowledge-based technologies

Physical/environmental	• City centre renewal
	• Neighbourhood renewal
	• Housing offer/upgrade
	• Transport infrastructure/public transport
	• Public spaces
	• Land reclamation and reuse
	• Environmental upgrading
	• Traffic control measures
	• Urban green spaces
	• Energy-efficient buildings
		• Development led projects
		• Port and water front remodelling
		• Contaminated land clean up
		• New public transport links
		  o within city, trams, bus-ways
		  o externally better train-links
		  o new or expanded airports
		• Beautifying city centre:
		  o public spaces, trees & gardens
		• Cultural attractions:
		  o concert halls
		  o art, music
		• Neighbourhood reinvestment
		• Estate regeneration
		• Reclamation and reuse of major industrial legacies
		• Environmental industries

Source: City visits

The focus of the efforts was to attract people into the city, increase investor confidence and improve the general experience of residents and visitors alike. Different cities emphasised different aspects of the framework, but most cities applied a majority of elements of the framework to their specific conditions. Below are some examples:

• Sheffield argued that economic recovery would not work without neighbourhood renewal and social integration. At the same time it prioritised public–private partnerships and put a strong emphasis on arm's-length structures in order to overcome the polarised political atmosphere of the city following industrial collapse. Sheffield also invested heavily in city centre projects such as the Peace Gardens, the Winter Gardens, a high-class tourist hotel and the restoration of the City Hall, in order to persuade outsiders and insiders alike that the city was worth investing in (see Figure 3.5).

- Bilbao upgraded the public transport infrastructure and restored the historical city centre neighbourhoods. It reclaimed the former industrial riverfront and directly commissioned and funded flagship projects such as the Guggenheim and the new bridge across the River Nervión. It significantly diversified its economy by encouraging higher education and the service sector.
- Belfast, because of historic community conflicts, focused major efforts on reconciliation and peace making, by creating shared public spaces. In the process it attracted major private investors and since 2000 has seen a striking growth in 'urban tourism', cultural enterprises and the value of city sites.
- Saint-Étienne relied on regional and national interventions to drive the recovery process within the city, reflecting the state ownership of dominant industries and central government dominance of social and public investment programmes. The city leadership has taken a major role in reclaiming land, restoring central squares and finding new uses for symbolic industrial monuments, such as the Imperial Arms Factory. It has improved the public transport infrastructure to connect it better to its dominant neighbour, Lyon.
- Leipzig took an early decision to save as much as possible of the historic inner-city housing and streetscape, rescuing extremely dilapidated, under-occupied traditional apartment blocks, fronting onto dense central streets, typical of pre-First World War East German cities. This 'Wilhelmenian style'

Figure 3.5: City centre project: Peace Gardens redesigned, with Sheffield's first 5-star hotel in the background

is lastingly appealing, costly to restore but unexpectedly attractive to younger, well-educated populations in a 'shrinking city'.[33] This new inner-city focus provoked an abrupt ending to the housing subsidies of the 1990s, which had encouraged building on the suburban fringe of the city and fuelled an urban exodus. Partial demolition of large outer estates helped to save inner-city streets. Highly complex funding packages, strong financial incentives, land reclamations, new uses and new planning priorities were required over a decade or more to make an impact. The gradual recovery of the city stemmed the population outflow and encouraged reinvestment.

- Torino, capitalising on its position in the foothills of the Alps, won its bid to host the Winter Olympics in 2006. Restoring its medieval city centre, reusing its older, obsolete industrial buildings, and generating new industrial high-tech enterprises on the back of the old put the city back on the map. A broad coalition of citizen groups forged new city-wide alliances that worked together to develop this high-profile 'rebirth'.
- Bremen adopted strong policies of social cohesion while maintaining many of its industrial engineering traditions by focusing on higher-tech, research-led new technologies. It invested in its universities and fostered science-based innovation. It restored its medieval city centre and encouraged a new kind of urban tourism.

Recovery measures

The recovery measures that created improved environments for reinvestment followed a comparable pattern across the seven cities. The cities' interventions can be grouped under six main measures: city centre upgrading; recycling derelict land and buildings; economic development; skills development and job transformation; building more integrated social conditions; and strong, publicly led partnerships. The 'recovery pattern book' that is in the making in these cities could be more widely applied. The common recovery measures across Europe show how a mix of economic, social and environmental measures was key to the progress towards recovery. Table 3.3 shows the common patterns of recovery measures.

All seven cities built on their heritage and culture, restoring old civic buildings and reusing industrial warehouses, mills and canals, creating popular pedestrian zones in city centres with imposing public spaces that the cities restored to their earlier role of citizen-gathering:

- In Saint-Étienne, central squares that were previously traffic roundabouts became traffic-calmed, attractive civic spaces, often with play equipment used by many families, children and older people where previously they had become decayed and congestion-ridden (see Figure 3.6).

Table 3.3: Common patterns of recovery measures

Measure	Leipzig	Bremen	Sheffield	Belfast	Bilbao	Torino	Saint-Étienne	Physical/ environmental	Economic	Social
City centre upgrading										
New and restored public spaces	✓	✓	✓	✓	✓	✓	✓	✓	✓	
Pedestrian zones, retail, entertainment	✓	✓	✓	✓	✓	✓	✓		✓	✓
Cultural initiatives, e.g. concert halls, museums, theatres, restoration of historic sites and buildings	✓	✓	✓	✓	✓	✓	✓	✓	✓	✓
New or upgraded public transport systems	✓	✓	✓	✗	✓	✓	✓	✓	✓	✓
Recycling land and buildings										
Land reclamation and reuse	✓	✓	✓	✓	✓	✓	✓	✓		
Expanding green spaces	✓		✓	✓		✓	✓	✓	✓	✓
Inner-city neighbourhood renewal	✓	✓	✓	✓	✓	✓	✓	✓		✓
Outer estate/neighbourhood renewal	✓	✓	✓	✓	✓	✓	✓	✓		✓
Economic development										
Inward investment measures – searching out new and expanding companies	✓	✓	✓	✓	✓	✓	✓		✓	✓
Financial incentives e.g for inward investors	✓	✓	✓	✓	✓	✓	✓		✓	
Relocation of existing businesses to the city	✓			✓	✓		✓		✓	✓
High-tech industry building on traditional manufacturing skills and history	✓	✓		✓	✓	✓	✓		✓	✓
Supporting new small enterprises through incubators	✓	✓	✓	✓	✓	✓	✗		✓	✓
Tourism	✓	✓	✗	✓	✓	✓	✗	✓	✓	✓
Skills development and job transformation										
Targeting low-income unemployed communities and minorities	✓	✓	✓	✓	✓	✓	✓		✓	✓
Targeting universities, developing diverse skills	✓	✓	✓	✓	✓	✓	✓		✓	
Linking employers to local labour	✓		✓	✓	✓	✓	✓		✓	
'Hand-holding' people into job access	✓	✓	✓	✓	✓	✓	✓		✓	
Building balanced social conditions										
Retaining and attracting new middle class by creating higher-grade 'offer' e.g through housing, culture	✓	✓	✓	✓	✓	✓	✓	✓	✓	✓
Integration of minorities		✓	✓	✓		✓			✓	✓
Community supports, initiatives, enterprises		✓	✓	✓	✓	✓	✓		✓	✓
Strong public and political initiatives										
Partnership structures	✓	✓	✓	✓	✓	✓	✓		✓	✓
City-region initiatives	✓	✓	✓		✓	✓	✓		✓	
Citizen involvement	✓	✓	✓	✓	✓	✓			✓	✓
Public political leadership	✓	✓	✓	✓	✓	✓	✓		✓	✓
Total	23	22	22	23	23	24	21	9	22	181

Sources: City visits and city reports

- In Belfast, the frequently bombed central zone became a crowded and integrated public space with shopping streets, parks and squares.
- Leipzig's central streets and squares were attractively restored to pedestrian use, frontages were renovated and empty flats reoccupied.
- Torino's magnificent central piazzas regained their former glory while continuing to house vibrant street markets with stalls, run largely by newly arrived immigrants from Africa.

All cities focused on the re-expansion of city centre attractions, retail and other services to compete with the lure of hastily agreed out-of-town shopping centres. To a growing extent, the strategy of making city centres into magnets for people and enterprise worked to restore value to devalued urban assets.

Figure 3.6: Neighbourhood planting: small-scale greenery in the 100 Squares project, Tarantaize (Saint-Étienne)

Environmental management

In the initial 'fire-fighting' stage of recovery, the most immediate worries were the economy and job creation. Given the vast environmental damage wreaked by their long industrial history, repairing the physical environment of cities was bound to receive priority, although the clear potential for jobs in environmental industries was almost completely ignored until recently. Rather they prioritised upgrading of the urban environment, which was understandable, given how ugly it had become. All the cities realised that public spaces, streets, parks, buildings and neighbourhoods could become environmentally attractive again. An emphasis on cleaning, repair, maintenance and security quickly paid off, encouraging inward investment and an end of population leakage. In these ways the cities directly tackled their immediate and local environmental problems in a desperate attempt to equalise conditions.

One of the biggest environmental challenges was decontaminating polluted land, a serious environmental hazard, following decades of spillage, chemical waste dumping, coal slag, iron ore, processing waste and dangerous extractive residues.[34] Some urban landscapes looked like moon scapes, scorched bare, brown and black. A huge reclamation programme was essential to any new uses. Bilbao, Leipzig, Bremen, Belfast and Saint-Étienne carried out the most spectacular land reclamation programmes, making large vacant spaces, covering hundreds of hectares of former industrial land near city centres, ready for reuse (see Figure 3.7). This activity not only restored the environmental assets of damaged land directly but also encouraged new investment and new, hopefully less polluting activity.

As climate change, energy efficiency, water and waste management, renewable energy and other new technologies to reduce greenhouse gases move higher up European and national agendas, more progressive, change-oriented cities are beginning to capitalise on this new environmental agenda as we will show later in Part 5.[35]

Figure 3.7: Former open-cast mines have been flooded to create attractive water landscapes, creating amenities and contributing to quality of life

City flagships

In order to galvanise external and internal support for the turnaround of places that seemed to have lost their rationale, city leaders had to present a powerful vision for the urban renaissance represented in their careful masterplans.[36] These plans had to unify and accommodate disparate interests so that the new vision for the city could attract widespread backing within and funds from without. Strong citizen support was vital. 'Flagship' proposals to transform the cities' physical, economic and cultural attractions through specific, highly conspicuous 'flagship' projects helped cities to bring partnerships together behind a unifying vision for the future of the city. Flagship projects could galvanise support in a demoralised and doubting public, publicise the determination of the city to do things differently and arouse the curiosity and interest of dynamic new investors. Cultural and sports venues and events, museums and the arts, imposing central squares, parks, water fronts, new public transit, all generated a new enthusiasm and won investors over. Several of the cities bid to host major sporting and cultural events on the back of which they acquired additional investment, even where the bid was only partially successful, as in Leipzig's bid to host the World Cup. Table 3.4 shows the key flagship projects each city adopted in order to build a new rationale for the city, to promote a new image and to attract new investment.

Flagship projects formed the vanguard of city recovery, because they symbolised for residents and visitors alike the dawn of the post-industrial era. They were born on the back of the careful work of building new institutions, attracting new money and generating new ideas. Sometimes the flagship projects served to kick-start regeneration; more commonly they underpinned and formed part of a much wider recovery process already under way; sometimes they were the key to unlocking capacity and facilitating a planned change of direction.

Many of the flagship projects were controversial and costly, and as yet, their wider, more lasting impacts are sometimes unclear. But they generally set failing cities back on the map and generated interest far beyond their immediate goal of city recovery. The spin-off benefits may be most conspicuous in the case of the Torino Winter Olympics, the Bilbao Guggenheim and the Belfast city centre 'shared spaces' regeneration. In Belfast, after 30 years of almost total inactivity in the city centre, public areas are now attracting all sections of the community and a rapid growth in tourists. These are remarkable and unimagined gains in the context of Northern Ireland, where the battle to hold in place the Good Friday Agreement of 1998 was long and hard. In the city, virtually street by street, schemes have been pursued to encourage social interaction in public spaces and to create a new atmosphere of spontaneous and informal contact, where previously there had been bitter and violent divisions. Organised events to build reconciliation also played a part.[37] Belfast symbolised in an extreme way the pain, the loss and the intricate rebuilding that accompanied dramatic change. The whole city became a kind of flagship for urban recovery.

Table 3.4: Flagship recovery projects in the seven cities

Cities	Flagship recovery projects
Leipzig	• Football World Cup bid (2006) • Cultural events celebrating local heroes Bach and Goethe • City centre and inner-city restoration • Re-establishment of historic trade fairs, traditionally hosted by the city • Application for Olympics 2012 (lost)
Bremen	• Technology park (linked to university) • Major waterfront mixed-use redevelopment (Overseas City) • Restoration of historic centre • Application to become Cultural Capital of Europe 2010 (lost)
Sheffield	• Major city centre regeneration project including public squares and gardens, renewal of main train station, new Retail Quarter, Peace and Winter Gardens • Advanced Manufacturing Park (linked to university) • Lower Don Valley regeneration programme (in planning) • Neighbourhood and housing renewal programmes
Belfast	• Development of entertainment, shopping and tourist facilities in the city centre • Waterfront redevelopment: Laganside (completed), Titanic Quarter (begun), North Foreshore (in planning) • Victoria Square and city centre pedestrianisation • Reopening of Stormont and restoration of civic functions • Application to become Cultural Capital of Europe 2007 (lost)
Bilbao	• Guggenheim Museum on Abandoibarra site • Waterfront mixed-use redevelopment scheme • Revived metro system designed by Norman Foster and further infrastructural projects (e.g. airport, port, train station) by renowned architects • Upgrading and expansion of metropolitan public transport system • Refurbishment of historic quarter
Torino	• Urban masterplan featuring 'central backbone' boulevard and new metro line • Winter Olympics 2006 • Restoration of historic city centre • Conversion of factory infrastructure to new uses • Torino Wireless ICT cluster
Saint-Étienne	• Design Biennale (founded 1999) • Design Village and Optics/Vision 'cluster sites' on site of Imperial Arms Factory • Zénith concert stadium (designed by Norman Foster) • Châteaucreux city-centre business services district and main train station restoration • Four major neighbourhood regeneration projects • New tram line • Application to become European Capital of Culture 2013

Source: City visits and city reports

The flagship initiatives had far-reaching consequences in setting the pace for recovery, creating a chain effect deriving from high-profile strategies. Urbanists now commonly refer to the 'Guggenheim effect', the 'peace dividend', the 'heritage dividend', 'industrial architecture' and 'urban tourism' as symbols of new roles for cities almost reminiscent of city shrines in the Middle Ages that turned modest urban centres into famed local capitals.[38] All ex-industrial cities and towns now seek to reuse their land and buildings in new and conspicuous ways, thus revaluing their earlier, often seriously devalued industrial legacies (see Figure 3.8).

Industrial architecture, heavy engineering, major urban infrastructure and restored natural environments all now find their place in recovering cities. The value of cities as centres of trade, services, culture, knowledge and innovation, building strongly on their industrial past, has proved to be a critical foundation stone of recovery, underlining the intrinsic worth of cities and the links between the past and the present. Interestingly, the US cities that we examine in Part Four have similarly used flagship projects to create momentum behind recovery.

Figure 3.8: Design Bienniale: the former Imperial Arms Factory being remodelled as the Design Village cluster site (Saint-Étienne)

Bidding for international events had two important consequences: it forced the cities to look outwards and aspire to international standards; and it galvanised local commitment around the intrinsic assets of the cities, their location and connectivity, their historic buildings and public spaces, their old and new image. It helped the cities win backing from private and public sponsors to develop new tourist facilities and spawn a host of new local services employing many low-skilled, part-time, female and immigrant workers, alongside more high-skilled, entrepreneurial 'knowledge' workers. These new service jobs were often criticised by leaders of traditional industrial unions as 'low value' and not 'real' jobs, but in recovery strategies they carried great weight, and often helped people into training, based around service skills and new opportunities, in surprising ways.[39] Bars and cafés, from Bilbao to Sheffield, have symbolised the change in atmosphere, as street spaces became sociable and thereby attracted activity that supported small new enterprises in a virtuous circle of recovery. The cities were acquiring a new rationale, based on innovation, culture and services.

Neighbourhood focus

The urgency of recovering population and attracting jobs generated new interest in the potential of 'compact cities' and the redensification of underused urban neighbourhoods.[40] This approach has helped cities to attract resources for neighbourhood upgrading. Often poorer neighbourhoods receive disproportionate investment both because they are more damaged, physically and socially, by industrial exploitation, and because their poor, under-used environments offer potential for new uses. As they stood, they had become a 'drag' on city recovery, as well as a social liability, a source of many new urban problems, such as higher crime, more family breakdown and rising ethnic and social tensions. Therefore their renewal became part of the wider recovery strategies of all the cities (see Figures 3.9a–b, 3.10 a–b and 3.11). The next chapter examines this important activity in more detail.

The 'Social Europe' philosophy of the EU,[41] supporting the equalisation of conditions and opportunities, led to special programmes designed to pioneer new ways of integrating communities, building skills in marginalised workforces and restoring declining cities, which the seven cities became experts at tapping into. Investing in poorer neighbourhoods within struggling cities became the main tool for raising their conditions closer to the average. The approach reflects a deep fear across Europe of social cleavage. Worries about the growing concentration of people without work and other vulnerable and poorly integrated groups were coupled with the growth of minority ethnic communities concentrated in the poorest areas of older industrial cities, creating a sense of urgency to the new programmes. The goal of creating greater social cohesion linked to reducing outward movement by more economically successful households was fundamental to city recovery. Table 3.5 highlights some social programmes that were developed by the cities with a strong neighbourhood focus.

Funding for renewal

In the 1980s and 1990s government leadership, recognising the essential future role of cities,[42] galvanised funding support on a scale that transformed physical conditions beyond recognition, offering cities the necessary resources to drive forward recovery programmes. But the city leadership had to work extremely hard to stitch together funding from regional, national and European bodies, to secure long-term investment in complex large-scale projects often lasting 10 years. There were multiple funding streams that each city drew on to support its various recovery projects. Grants and subsidies were needed for conspicuous, landmark

Table 3.5: Conspicuous neighbourhood renewal and social programmes linked to jobs in each city

Cities	Special programmes *Neighbourhood inequality, social integration and social programmes, targeted instruments for regeneration*
Leipzig	• *Stadtumbau Ost,* a federal funding programme to tackle housing vacancies, demolition, and refurbishment • Employment agency, matching workforce with companies willing to relocate • Also offering help for unemployed to access new jobs
Bremen	• *Wohnen in Nachbarschaften* (WiN) (Living in Neighbourhoods programme), now part of the Socially Integrated City programme targeting the 10 most deprived neighbourhoods • *Stadtumbau West,* demolition, remodelling and rebuilding programme • Innovation in employment, matching previous workforce to new jobs
Bilbao	• Neighbourhood renewal focus on problematic inner-city neighbourhoods and the Old Quarter, through the city agency Surbisa • Lan Ekintza, skills and employment programme • Renovation of outer neighbourhoods, e.g. Barracaldo
Belfast	• Community environmental programme, Groundwork and Peace III • Social house building programmes in inner and outer neighbourhoods • Gasworks Employment Matching Service (GEMS) targets disadvantaged residents in neighbourhoods close to Laganside regeneration to link unemployed to new jobs
Sheffield	• Closing the Gap neighbourhood renewal strategy • New Deal for Communities/Sure Start • Housing Market Renewal (HMR) programme • Construction JOBMatch employment programme to help new firms recruit locally • JobNet, city-level job recruitment scheme with neighbourhood-based drop-in centres in partnership with Kier Construction and other companies
Torino	• 14 participative neighbourhood renewal programmes run by a dedicated department within the city council, operating at ground level within deprived neighbourhoods
Saint-Étienne	• Large-scale neighbourhood renewal in four neighbourhoods, largely funded by the national urban renewal agency *Agence Nationale de Renovation Urbaine* (ANRU) • Attempts to help unemployed into new construction jobs

Sources: City visits and city reports

projects and for many lower-level, local initiatives across the cities over decades. Most programmes required contributions from the city itself. European funding also played a driving role in all the cities, but it was only part of a much more complex and diverse funding structure.

External funding was particularly vital for social inclusion programmes since many social problems were intensified by the shrinkage of local resources. Inputs into the poorest neighbourhoods offered indirect rather than direct payback, as social conditions improved. For example, the creation of jobs relied mainly on private enterprises growing again, but the skills training that was essential to enable local people to fill those jobs needed public support.

Figures 3.9a-b: Neighbourhood focus: Victorian bath house converted to Healthy Living Centre, Upperthorpe (Sheffield)

3.9a

3.9b

Figures 3.10a-b: Neighbourhood renewal: conversion of former fire station into new homes, café and childcare centre, Gröepelingen (Bremen)

Overall public investment was the critical lever in attracting private funds, but the total amounts of money spent by the cities and the diverse sources of funding are obscured by many complex factors:

- extended and multiple timescales
- opaque organisational budgets
- matched funding arrangements between different sources, sometimes involving 'in-kind' support
- the subsidised involvement of private investors
- the bending of mainstream public sector programmes, such as education, transport and health, to provide additional leverage
- aggregation at city, regional and even national levels of particular funding streams into a single investment agency or funding 'pot'
- the sheer complexity of partnership agreements.

Table 3.6 shows the diverse sources of funding for different programmes, used both for more conspicuous flagship projects, such as the Winter Olympics and the Guggenheim, and the more mainstream and mundane ones, such as estate renewal.

Table 3.6: External funding streams in the seven cities, 1995–2006

External funding sources	Cities						
	Leipzig	Bremen	Sheffield	Belfast	Bilbao	Torino	Saint-Étienne
Urban/EU EU (Objectives 1 and 2)	✓	✓	✓	✓	✓	✓	✓
EFRE (European Fund for Regional Development)	✓	✓	✓	✓	x	x	x
National/federal	✓	✓	✓	✓	x	✓	✓
Regional/provincial	✓	✓	✓	✓	✓	✓	✓
Local city level resources	✓	✓	✓	✓	✓	✓	✓
Regulated private sector, e.g. bank foundations, planning agreements	x[1]	x[1]	✓	✓	x[1]	✓	✓
Special publicly funded agencies at regional level, e.g. regional development agencies in the UK	✓	✓	✓	✓	✓	✓	✓

Note: [1] Private investors and major private companies invested heavily in these cities but they relied on public infrastructure investment to provide a viable public framework within which their efforts could be made to work.

Sources: City documents and reports; EU

The lack of transparency and the multiplicity of delivery bodies and agencies means that for most cities there is incomplete information on the amount of funding that has been invested and the data that is available is distorted by many factors, such as the size of populations affected, wider economic influences, measurable inputs in kind, and so on. Four factors, which determined the shape of funding, were common across the seven cities:

- reliance on public resources
- complexity of funding streams
- range and multiplicity of schemes at different levels of the city from infrastructure and monumental flagship projects to community-level programmes
- visible scale of investment.

On the back of large-scale public investment, cities were able to attract new private enterprises looking for opportunity. The private inward investors who were vital to economic recovery were attracted by the support they received from the city leaders and by the publicly funded initiatives, which they were willing to partner, both in the upfront investment and in the skills development that supported their enterprises. The same applied to new incoming residents, to higher education institutions, to their research teams and the incubator spaces they supported.

Although many of the public funding streams were relatively short term and precarious, coming and going with political changes, nonetheless new phases of funding seemed to flow on from earlier programmes, and city recovery programmes secured continuing public resources over decades, accompanied by a flow of private investment. The cities proved endlessly inventive in their attempts to win more support.

Since 2008, inward investment and public funding have begun to dry up, and many ambitious regeneration projects have been on hold, or on a slow burner with the global economic recession that began in 2007.[43] There is likely to be a period of 'investment stagnation' during which the cities will struggle to hold onto their gains. We return to this question in Chapter Sixteen.

Expanding enterprise

Many new firms and enterprises moved to the seven cities following on from the immense recovery efforts, creating many new jobs. Private companies seeking out opportunities for expansion in declining cities with under-used capacity created many new-style service industries and high-tech innovative enterprises, although there was often a link between the cities' historic functions and their new economies, which built on earlier industrial expertise). Alongside the growth in new enterprises, many existing firms that had declined severely over the late 20th century took on a new lease of life. Table 3.7 shows key growth sectors and the connection with the earlier industrial heritage of the cities.

Table 3.7: New investors in the seven cities

City	Jobs *Inward investment, employment and growth sectors*	Examples of major firms relocating or expanding since recovery began	Links to earlier industry and skills
Leipzig	• Logistics • Car production • Media and publishing	DHL/Amazon	Logistics linked to ancient trade centre roles
Bremen	• High-tech, university-linked development • Maritime and harbour services • Logistics • Food technology • Aerospace industry • Advanced engineering • Environmental engineering	Airbus (EADS)	Expansion of many existing food manufacturers with new technologies
Sheffield	• University-related services • Advanced manufacturing and engineering • Medical technology • Business services, e.g. call centres • Construction	Boeing research; Polestar print works; Nationwide Building Society	Laser development linked to knife technology
Belfast	• Business services, e.g. call centres • Tourism • Retail • Public sector (40% of jobs) no longer growing	Halifax; developer of Titanic Quarter; Harland & Wolff	Creating investment appeal by reclaiming the port area which built the *RMS Titanic*
Bilbao	• Advanced industrial manufacturing • Major international banking • Tourism-related services • Technology park	BBVA[1]	Advanced international banking and tourist recovery linked to traditional Basque investment tradition
Torino	• Restructured car industry • Industrial design • Telecommunications, e.g. wireless technology • Tourism	Fiat	Hydrogen engines linked to car manufacture
Saint-Étienne	• Medical technologies • Business services • Design • Optics • Retail • Advanced mechanical engineering • Construction	Casino HQ	Optics and zoom lens linked to earlier arms lenses

Note: [1]Banco Bilbao Vizcaya Argentaria faces major restructuring following the banking crisis of 2008.
EADS = European Aeronautic Defence and Space Company

Sources: City visits and city reports

Figure 3.11: New health clinic built on the site of a demolished block in Quartiers Sud-Est (Saint-Étienne)

There are many examples of a new entrepreneurialism growing in old industrial cities:

- Saint-Étienne is developing specialist optic lenses, within its Optics cluster, based on the site of the Imperial Arms Factory. This initiative grew out of its earlier experience in armaments that required precision engineering to produce gun lenses, for accurate firing. A Saint-Étienne optics company invented the zoom lens for modern cameras, based on this tradition.
- Sheffield has developed health-related laser technologies for medical science, based on its earlier expertise in stainless steel, knife making and metal processing technologies.
- Bremen's traditional role in high-level engineering led to their decision to go for a university and science-based approach to developing an advanced aeronautics industry and advanced shipping. This led to Bremen partnering the European Airbus development (see Figure 3.12).
- Torino not only restructured and reshaped its earlier highly successful car industry, but also its earlier communications industry, superceded by modern IT.
- Leipzig, as an ancient trade route and trading centre, again became a major world-wide distribution centre when Amazon and DHL both decided to place one of their few worldwide distribution centres there. A major factor in this success was Leipzig agreeing to host a 24-hour airport, essential for modern logistics but too damaging for most cities to countenance.

- Belfast and Bilbao have rapidly expanded their tourist potential, building indirectly on their uniquely troubled but high-profile histories, while simultaneously aiming to draw a veil over their divided past, with symbolic, unifying, high-profile new developments.

Figure 3.12: Airbus development (Bremen)

In different ways, all the cities are beginning to claw back their position and to create a new generation of small and medium-sized enterprises. They are also beginning to see the fruits of their scientific, engineering and precision manufacturing skills in the growth of new environmental or 'green' technologies, which we discuss in Part 5. Specific examples of expansion abound. Commercial rental property in Sheffield in the years between 2004 and 2007 gained value more rapidly than the national average, some of it without public subsidy.[44] A highly rated hotel opened in the Cathedral Quarter in Belfast in an old bank in 2006. It was restored entirely with private money, and is listed as one of the five very best small hotels in Europe.[45] These investments could lose their purchase in the more difficult economic conditions we have faced since 2007, but urban history is engraved with such risks and these cities have shown a resilience that was not foreseen even 10 years ago.

Cities bounce back: population and employment change

The seven cities have slowed their population decline over the past decade and shown actual regrowth in five of the seven cases. Even in two of the cities, Saint-Étienne and Belfast, where population decline has continued, it is no longer a strong trend. Population stabilisation makes an immediate positive impact on housing, services, local economic activity and therefore jobs, even where it does not yet show an absolute rise. Figure 3.13 shows changes in population up to 2005, with a clear if small growth in five cities from 2000.

Figure 3.13: Population change per decade, 1970–2005 (%)

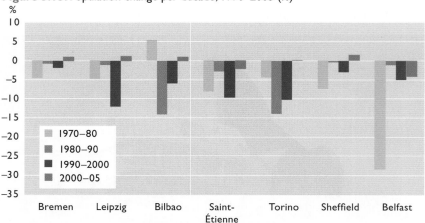

Note: The baseline for each decade change is the beginning of that decade.
Sources: National and regional statistical bureaux

Changes in unemployment have gone hand in hand with population recovery. Some of the cities now outperform the national picture in employment rates although the rate of job creation, the flows in employment and the scale of new investments to the cities fluctuate with the wider economy, which is now suffering. The overall position up to 2005 reflects a stabilisation of job losses, reductions in registered unemployment and in the cases of Sheffield, Torino and Bilbao, an actual regrowth in both population and jobs. The two most notable exceptions to the general decline in unemployment are the German cities where manufacturing traditionally formed a higher share of total employment and industrial job losses continue. In addition, the high costs of German reunification over the 1990s had a debilitating effect on the economy of Leipzig particularly, but also other former industrial cities, such as Bremen. The dramatic change of economic system from a communist to a Western market model made the transition extremely difficult. Leipzig has in the last five years attracted several very large international investors, offering potentially thousands of new jobs and generating many smaller service enterprises to accompany the significant job growth. Both cities still face major budgetary problems, which could have knock-on impacts on local job markets. However, from 2005 to 2008, as Germany's economy grew and manufacturing expanded again, both Leipzig and Bremen benefited. Figure 3.14 shows that in four of the seven cities unemployment has now fallen below the national average, with changes over 15 years underpinned by a decline in the rate of unemployment in all the cities except Leipzig.

Figure 3.14: Unemployment rates in 2005 in the seven cities and their countries (%)

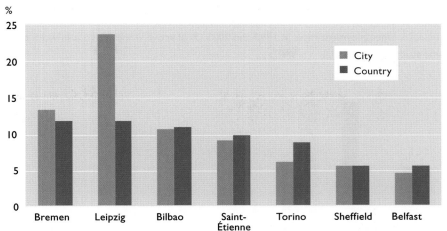

Note: If not available for 2000, 2005 data taken from closest available year. Belfast: Northern Ireland
Torino: province level
Sources: City statistics; EU

Declining unemployment

The pattern of work for most of the cities reflected progress, suggesting growing participation by the workforce in alternative jobs. At the same time, both Belfast and Sheffield experienced a large fall in officially registered unemployment, but still experience high levels of economic inactivity, with many people opting out of the job market through difficulties in adapting to the new economy. They therefore no longer show up in official work statistics, although they do show as benefit claimants. Figure 3.15 shows the major changes in levels of worklessness, with a 15% fall in Bilbao and Sheffield, and a 10% fall in Torino and Belfast.

There have also been big changes in the distribution of jobs between different sectors. We have analysed this closely for the German city of Bremen. Figure 3.16 shows how Bremen experienced job growth in service sectors but continuing job losses in other sectors, particularly its core traditional industries.

In Leipzig, a similar pattern of decline and regrowth emerges. Figure 3.17 shows the changing structure of jobs in the city over a 10-year period with a decline in traditional manufacturing and construction jobs, and an increase in service-related jobs. A similar shift to the service sector is common across industrial cities.[46]

Our findings on population and employment reinforce the ground-level evidence that the seven cities are indeed recovering, based on three main measures to gauge the cities' emerging condition: a slow down in job losses, a stabilisation of population and a redistribution of employment. In practice, this pattern reflects some new economic growth to compensate for the continuing job losses in manufacturing. The changing economy of cities has not yet pushed employment figures back to where they were in their almost forgotten manufacturing heyday but it demonstrates the resilience of cities in contrast with the belief that losing industry meant losing the economic rationale of these cities.

Figure 3.15: Unemployment rates in 1990 and 2005 (% of active workforce not in work or full-time studying or training)

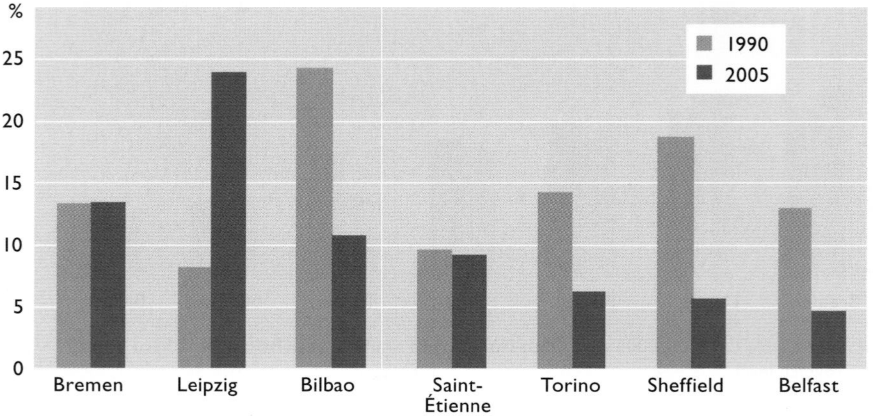

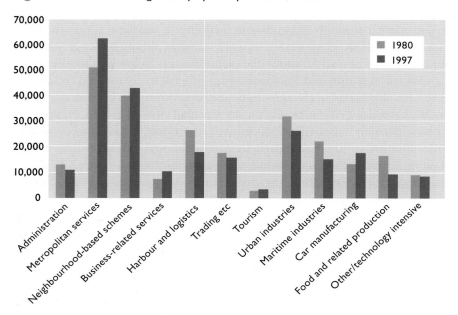

Sources: Stat. Landesamt Bremen, Stat. Bundesamt, Bundesanstalt für Arbeit, Stat. Landesamt Sachsen, Stat. Bundesamt, Bundesanstalt für Arbeit, Eustat, Inst. Nacional de Estadística (INE), Inst. National de la Statistique et des Études Économiques (INSEE), Inst. Nazionale di Statistica (ISTAT), Office for National Statistics (ONS), Northern Ireland Statistics & Research Agency (NISRA), Dept. of Finance and Personnel (DFP), Office for National Statistics (ONS)

Figure 3.16: Bremen, change in employment per sector, 1980 and 1997

Sources: Prange and Warsewa (2000); Statistisches Landesamt

Figure 3.17: Leipzig, change in employment per sector, 1991 and 2004 (%)

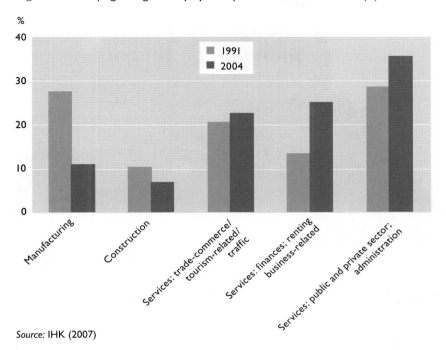

Source: IHK (2007)

Resilient cities

Over a decade or more of city centre restoration and economic recovery, a new urban image has emerged. The renovation of older housing and other buildings created a new atmosphere of 'residential appeal', as Saint-Étienne called it. Street activity increased in central and inner areas as people moved back and small new businesses opened. Pedestrian streets and public spaces based on traditional urban design increasingly limited, slowed or excluded traffic.

A combination of public investment and local leadership has fostered resident interest, generated service activity and encouraged cultural enterprises. It has attracted visitors, new urban tourists and residents who enjoy the remodelled monuments to earlier industrial achievement and the cultural and social life of cities (see Figure 3.18).

To a large extent, existing but previously unpopular housing has filled up with the growth in smaller households and has regained life. Nonetheless, smaller households mean less people, so more households are needed to sustain a population density in urban neighbourhoods that is essential to support many vital city services, such as frequent buses and local shops. Inevitably, smaller households will have to occupy smaller spaces to make this possible.[47] The aim over time continues to be the greater expansion of inner-city and city centre populations, which in turn will generate more service activity, a greater sense

Figure 3.18: Restoring and remodelling old industrial buildings: restored wharf houses creating new ateliers for artists and University of the Arts Department (Bremen)

of security and vitality. The redensification of cities supports more local services and greater economic activity. It also supports higher quality environments, more public transport, more pedestrian and family-friendly streets and potentially more energy-efficient use of resources.

At the same time, the expansion of metropolitan suburbs has not yet stopped, although there are signs that this outward drift too is beginning to slow. Some governments, notably the UK, Germany and France, have reduced incentives to 'sprawl' and increased incentives towards renovating existing homes and other buildings, alongside reusing brownfield sites.

However, the seven cities depend heavily on public funding and they still have major social, environmental and physical legacies that limit their capacity to adapt. A lot has been achieved but much remains to be done. Economic prospects are now clouded with uncertainty as the cities are all heavily dependent on wider economic conditions. As they have diversified their economies and developed a new skills base, they may show more resilience in the harshly competitive environments they face, compared with the late 20th century when they faced economic collapse. Their recent experience of rebuilding their physical, economic and social fabric following that collapse gives them invaluable experiences, methods and insights, well-oiled vehicles for change and a broader base of support for local leadership and innovation.

As we know from the financial turmoil of 2007 and 2008, a future left only to the market, devoid of significant public involvement, could weaken the progress of cities, which have relied on the injection of major public support. Private investors have been willing to invest in new initiatives without direct public 'carrots', but on the back of a strong public infrastructure and visible progress towards recovery, directly supported by governments. These firms operate in the market but within an active public framework. They benefit from the infrastructure, services and public realm, funded collectively by cities through the tax base. This public framework for supporting cities and communities is common across Europe, although it takes different shapes in different cities. It is less common and less well developed in the US, as we show in Part Four.

A combination of restored image, recovering population, inward investment, new enterprise and public backing has helped the cities to weather their post-industrial decline and to begin to recover. Their future will certainly involve many more storms that they may now be better placed to weather, building on their partnerships and their diversified economies. The next chapter looks more closely at smaller-scale, more local efforts to reintegrate marginalised areas and populations.

FOUR

Neighbourhood interventions: can small scale make a difference in big cities?

Improving poorer areas and integrating poorer communities

Over the long period of industrial growth and decline, urban populations were distributed according to their incomes, education, origins and functions in the economy into different parts of the city. Even poorer, working-class areas often had a hierarchy of more skilled and less skilled, more stable and less stable, leading to the ever-greater marginalisation of the poorest areas from city prosperity. Big neighbourhood inequalities have long been highly visible in cities, specifically with regard to income, housing conditions, school performance, crime, graffiti and vandalism. But as deindustrialisation took hold, these gaps widened.[48]

'Out of bounds' areas harmed the cities' attempts to generate new investment, and weak market cities have had many more difficult areas than average, because of their greater job and income losses. As a result, European cities struggling towards recovery focused major efforts on tackling these problems – disadvantaged and declining neighbourhoods loomed large in the thinking of city leaders in former industrial cities. Recovering cities desperate to attract new investors and employers needed three main attributes, in addition to attractive, lively city centres and good transport links to other cities:

- attractive housing and integrated, accessible, well-serviced neighbourhoods within the city;
- a skilled, trained, adaptable workforce at all levels to take up opportunities in new services;
- strong crime control, safe streets, traffic calming and quality urban environments.

Large, conspicuous enclaves of decay, poverty and crime deter progress and give the city a negative image.

Special social and neighbourhood projects in each city became increasingly prominent as they uncovered ways to tackle entrenched social dislocation. There were many more local initiatives than we could include in our study, each with its own particular setting, evolution and impacts. In this chapter we summarise the different approaches to overcoming poverty, neighbourhood decay, barriers to work and skills mismatches in the poorest areas, drawing on initiatives in each city.

Old working-class areas and post-war subsidised housing estates have high concentrations of low-skilled and out-of-work populations, with poor people ever more concentrated in the worst areas as better-off people have moved away. Sheffield illustrates the gap in income, jobs and conditions most acutely, with 14 years' lower life expectancy in the poorest neighbourhood compared with the richest. But Saint-Étienne, Belfast and Torino also have very high levels of inequality. [49]

Some communities are so deprived, with such limited incomes, that they appear starved of resources, facilities and services. In fact, in most European cities they often receive disproportionate help through public attempts to remediate acute problems. As new problems often overtake the solutions, neighbourhood programmes often seem to fail. Old industrial skills and a manual tradition have proved very hard to change even over two or more generations. There is a local mismatch between available labour and available jobs, combined with poor neighbourhood schools, low skills and a lack of working parental role models, which can affect both opportunities and aspirations. A strong tradition of manual work and a growth in part-time service jobs do not always blend.[50]

Multiple special programmes targeting the worst areas have followed in quick succession since the 1970s. Each wave of programmes is time and resource-limited, so some fundamental problems remain. Special programmes are never in place long enough to reverse such deeply embedded trends and social disarray. Bigger policy decisions, driven by the global and national economy, international and internal migration, government housebuilding and other targets can undermine and limit progress. Therefore, neighbourhood decay, community vulnerability and skills mismatches remain big challenges, which all seven cities were tackling in somewhat similar ways.

City governments developed targeted programmes to tackle four main types of deep-set disadvantage:

- inner area renewal;
- the rescue of large estates, usually on the periphery of cities;
- community enterprise and community programmes directly aimed at disadvantaged or vulnerable social groups: youth, families, minorities, out of work, disabled etc;
- skills development and 'hand-holding' into work, aiming to link potential recruits to the job market with prospective employers.

All the seven cities adopted at least three of the four approaches, invariably concentrated in the same areas. All the programmes we examined, whether focusing on physical renewal, social and community programmes or jobs and skills, were created and supported at city level but implemented on the ground within neighbourhoods. They offered additional facilities and activities, more social support and training. Table 4.1 shows the way the programmes and projects operated. Table 4.2 shows how each city prioritised neighbourhood renewal, applying local investment to inner and outer city projects.

Table 4.1: How projects operate at city and neighbourhood level

Leipzig	• The city government has developed a strategy to increase the residential and commercial appeal of run-down, vacant neighbourhoods, combining funding from government and the EU • Individual projects are developed to suit each neighbourhood, coordinated by the city council
Bremen	• The city government pools funding from government programmes and allocates it to deprived neighbourhoods • Neighbourhood projects focus on the social integration of socially excluded (the case study areas have a high proportion of minority ethnic population)
Sheffield	• JOBMatch is a Sheffield-based programme to attract companies to Sheffield, offering a free human resources consultancy service to inward investors • JobNet is a sister programme set up in the city to run 15 neighbourhood-based drop-in job centres which offer personal employment advice and guidance to local residents, and advertises the jobs that JOBMatch adds to its database, alongside other local vacancies sourced by its employer liaison team
Belfast	• Belfast City Council is developing landmark regeneration projects to restore confidence in the city and reconcile divided communities • Skills development and job access form a central part of this regeneration effort • GEMS is part of larger regeneration programme in central and inner Belfast, supporting local people in accessing new service sector jobs; it borders on interface areas of deprived Protestant and Catholic neighbourhoods
Bilbao	• Lan Ekintza is a social-support organisation, coordinating efforts by public and private bodies working in social fields to help low-income residents and new small enterprises. It also: • provides assistance during the creation of new businesses as well as existing small and medium-sized companies • offers training and skills development to help the workforce cope with economic restructuring • offers assistance in finding jobs • provides specific programmes targeting migrant populations
Torino	• The *Projetto Speciale Periferie* (PSP) (Plan for Marginal Neighbourhoods) unit runs 15 different neighbourhood regeneration projects funded by different programmes, using a novel integrated approach to delivery that brings together all municipal departments that serve neighbourhoods. It coordinates and (where necessary) funds extensive participation for each project • Neighbourhood projects are individually designed and piloted by a local working group featuring representatives from the community and the PSP, which run regular wider consultations with residents
Saint-Étienne	• The ANRU programme is regenerating four large deprived neighbourhoods in Saint-Étienne, two in the historic core and two on the periphery. It is upgrading over 6,000 homes, with some partial demolition. Its aim is to improve the residential appeal of the city by improving the poorest homes and environments and to integrate the poorest communities into the city • The regeneration of Tarantaize, one of the inner areas, aims to create a more socially mixed community through improving the neighbourhood's residential appeal, using rehabilitation/reconstruction/de-densification of the existing stock and an upgrading of existing infrastructure, transport and cultural amenities

Table 4.2: Three types of targeted neighbourhood programmes in the seven cities

	Neighbourhood renewal	Inner-city renewal	Outer estates
Leipzig	City-wide housing and urban renewal – all older inner areas and major peripheral estates were targeted	Comprehensive renewal of extremely decayed street properties with multiple forms of investment, some demolition, open space creation, incentives for restoration, e.g. Leipzig	Extremely large 1970s communist-built housing areas, far from city centre, with fairly good facilities and amenities, more mixed social make-up, but falling demand and decay; major upgrading and some demolition, e.g. Grünau
Bremen	10 poorest neighbourhoods targeted through WiN, including inner and outer areas	Combined approach – facade improvement, subsidies for upgrading, new facilities, social support, community events, very little demolition, e.g. Gröpelingen	Several extremely large, unpopular, hard-to-manage estates of 1,000+ units. High minority ethnic population. Some partial demolition and remodelling but majority upgraded; intensive residents' consultation and representation, e.g. Osterholz-Tenever
Sheffield	'Face lift' on inner-city terraces, some major social housing estates rebuilt, following demolition – at least 20 areas targeted in both inner and outer city	Different neighbourhood renewal programmes for different inner areas, e.g. New Deal for Communities in Burngreave; Housing Market Renewal in other areas – all involving upgrading and some demolition, e.g. Burngreave, Fir Vale	Some very poor large outer estates demolished and rebuilt as mixed housing, others improved through estate renewal, e.g. The Manor, Norfolk Park
Belfast	All social housing estates and all low income inner-city areas targeted with social programmes	Inner-city areas are the hardest to tackle because the sectarian divides are so strong and communities very close to each other are often still divided by peace walls, e.g. east-west Belfast	Many new publicly rented homes built in outer areas since The Troubles began in 1970s – mainly good quality but socially deprived, some estate renewal
Bilbao	All the poorest areas were targeted for renewal, Barrio Viejo in the city centre and Miribilla further out. Barakaldo is one of the poorest outer suburbs	Concerted upgrading of historic medieval Barrio Viejo and also the more recent 19th-century run-down neighbourhoods near the centre – big improvements carried out, very little demolition, e.g. Barrio Viejo	Several dense high-rise outer areas built with some subsidies in the 1970s but mostly privately owned; some demolition and rebuilding but mainly renovation and upgrading, e.g. Miribilla, Barakaldo
Torino	14 poorest areas of the city targeted through the neighbourhoods programmes, some city centre, some outer estates	The historic inner areas are dense, attractive and potentially valuable but often very run-down and crowded with immigrant households, e.g. Porto Palazzo	Some of the poorest, most decayed areas of the city are in outer housing estates built in the 1970s, now the target of upgrading, e.g. Via Arquata, Mirafiori
Saint-Étienne	Four *Grand Projects de Ville*, two inner-city, two large outer estates, were upgrading significant and conspicuous neighbourhoods	Two large inner neighbourhoods with cheap, dilapidated properties, low-income households, large concentrations of minorities – targeted with government funds for upgrading, environmental improvements, very little demolition, e.g. Tarantaize	Several large outer estates built for social housing. High minority concentrations, serious decline in amenities, services, standards. Big national reinvestment programme targeted two biggest for upgrading and environmental improvements, e.g. Quartiers Sud-Est

One way that the cities maximised the impact of intensive, local programmes was to change the way they related to local communities, both in inner and outer areas, whether in tackling neighbourhood renewal or skills development. A strongly participative approach was the hallmark of the special neighbourhood projects in several of the cities. Torino, Bremen, Sheffield and Belfast had particularly striking approaches to transforming relationships with residents through a community-oriented, 'bottom–up' approach to consultation and involvement. It would have been impossible to tackle the extreme conditions of the poorest neighbourhoods while ignoring the existing community. Table 4.3 shows the participative structures and the role of community partnerships in disadvantaged neighbourhoods in the seven cities.

Table 4.3: Participative structures, community partnerships and resident involvement in the seven cities

	Participative structures	Community partnerships
Leipzig	Grünau – close community liaison over upgrading and structural decisions about whether to proceed with limited demolition. Similarly, decisions about demolition, new open spaces and building renovation in the inner city required close involvement with residents	Huge citizen push on many fronts but seems mostly politically led following reunification. Outer estates (e.g. Grünau) were more traditionally populated, so more community activity
Bremen	Local resident representatives took part in participatory budgeting for social programmes, allowing community priorities to prevail	Lots of community involvement in special social programmes, lots of 'hand-holding', many special community spaces and facilities
Sheffield	Community-based enterprises and close local involvement programmes – area representatives for all upgrading programmes shared in decisions with officials	Lots of community representation and grassroots organisations but uphill struggle to influence major policy; also some fragility, due to funding difficulties
Belfast	All activity has to be brokered across community divides within the troubled areas, involving many levels of representation	Inescapable negotiation of all moves with different communities; highest involvement possible
Bilbao	High citizen engagement due to political dynamics of the Basque Country has resulted from efforts to help residents in low-income areas	Some community-level initiatives, e.g. in upgrading areas in thr historic centre by Surbisa and social programmes in Barakaldo
Torino	Neighbourhoods Unit was set up to encourage and allow priorities to be shaped by resident participation at a local level	Big efforts at consultation and involvement during strategic plan deliberations (1998–2000) but almost inevitably diluted over time
Saint-Étienne	Resident representatives' committee feeds into the *Grands Projets*, although high-level decisions are hard to influence; close community liaison over rehousing of residents within renewal areas	Some resident consultation and involvement (regarded as 'tokenistic' by some)

The cities faced many long-run barriers to these new ideas. Trust was often missing between the town hall and community leaders, but also more worryingly, mistrust, suspicion and alienation often lay deep within communities. The extreme disruption to social and economic security that arose from the demise of major employers and of other recognised local institutions, such as local shops, has left a legacy of anger and disillusionment in the most harshly affected communities. Table 4.4 sets out some of the barriers and challenges that the cities face at community level.

Table 4.4: Community barriers and challenges to community cohesion

	Barriers	Challenges
Leipzig	People were hard to attract into the vacuum left by the abrupt collapse of the GDR	Restoring collapse of confidence in city prospects; revitalising city streets and shops; renovating deeply decayed, derelict properties; making good abandoned spaces
Bremen	Strong polarisation and semi-segregation in run-down areas caused deep civic unease	Strong social welfare tradition within city did not extend to inter-ethnic relations.
Sheffield	Big minority concentration in poorest inner areas	Overwhelmingly white but poor outer estates have proved very hard to integrate socially; strong refugee communities causing some resentment and divisions with more established ethnic groups and the white population
Belfast	There were 56 'peace walls' after the Peace Agreement in 1998, left in place to ensure no return to the previous communal violence	Thirty years of violent community clashes on the streets of Belfast have created physical and psychological barriers unparalleled in the other cities
Bilbao	Bitter feelings of isolation and loss of status in the worst-hit local communities	Bilbao has been wracked with terrorist violence as well as losing its prestigious industrial and economic dominance
Torino	The city has lost much of its former national influence, status and wealth	Poorer social housing areas has become run down in dense inner areas, as they depopulate and have become crowded again with mainly African immigrants
Saint-Étienne	So strongly working class was the influence of the mining tradition, local culture and remaining population of the city that it has proved extremely resistant to change	The city has lost so much population to the suburbs that its city centre has become uniquely poor and decayed in France; the absorption of immigrant communities dating back to the 1960s and 1970s has been a particular challenge

Many of the cities have large minority ethnic populations concentrated in the poorest areas, both within inner cities and in outer estates. There are often tensions between more settled, indigenous working-class communities and newcomers of foreign origin. One reason for targeting the poorest areas is to overcome ethnic tensions and to help integrate communities that otherwise might stay permanently on the edge of mainstream society. Operating at community level and adopting a strongly participative approach is designed to help overcome the truly major barriers to integration faced by the seven cities.

A particular worry concerns the children of immigrants who, on the one hand, are finding themselves 'between two worlds', and on the other, might go to almost 'ghetto–like' schools, where contact with 'local' children is almost impossible.[51] The physical renewal of properties cannot address such complex human problems, and most of the programmes have at least some focus on helping minority populations overcome disadvantage to become more integrated. This ongoing and deeply worrying challenge has only partially been met. Table 4.5 outlines some of the approaches that helped to address this problem.

Table 4.5: How the seven cities developed programmes to help integrate minorities in disadvantaged areas

	Focus on integration	Specific projects or programmes
Leipzig	Very few minorities and large-scale housing abandonment, so the issue is holding onto and attracting back more skilled residents in order to reinforce a more mixed, more stable population	Strong incentives to upgrade existing urban stock
Bremen	Major concentrations of minority ethnic groups in poorest inner and outer areas has attracted special social investment through (WiN/*Soziale Stadt*); cultural and inter-faith celebrations bring together different communities.	Multi-cultural festivals; upgrading and neighbourhood projects targeting the poorest areas with highest minority concentrations
Sheffield	Community trusts operate in ethnically mixed areas and offer services for minority communities, e.g. NUCA. Attempts at creating more socially mixed communities through upgrading and redevelopment, although the city is still very socioeconomically polarised	Anti-racism programmes run by council
Belfast	Peace III programme (EU) to heal divisions, careful cross-sectarian conciliation efforts throughout the city, including particularly interface and front-line areas; strong focus on city centre activities that break down religious divisions; some new immigrant communities	Peace III programmes cross religious divides and create common ground, shared by all communities
Bilbao	Special efforts in areas of need where newer foreign immigrants have settled, also in poorer older areas with high concentrations of working-class residents, often migrants from other parts of Spain (south and far west)	Some neighbourhood renewal and job programmes targeted at minority areas; improvement programmes are helping to integrate southern Spanish migrants from 1960s and 1970s, as well as more recent arrivals
Torino	Some neighbourhood projects prioritise immigrant needs, and several of the targeted deprived inner areas have very high concentrations of new minorities in extremely crowded conditions	Porto Palazzo programme is targeting illegal immigrants and helping them to integrate economically and socially
Saint-Étienne	As in Italy, there is a tradition of officially recognised community 'associations' which do important work on the ground targeting youth, but also concerning community relations and resident capacity building; the city council is attempting to create a more social mix in the most deprived neighbourhoods by upgrading housing and amenities; it is working mainly with children and young people	Inner-city upgrading targeting high minority areas.; youth, children's and community centres are all targeting minorities

None of the programmes we saw matched the scale of the challenge of integration. However, without these special efforts, minorities might have remained outside the possible benefits of local programmes. As it was, the efforts at inclusion at least meant that some minority ethnic children would grow up with an awareness of belonging to a wider community than their parents. The city authorities and the wider community also derived benefit from these programmes. Decision makers, civic bodies, schools, health services, churches, employers and emerging new structures all have to accommodate the idea that European cities comprise many communities, some of which are being excluded by virtue of their origin, some by misfortune, some by the twists and turns of the economy. It is not good for the future of any city to allow this separation to fester. Inner-city run-down areas have the biggest concentrations of newly arrived and vulnerable residents.

Inner-city neighbourhood renewal

The seven cities have many distinct neighbourhoods with serious problems of physical decline, although very different problems are confronting inner and outer areas. The programmes targeted local areas of around 5,000 people. We consider inner and outer areas separately, because of the different challenges they pose, even though many of the problems have similar causes. However, the conditions and outcomes were very different in the two types of areas.

Inner areas have old decayed stock, often over a century old, following a clear street pattern laid down before the First World War, with little amenity space but lots of street facilities, public transport and easy access to the city centre, a vitality and mix of uses that has not been completely lost.

The underlying aim of inner-city renewal is to reintegrate low-income, often ethnically distinct, communities into the main core city. The cost of replacement housing is prohibitive because inner cities have a mix of good and bad housing. It is actually cheaper to renovate most of the stock, even though some of it is highly dilapidated and therefore costly to repair. The option of demolition would create intense problems of relocation for the vulnerable communities in these areas. The main focus of renewal is therefore on refurbishment, remodelling buildings and improving facades and street environments.

Demolition, where it was carried out, was almost always controversial and intrinsically unpopular because it represented the destruction of valued and expensive resources. It reflected a failure of viability and at least in the short term it damaged the image of the area (see Figure 4.1). However, where there was spare housing capacity, as in Leipzig, Saint-Étienne and Sheffield, some partial, carefully targeted demolition could remove eyesores and restrict supply in a way that made the surviving homes more attractive, making demand for the limited remaining 'rescued' homes more certain. The reuse of the bare spaces, created by demolition, for open space, community facilities or play areas made some inner areas more family-friendly and more attractive to existing and new residents.

Figure 4.1: Small demolition site in inner Saint-Étienne

The upgrading of inner areas retained their overall structure, beautified their often inherently attractive street fronts, improved their street environments and amenities, and restored their viability although much remained to be done. The upgrading of inner areas offered relatively easy gains compared with outer areas:

- The built form is more traditional, more adaptable and has more potential to be made attractive than newer outer estates. Therefore it is easier to convert to modern standards.
- Inner areas are nearer the centre, on better transport routes, with more mixed uses, diverse owners and facilities. People accept a greater social mix within dense inner areas, leading to more informal social contact and integration, if not more explicit mixing.
- The street patterns and clear frontages of older areas are familiar and appealing to a wide band of residents. They provide shops and other mixed uses, offering closer street surveillance because of density. Proximity between homes and street activity entice more people onto the streets, making them more secure.
- The challenge of renovating older street properties relates to the age of some building elements, the lack of modern amenities and general neglect, rather than to the main structures of the buildings that are almost always sound. Although they need adapting to modern household patterns and living requirements, even these problems make the investment required far lower than replacement costs.[52]

- Reclaimed streets look strikingly attractive to younger, more professional workers and students, a category of new urban residents we call 'urban pioneers', who move into poorer inner areas, partly attracted by the ethnic diversity, mixture of uses and proximity to the city centre. They then invest their energy into making these areas more attractive. Small businesses and start-up enterprises find inner areas cheap and convenient, so live–work is a common pattern in renovated houses. This process of 'low-level gentrification' is far more beneficial to declining cities than simply continuing to lose population.[53]

Table 4.6 shows the broad spread of renewal actions taken within inner areas.

Table 4.6: Specific examples of renewal actions in inner areas

	Facelift to facades	Street improvements	Incentives to private landlords to upgrade	Some newbuild	Limited demolition	Creation of new open spaces	Improved facilities	Renovation of homes
Leipzig	✓	✓	✓	✓	✓	✓	✓	✓
Bremen	✓	✓	✓	✓	–	✓	✓	✓
Sheffield	✓	✓	–	✓	✓	✓	✓	✓
Belfast	✓	✓	–	✓	✓	✓	✓	✓
Bilbao	✓	✓	–	✓	–	–	✓	✓
Torino	✓	✓	–	–	–	✓	✓	✓
Saint-Étienne	✓	✓	–	✓	✓	✓	✓	✓

Impacts of inner-city renewal

The special project areas that we visited had a basic traditional street front layout, with run-down terraced houses or six-storey continental apartment buildings, also in terraces. Many small, inconspicuous facilities and enterprises were 'tucked into' these streets, creating an atmosphere of activity that made inner areas feel alive, even though they were poor. However, a pervasive atmosphere of poverty reflected both the status of the indigenous community that survived in the areas and the conspicuous newcomers, in most cases immigrants from abroad or from far-flung poorer regions of the country (for example Andalusians in Bilbao and Sicilians in Torino) (see Figures 4.2 a–d).

The neighbourhood renewal projects offer a vision of the ideal urban neighbourhood, accessible, attractive, historic, offering cheap but potentially good-quality homes, multiple amenities including reclaimed spaces, community facilities, reopened small shops, workshops and so on. The major incentives to upgrade homes, offered by governments at only a fraction of the cost of replacing

Figure 4.2a-d: San Salvario (Torino); Tarantaize (Saint-Étienne); Burngreave (Sheffield); Gröpelingen (Bremen)

homes, seemed to win over private owners and landlords. Much of the upgrading still remained to be done in the areas in 2007–08, but the improved facades and better environments already had an immediate visual impact and the community facilities were impressively active and well used (see Figures 4.3a–b).

4.2c

4.2d

All the area programmes were managed through community-based offices (sometimes in community centres), and became the organising bases for community liaison and community development. So the tools of neighbourhood renewal became intrinsic to success and part of the changed relationships that were part of the original challenge. Often the high-level renewal programme teams remained headquartered in the city centre but had frequent local contact and in-depth knowledge of the areas through visits and local meetings. They

Figures 4.3a-b: Restored main square: the Porta Palazzo regeneration project centred around the open air city centre market where many illegal immigrants work (Torino)

4.3a

4.3b

had no choice but to spend time on site because decisions had to relate to many different individual and site-specific needs. The project managers had to work, block by block, house by house, site by site, in order to rescue and restore as many buildings as possible, while winning over landlords, tenants, local businesses and community organisations.

Many complex negotiations were involved with householders, neighbours, planners, utilities, funders, surveyors, architects and technical advisers. The amount of detailed, painstaking ground-level work was decisive in changing conditions from within. This was key to rapid progress as project leaders became committed to the communities they were trying to help. Part of their mission everywhere was to retain as well as attract residents in order to keep the areas functioning. The actual disruption to the areas was much smaller than it would have been with wide-scale demolition because house improvements did not generally involve major structural change. The care that was taken to support residents and to meet their common wish to stay reinforced relationships and added a human dimension to the work that local staff told us they valued.[54] The future of these inner areas seemed brighter and more promising than previously, and our studies showed just how significant the gains were.

Rescuing large outer estates

Peripheral housing estates proved far harder to restore successfully and to integrate fully into the rest of the city. Their location, often several kilometres from the centre, and their overwhelming architectural form set them apart. Nonetheless, all the seven cities tried to achieve a positive outcome since they could not afford to lose such large areas of potentially valuable housing. The fact that they were usually separate, monolithic, mono-functional, poorly connected, imposing structures with many distinctive, unattractive features meant that they were seriously challenging. They were harder to upgrade because they were invariably built in concrete and steel, in stern-looking, hard-to-adapt blocks, with many communal, but ill-defined spaces between homes. Their appearance was generally alienating, and over time they had become deeply unpopular and marginal to the city. On the other hand, they were still a big housing resource, usually with 2,000 or more modern homes, which could not easily or cheaply be removed and replaced. They too had become part of the urban landscape, and were defended by at least some of their residents (see Figures 4.4a–b).[55]

The large estates we visited shared certain hard-to-change characteristics that undermined their long-term viability. They were too separate from the city to be easily integrated, and had fewer transport links, fewer local services, jobs or facilities than inner areas. Low-income households without cars are heavily reliant on public transport. Even with good bus and train links, as in Osterholz-Tenever (Bremen), Grünau (Leipzig) and Barakaldo (Bilbao), outer estates are up to fifteen kilometres from the city centre. All the estates were originally built under government incentives to house low-income residents and were predominantly for rent from social or public landlords. As industrial jobs vanished, so the populations they housed became poorer, and today they have unemployment levels that are double, triple or further above the city average.[56] Everywhere large, modern social housing estates seem to drift to the bottom.

Figures 4.4a-b: Large outer estates: Saint-Étienne; Bilbao

The estates were built to standard patterns and styles, often across national boundaries, in large blocks of flats and, although there are more houses than flats in social housing estates in England and Ireland, this has not overcome the problems of isolation and mono-tenure, mono-class renting and the concentrated poverty of subsidised housing areas. Generally the social and physical infrastructure is too limited to accommodate the full range of necessary activities for households on low incomes, although on very big estates like Grünau in Leipzig the large but declining population of tens of thousands supports a complex of shops and other services.

The low-income communities in outer estates are often from diverse backgrounds, with high concentrations of minority ethnic communities, which have proved hard to integrate. This problem has been made much worse by the general levels of poverty and the distance from job opportunities. There is therefore a local need for social supports of all kinds, with big calls on additional funding, special programmes, help with children, youth and family problems. The lack of locally based jobs accelerates the decline in environmental conditions since public funding and subsidised rents are not sufficiently dedicated to basic jobs to maintain estate conditions.

People in work usually try to move away or avoid moving in if they possibly can, making population turnover and community instability big problems. It is hard to adapt the local skills base or to remotivate residents who have lost jobs. The distance from other core economic activity and the poor work experience of the population all alienate potential employers, making it even harder to bridge the gap into work or to attract a different type of population base. This combination of economic, social and physical problems makes the renewal of estates seem harder, more elusive and more questionable.

Why governments intervene in outer estates

With these complex, interlocking built-in problems, why have all the cities poured large resources into estate rescue? There are a number of crucial reasons that made the targeted rescue programmes on mass housing estates inevitable:

- Massive investment is tied up in the physical infrastructure of estates: they are very costly to demolish as they are built in concrete and steel reinforced blocks.
- The general anxiety of European governments to invest in the poorest areas, recognising that they are constantly left behind, has made outer estate rescue programmes possible. The governments drove their creation in the first place just as the industrial era was coming to an end, so they accepted some responsibility for the plight of their populations.
- There is a real reluctance among many social landlords to destroy structurally sound housing leading to replacement costs that are at least double and often triple the cost of upgrading. The impact of demolition on communities is

highly damaging and the process itself is complex and slow, particularly if residents resist the process.

- The communities concentrated in outer estates cannot simply be removed. They have high social needs and a fragile social support structure. It is hard to imagine dispersing so many people into existing homes and spaces even though most of the cities have spare capacity.

- Even with substantial demolition of up to a third of all dwellings, as in German outer estates such as Osterholz-Tenever and Grünau, a majority of blocks have been upgraded and produce quite a dramatic visual impact. In the outer estates we visited, the demolished blocks were often the furthest away from the centre of the estates where facilities were usually located. These blocks were often the largest and hardest to manage. Their removal increased the viability of remaining housing areas.

- Estate rescue, involving remodelling and restoring difficult estates and managing them carefully has a successful track record.[57]

Why demolition is not more widely adopted

It is very hard to uproot whole, large, isolated estate communities without generating opposition and unmanageable community tensions, in spite of the ongoing problems. For example, in Grünau there is intense opposition to extending the planned demolition in the future, even though the estate still has many empty flats and would possibly be more attractive if it was smaller. There is hope that over time demand may rise, but there is also a sense of not knowing what the future holds.

The fear of uprooting 'settled' minorities who made a niche for themselves as surplus space became available is grounded in the volatile relations between minority groups, particularly young people, and authorities. Minorities would be hard to disperse and integrate into homes elsewhere in the city. It seems more promising to work with the existing community and to attract in other groups, which is beginning to happen at Osterholz-Tenever in Bremen and Quartiers Sud-Est in Saint-Étienne. Interestingly, in virtually all white estate communities in Sheffield and Belfast, similar community defences have been aroused. In the Manor Estate in Sheffield, a large older 'cottage' estate on the edge of the city, the rebuilding of the estate, following a decision to demolish it for structural reasons, has involved rehousing many residents locally, recognising community ties that have built up.

The *Muraille de Chine* (Wall of China) in Saint-Étienne's Quartiers Sud-Est, one of four special *Grands Projets de Ville*, was an extreme, Corbusian example of unmanageable mass peripheral housing, with several hundred flats in a single giant block. When it was removed in the late 1990s, the residents, many North African in origin, and very poorly integrated, were rehoused in other parts of the estate. While it certainly did not solve all the problems of the estate, it reduced many social and management pressures, and it reinforced public support for a very marginal community. On the other hand, the estate has remained unsettled with many visible community tensions and unresolved social problems, clearly demonstrated by the disorders in 2005.[58]

Over time, the estates have become more established as better links to the city centre have been established and spare scraps of land between the city and peripheral areas have filled up. Public transport has improved to some outer areas to overcome isolation. For example Barakaldo, Bilbao, a poor, densely built-up, high-rise, working-class suburb, which is technically a separate municipality from Bilbao, is far more integrated with the city now. Large peripheral estates tend gradually to be improved by public action.

Meanwhile, the homes themselves were usually built to reasonable standards and were not generally the main focus for upgrading. The large outer estates were all built post war and are often fairly modern in their basic amenities. Residents usually describe their flats as satisfactory but their environments and social conditions as poor.[59]

Impacts of estate renewal

There were many changes that influenced the progress made on the outer estates, in spite of their problems:

- A big factor making estates work better and become more acceptable is the change in physical appearance. Cladding, decorating and greening the outer walls of blocks have made them brighter and softer on the eye.
- The common areas and surroundings of renovated blocks are more secure and useable, through on-site management and maintenance. Also, the renewal programmes have generated more care both within the community and from landlords.
- Strong entrance doors with unbreakable glass have been installed, opening into clean, attractive supervised foyers with a concierge who recognises people, takes parcels and post and helps people with shopping. Communal entrances become civilised, controlled, attractive spaces, instead of threatening no-man's-lands, which residents have to cross to get home or to get out, making them feel alternately prisoners and excluded.
- Demolition eliminated the most difficult to manage, biggest and most unpopular blocks, thereby reducing the overall size of the estate, making them more manageable.
- The new investment has encouraged more diverse uses and some new jobs.
- The greener, more carefully maintained environments have had a softening impact on the previously hard, concrete surroundings.
- The overall upgrading has led to more flats being occupied and more aspiring residents moving in, following concerted efforts at marketing. This has made them more financially viable and raised the morale of staff, community leaders and residents.

- Social programmes, particularly targeting children and young people, have helped build confidence and communication.
- The upgrading of facades, communal entrances and surrounds has transformed the previously forbidding appearance of giant-sized blocks, making them stand out even more dramatically on the sky lines, but in a way that appeals rather than deters (see Figures 4.5a–b).

Figures 4.5a-b: Upgrading in Osterholz-Tenever (Bremen); Via Arquata (Torino)

There are still many questions about young people's futures in these areas; estate structures have still not been sufficiently modified or integrated to make them secure in the long term. Despite progress, the estates are very much on the edge of cities, making them socially and economically more precarious than in generally recovering inner cities. The battle to create a better social mix is much harder than in more proximate areas. It is also harder to generate new enterprises or attract private investment. In spite of many improvements, they remain essentially 'social housing estates'. Table 4.7 shows examples of mass housing estates in six of the cities, their problems and progress.

Table 4.7: Problems and progress on outer estates

	Problems	Progress
Leipzig: Grünau	Massive East German 'new town' with 35,000 homes, in high blocks far outside the core city; popular until reunification, then serious population outflow	Big injection of federal funds for estate upgrading, some selective demolition around edges and improved facilities; has become more viable through shrinkage
Bremen: Osteholz-Tenever	Planned as giant new settlement in the 1970s, but building stopped half way at 3,000 units due to overwhelming scale, popular rejection and financial problems	About 10 large blocks are being removed, opening up room for play space and community facilities; overall upgrading externally and internally, making estate much more attractive to wider social groups
Sheffield: Park Hill[1]	Imposing concrete block structure in the city centre, built in the mass housing zenith of the late 1960s and early 1970s; very problematic management and maintenance; now listed by English Heritage as an architectural monument	Big regeneration project with Urban Splash, a city-based regeneration company, partnered with the city council and a non-profit housing association; the flats are being totally refitted and the estate will offer high-rise, mixed-use city centre living; in contrast to the others this estate sits just above the main railway station
Bilbao: Barakaldo	Large, dense suburb of high-rise blocks, receiving government subsidies, mostly occupied by former ship and steel workers from southern Spain; low-income, poor facilities, outside main city	Some upgrading and general improvements; also strong social development programmes
Torino: Via Arquata	Blocks of social, subsidised housing on the edge of the city; became very run-down, dilapidated and poor as jobs in a nearby factory went	Careful block improvements accompanied by street upgrading, expansion of pedestrian routes with attractive planting; strong resident involvement
Saint-Étienne: Quartiers Sud-Est	Large concrete HLM on edge of Saint-Étienne, renowned for its *Muraille de Chine* (Wall of China), its large minority population and its occasional disturbances	Improved environment, gradually upgrading of blocks; older part of estate (dating from the 1950s) is very well maintained and attractive; investment in community facilities

Note: [1] We include Park Hill in the city centre because of its architectural importance as a mass housing estate and because its social and management problems closely reflect wider mass housing problems. HLM= *habitation à loyer modéré* (rent-controlled housing)

On balance, the long-term outlook for the estates is still unclear, even after the investments of the past decade. There was a view, sometimes aired, that at least in some places the estates might be costing more money than they were worth and might in the long run outlive their role. On the other hand, the need for affordable homes seems likely to expand and there are no obvious signs of large-scale replacement programmes of low-cost housing for poor populations. They are therefore likely to go on providing a valuable resource for low-income communities for a long time to come.

Neighbourhood renewal areas with their shortage of work, general decay and accumulated social problems are an intense microcosm of the much wider problems of weak market cities. Social polarisation between areas of a city has shaped the political priority given to neighbourhood renewal. The programmes are as much social as physical, even though most spending has been focused on physical conditions.

City decision makers realised that physical change did not of itself solve social problems, and nor did shifting needy and problematic populations around. Given that communities were established in mass estates and that inner cities were being revalued, city leaders have opted increasingly to support rather than remove existing communities, retaining many embedded social problems within estates on the edge of cities, or within older, poorer streets and places in the inner city. The earlier experience of moving people from old slums into multiple new estates around the edge of cities proved so problematic that it now seems better to address problems directly than to redistribute them across new areas of the city. The long timescales for resettling families makes the task of rehousing such vast numbers daunting. In any case, the cities are now far more built up than before. Suburban communities oppose further building, and sprawl is increasingly contentious as environmental pressures mount.[60]

Meanwhile, there is a growing shortage of cheap housing across Europe.[61] As social housing subsidies have declined, new kinds of demand have risen, partly due to immigration, partly due to family change and the growth in lone parents and partly due to the loss of former industrial jobs and the rise in economic inactivity and inequality. This means that lower-income areas, whether estates or inner cities, are simultaneously more socially precarious and more valuable than they were when they were built.

Community retention and a greater social mix are particularly important because inner cities and outer estates have lost so much population. One common reaction is to sell the improved empty homes to working households to improve the neighbourhood economy and support social integration. At Osterholz-Tenever the upgrading manager explained the lengths they were going to to recruit new tenants "in work, who could pay rents and maintain conditions. The flats themselves are beautiful as you can see". The show flat was modern, spacious, secure and very good value. "There's more a psychological than practical barrier to surmount."[62]

The other common pattern is to offer local rehousing to those affected by demolition, but who want to stay in the neighbourhood, since filling empty units is a primary goal. Saint-Étienne regeneration staff have invested major efforts in retaining the existing population and 'hand-holding' vulnerable residents into new homes. As one senior official explained, "We learnt our lessons from previous demolition. It doesn't solve problems – we destroyed our communities."[63] Improving social conditions is easier from a base of residents attached to their homes and areas.

Community action and participation

Community involvement in decisions, community facilities for local activities, community-based services and social support for the most precarious households could transform conditions, since many earlier problems stemmed from neglect and poor local management, rather than simply the intractability of problems. There have been many experiments since the late 1970s and early 1980s in all the countries that show the value of community involvement in inner areas and estate renewal.[64] Community development programmes were developed to stabilise inner and outer areas with diverse populations, many incomers and relatively high population turnover. Most social programmes were time limited with uncertain long-term funding.

In spite of the differences between outer and inner areas, community-based renewal activity followed a common basic pattern in all the cities, which is summed up in Box 4.1.

Box 4.1: Community-based renewal activity

- Some *selective demolition* of obsolete housing, particularly large 1960s blocks and semi-derelict 19th-century terraces
- *External upgrading* of houses and blocks
- *Incentives* for private owners to do up their rented property
- *Reclamation of derelict* open spaces and former demolition sites, usually for open space and play areas
- Creation of *children's play areas* in communal areas of estates or open spaces in older areas
- Efforts to attract *better-off, in-work* residents to fill empty upgraded houses to create more balanced communities, while also retaining and rehousing locally the existing community
- *Attempts to stem the decline* of local shops and schools, offering special terms and incentives and upgrading premises
- General recognition of the *value of these areas* and their local assets, offering capacity for community uses and support for the development of community activity
- Recognition in almost all cases that *areas with even the most severe problems can be reclaimed*
- Intense *investment, attention to detail and 'hand-holding'* of local residents
- Care, repair and *local management*, making neighbourhood survival more likely

---

Most renewal programmes include a process of consulting residents so that they can feed in their own priorities and share information on their particular needs. There have been big debates in several cities about whether this involvement is purely tokenistic, but our impression from visits to all the neighbourhoods was that care was being taken by local government and renewal teams to win the support of residents for neighbourhood renewal. Without their cooperation, local rescue programmes were unlikely to succeed. Table 4.8 gives examples of community-based programmes and initiatives supporting residents.

Table 4.8: Examples of community-based programmes and initiatives supporting residents

Leipzig	*Soziale Stadt* Programmes were directed to the most deprived areas. In east Leipzig with its high levels of social welfare dependency, highest city-wide share of immigrants and less attractive urban spaces, funds were invested in creating public spaces on land cleared from demolished housing, neighbourhood management activities and support for small business owners in order to support the local community and improve the overall appeal and image of the area
Bremen	*Wohnen in Nachbarschaften (WiN)* A special city programme developed by the city-state government to fund and organise social programmes in the poorest neighbourhoods
Sheffield	*New Deal for Communities* A 10-year programme, combining Burngreave community involvement, community-based projects targeting families, young people and minorities, the expansion of local facilities and skills development. The programme closed abruptly in 2009 when it ran out of money, threatening the continuation of some programmes
Belfast	*Peace III programme* A 10-year EU-backed programme aiming to reconcile divided and hostile communities within the city by providing shared spaces created and used by different communities working together
Bilbao	*Surbisa* A neighbourhood renewal agency set up in 1985. It targets help at the poorest and most vulnerable residents
Torino	*Projetto Speciale Periferie (PSP)* Set up by the city council, this programme has worked closely with residents to provide needed social facilities and improve local environments. It has helped develop several social enterprises
Saint-Étienne	*Associations de Quartiers* In inner-city neighbourhoods and outer estates, community-based organisations run community centres providing children and youth programmes with funds from the municipality. They also represent residents' views to official bodies

Note: Some of these programmes have now ended

A limitation on the degree of involvement is the inevitable differences within and between communities; the emergence of local leaders can lead to some views rather than others dominating and clashes of control can arise between the delivery teams and local activists. While consultation and decision making were important but often fraught with difficulty, the actual provision of services and the delivery of visible improvements took precedence since programmes needed to show results if they were to survive.

Residents' priorities are invariably the local environment, maintenance, cleaning and security. Community involvement depended therefore on local intensive management, cleaning and repair. Simple, relatively low-cost, but ongoing measures had disproportionate impacts and showed an immediate return. By making shared and common spaces more useable by all groups, young people can more easily be accommodated. Therefore, progress depends on the quality of neighbourhood environments. Greener environments transformed even the most unpromising areas in Saint-Étienne, Leipzig and other cities (see Figure 4.6a-b).

Figures 4.6a-b: Reclaimed demolition site (Leipzig); greening harsh environments (Saint-Étienne)

New facilities were created within renewal areas, often within existing buildings, in order to support resident activity, including community programmes focused on children. Many unused, potentially attractive but run-down large buildings including churches, schools, wash houses and shops were converted to community uses with government support. Many community facilities grew from the renewal programmes we visited (see Figures 4.7a–c).

Figure 4.7a-c: Healthy Living Centre NUCA (Sheffield); San Salvario Centre (Torino); Children's programme (Saint-Étienne)

Social enterprises

A tool that became popular in cities trying to restore and reintegrate marginal communities was the social enterprise model. A social enterprise operates not for profit with a social purpose, offering services and activities that are beneficial to the community, using innovative and entrepreneurial methods, including income-generating activities, to support their social purpose. Social enterprises have to prove their value through the numbers wanting and using their services. Community-based social enterprises operate within a specific neighbourhood and have strong community representation within their decision-making and delivery structures. They promote self-help, involving people in solving problems for themselves. Any surplus income is ploughed back into the social business. We found out about some inspiring social enterprises in most of the cities. In Torino, Sheffield, Bremen and Saint-Étienne we visited them and recognised a clear, common approach involving communities directly in tackling local needs, to prevent the hardest social problems from unravelling (see Figures 4.8a-d). Box 4.2 provides details of six social enterprises in three of the cities and Table 4.9 describes community enterprises in the seven cities.

Figures 4.8a-d: Community café in Gröpelingen (Bremen); NUCA youth activity (Sheffield); Cascina Roca Community Centre based in a converted farmhouse showing the children's facility and café (Torino); Local youth using new leisure facilities with LSE researcher Jörg Plöger (Belfast)

Box 4.2: Details of community-based social enterprises in three of the cities

Bremen

Gröpelingen

The WiN programme, a social and physical renewal programme targeting Bremen's poorest neighbourhoods, supports several community-based social enterprises in Gröpelingen. A local disused fire station has been converted into a community café, run by people with previous serious mental health problems, as part of a wider training programme. There is also some warden-supported housing built in. Nearby is an attractive adventure playground, set in trees, with animals, an advice and neighbourhood management centre and another community café.

Osterholz-Tenever

The very large and imposing high-rise estate on the edge of Bremen houses a very highly concentrated low-income community, over half from foreign immigrant households. The WiN programme, alongside major investment in physical restructuring, has supported multiple community investments, including a large new community centre for local meetings, offices, youth and other social activities. A share of the local budget is reserved for community activities proposed and organised by residents, including clubs for children and young people, cafés, training schemes and holiday programmes.

Sheffield

NUCA (Netherthorpe and Upperthorpe Community Association)

NUCA grew with the help of Objective 1 European anti-poverty funding. The inner-city area houses many minority communities, including a substantial Yemeni refugee population. An old disused public baths with swimming pool was converted into a healthy living centre, with sports, alternative health and swimming in the modernised pool. Many other activities for young people, families and minorities have grown out of the core activity around health. This includes a job link programme, offering training, advice and support to help local people into work.

Manor and Castle Trust

In the mid-1980s a very large brick-built inter-war council estate, called the Manor, became the subject of a highly controversial transfer of ownership, demolition and rebuild plan, as a way of securing additional investment. Twenty years later many existing residents have been rehoused in newly built properties within the Manor and a strong and successful community association provides many local services, as well as representing the local community in many public arenas. It generates income from its activities in order to support the services it offers.

Torino

San Salvario

The Associazione San Salvario is based in a small shop front, where Nutella chocolate spread was first made, in the heart of a dense, crowded, high immigrant neighbourhood adjacent to the main station. It involves the community in upgrading facilities, providing services and advice encouraging local activity and investment and attracting partners to fund these. It is converting a large public bath house into a community centre with a café, youth, training and meeting spaces and many other needed activities. It plans to grow tomatoes on the roof! The centre is part-sponsored by Vodafone.

Cascina Roca

Mirafiori is the large factory and housing area in outer Torino, where Fiat is based. Unemployment and high inflows of low-skilled workers mark the area. The community has been deeply involved in converting a surviving old farm house, previously swallowed up as the city grew, into a local community enterprise centre. It offers a high-quality training space, sports and youth facilities, a café, an outdoor courtyard-style recreation area and small meeting rooms. During our visit, a music group of older Piedmontese residents was singing their traditional songs in dialect.

Table 4.9: Community enterprises in the seven cities

	Community enterprises
Leipzig	Spinnerei, inner-city, west Leipzig, formerly totally derelict textile mill, now a centre for artists, small local enterprises and resident activity within the inner core of west Leipzig where abandoned housing is being reclaimed
Bremen	Gröpelingen café, advice centre, city farm in old port area
Sheffield	Netherthorpe and Upperthorpe Community Association, providing swimming youth and children programmes
Belfast	'Ex Maze' prisoners acting as tour guides in former troubled areas, welcoming bus loads of foreign tourists, and showing them round their troubled areas
Bilbao	A training centre of Mandragon cooperatives based in Barakaldo, encouraging local enterprises
Torino	Associazione San Salvario in city centre adjacent to main station. Cascina Roca at Mirafiori
Saint-Étienne	Community and youth programmes in Quartiers Sud-Est; *maison d'emploi* in inner city to help unemployed people get jobs

Value of small-scale neighbourhood projects

Participation takes time and effort to develop. Resident capacity building is resource-intensive, and plugging into existing local networks is vital; for example, Sheffield helped to attract new firms to the city by recruiting potential workers from established low-income communities. Understanding local priorities through the neighbourhood forums in Torino, brokering community tensions through the peace process in Belfast and retaining the established community in Saint-Étienne through local outreach all involved intensive 'hand-holding' efforts. The barriers to trust were immense. The programme organiser in Tarantaize, Saint-Étienne told us, "We have to knock on every door and help every family understand what we are trying to do. Then we help them stay and get the benefit. This is one of the poorest and oldest areas of Saint-Étienne, dating back in parts to medieval times. We really want the community to survive."

In sharp contrast to the hopes of the community organiser, a youth worker living in an outer estate in Saint-Étienne told us angrily, "It is always the same, they just herd residents into blocks and we get nothing. Things will never improve, we will never get jobs." His 'cry for help' provides the strongest rationale for 'hand-holding', offering work experience and training to young people, which is what the Quartiers Sud-Est youth programme was doing with him. Quartiers Sud-Est, where this young man lived, was one of the areas where violence erupted in October 2005 during the large-scale riots in outer estates across France. Fear of youth disorder is one of the drivers behind the commitment to integration among city leaders. We were struck by the fact that using local channels, the *Grand Projets de Ville*, driven by funding from Paris, were forced to respond to local voices, and were trying to help young people. The neighbourhood projects offer a lifeline to marginal people, even though their methods have sometimes been contested. As long as they do not threaten the residents' fragile foothold in these areas, the money

?a: Graffiti attacking gentrification
(?e)

spent on their homes and communities seems to help, in spite of occasional accusations of gentrification, a form of displacement through upgrading (see Figure 4.9a). In practice, outsiders tend to move in where homes are empty, then upgraded, as in Leipzig (see Figure 4.9b).

The people working in the projects on behalf of the city or bigger agencies showed imagination, understanding, enterprise, patience and skills in brokering the divides, ethnic, economic, social and geographic, between the poorest parts of cities and the rest. Their core task and mission was to achieve a real transformation within the most difficult areas of the city, using known tools but operating in more direct, more personal and more engaging ways than in the past. The impact on wider conditions would be spread over many years of often inconspicuous, detailed, ground-level effort. On

Figure 4.9b: Gentrification (Leipzig)

the other hand, it is hard to see how without these efforts, bridges can be built between the most marginal communities and the rest of the city. City leaders see community renewal as the lifeblood of city recovery. Sheffield's chief executive summed it up this way: "We know our city is one of the most divided. Only if we can integrate the deprived neighbourhoods into the city, will we succeed."[65]

Jobs and skills for the new economy of urban recovery

No form of neighbourhood renewal can succeed without tackling the local economy, the poverty of residents and the skills mismatch between current and former employment opportunities. The skills development projects we uncovered were integral to equalising neighbourhood conditions as regaining work is vital to the recovery of cities. The integration of a discarded industrial workforce into the new economy is vital for the economy of the city and particularly for its poorest communities.

Many incoming investors bring their higher skilled and professional workers with them, the 'new incomers', but need to know that there is a useable skills base within the city. They need to recruit a local workforce and look for job-ready, qualified workers. In addition, they look for local services, amenities, adequate housing conditions, education and a local environment that will appeal to and help retain their staff.

Higher education has a vital role to play in the new job market. Most cities have strong technical universities with engineering traditions. They recognise the future potential that lies in expanding higher education linked to the new 'knowledge' economy. Bremen has based its overall economic restructuring on a strategy of high-level research, scientific advances and business development linked to its technical universities. Torino has used its polytechnic to support start-up businesses in communications, engineering and transport. Sheffield's universities likewise are directly connected to the city-wide partnership, Creative Sheffield, to foster economic development. Belfast's are linked to the new science park in the Titanic Quarter.

In low-income neighbourhoods, special skill building has been developed to train disadvantaged and unemployed workers whose experience was no longer in demand, to help them prepare for a very different kind of work that now relies more on interpersonal communication skills and less on physical strength. Helping young people from a background of parental unemployment to develop and value more service-oriented skills is a crucial stepping-stone to new jobs. This often requires micro-level work on an individual basis within wider programmes to support local training and job access. Skills development runs in parallel with the physical reinvestment that makes poorer areas more attractive and encourages new enterprises to come to the cities.

There are still many groups outside the new economy and city governments want to close the gaps by building people's confidence in their own abilities, creating new routes into work. Specific local skills projects at community level and wider skills programmes at city level underline the connection between local social issues, jobs and the wider economy (see Figures 4.10a–c):

- Saint-Étienne, which had focused less on jobs and skills and more on renewing the physical infrastructure, opened a *maison d'emploi* (employment centre) in 2007 in its poorest inner neighbourhood close to the city centre, to link local people into jobs. The city required local construction contractors for neighbourhood regeneration to hire a minimum percentage of local residents.
- Sheffield not only helped employers by identifying suitable local workers; it provided training, advice and access to jobs for local residents outside the workforce.
- Belfast trained ex-paramilitary prisoners released in inner neighbourhoods as tour guides to show inquisitive tourists around formerly troubled areas.
- Bilbao, through its social agency, Surbisa, supported a job access and training programme, working in the poorest inner neighbourhoods, targeting the most vulnerable groups.
- Torino, through its neighbourhoods programme, supported special drop-in centres that helped people with job applications, training and business support.
- Leipzig set up its own employment agency to recruit unemployed, well-qualified workers for the new companies that were moving in.
- Bremen trained unemployed residents to work in community enterprises.

Figures 4.10a–c: Apolie Centre bread-making cooperative (Torino); Lan Ekintza Awards (Bilbao); Bremen Technology Park

4.10b

4.10c

While the skills programmes are specific to each city's conditions they share a core aim of offering new and different opportunities to people who otherwise might be out of work, with a linked goal of persuading prospective employers that they will find suitable, job-ready staff. Skills initiatives are grounded in the manufacturing history and ex-industrial culture of the areas, identifying local

Table 4.10: Imperatives behind job programmes

	Job drivers
Leipzig	To attract more jobs; major plank of economic recovery strategy; targeting large scale employers
Bremen	Decision to build on high-skills/engineering tradition to generate new jobs; within poorer neighbourhood, community-based enterprises offering opportunities to most marginal people
Sheffield	Driven by extreme job losses; low-skilled residents concentrated in marginalised neighbourhoods, need help to reintegrate into the mainstream employment market
Belfast	Driven by extreme unemployment levels and high dependence on public sector jobs; social exclusion and general deprivation are heavily concentrated in the former working-class, industrial and shipyard areas
Bilbao	Strong focus on diversifying the industrial economy into professional, financial and knowledge jobs; special 'hand-holding' skills projects in inner immigrant areas
Torino	To link extremely marginal, often illegal, immigrants to jobs
Saint-Étienne	Complete closure of all mines and loss of state subsidies has caused high unemployment and a serious mismatch of skills

economic opportunities and the needs of local communities. Table 4.10 shows the drivers behind the job programmes that have developed in each city.

The employment projects we studied aimed to help a broad range of potential jobseekers: former miners, shipyard workers and industrial workers; unemployed semi-skilled and unskilled manual workers of all kinds; engineers; technicians and related back-up workers; new immigrants often drawn in to help with construction projects and other casual work, and stranded by economic decline; marginal and semi-disabled workers; women; and minority ethnic groups, all too often under-represented in the new economy of industrial cities.

Each programme is delivered at a local scale, through community-based enterprises and projects. Yet the ambitions are far reaching and the programmes are established at city and regional level, usually with national and EU support. Funding comes from a mix of sources, including the EU, but mostly from national government and local public bodies. The goals and mechanisms of each programme are shown in Table 4.11.

The private sector has helped mainly through its willingness and desire to recruit locally, knowing that there is an available workforce and ready-made infrastructure. Kier Construction in Sheffield is a good example of a company that recognised its own interest in helping the city to train the local unemployed workforce for jobs in construction. It formed a partnership with the local council and local communities to offer training and jobs. Table 4.12 sets out the way the job programmes evolved in each city and Box 4.3 describes the job construction partnership Kier Construction set up.

The skills programmes were based in poorer neighbourhoods, even though they were part of bigger programmes to help unemployed people into work, to help employers find an adequate workforce and to combat social exclusion, poverty and worklessness. Bremen is an exception because of its focus on university and research-led technical skills even though the city has also developed job training in poor neighbourhoods. Table 4.13 describes the specific local projects, what they hoped to achieve and how they worked in practice.

Table 4.11: How the seven cities changed their skills base

	Goals and mechanisms and approaches in skills programmes
Leipzig	In-work training and adjustment to new technologies; changes working practices in favour of new style of working; leads to major investors coming in; local jobs recruitment
Bremen	Focus on higher education, helps graduates develop business ideas; innovation is central to city strategy; chain effect on technical developments; links between science and wider economy, thereby leading to more local job recruitment
Sheffield	Apprenticeship-style on-the-job training for new recruits; training for tenants in building skills so they can supervise local contract repair work; new ways of working for builders and council-supported employment leading to industry-accredited qualifications
Belfast	Service skills development for ex-industrial workers; also special service projects in cooperation with local people
Bilbao	Job links training for most marginal workers; higher-level economic and skills development to allow economic diversification
Torino	Developing job-readiness skills; preparing people to develop micro-businesses through training in business planning
Saint-Étienne	Creating open-door job centres in poor areas of the city centre; building in local labour clauses to building contracts; adapting the National Mining College to the new economic realities

The implementation of job access programmes requires funding priority and local leadership as the programmes are working against a backdrop of local disillusionment and frustration. Political commitment is paramount, but two factors pushed jobs up to the top of the local political agenda. One was the intense social and political strain the cities experienced between the mid-1970s and the early 1990s. There were often explosive clashes within the cities, resulting from the tensions of economic change. Belfast is an extreme example of this, obviously made worse by the political problems.

Developing jobs skills is difficult, long deferred and hard to match directly with available jobs. We noticed in every programme certain conditions that seemed to be prerequisites for success. The more practical challenge is the hands-on task of helping disadvantaged and unconfident individuals overcome all the personal difficulties they face, which are often intensified by entrenched social and economic problems. Table 4.14 sets out the barriers that job preparation programmes faced and the key conditions they had to meet to succeed.

On the ground within each city, job programmes drew hundreds of previously marginalised residents into employment. It is hard to measure the full impact of generally small-scale projects on the local community and the wider city, but it is clear that a ripple effect occurs by looking at the impact of job failures. We know that relatively small groups of disaffected young men (at most a few hundred, but more commonly a few dozen) can cause havoc in a city, leading

Table 4.12: Structure of the job programmes

	Who runs programme	Scales of operations and impact	Funding
Leipzig	Independent company founded by city council, now independent with city council as biggest shareholder	City-wide with regional impact; channelled more than 3,000 jobseekers (approximately 50% of whom were unemployed) into new jobs	2001–05: €2.5 million (around two thirds from the city council) Since 2006: 60% public; 40% private companies
Bremen	City council	City-wide including Bremerhaven	1984–94: local government 1994–2004: €2.6 billion; federal government (special aid) Since 2004: €200 million; mixed (local government, federal government, EU) Very high cost
Sheffield	City council's employment unit Five construction companies	Phase I: city-wide, 100 trainees Phase II: city-region-wide, 500 trainees	Phase I (100 trainees): £1,300,000 from construction companies (through contracts) £672,000 from Decent Homes and Housing Market Renewal £84,000 from EU
Belfast	Set up by Belfast City Council and South Belfast Partnership with other board members	Originally six deprived wards in south and east Belfast, now covers all Northern Ireland Unemployed: 327 into employment (after two years); 343 into training/ education (after two years)	2002–05: €1.2 million; mixed funding by local government, Laganside Corporation, central government bodies, EFRE Since 2006: multiple sources
Bilbao	City council	City-wide	Province, region and city
Torino	Local community-based association, set up by enterprising immigrants	Neighbourhood-based Drop-in centre had 730 users in 2006 Part of wider neighbourhood regeneration programme	Per annum: €30,000 (75%) from bank foundation *Compagnia di San Paolo* €8,400 from Province of Torino €9,900 from Apolié
Saint-Étienne	City council and government	City-wide	French national government

to widespread outbreaks of disorder. Similarly relatively small groups of young people undertaking training and getting jobs can generate an equivalent benefit, offering new role models and a more hopeful future. Families, peer groups, local social gathering places, even local crime networks, are affected by fairly small changes in the way school leavers and potential job recruits see their futures.

Box 4.3: Kier Construction's JobNet partnership

Kier Construction in Sheffield won the contract to carry out the Decent Homes upgrading programme for the city. Its approach illustrated both the economic and the social benefits. The company faced recruitment problems for relatively low-skilled jobs in a city with high levels of under-employment and economic inactivity because of the poor image of construction work. The training subsidies from EU Objective 1, the Regional Development Agency, the Learning and Skills Council and the city itself fund the training and 'hand-holding' recruitment of local residents into real construction jobs. It offers full apprenticeships with funded training, placements and qualifications. This has created a mutually beneficial partnership between the city, Kier Construction and disadvantaged communities. The programme has run for four years and the ideas it embodies of training, support and real jobs is being extended into much wider areas of the city as well as different types of work. Kier Management, another branch of the company, now plans to offer training to redundant security workers to become car workers for sheltered schemes. The focus on training and job change has particularly attracted young people, but the programmes also specifically target groups that may be excluded longer term. Kier is now proposing to Sheffield City Council that it develops further care-oriented training programmes on a similar basis, to fill vacancies in low-valued service jobs.

We attempted to gauge the impacts of the programmes, and Table 4.15 shows measurable impacts resulting from the job programmes.

Dedicated skills and job programmes introduce new avenues to work that become visible close to the ground. Cities support training initiatives, university compacts, employer recruitment, relocation, business start-up centres, new enterprise 'cluster' facilities, as well as hand-holding, employment-linking initiatives, to contain wider social problems and to create wider economic and social benefits.

We found that small-scale programmes had quantifiable outcomes, albeit sometimes on a micro scale. The programmes brought wide benefits to the cities far beyond immediate job creation, job access and skill-building objectives:

- The skills projects demonstrated the value of bridges between low-income, often demoralised, communities with the 'wrong' skills and new job opportunities; programmes in Torino and Sheffield exemplify this.
- Building bridges between employers and the potential workers they might overlook persuaded employers that a valuable labour force potential was to be found within low-income communities and low-skilled groups in weak market cities. Belfast, Sheffield, Leipzig and Bilbao helped large private sector employers tap into parts of their former industrial workforce they would have difficulty recruiting independently.
- The companies that the cities want to attract are often searching for large, cheap sites. All the seven cities studied offered big spaces with good access to

the city centre, to other cities and internationally. All the cities are reclaiming large tracts of obsolete industrial and port land that will help diversify the local economy and create jobs. All the cities have attracted investors who have created jobs and at least indirectly supported training.

• Universities, research activities and high-tech companies can combine resources and help strengthen the local economy in older industrial cities. Bremen

Table 4.13: Shape of the different job programmes

	Employment organisation	Aims	Methods/approach	Target beneficiaries
Leipzig	Personal services to businesses (PUUL)	To provide employment-related services for investors To increase job market access for the unemployed	Pre-selection of workforce; training of the unemployed	Unemployed (local and regional); existing and potential new companies
Bremen	Development strategy to promote innovation (City of Science)	To overcome structural crisis by fostering specific economic sectors	Extension and restructuring of 'science landscape' Links between higher education and local economy	Students, graduates; some start-up enterprises; local/ regional companies; local workforce
Sheffield	Construction JOBMatch	Training for hard-to-reach groups in construction skills to meet industry demand for new workers	Supported work programme with built-in training, plus wrap-around basic skills training	Women; minority ethnic groups; long-term unemployed; individuals from deprived areas
Belfast	Gasworks Employment Matching Service (GEMS)	Link between the long-term unemployed and new job opportunities through regeneration on Gasworks site (Laganside redevelopment)	Training, job market skills, help with applications Link employers with local area. Create local participation	Unemployed in a number of deprived east and south Belfast wards
Bilbao	Lan Ekintza employment training	To help vulnerable minorities into jobs	Training Advice Access to vacancies	New immigrants; left behind populations
Torino	*Associazione Apolié*	Information and guidance to support access to jobs for immigrant job seekers Broker training and apprenticeships	Personalised approach; one-to-one interviews with employment counsellor in drop-in centre Cultural mediator helps bridge to Italian system Legal advice on visas and work permits from in-house lawyer	Job-seekers of all ages in deprived immigrant neighbourhood
Saint-Étienne	*Maison d'emploi*	To attract local unemployed into work	Link to training and jobs	Ex-industrial workers

Source: Power et al, 2008

exemplifies this but Saint-Étienne, Sheffield, Bilbao, Belfast and Torino also offer a high level of technology, design and engineering; as well as targeting low-skilled and marginal communities. Leipzig's ancient university and its population of current and former students have made it a favoured location for new entrepreneurs and helped generate an 'artistic entrepreneurialism' that has gained international recognition. (See Figures 4.11a–c)

Table 4.14: Barriers and requirements of skills programmes

	Key barriers and challenges	Key requirements for programmes to work
Leipzig	High unemployment, many long-term unemployed; municipal debts versus oversized infrastructure for less population; many new jobs tap into regional rather than local labour markets	Good political leadership and cross-departmental cooperation; early recognition of urban crisis and subsequent change of urban development strategy; willingness to go 'the extra mile' to ensure inward investment
Bremen	Forced to cut budget due to threat of bankruptcy again (another special aid by federal government uncertain); how to link low-skilled workforce with the new economic sectors; lack of company headquarters, dependency on decision made elsewhere lack of high-skilled services	Freedoms and responsibilities linked to city-state status; federal government aid (1994–2004) enabled design of Special Investment Programme (ISP); a clear long-term strategic vision focusing on technology and innovation
Sheffield	Getting funding together (mainstream training funders not keen to fund non-traditional programme); winning construction companies over to programme; recruiting hard-to-reach individuals and those who would not traditionally consider construction	Sustained leadership and support from council's chief executive; in-depth understanding of local communities' needs; ability to use regeneration funding to finance programme; ability to build programme into construction companies' delivery contracts; lead construction company partner Kier Sheffield LLP championed programme to other construction companies
Belfast	Structure of 'old' government arrangements Difficulty to match new jobs with existing skills base The consequences of long-term exclusion	Creation of unique and innovative partnership model; attempt to link large regeneration efforts with local communities; political leadership willing to overcome crisis
Bilbao	Still heavy reliance on industry Difficult political situation	Hand-holding; diversifying economy; targeting vulnerable groups and areas
Torino	Convincing informal workers to formalise their work, despite disincentives Overcoming cultural barriers to female employment in immigrant communities	Personalised, relationship-building approach, which deals with cultural as well as skills issues; on-site experts to advise and support, e.g. lawyer, enterprise counsellor, cultural mediator
Saint-Étienne	Very old fashioned 'socialist' industrial economy and council resistance to change	Building contract hire requirements tied to neighbourhood renewal

Table 4.15: Measurable impacts of programmes

	Impacts of programmes
Leipzig	Channelled more than 3,000 jobseekers into new jobs (approximately half were unemployed); significant job creation especially in car manufacturing and logistics sectors
Bremen	Increased share of high-tech employment; several successful companies in economic niche markets (environmental technology, maritime logistics, aerospace); higher education institutions labelled 'centres for excellence' (2005); filtered down into services offering jobs in poorer communities
Sheffield	High retention rate among trainees; good performance of current trainees; expansion of programme across the city-region; 23% of trainees achieved their construction qualification six months early; over 50% of trainees come from the city's most deprived neighbourhoods; eight times more women and almost six times more black and minority ethnic workers are recruited than nationally
Belfast	327 unemployed into employment (after two years); 343 unemployed into training/education (after two years)
Bilbao	Opened up job opportunities; celebrated new training successes
Torino	Total of 730 users during 2006, 82% of whom were immigrants; survey of users in 2006 showed 75% were in permanent employment; two new businesses and two associations created by users during 2006
Saint-Étienne	Helped most fragile inner communities; too early to measure impacts

Figures 4.11a-c: Incubators (Torino); new science park (Belfast); Spinnerei, old industrial complex that is being gradually restored as a centre for artists, small workshops and new enterprises (Leipzig)

How skills, employment and social goals came together

The skills programmes arose because of a wider social need to upgrade community conditions, both physically and economically. The combined approach of job creation, skill building, social integration and environmental upgrading undoubtedly contributed to city recovery. Only with the necessary new skills would new jobs take root in old industrial communities. The industrial sectors in all the cities, shrunken as they are, continue to be vulnerable. In the recession, following the international banking crisis, job growth prospects have faded. Cities are witnessing jobs being shed. Local projects within communities make a vital link between the public interventions to rescue European economies, and the communities that most need them. The skills programmes, having been closely linked to the socially oriented approach of neighbourhood renewal programmes, are now more necessary than ever. Table 4.16 shows how skills projects help with wider social conditions.

Table 4.16: How the skills and employment programmes filter benefits into community conditions

	Community conditions
Leipzig	• The city and regional programme had a big overall effect on city recovery, community viability and attracting new employers. It generated income and helped retain a youthful, graduate population
Bremen	• The programme has had a major impact on city innovations, economic development and job growth • High-tech industries diversify the economy and generate ancillary services • Local community programmes address the harshest social problems and conditions
Sheffield	• Directly upgrades low-income areas as part of the Decent Homes programme, which combines job training, employment and local physical improvements • Neighbourhood focus • Employer links to local workforce
Belfast	• Part of major urban regeneration schemes, explicitly recruiting long-term unemployed in the former dock area
Bilbao	• Part of a city and region-wide drive to diversify the economy and create alternative work
Torino	• Part of wider neighbourhood regeneration project • Based in neighbourhoods with the highest immigrant concentrations • Breaks down barriers to integration
Saint-Étienne	• Urgent need to give new sense of direction and social purpose to an almost entirely industrial city • Jobs and skills development rising in significance • New job recruitment centre (*maison d'emploi*)

There are many common threads running through the skills programmes. Even though each programme is distinctive, tailor-made to each city, and to particular communities within cities, some common lessons have emerged across all the cities. Box 4.4 sets out some of the wider lessons from the programmes.

The general recovery in employment levels across the cities up to 2007 underlines the bounce-back that the cities showed. Yet the big chain effects of industrial collapse, skills mismatches and physical decline have been heavily concentrated in the poorest neighbourhoods of former industrial cities where unemployment is highest and housing and environmental conditions most problematic. In the worst affected areas that we visited, 40 per cent or more of the adult working-age population was not in work, studying or training.[66] For young people the rate is even higher. Up to one third of the population of our

Box 4.4: General lessons from the skills programmes

a) **Focus on jobs**
- Jobs are a driving purpose of the cities' special programmes and overall strategies. The programmes are all based on skills development in order to qualify the workforce for future economic demands, that is, jobs
- City governments and business leaders recognise the need for a higher tax base to fund new infrastructure, having lost tax resources heavily through deindustrialisation. New jobs and an employed workforce helps this

b) **Skills context as driver**
- All the cities need to adopt the new skills requirements of new companies and want to spread skills more widely among large disadvantaged populations
- In a rapidly changing job market it has become important to get people into work they are qualified to do
- Cities also want to attract higher education institutions into partnering new skills programmes with knock-on benefits for people lower down the job ladder
- Companies looking for more skilled workers are important partners in the programmes

c) **Professional development and skills orientation**
- Training is an essential ingredient of all programmes
- Employer-based training complements the more basic training the programmes offer
- The programmes directly offer new-style workplace experience to target groups. This helps employers by providing a relatively low-cost workforce
- Promotion of higher-level skills and people-based skills is common to all programmes
- Linking universities into company formation and new jobs helps grow innovative small businesses needing back-up services
- Most cities support business incubator centres and new business parks tailored to inward investors

d) **Young people**
- Holding onto young graduates is a common goal across cities, but only Bremen focused on universities as key levers into innovation and the new economy
- Sheffield has the strongest focus on youth in poorer areas

e) **Social integration**
- Efforts to include immigrants and minority ethnic groups in work programmes require special effort if this is to work in practice
- 'Hand-holding' disadvantaged people into training and work is the only way to ensure success with more marginal groups, particularly minorities, low-skilled youth and long-term unemployed
- All cities share the goal of integration
- Helping people into work combats social exclusion

f) **Community conditions**
- Social conditions deteriorate through lack of work and the converse appears to be true

continued/

Box 4.4: continued

- A majority of skills and job programmes have a direct community focus, particularly in deprived areas
- Disadvantaged areas are seen as a job resource and as places where job and skills growth have the biggest impacts
- Many community programmes generate local jobs and job training

g) **Sustainable development**
- Environmental concerns do not figure directly in any of our skills case studies but indirectly all the cities prioritise sustainability by virtue of their efforts to find a new rationale for cities and their residents
- Economic activity and jobs are vital to the survival of communities
- Jobs and re-investment are a prerequisite of city recovery
- Sustainable communities mean places with work, economic regrowth, alongside more attractive conditions, helping existing communities and protecting environments
- Many local jobs in the future will derive from environmental technologies and retro-fitting existing buildings and infrastructure to raise energy efficiency standards
- The goal of creating sustainable, long-term jobs is universal

cities, mostly in inner areas, but also in large, government-sponsored post-war estates on the edge, were caught up in a spiral of physical disinvestment and social unravelling. Yet the commitment to helping these areas and integrating their impoverished communities is high on the agenda of the cities, more so as financial troubles bite deep and cities rebuild momentum for recovery, reviving demand for both homes and labour.

Many of the projects and programmes we visited made a real difference in people's lives. Local neighbourhood projects in each city showed the micro-level at which it is necessary to work in order to make new social and economic opportunities a reality. A strong lesson from neighbourhood renewal, community enterprise and skills programmes is the need for a local delivery mechanism, building trust and consensus, linking big plans to local realities. Only through close-grained work within low-income communities can cities make a real difference in the lives of people who are at the very margins of the new economy. In the next part of the book we look at each European city's story, case by case.

Part Two
Learning from 50 years of boom and bust: seven European case studies

Part Two

Introduction

Each city has a particular story to tell, with its own place in the history of its country and the development of its wealth. The pattern of industrial collapse is alarmingly similar, but the local political crises it spawned are particular to each setting. For this reason, we decided to include seven case studies to provide flesh and bones to the broad canvas we have so far offered.

The lived experiences of each city, its local setting and cultures, its changing leaderships and operations, its position in the European urban context, is specific, detailed and revealing. Although each case study offers highly abbreviated accounts, it summarises the main ups and downs of urban industrial growth and decline, and then regrowth after crisis, to mirror in particular places the story so far.

Three years of visiting the cities and meeting with city actors provided us with a wealth of material including observations, quotations, local reports, photographic records and evidence collected at events, in visits to new industries, local universities, public spaces and local monuments. We learned to know and recognise local landmarks, to 'get under the skin' of problems and progress, to move alongside the local people who knew so much about their city and whose voices are so rarely heard.

The record provided by the case studies offers concrete evidence of change and progress, direct accounts of what really happened and insights into the patterns that we uncovered by linking up ground experience from each place with the bigger picture of urban change, so often described by academics and urbanists.

The seven cities were chosen as typical examples of post-industrial crisis and recovery efforts within each country. However, as our understanding grew, we recognised four groupings within our sample:

- cities in political turmoil represented by Belfast in Northern Ireland and Bilbao in the Basque Country;
- cities of mono-industrial manufacturing production, represented by Sheffield in England and Saint-Étienne in France;
- regional capitals with historic leadership roles, represented by Torino in Italy and Bremen in Germany;
- cities in the former socialist countries of eastern Europe, represented by Leipzig in Germany.

Readers can choose the case studies they want to know more about in Part Two or can simply move on to Part Three, which pulls together the evidence from all seven cities to provide a framework for measuring recovery and an overall assessment of their progress.

FIVE

Leipzig

CITY CONTEXT

Leipzig is located in the east German state of Saxony, 150km south west of Germany's capital, Berlin (see Figures 5.1 and 5.2). With 4.3 million inhabitants, Saxony is the most populous of the new *Länder* (regions) that were formed after German reunification.

Figure 5.1: Map of Germany

Figure 5.2: Map of the federal German state of Saxony

Leipzig's traditional role was that of a commercial and trading centre for Saxony and beyond. With 500,000 inhabitants it is the second largest city in East Germany, after Berlin and the thirteenth largest among all Germany's cities. It originates from a Slavic village founded around 900 AD, and was accorded town status in 1165. Its favourable location at the crossroads of central and eastern European trading routes made it a major market centre in the late Middle Ages and its trade fair is the oldest in Europe. Leipzig is also home to Germany's second oldest university (founded in 1409).

Most German cities experienced their most dramatic urban transformation and rapid industrialisation during the so-called *Gründerzeit* (foundation era).

This period began after the victory against France in 1871 and the creation of the German nation-state, and ended with the outbreak of the First World War in 1914. The former kingdom of Saxony became an independent region and Leipzig emerged as a leading national city. Much of the older housing in German cities was constructed during this period, in dense four-to-five storey apartment buildings. Leipzig industrialised rapidly during the late 19th century, mainly driven by publishing, textile and metalworking industries, leading to unprecedented population growth (see Figure 5.3). The city's population more than quadrupled between 1871 and 1900, from 107,000 to 456,000. Leipzig reached its population peak in the 1930s with over 700,000 inhabitants, making it the fourth largest German city. Further industrialisation in the inter-war period (1918–39) in electrical, chemical, mining and energy sectors, added to the existing industrial base.

Figure 5.3: Leipzig, population development, 1850–1989

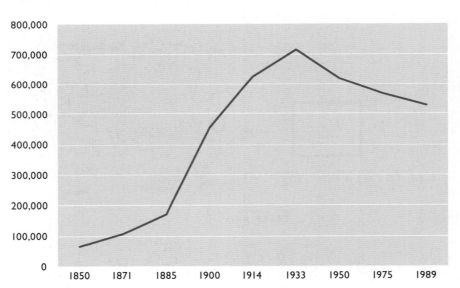

Note: Time axis not calibrated.
Sources: Statistisches Landesamt Sachsen; Stadt Leipzig Department of Urban Development (2006); Nuissl and Rink (2003)

Leipzig suffered less damage during the Second World War than other major German cities. However, the division of Germany into two states in 1949 led to state functions being concentrated in east Berlin and regional governments being dissolved. The German Democratic Republic's (GDR) orientation towards the eastern bloc disrupted Leipzig's traditional commercial ties, although industrial activity was soon revived by the creation of large industrial conglomerates (*Kombinat*) based on existing industrial sectors (see Figure 5.4). It continued to host the annual international trade fair, as the showpiece of the eastern bloc's industrial production, helping Leipzig to retain a few commercial links with the West (see Figure 5.5). However, Leipzig was the only major East German city to

Figure 5.4: Heavy machinery for open-cast mining produced by Kombinat Takraf (Leipzig)

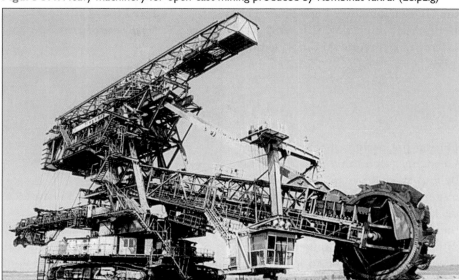

Figure 5.5: Impressions from Leipzig's trade fair during the GDR period

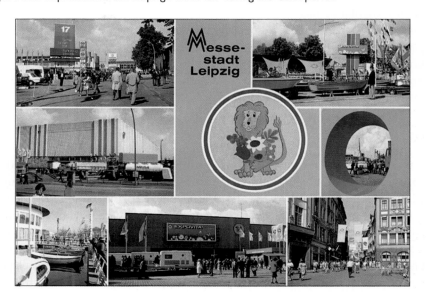

experience considerable population losses before 1990 – the population declined from 713,000 in 1933 to 530,000 in 1989.

Towards the end of the 1980s, the eastern bloc disintegrated following the collapse of the socialist regimes. Citizens of Leipzig played an important part in East Germany's political transformation. Their weekly Monday demonstrations were an important factor in the 'Peaceful Revolution', accelerating the collapse of the GDR regime (see Figure 5.6). The Berlin Wall came down in 1989 and Germany was reunified on 3 October 1990.

Figure 5.6: Monday demonstrations in Leipzig

CRISIS

During the period of separation East Germany's economy had fallen far behind West Germany's. Leipzig had experienced slow but continuous decline throughout the socialist era and then rapid decline in the years immediately following reunification. Integration into West Germany through the adoption of its constitution, political and legal systems, and adaptation to a new economic model were a shock. Leipzig, along with other cities in the new *Länder* and other transitional economies, displayed particular patterns of urban decline which came to be labelled 'shrinking cities'.[1] The most obvious signs of crisis included:

- industrial collapse
- environmental damage
- increasing social problems, especially unemployment
- population decline
- uncontrolled suburbanisation and sprawl on the urban periphery
- housing crisis, signified by decay and high vacancy rates
- overburdened public administration.

Industrial collapse

East Germany's industrial collapse was profound and sudden: between 1990 and 1993 over half of the four million industrial jobs were lost.[2] New economic conditions were attached to the 1990 currency reforms, which replaced the East German mark with the West German Deutsche mark. Firms were unable to pay employees, meet production costs or invest in much-needed technology.[3] The agency created to handle the privatisation of state-owned East German industrial conglomerates (*Treuhandanstalt*) was widely criticised for selling allegedly non-competitive companies and their assets too quickly to West German and international investors.[4] Almost 300 of Leipzig's 800 privatised companies were closed.[5]

Deindustrialisation in Leipzig was particularly severe. In only seven years (1989–96) 90,000 manufacturing jobs were lost, a 90 per cent decline (see Figure 5.7). None of our other case study cities experienced such acute losses. In 1991, 27 per cent of the workforce was still employed in manufacturing, but this fell to 11 per cent by 2004.[6] Although the service sector expanded it could not compensate for such dramatic losses.

Figure 5.7: Number of employees in manufacturing, 1989–96

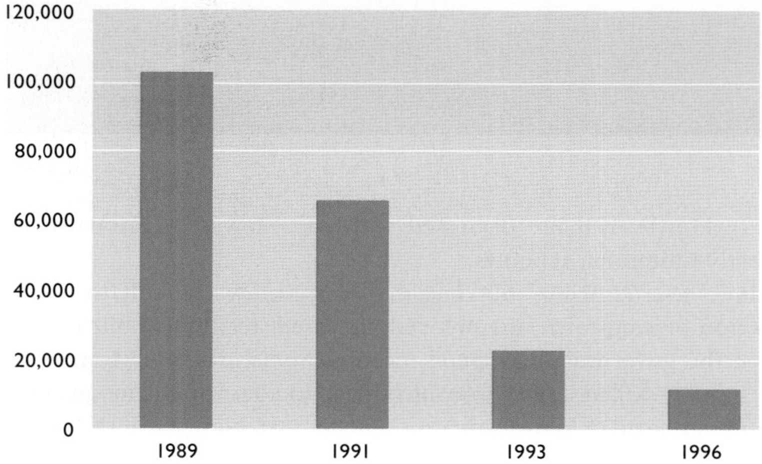

Source: Stadt Leipzig Department of Urban Development (2006)

Environmental damage

Leipzig is close to the former GDR's industrial heartland, and the concentration of heavy industries caused serious air, water and soil pollution. There had never been a significant environmental or green movement in East Germany and by the end of the 1980s the chemical industries, coal-fired power plants and open-cast lignite mining of Leipzig and its surroundings areas had generated a massive environmental burden (see Figure 5.8). The collapse of the industrial sector had serious social consequences but a direct positive impact on some environmental conditions and aspects of quality of life.

Increasing social problems

The loss of industrial employment was not compensated for by the creation of new jobs. Unemployment became the most serious social problem, reaching almost 20 per cent by the late 1990s. Leipzig's unemployment rate was substantially higher than for Germany as a whole and, in 2005, even surpassed the East German rate

Figure 5.8: Heavy industry, early 1990s

(see Figure 5.9). However, many dismissed workers received generous social packages and early retirement schemes.

With economic restructuring, jobs became increasingly difficult to access and the proportion of long-term unemployed increased steadily. Labour market problems forced the government to spend more on social welfare. Meanwhile, the emergence of high-skilled service jobs introduced socioeconomic inequalities, which were almost unheard of in the earlier socialist context. New social values and

Figure 5.9: Unemployment rates for Leipzig and Germany, 1990–2005 (%)

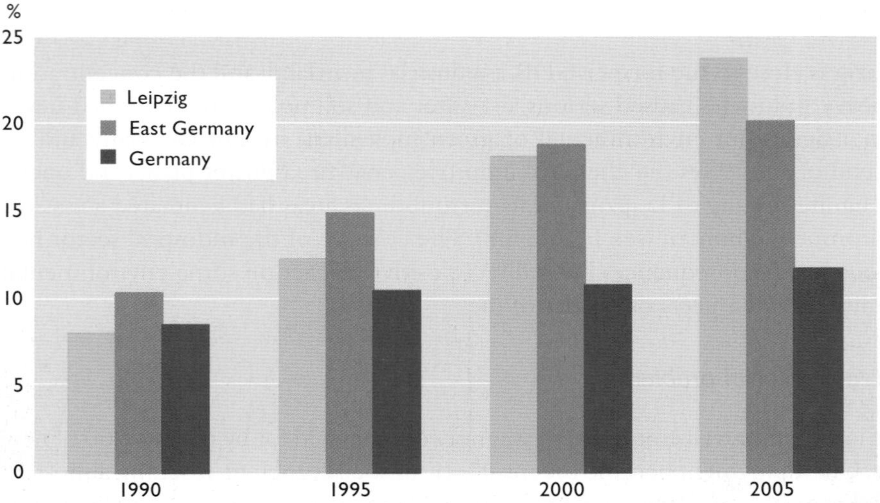

Sources: Statistisches Bundesamt; Statistisches Landesamt Sachsen; Bertelsmann Stiftung (all online)

consumption-oriented lifestyles, coupled with high levels of welfare dependency, often caused psychological stress and frustration.

Population decline

Population decline accelerated after reunification (see Figure 5.10). Three demographic processes contributed to this dramatic decline.[7] Suburbanisation was the most important and responsible for approximately half the losses. The movement of predominantly skilled, economically active people aged between 20 and 40, towards more prosperous and dynamic West German regions was responsible for about a quarter of the decline. Finally, declining birth rates reduced the population by approximately another quarter.

Suburbanisation and sprawl

Due to strict regulations on settlement patterns, East German cities had practically no suburban hinterland until 1990. Following reunification, the mostly rural municipalities surrounding Leipzig were transformed by residential and commercial developments in a process dubbed 'Wild East suburbanisation', which lacked planning and sustainability (see Figure 5.11). This was driven by the availability of substantial federal subsidies. Eastern local authorities had

Figure 5.10: Population development, 1989–98

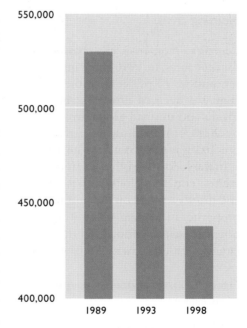

Sources: Statistisches Landesamt Sachsen; Stadt Leipzig (both online)

Figure 5.11: Suburban developments of the mid-1990s

to adapt to the new Western land-use planning system and investors from the West took advantage of this. Most new suburban developments were not accompanied by investments in public transport, leading to a dependency on private cars. Suburbanisation reached its peak between 1995 and 1998.[8]

There was initially little incentive to invest in the decaying and unpopular inner-city housing stock. The government was committed to re-establishing pre-war ownership of properties expropriated during the socialist regime. It favoured restitution of properties to their previous owners rather than compensation payments, leading to long delays in renewal. The tax base of the city fell and city centre activity declined through competition from new shopping malls on the periphery.

Housing crisis

Leipzig's urban crisis was characterised by a dilapidated housing stock with high vacancy rates. In 1990 three quarters of the city's 258,000 housing units required renovation, 13 per cent of the stock was in a very bad condition and nine per cent was deemed uninhabitable.[9] By 1989 almost 30,000 housing units were vacant and this had grown to approximately 62,500, or 20 per cent of the stock, by 2000.[10] Yet almost 60 per cent of the city population were still occupying pre-1918 housing units in the 1990s, many of them very dilapidated.[11]

In the socialist era, the main emphasis was on the construction of large *Plattenbau* estates (concrete blocks). These were built on a huge scale from the early 1970s and mostly located on the periphery of cities. Figure 5.12 shows the age of empty properties in Leipzig. Over 30 per cent of the population lived in these socialist housing estates. Grünau, on the city's western edge, was East Germany's second largest such estate, with 75,000 inhabitants (see Figure 5.13).

Figure 5.12: Age of vacant housing stock in Leipzig, 2000–05, showing declining numbers of empty units

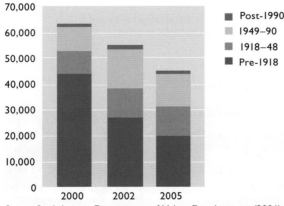

Source: Stadt Leipzig Department of Urban Development (2006)

Figure 5.13: Mass-built estates on the periphery (Grünau)

Overburdened public administration

Leipzig struggled to meet the growing demand for public services. While the numbers dependent on social welfare increased, the tax base reduced as the population declined and companies closed. One major characteristic of such 'shrinking cities' is their oversized public infrastructure, used by a declining population. Yet because of fiscal pressures, Leipzig's administration had only limited flexibility to confront its problems and design long-term recovery.

RECOVERY ACTIONS

From pro-growth to adjustment

In the period immediately following reunification, the German economy was expanding and there was a strong belief that East Germany would quickly catch up with West German standards. For this reason, pro-growth strategies were adopted throughout East Germany in the 1990s. Leipzig became known as a 'boom town', mainly due to the manifold construction activities.[12]

However, the pro-growth strategies were far too optimistic and generally failed across East Germany. In the second half of the 1990s, driven by strong city leadership, Leipzig was the first major East German city to recognise the need to adopt more realistic approaches to urban development. The new approach can be summarised under two broad headings:

- '*Fix the problems*': mostly aimed at strengthening the inner city to increase its attractiveness to compete with the suburbs, both in residential and commercial activity.
- '*Think big*': aimed at establishing Leipzig as an economic and cultural centre within the emerging European city network. This included major efforts to attract large companies and promote large-scale events and developments.

The City of Leipzig embraced economic restructuring, actively transforming its industrial past and re-emerging as a service and trade centre. The construction of a new trade fair replacing the outdated old complex underlined the goal of re-establishing the city as an important hub for trade and commerce (see Figure 5.14). Another plan was to establish Leipzig as a leading regional centre for banking and finance.

Figure 5.14: New trade fair: reviving traditional function

Major investment was made in revitalising the decayed urban centre as its limited city centre functions were losing ground to suburban developments. One project was to modernise Leipzig's large train station, incorporating a new shopping mall, the first such project in Germany (see Figure 5.15). By the late 1990s, the city centre had regained activity, attracting inhabitants and tourists alike, and confidence, with retail and some office developments. Many historic buildings were refurbished, including the medieval and 19th-century town halls, churches, merchant houses and Leipzig's typical historic shopping arcades.

Figure 5.15: Main train station, refurbished and now equipped with a shopping mall

Urban renewal

The particular problems of a 'shrinking city' put housing high on the political agenda. With rising vacancy rates in inner-city neighbourhoods, the housing market had become increasingly dysfunctional. Urban renewal was seen as essential in the fight against population loss. While competing with economically more dynamic West German regions was considered difficult, it was argued that the city could compete with its own suburbs by fostering a supply of attractive inner-city housing, for example in the refurbished older housing stock, alongside other urban amenities.

From 1998, the city council convened several urban roundtables (*Stadtwerkstatt*), bringing key stakeholders together to discuss plans. Three major solutions were identified:

- enhance the attractions of the inner city to compete with suburban developments;
- recognise that investment in saving all areas was impossible;
- accept the need for some selective demolition, with positive effects on the urban environment, lowering densities, creating more individualised housing, more green areas and public spaces.[13]

Strategic urban development plan (2000)

In 2000 the city published an urban development plan that specifically targeted housing and urban renewal, defining a joint strategy for older housing, large estates and new construction. The main aims were to increase the competitiveness of well-equipped inner-city neighbourhoods and to consolidate the housing market. The city thus decided to support the renewal of selected areas and to demolish between 15,000 and 20,000 properties (around seven per cent of the total stock) by 2010.[14]

Funds were channelled into three large areas that were particularly needy as the city drew on several external funding streams.[15] From 1997 to 2003, €30 million to €40 million were available from local, regional, federal and EU (Objective 1) sources. East Leipzig, with the highest levels of deprivation, received funds from the *Soziale Stadt* neighbourhood renewal programme, funded by the federal and regional governments. In west Leipzig urban renewal funding came from the EU's Urban II programme.

Housing Vacancy Commission and demolition programme: Stadtumbau Ost

In 2000 the increasing problems with housing vacancies across East Germany led to the formation of an interdisciplinary expert commission bringing together leading urban experts chaired by Leipzig's then mayor. This Expert Commission on the Restructuring of the Housing Market in East Germany became known as the Housing Vacancy Commission. Almost one million housing units were vacant in East Germany by the late 1990s. The Commission recommended demolishing between 300,000 and 400,000 East German homes over 10 years, representing a significant shift in thinking.

As a result of the Commission's findings in 2002, the federal government launched a major programme, *Stadtumbau Ost*, to help East German cities overcome their housing market crisis. While the term *Stadtumbau* translates literally into 'urban conversion', in practice it usually meant demolition. Thus, alongside new construction and renovation of the existing stock, demolition became the third pillar of federal urban policy. Nearly €3 billion came from regional and federal funds between 2002 and 2009. Since 2001, over 9,200 units have been demolished in Leipzig, with two thirds of the demolitions in large outer housing estates, mostly in Grünau.

Urban renewal instruments

The urban renewal strategy also aimed to improve the urban environment, quality of life and housing choice within inner-city neighbourhoods to attract people back into the city. Leipzig pioneered policies designed for the specific East German situation. It came up with a number of innovative ideas, as shown in Table 5.1.

Table 5.1: Instruments and programmes for urban renewal

Instrument/ programme	Description	Aims	Impact
Town-houses (*Stadthäuser*)	Construction of owner-occupied semi-detached town-houses in the inner city	Create attractive housing choices in order to compete with suburbs	By 2007: 100 houses, but developers often prefer suburban locations with less regulation and possibility to develop larger areas
Tenant refurbishment incentive	Tenants receive financial assistance to refurbish their blocks	Provide necessary refurbishment to semi-derelict buildings	Limited success: housing market offers large choice of inexpensive housing anyway
Self-user programme (*Selbsnutzer*)	City helps organising and advising 'owner groups' for buildings	a) Provide housing for middle classes; stop suburbanisation b) Consolidation of older housing stock	2001–07: approximately 300 families (half in older housing units, half in new town-houses, see above)
Guardian houses (*Wächterhäuser*)	Temporary rental-free lease of decaying buildings in strategic locations, occupiers required to make necessary repairs; coordinated by not-for-profit group	Save endangered buildings from further dereliction; positive signal for area Side-effect: housing option for creative groups (e.g. students, artists)	Small symbolic impact; eight buildings
Temporary use of private property as public spaces (*Gestattungsvertrag*)	Contract between city and land owner; city allowed to temporarily use privately owned land as public space, e.g. local park; duration of lease usually 10 years; owner responsible for demolition and clearing of site, but freed from property taxes and site security	Increase quality of life and attractiveness of area; create beneficial intermediate solutions for owner and city	Successful: 106 contracts (1999–2005); funding: €6 million (until 2006)

Sources: interviews with representatives from the Departments of Urban Renewal and Housing and Urban Planning, City of Leipzig

The reclamation of former mines just outside the city shows how quality of life can be improved through environmental reclamation. The landscape to the south of Leipzig was scarred with the legacy of open-cast lignite mines, the last of which closed in the late 1990s. This area is undergoing an impressive process of 'landscape transformation' with former open-cast mines being decontaminated and flooded to create a large lake district for leisure uses, such as swimming and sailing.[16]

Major investments in urban regeneration

From the early 1990s many major investments were made to modernise the transport and utilities infrastructure (see Table 5.2). Leipzig is now well linked by new and modernised highways. A new fast-train link has reduced travel time to Berlin to just over one hour. Another major transport investment is the city tunnel to improve suburban and regional train connections. In addition to road and rail investments, Leipzig-Halle airport on the northern development axis just outside the city was modernised and extended. With 24-hour flight access it is developing into a major hub for air cargo and logistics. The cargo handling centre near the airport was also developed with public sector funding in the mid-1990s.

Table 5.2: Major public sector investments in Leipzig and surroundings

Location	Project	Sector	Period	Investment (million €)
City	Technical infrastructure (gas, electricity, water)	Technical infrastructure	1993–94	1,000
	Main train station (modernisation, shopping mall)	Transport infrastructure, retail	1996–98	260
	Fine arts museum	Museum, arts	2000–04	73
	City tunnel	Transport infrastructure	2003–10	572
	University campus (modernisation)	Higher education	2004–09	150
Urban fringe	New Leipzig Fair	Trade fairs, commerce	1993–95	2,060
	Leipzig airport (modernisation, expansion)	Transport infrastructure	1993–00	660
	Leipzig-Halle cargo handling centre (GVZ)	Transport infrastructure, logistics	1993–94	50
	Medical scientific centre	Health services	1992–96	1,500
	(Re)development of enterprise areas	Business/industrial park	1993–96	1,200
	Various media-related projects (e.g. Media City, printing quarter, etc.)	Media, publishing	1993–2003	1,150

Sources: Nuissl and Rink (2003); Stadt Leipzig/Office for Economic Development (2005)

Attracting new companies

Recognising that subsidies and other public funding would be limited, Leipzig shifted its economic development strategy in the late 1990s. The almost complete absence of large private sector companies drove the city to a stronger emphasis on attracting major new companies and adapting to the new employment situation. Several companies have since located new production or service sites in Leipzig. The most significant were in car manufacturing and logistics (see Figure 5.16). Both BMW and Porsche decided to build new plants in Leipzig to produce

Figure 5.16: Development corridor: highway exit for BMW plant, Quelle warehouse and new trade fair complex (north Leipzig)

new car models, and including suppliers, this sector has created some 6,000 new jobs in the region so far.[17] The renowned international architect, Zaha Hadid, designed BMW's plant. The first major logistics company to invest in Leipzig was the mail order company Quelle. DHL and Amazon followed more recently, locating their European distribution headquarters in or around Leipzig. About 5,000 predominantly low-skilled jobs have been created in this sector so far. An estimated further 4,000 are planned for the DHL centre by 2010.[18] With the EU's expansion, Leipzig is now at the centre of Europe's transport networks. This success is closely related to the heavy subsidies to transport infrastructure.

There were several other decisive factors, including the availability of cleaned-up brownfield land, a ready workforce and increasingly deregulated labour laws. The city's land supply strategy ensured that land was available for potential investors with generous public subsidies, especially for site preparations. The city also realised that, in order to attract companies, it needed to design special business services such as the job agency PUUL, to help link incoming companies to a large, relatively well educated workforce.

Cluster approach

The city's economic development policy adopted a cluster approach, first developed by academics, then promoted by a lobby group of large regional companies called Economic Initiative Central Germany (*Wirtschaftsinitiative Mitteldeutschland*). Five strategic clusters were identified: car manufacturing and suppliers; media, IT and communication technology; health, biotechnology and medical technology; energy and environmental technology; and a cross–cluster group including the trade fair, financial services and logistics.

Urban marketing and events

Leipzig made considerable efforts to promote its position within the European urban hierarchy by supporting major events connected with international culture and sport. It applied to host the Olympic Games in 2012 and secured the German selection in 2004, but was not among the five international finalists. Nonetheless, the activities and local media coverage for this bid were a major boost to the city and its inhabitants. The city also hosted several games for the 2005 Football Confederations Cup and the 2006 Football World Cup.

Leipzig has a significant cultural heritage on which to draw and has been organising events around famous former citizens such as the composer Johann Sebastian Bach and poet and playwright, Johann Wolfgang von Goethe (see Figure 5.17). The Leipzig art scene, displayed most prominently in the work by the New Leipzig School of painters, has recently attracted significant national and international attention. This success can be attributed in part to the Academy of Visual Arts Leipzig and to the city's low rents for large studio spaces. An old textile works complex, the Spinnerei, for example, was gradually taken over by artists while the city council quietly encouraged its organic development (see Figure 5.18).

Figure 5.17: Statue of the composer Johann Sebastian Bach

Figure 5.18: Marketing the cultural past, former spinning works by artists

Social programmes

In Leipzig, interventions with a social focus have received only limited funding by comparison with large-scale projects for economic development and the physical regeneration of east Leipzig, west Leipzig and Grünau in particular. East Leipzig shows the highest concentration of disadvantaged social groups and welfare-dependent households. Some of the initiatives to tackle specific problems are outlined here:

- *Integration of immigrants:* although high by comparison with other East German cities, the proportion of foreigners in the population is significantly lower in Leipzig than in most West German cities (seven per cent). In east Leipzig, however, 15 per cent of residents are foreigners, mostly from Iraq, the Ukraine, Vietnam, Turkey and Russia. The neighbourhood management office in east Leipzig runs an integration project, which receives EU funding.
- *Urban renewal:* projects in east Leipzig include the local park, Rabet, which was developed following the demolition of decayed buildings (see Figure 5.19). The park forms part of a green corridor running through east Leipzig, which has less access to green spaces and attractive public amenities than other areas.
- *Local skills: Lokales Kapital für soziale Zwecke* (LOS), a local social investment programme, receives EU Social Funds to provide small-scale financial support for projects to improve residents' skills and qualifications, especially targeting the long-term unemployed.
- *Support for small- and medium-sized enterprises (SMEs):* some local businesses in the area benefit from funds from the federal government.

Figure 5.19: New neighbourhood park on land cleared from demolished housing (east Leipzig)

SIGNS OF RECOVERY

The dramatic political transformation following the collapse of the Berlin Wall in 1989 made the crisis in Leipzig more extreme and sudden than in western European former industrial cities. Signs of recovery, following the un-sustained post-reunification boom, were visible from the late 1990s.

Population: strong decline, slight recovery

Leipzig's population reached its lowest point in 1998, with 437,000 inhabitants. According to recent figures, the city now has 502,000 inhabitants. Most recent population gains follow the city's incorporation of surrounding municipalities in 1999.[19] Therefore, analysis of population figures alone cannot explain recovery. Urban renewal efforts have created attractive and inexpensive inner-city housing that is increasingly reoccupied.[20] Suburbanisation quickly lost its impetus, in part explained by the end of federal subsidies, poor transport connections and more attractive housing options within the city. In contrast to many other western European metropolitan areas, the Leipzig region now shows a trend of population decline in the suburban municipalities and growth in the city (Figure 5.20).

Figure 5.20: Population development in Leipzig and surrounding municipalities, 1995–2003 (%)

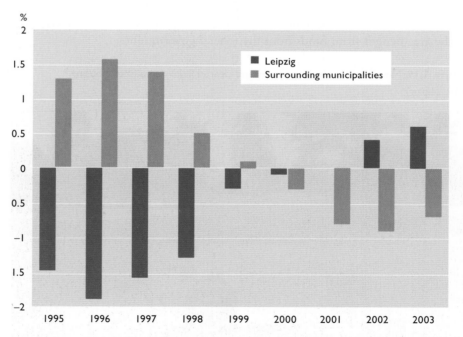

Source: Statistisches Landesamt Sachsen, quoted in Stadt Leipzig Department of Urban Development (2006)

Leipzig has successfully attracted younger households. The largest group moving to the city is aged 18 to 30,[21] partly due to the rising numbers of students at the University of Leipzig, which has strengthened its position as a leading regional higher education institution. Changes in taxation policy have supported the increase[22] (see Figure 5.21). Given the underlying demographic trends in East Germany, even maintaining the population at the current level would be a major achievement.[23]

Figure 5.21: New university buildings

Economic development

Leipzig's deindustrialisation reached an almost unprecedented depth with incredible speed, followed by an early strategy of creating a centre for banking and finance which failed and a construction boom which could only briefly absorb manufacturing losses. Yet towards the late 1990s, Leipzig has 'gone the extra mile' to foster economic success, providing additional services to potential companies and simplifying bureaucratic decision making.

The situation improved in the late 1990s, and even more so in the first half of the 2000s. Leipzig's success in attracting BMW against competition from 250 other German and foreign cities was particularly important, although current troubles in the car industry do not bode well.[24] The media, IT and communication technology cluster, with its 33,000 employees, is also important. It reflects growth in publishing and printing, but mostly depends on the regional publicly owned broadcaster. The other clusters show relatively little development.

Employment in manufacturing has increased since the mid-1990s, although only 11 per cent of the workforce is now employed in manufacturing, considerably lower than other German cities (see Figure 5.22). Nevertheless, some traditional sectors such as printing/graphics and machine engineering have modernised into niche markets, albeit with much reduced workforces.

Figure 5.22: Leipzig: rising number of employees in manufacturing, 1996–2004

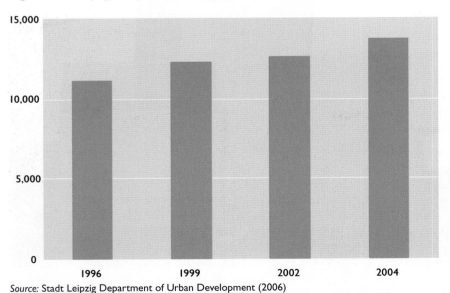

Source: Stadt Leipzig Department of Urban Development (2006)

Progress of urban renewal

Leipzig's innovative programmes and funding mechanisms, later copied by cities with similar problems, provided clear signs of positive renewal. By 2000, three quarters of the remaining pre-1918 housing had been refurbished. The numbers living in pre-1918 housing rose from 260,000 in 1998 to 300,000 in 2005, despite ongoing population losses and demolition.[25] The total vacancy rate dropped from 20 per cent or 62,500 housing units in 2000 to 14 per cent or 45,000 units at the end of 2005. Demolition under the *Stadtumbau Ost* programme, particularly those targeting the older housing stock in more central areas, attracted substantial criticism.[26] Gentrification is becoming evident in the more desirable inner-city locations.[27]

East Leipzig still shows the highest levels of deprivation in the city,[28] with vacancies still comprising around a third of all properties. There remain high levels of welfare dependency and unemployment, low incomes, low educational levels, many one-parent households, which all reflect ongoing polarisation and need. However, the influx of migrants may partly compensate for ongoing population losses and boost small enterprises. West Leipzig recovered more strongly; the proximity of high-quality green spaces and an overflow of demand from the adjacent and already-gentrified Südvorstadt have helped (see Figure 5.23).

Figure 5.23: Large green public spaces close to the city centre

Estates built during the socialist period, meanwhile, became more problematic. Although massive investment went into renovating this segment (see Figure 5.24), Grünau alone lost more than a third of its population between 1996 (76,000) and 2005 (48,000).[29] This estate, once sought after for its modern housing conditions, now shows increasing signs of social deprivation and houses an ageing population.

Figure 5.24: Grünau housing estate, refurbished blocks

Even optimistic projections suggest that it may only stabilise on a much smaller scale.[30]

Unemployment continued to rise in Leipzig until 2004, when it reached almost 25 per cent. Mostly due to national economic growth, unemployment has decreased since then but the proportion of long-term unemployed is still high. While the city has been relatively successful in attracting new companies, new jobs, for example in the service and logistics sector, have not compensated for the losses, with many in less secure, more temporary and lower-paid employment. Being located in a weak region has also meant that jobseekers from surrounding municipalities have taken many new jobs in Leipzig. The current economic recession will have a further detrimental effect on the labour market and unemployment remains Leipzig's most crucial and difficult social problem.

Regional and wider metropolitan cooperation

Collaboration across the region has recently gained ground as a way of expanding the city-region's economy and reducing public expenditure. Leipzig and the regional capital of Dresden, a city similar in size, have long experienced weak collaboration. The Saxony triangle, formed by the three major regional cities of Leipzig, Chemnitz and Dresden, was developed to foster regional cooperation but there are doubts about its progress.[31] The city-region of Leipzig and Halle, the neighbouring city with 270,000 residents, is much more popular. However, these two cities belong to different regions (Saxony and Saxony-Anhalt), making decision making difficult. Nevertheless, Leipzig and Halle already cooperate, share an airport and offer inward investors a common labour pool. Land suitable for new industrial parks is increasingly scarce in Leipzig, so the city is cooperating with nearby municipalities, including Halle, to attract companies to the region in order to jointly benefit from spin-off effects.

CONCLUSION

Leipzig has undergone a dramatic transformation since Germany's reunification, while dealing with significant problems, such as its shrinking population and steep manufacturing job losses. Nevertheless many challenges remain, including budget deficits, the need to retain a viable economic base with growth in sectors such as research and development and the uncertain future for the *Stadtumbau Ost* regeneration programme. While some areas like east Leipzig are struggling with a concentration of social deprivation, others like west Leipzig are recovering more strongly.

Leipzig now leads the way for East German cities in leadership, innovation and its pragmatic approach to change. The tradition of citizen involvement in local affairs is a strong component of this success. The city's overall success has drawn leading actors into the national government and to other cities. Larger projects were helped off the ground by the so-called 'Leipzig model', based on consensual decision making and cross-cutting political leadership, which was particularly important in Leipzig's recovery.

Figure 5.25: Timeline of important events in Leipzig since the late 1980s

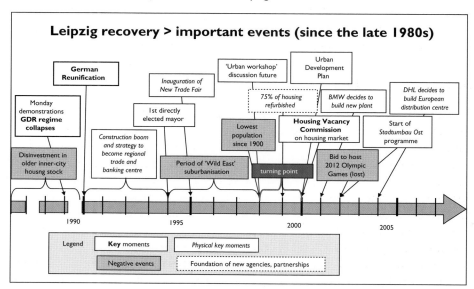

SIX

Bremen

CITY CONTEXT

Bremen in north-west Germany is located on the River Weser, which reaches the North Sea some 60km down river (see Figure 6.1). The city of Bremen (population 548,000) and its downriver sister-city of Bremerhaven (population 117,000) form the city-state of Bremen. Under the German federal system, the city-state has regional government powers.[32] The city-state of Bremen is governed by a senate with legislative powers bestowed on their *Burgerschaft* (parliament). In this chapter we focus mainly on the City of Bremen. Where necessary, we will distinguish between city-state and city level.

The first settlements in Bremen date back to the 1st century AD. In the 13th and 14th century, Bremen was an intermittent member of the prosperous Hanseatic League, an important late-medieval trading union with its economic centre in the Baltic Sea region. Its special political and legislative status – as an independent city-state – gave it a high degree of sovereignty from the 17th century onwards. After the unification of Germany in 1871, Bremen was formally recognised as a city-state with the official title of Free and Hanseatic City of Bremen.

Urban development only began in earnest in the 1800s. Harbour and trade-related activities sustained the economic development of the city, facilitated by Bremen's location at a

Figure 6.1: Germany, location of Bremen

ford on a navigable river with easy access to the sea. From the early 19th century, Bremen's commercial elite pressed for expansion of the harbours.[33] The result was the foundation of the coastal town Bremerhaven in 1827. The new port facilities in this Bremen enclave were to guarantee the access of larger ships.[34] In 1888, the large overseas harbour was built just north of the city as a response to advances in shipping technologies and in order to create a free trade zone, outside the tariff union of the new German nation-state founded in 1871.

Industrialisation and booming overseas trade fuelled a rapid growth in population, from 100,000 in 1880 to nearly 350,000 by 1930 (see Figure 6.2). This growth, and the consequent housing demand, catalysed rapid expansion of the built-up area and transformed the medieval city. Figures 6.3a–b shows the layout of Bremen at the end of the medieval era and at the beginning of the 20th century. Today, Bremen's harbour is the second largest in Germany, fourth in Europe and the 22nd largest in the world.

Figure 6.2: Population development, 1812–1970

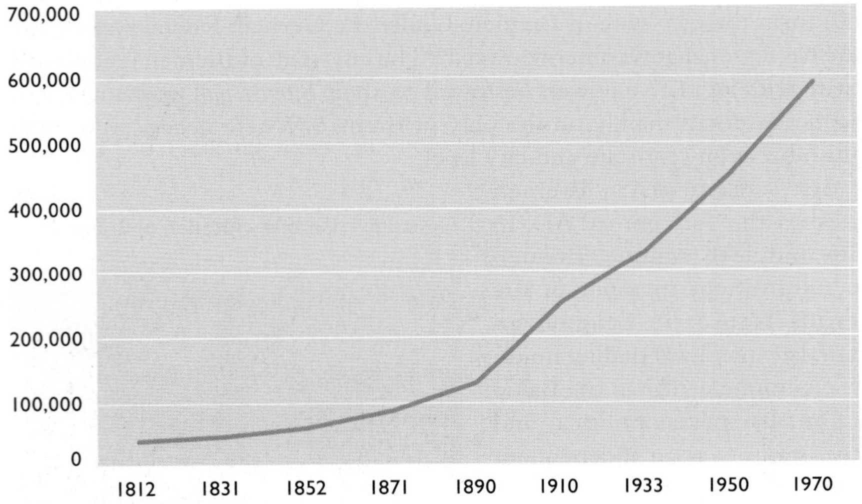

Source: Statistisches Landesamt Bremen (online)

During the 20th century, Bremen's economic base gradually shifted from trade and harbour activities towards industrial activities[35] and it soon became a major industrial city. While shipbuilding was the most important sector, car and airplane production developed quickly. In the 1920s and 1930s an important arms industry emerged (producing for example warships, weapons, warplanes, transporters). Both the harbour and its industries made Bremen a major target for air raids during the Second World War, destroying or damaging large parts of its several harbours. Industry became the driving force of Bremen's economy during the post-war boom of the 1950s and 1960s. New industrial sectors emerged, such as machine and engineering industries and food processing. After the war the US troops in Germany used the harbour for the movement of troops and goods. Bremen still has several harbours and, although the modern container facilities are located in Bremerhaven, most bulk cargoes are still shipped to and from the harbours in Bremen.

Figures 6.3a-b: Bremen, development of built-up area, around 1500 and 1900

CRISIS

The world entered a phase of deep recession after the oil crisis in 1973 as economies shifted from Fordist to post-Fordist modes of production. Although Bremen's economy proved fairly resilient at first, it entered the crisis in the late 1970s.[36]

The city's industrial crisis is closely associated with the decline of the shipbuilding industry. The city's largest employer, the shipbuilding company AG Weser, founded in 1843, collapsed in 1983 having employed 16,000 workers at its peak. In 1997, the second largest shipbuilding company, Bremer Vulkan AG, founded in 1805, also collapsed, resulting in further job losses.[37]

For a 'harbour city', the loss of its most symbolic industry was a serious blow, but this was only the tip of the iceberg. Additional redundancies were caused by the restructuring and increasing mechanisation of harbour-related activities and other industrial sectors.[38] However, some job losses were compensated for by new industrial jobs in the Mercedes-Benz plant, which opened in 1979. Meanwhile, semi-skilled and unskilled harbour workers found it very difficult to re-enter the labour market. The loss of low-skilled work was felt most in the traditional working-class neighbourhoods located close to the old harbours. The 'old' economic base was disappearing rapidly, with no alternative in sight.[39] The overall share of jobs in manufacturing dropped from 33 per cent in 1970 to 19 per cent in 2005.[40] The arms and defence industries were also seriously affected, especially after the political changes in Europe following the collapse of the Soviet Bloc in 1989.

Although the process of deindustrialisation continued through most of the 1990s, the crisis was worst around the mid-1980s. From 1980 to 1985, unemployment jumped from five to 15 per cent and was almost double the West German average. In Bremerhaven, declining economic sectors, such as deep-sea fishing, food processing and shipbuilding, pushed the unemployment rate to almost 20 per cent in 2004, one of the highest rates for any West German city.

In the 1970s, Bremen also began to lose its role as a prime retail, office and residential location, due to three factors. First, residential and retail suburbanisation increased rapidly, forcing the city centre to compete with shopping centres outside its boundaries. Second, from the 1970s, Bremen followed a polycentric model of land-use planning, giving intermediate centres equal status with the city centre. This was only reversed in 1992. Third, structural economic change undermined the harbour and trade-related businesses, making the old central port infrastructure obsolete. In the city centre, approximately 20,000 service sector jobs disappeared in the 1970s and 1980s, many related to harbour activities, such as logistics, trading, transportation and storage. Consequently, many buildings fell into disuse, especially in the Schlachte area on the River Weser. A few years later, this loss of employment was matched by population decline. After reaching its peak around 1970, Bremen's population fell to its lowest level in 1987, having lost 50,000 inhabitants (see Figure 6.4). This decline was due not to migration to more

Figure 6.4: Population decline, City of Bremen, 1970–2005

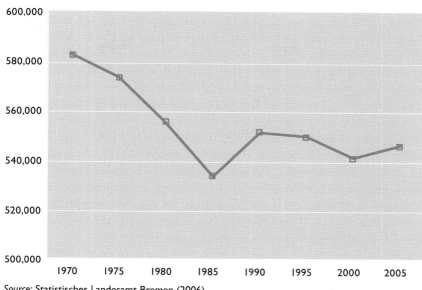

Source: Statistisches Landesamt Bremen (2006)

dynamic regions, as was the trend in most East German cities, but rather due to suburbanisation, natural population decline due to low birth rates and the return of many former migrant 'guest workers' to their home countries.

Low-skilled, elderly or migrant workers were hardest hit and increasingly excluded from the labour market, as the growing service sector did not supply a sufficient number of new low-skill jobs. There was a shift in low-paid jobs towards less-secure employment and more part-time working. Traditional working-class areas, previously close to major employment sectors, such as Gröpelingen, suffered most severely. In addition, some large peripheral housing estates, such as Osterholz-Tenever, became 'problem areas' as they accumulated poorer households.

RECOVERY ACTIONS

During the post-war period, Bremen was governed exclusively by the centre-left Social Democratic Party (SPD). Following the 1991 elections, the SPD, still the strongest political party, was forced to form coalitions and make political compromises. The first coalition was with the smaller liberal Free Democratic Party (FDP) and the Green Party. Clashes over proposed development zones, among other issues, caused the coalition to break down. From 1995 to 2007, Bremen was governed by a coalition of the two major German parties, SPD and the centre-right Christian Democrats (CDU). Much of the substantive recovery action, described below, was undertaken during this period. After the 2007 election, the SPD again formed a coalition with the Green Party.

Bremen's innovation-based approach

The outcome of the intense political problems posed by the crisis was a consensus that the city had to reposition itself. This 'change of path' was to be achieved by encouraging a new economic base that could meet future challenges.[41] Subsidies were cut and economic policy reoriented, moves that were hotly contested in Bremen where the governing SPD had strong traditional links to manual workers and trade unions. The cornerstone of the new approach and the first coherent attempt at economic restructuring was the economic policy action plan, or *Wirtschaftspolitisches Aktionsprogramm* (WAP), which began in 1984. The action plan, developed by the Bremen Economic Research Institute (BAW), revolved around two main objectives: restructuring Bremen's scientific landscape and strengthening the regional economic base. WAP offered significant investment opportunities and was mainly funded by the *Land* (or region) of Bremen, supplemented by EU money (Objective II).[42] In 1994, WAP was integrated into the substantial government-backed Special Investment Programme (ISP).

ISP offered an even greater opportunity to invest in economic restructuring and was made possible after Bremen was granted substantial financial aid totalling €9 billion from the federal government to deal with its long-run financial crisis. Rather than following a strategy of simple debt redemption to resolve its negative financial legacy, Bremen secured the federal government's agreement that the money saved on interest payments could be used for a strategic large-scale investment programme, the details of which are shown in Table 6.1.

Table 6.1: Special Investment Programme (ISP): main areas of activity

Activity	Examples of funded projects	Investment (€ million)	
Research, innovation and technology	New research institutes; research facilities; transformed university departments; links to new businesses		653
Development of new industrial and office parks	Airport City, Logistics Centre, Technology Park, Overseas City	Business parks: approximately	670
Transport-related projects	Transport infrastructure for new employment areas; harbour and airport investments; new tramlines	Traffic infrastructure: approximately	460
Tourism related projects – strengthening the city centre	e.g. tourism, Space Park, events/congresses, city centre	Urban revitalisation: City centre (retail, tourism): Suprastructure, events: Total:	201 205 172 578
Other spending			293
Total			2,654

Source: Prognos (2002)

Restructuring the university sector

The University of Bremen was founded in 1971 with a focus on social sciences and a reputation for being a leftist institution. With its status as city-state providing power over educational policy, Bremen decided to restructure the university towards high technologies, engineering and natural sciences in the 1980s to accompany the process of economic restructuring. New faculties were created and existing science faculties expanded to strengthen links between logistics, maritime sciences, aerospace and higher education and attracting off-shoots of renowned research institutes such as Fraunhofer, Max-Planck (both in Bremen) and Alfred-Wegener (Bremerhaven). The private International University of Bremen was founded in 1999 and renamed Jacobs University in 2007, following a €200 million donation from the Jacobs Foundation. As a result of the investments and their success, the Association of German Foundations and the Ministry of Education awarded Bremen the title 'Centre of Excellence' in 2005 for the performance of the six institutes of higher education. To the surprise of some, Bremen was also named a City of Science and has been acknowledged for its excellent higher education sector. External funding and the internationalisation of courses helped with this.

Delivering recovery projects

Providing attractive areas for office and industrial (re)location involved modernising existing areas, such as Airport City, redeveloping brownfield and dockland sites, such as Overseas City and developing new strategic sites, such as the Bremen Technology Park. To attract inward investment, the City of Bremen founded an investment agency, *Bremer Investitions-Gesellschaft mbH* (BIG), in 1998. Its main objective was to promote the new business parks and urban regeneration projects.

A major investor in these new developments was the EU. The state of Bremen has been receiving EU Objective II regional funding since 1994. This programme identified two main priorities: innovation and knowledge; and strengthening and upgrading urban residential and economic areas.[43] In the first funding period (1994–99), €133 million was available and supported: environmental protection (44 per cent of the total); strengthening the service sector (35 per cent); and diversification of the industrial sector (20 per cent).[44] The focus was on overcoming industrial decline and adapting to change. Between 1994 and 1999 Bremen also had access to funding from other EU programmes:

- Resider offered support for regions that suffered a crisis in the steel industry (€3.2 million).
- KONVER II gave support for regions that depended on military and arms industries (€5.6 million).

- PESCA supported regions suffering from declines in the fishing industry (€2.6 million).

During the second funding period (2000–06), available funds were increased to €226 million. Over half was dedicated to strengthening the service sector (57 per cent), but the shares for environmental protection (25 per cent) and diversification of the industrial sector (nine per cent) were both reduced. A new theme, 'assistance for urban problem areas', was added and constituted eight per cent of the funds. In the current period (2007–13), Bremen will receive €142 million of regional funding.

Below we detail some of the key recovery projects.

Technology park

The decision to develop a technology park was influenced by the success of Silicon Valley in the US. The Bremen site developed slowly with funding from WAP and began with the 1986 creation of a business incubator, the innovation and technology start-up centre (BITZ), to provide university graduates with offices and the infrastructure to start their own businesses. This 'organic' approach proved so successful that in 1988 it was decided to develop the technology park itself on 75 hectares of land surrounding the university. The real 'turbo-booster' for the park came with the above-mentioned ISP in the 1990s.[45] The programme not only provided funding to develop the site, but also to strengthen the scientific base by investing more in university faculties and research institutes. Figure 6.5 shows the business incubator and Figure 6.6 shows the university that is in its immediate area. The Bremen Technology Park is now the third largest of its kind in Germany, with 6,200 employees. It mainly hosts companies from aerospace, aircraft, environmental and medical technology industries. Approximately three quarters of these 320 companies have relocated from other areas in Bremen. Its balance of public to private investment, a ratio of 1:8, is the lowest for all business/industrial parks in Bremen, indicating a high success rate.[46] An attraction of the Technology Park to the wider public is the Universum Science Centre, an interactive museum with striking architecture.

Overseas City

In the inner city, both sides of the river have been redeveloped since the mid-1990s with ISP funding. In 2001 work began on the large Overseas City (*Überseestadt*), a waterfront redevelopment scheme on 217 hectares of the mostly abandoned Overseas Harbour (see Figure 6.7).[47] The project received considerable public funding, particularly for land remediation and infrastructure such as the new tramline. A particular characteristic is its mixed land uses: there is still some

Figure 6.5: The business 'incubator', BITZ innovation centre

functioning food processing industries, such as Kellogg's; a new wholesale fruit and vegetable market has been located there; and old storage buildings have been restored for university, arts and office use and as upmarket residential loft apartments.

Airport City

Airport City is a 128-hectare revitalised business and industrial park, that developed around the airport in the mid-20th century. It

Figure 6.6: The university, now 'embedded' in the Bremen Technology Park

attracted considerable funds through ISP as well as €13 million of Objective 2 European regional funding for environmental protection and site rehabilitation in the 1990s. Its revival is linked to the recent success of the aerospace industry, especially of the European Aeronautic Defence and Space Company (EADS) and its suppliers. The other main sector is aircraft production, which has a long tradition in Bremen, initiated by Focke and continued by Airbus today.

Figure 6.7: Aerial view and model of the Overseas City redevelopment site

The logistics sector has also expanded around the airport. Airport City is now Bremen's largest business park, with 13,500 employees in 450 companies.[48] The regional airport of Bremen, owned by the City, has experienced a considerable increase in passenger numbers since Ryanair decided to make it one of their major hubs in 2007, offering flights to 17 destinations. The airport is close to the city centre, connected by a new tram service. Road access to the area has been financed by central and regional governments.

City centre revitalisation and urban renewal

City centre revival started in earnest in the 1990s, and in 2004 some buildings in the centre were awarded world heritage status by UNESCO. ISP funds offered a unique opportunity for major projects in this area, including the redevelopment of the Schlachte riverfront area with new bars and restaurants, a modern arts museum, new public spaces and tourist appeal; the upgrading of the shopping district to improve Bremen's weak retail index;[49] the restoration of landmark buildings, including the modernisation and restoration of the Kunsthalle art gallery, the Goethe theatre, the Focke museum, the town hall (see Figure 6.8) and others; and

Figure 6.8: Bremen's imposing medieval town hall

the development of the Stephani Quarter on the northern edge of the city centre as a media cluster around the new offices of the regional broadcasting company.

Neighbourhood and housing renewal

Alongside restoring its centre, the city invested in its inner and outer neighbourhoods. This involved a shift from the traditional Social Democrat approach, based on equalising living conditions regardless of their socio-spatial distribution, toward a more spatially targeted approach. The funds were thus linked to the most disadvantaged and deprived areas.

Neighbourhood renewal activities were supported by two similar programmes: Bremen's neighbourhood renewal programme *Wohnen in Nachbarschaften* (WiN) (Living in Neighbourhoods) and the *Soziale Stadt* programme funded equally by the federal and regional governments. Bremen launched the WiN programme in 1998, developed from a previous programme targeting specific problems in large housing estates. Its integrated approach towards social cohesion and empowerment in disadvantaged neighbourhoods meant that WiN anticipated most of the features of the large-scale federal-regional *Soziale Stadt* programme which started in 1999.[50] Bremen has now integrated the two programmes. Today, 10 areas in Bremen, and one additional area in Bremerhaven, receive funding from one of these programmes.[51]

Physical remodelling

In 2002 the federal government launched the *Stadtumbau Ost* programme to give East German cities an instrument of intervention to stabilise their housing markets, which had been affected by high vacancy rates and decay (see also Chapter Five on Leipzig). While *Stadtumbau* means urban remodelling, the programme is most widely known for its emphasis on the demolition of surplus, poor-quality housing. A corresponding *Stadtumbau* programme was designed for West Germany to respond to its rising vacancy rates caused by unemployment and population decline. Bremen actively lobbied for inclusion in this because of its own housing problems following industrial decline.[52] *Stadtumbau West* focuses on finding innovative solutions to housing market problems and in Bremen the programme focuses especially on Osterholz-Tenever. This large peripheral housing estate had deteriorated rapidly during the 1990s due to mismanagement by new owners, inappropriate lettings policies for public housing and the increasing stigmatisation of the whole area.[53]

Social integration

Because of the growing social problems in declining housing areas, the physical investment programme was accompanied by social investment programmes. A major driver was the need to integrate residents from a migrant background. Like other industrial cities in West Germany, a relatively high proportion of Bremen's population comes from a minority ethnic background. According to official statistics, 13 per cent of the city's inhabitants are foreigners, one third of whom are Turkish. In addition, there are earlier immigrants who have acquired a German passport and ethnic German settlers from East European countries. By including all those from a foreign migrant background, the proportion of the city population that is from a migrant background increases to 27 per cent. The composition is shown in Figure 6.9; the high concentration of minorities in Osterholz-Tenever and Gröpelingen is particularly clear. Bremen, with its long tradition of progressive social policy and large number of residents from a migrant background, devised a city-based cross-departmental approach to integration.[54]

Figure 6.9: Percentage of people with foreign migrant background at country, city-state and neighbourhood levels, 2006

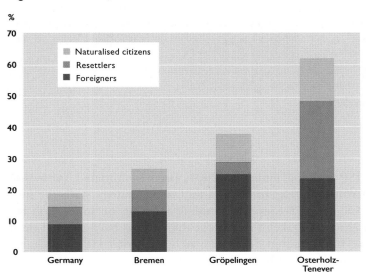

Sources: Statistisches Landesamt Bremen (online); Statistisches Bundesamt; www.focus-migration.de

SIGNS OF RECOVERY

The city's various efforts have prompted economic and physical changes, and it remains one of the country's major industrial cities. Although only Germany's 10th largest city, it has the fifth largest manufacturing workforce.[55] Its main industrial sectors include: car production (dominated by DaimlerChrysler); food and beverages (major companies include Jacobs, Kraft, Hag and Beck's); aircraft and aerospace (Bremen holds a leading position in these sectors; companies include EADS involved in the manufacturing of the Airbus); defence (for example OHB Technology and Atlas Elektronik Group); and shipbuilding (while the main employers have disappeared, smaller companies have survived and even prospered in niche markets, such as the construction of special purpose ships).

Impacts of innovation

Recent studies have tried to measure the impact of technology-focused investment on employment in Bremen. Table 6.2 shows that employment in technology sectors was above the German average between 1999 and 2004. Increases in employment in research and development are particularly striking.

Table 6.2: Indicators for innovation employment trends, Bremen city-state (1999–2004) (%)

	Bremen (city-state)	Germany
Advanced technology	+2.8	+0.7
Knowledge-intensive services	+3.2	+3.7
Research and development	+7.2	+1.0
Employees with higher-education degree	+11.7	+7.7

Source: Stenke and Wilms (2006)

Innovision 2010

In 2002, before ISP funding ended in 2004, Bremen initiated Innovision 2010, a cross-departmental programme as a follow-on strategy. With the most recent period of Objective 2 European funding focusing on innovation and knowledge (starting in 2007), key funding for the city has been secured up to 2013. Although the €200 million does not match the earlier ISP funding, it is still a significant commitment. One ambitious objective is to place Bremen in the top 10 technology cities in Germany, drawing on seven economic clusters, including the traditionally strong aircraft and aerospace, logistics and maritime sectors, as well as TIME (telecom, IT, media and entertainment), environmental technologies, health technologies and design sectors.[56] The move from Harbour City to a City of Science continues apace. Table 6.3 shows the impact of the ISP in Bremen up to 2001.

Table 6.3: Employment and funding effects of the Special Investment Programme (ISP) in Bremen (until 2001)

Directly employed in ISP-funded institutes	1,008
Indirectly employed (e.g. companies cooperating with ISP-funded units)	210 (regional)
New jobs in spin-offs (since 1997)	79
External funds acquired by all ISP funded units	€38.9 million
Private investment induced through cooperation with ISP-funded units	€51.5 million

Source: Prognos (2002)

The weaker side of city recovery

The precarious and still unresolved budgetary situation of the city-state of Bremen threatens some components of the strategy, such as further investment in the modernisation of its university. Other activities have not blossomed in the way innovation has. A significant proportion of the ISP funds were invested in tourism and leisure projects, and investments in purpose-built attractions have been largely unsuccessful. The most well-known failure is the Space Park project, a proposed entertainment centre featuring aerospace technology located on the former AG Weser shipyard. After about €180 million of public and €420 million of private investment, the project collapsed, before opening to the public. In 2007, the site was sold at a bargain price to an Irish investor who is planning a shopping development on the site. This may suggest the still halting recovery of more precarious areas. Another failure was the attempt to launch a musical theatre. Bremen also applied to become Germany's European Capital of Culture in 2010, but lost to Essen. Despite these conspicuous blows to the city's efforts, Bremen stuck to its recovery trajectory, as earlier sections have shown.

Labour market changes

Over the 1990s, Bremen lost more jobs than it gained and unemployment has stagnated at a level above the German average, at around 14 per cent. In addition Bremerhaven has one of the highest unemployment rates of any West German cities. This suggests that while the number of high-skilled jobs has increased, the employment opportunities for lower-skilled jobseekers are still limited. The social inequalities generated by high unemployment foster deprived areas with high levels of social welfare dependency. In response, Bremen founded an employment and training agency, BAG (*Bremer Arbeit GmbH*), partly financed through the European Social Fund, to try and overcome these barriers.

A major challenge: the future of the city-state

One of the most crucial factors in Bremen's ability to achieve sustained urban recovery is finding a way out of its long-run budgetary problems and increasing debt. Even with generous federal aid, after the successful constitutional case in 1992, Bremen was unable to control its chronic budget deficit. Its debts increased from €8 billion to a record €12 billion by 2005, making Bremen the most indebted German *Land* per inhabitant. As a result, most departments are not allowed to spend for most of the year and all are affected by efforts to cut costs. Without new financial aid, Bremen will face bankruptcy and its recovery process will be jeopardised. One option to control the budget involves greater privatisation of public functions, which some fear would involve Bremen ceding some power over service provision to the private sector which, with its emphasis on profits, threatens social cohesion, quality of life and housing standards. For now, Bremen's budget problems are unresolved, and its future political and regional status remains a matter for ongoing discussion.

Regional and metropolitan cooperation

Meanwhile, the issue of regional cooperation has become more prominent. The federal state of Bremen and the surrounding state of Lower Saxony began a joint regional planning approach in the 1970s to coordinate large-scale developments such as the proposed deep-water harbour in Wilhelmshaven, the construction of a coastal highway and the location of the four Airbus plants in the region. Bremen is also discussing regional development issues with the booming area of Oldenburg to its south west. Since 2002, Bremen has been involved with 35 adjacent municipalities in a cooperative approach to regional planning, mainly addressing conflicts between municipalities. Bremen's interest in metropolitan and regional cooperation is driven by:

• the desire to influence land-use decisions in surrounding municipalities, such as the location of large-scale retailers;
• the ability to realise larger regional infrastructure projects; and
• the implementation of a metropolitan area strategy, for example with regional marketing.

Following discussions about competitive city-regions, the European metropolitan region of Bremen-Oldenburg emerged in 2005. With a population of 2.37 million it is the smallest of the 11 metropolitan regions in Germany. Its main aim is to foster regional economic development, promoting regional business through the Chambers of Commerce.

CONCLUSION

Compared to other case study cities, Bremen, possibly alongside Torino, seems to have undergone the most significant recovery. Although the city of Bremerhaven is still showing decline on most indicators, the larger city of Bremen has halted population decline and shown recent improvements in employment. While the loss of manufacturing employment has not yet been matched by an equivalent growth in new employment, the number of service sector jobs is increasing more rapidly. There are, however, several factors which call into question how the city will fare in the future, including the consolidation of public finances, dealing with increasing social polarisation and guaranteeing the long-term durability of the innovation strategy. While generous federal aid between 1994 and 2004 allowed Bremen to design an ambitious investment programme, the city will not have such access to external aid in the future.

Although the decline of harbour activities has contributed to the urban employment crisis, Bremen has been able to establish itself as a node in the global transport and cargo networks, continuing its maritime tradition without the 'hardware'. About one third of all employment depends directly or indirectly on harbour-related activities (for example logistics, shipping, storage, trading). But competition among Europe's major ports is strong. Cities that do not adapt their facilities quickly enough to the sector's requirements can easily lose market share. Therefore, in its role as city-state, Bremen is constantly lobbying the federal government for funds to improve its transport infrastructure.

Further investment has gone into revitalising the city centre but culture-driven regeneration based on entertainment and tourism has not been very successful. Several experts describe Bremen's service sector as underdeveloped, with few major company headquarters. The creative service sector is also underdeveloped. Nevertheless, Bremen seems to have a good basis for addressing future challenges.

Finally, social exclusion remains a serious concern for those who are not ready to fit new job profiles, especially people from a migrant background, the long-term unemployed and the low-skilled. Nevertheless, efforts are underway to reverse the social pressures in deprived neighbourhoods. There is a political consensus that urban social problems need special attention and therefore specific funding to overcome the worst effects of structural adjustment.

Overall Bremen is pulling away from its period of decline, but like all the cities in our study, continues to face ongoing economic and social challenges.

Figure 6.10: Timeline of important events in Bremen since 1980

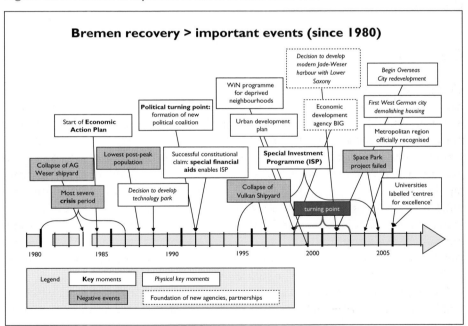

SEVEN

Sheffield

CITY CONTEXT

Sheffield is located in the South Yorkshire conurbation (see Figures 7.1 and 7.2). In 2001, the city had an estimated resident population of 513,234, with a population density of 1,395 people per km². Sheffield is England's fourth largest local authority in terms of population.

Figure 7.1: Map of the UK

Figure 7.2: Map of Sheffield local authority area

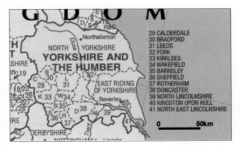

The nearby towns of Rotherham, Doncaster and Barnsley surround the core city of Sheffield and contain the coalfields which fuelled Sheffield's steel industry (Figure 7.3). The wider city-region comprises 11 local authorities, and in 2005 had an estimated population of 1,736,600.[57]

History

Sheffield nestles in a natural basin surrounded by seven hills, at the confluence of two major rivers, the Don and the Sheaf, from which Sheffield gets its name. The Peak District National Park, which borders the city along its western periphery, constitutes roughly one third of the city's land.

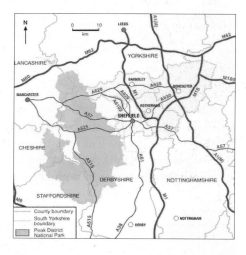

Figure 7.3: Map of Sheffield and the South Yorkshire sub-region

The first settlement in the area dates back to the 7th century. Local production of metal began in the early Middle Ages and was sustained by a coincidence of natural resources, namely iron ore for smelting, oak woods for charcoal and fast-flowing streams for water power. Sheffield expanded as a result of the production of its famous knives and the associated trade activities.

Industrial revolution, pioneering industrialists and large-scale production

During the 18th century the concentration of steel-making entrepreneurs and activity in the city sparked several pioneering innovations that won the city an international reputation. The crucible process produced a better quality of steel and the 'Sheffield plate' technique for fusing silver onto cheaper copper products proved highly popular. With its concentration of industries, new technologies and inventive spirit, Sheffield became a leading city of the industrial revolution in late 18th-century Britain, with a dramatic expansion of its metal-working industry.[58]

By the late 19th century, powerful local steel-making companies drove the city's economy. A local engineer, Henry Bessemer, invented the Bessemer converter to enable the mass production of steel (Figure 7.4).[59] The invention of stainless steel in Sheffield in 1913 also broke new ground, producing a cheaper and more durable material that proved internationally popular.

At the turn of the century, the light metal goods and heavy steel production and engineering industries were flourishing, employing around 75,000 people by 1911.[60] The nearby pits in Barnsley and Doncaster underpinned Sheffield's industrial success, providing cheap local energy.

Population growth and diverging housing conditions

The city's population grew in step with its industrial success, nearly tripling between 1801 and 1851 from 60,000 to 161,000 (see Figure 7.5).[61] Closely

Figure 7.4: Bessemer steel machine (Sheffield)

packed homes were hastily erected to house migrants from the surrounding countryside and regions. Much of it was built along the Lower Don Valley on the eastern side of the city, close to the expanding steel works (Figure 7.6). Factory owners built their mansions in the picturesque west of the city bordering the Peak District, away from the smoke stacks in the east. Their pattern of social segregation still characterises the city today, an affluent west and a deprived north and east (Figure 7.7).

Figure 7.5: Population development, 1801–1983

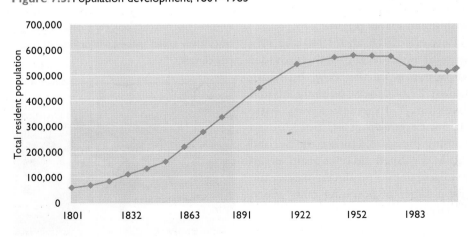

Sources: ONS census data; ONS mid-year estimates; Vision of Britain, 2007

Figure 7.6: Patterns of industrial land use, Sheffield and Lower Don Valley

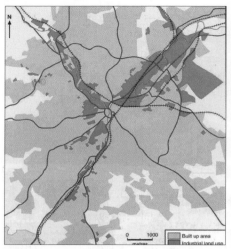

Note: Red areas indicate traditional industrial areas.

Figure 7.7: Index of Multiple Deprivation, by ward, Sheffield compared with the UK average, 2000

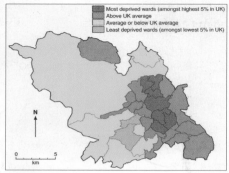

Note: Brown areas indicate high-deprivation areas.

Inter-war and post-war slum clearance and rebuilding

Sheffield served as a major centre for the manufacture of armaments during the First World War. By the end of the war, the city's population had reached half a million. In 1919, faced with poor housing conditions and overcrowding in the city centre, the city council commissioned a new urban plan for Sheffield. This plan eliminated all city centre slums, displacing 125,000 people into new low-density satellite settlements around the centre.[62] It also created a series of open spaces running up from the city centre into the Peak District,[63] giving Sheffield its attractive layout of 'villages' interspersed with green spaces (Figure 7.8).

Between 1919 and 1940 the city council became the main provider of housing in the city, building almost 27,000 new publicly owned dwellings.[64] In practice very little clearance was carried out due to housing pressures. During the Second World War, Sheffield once again served as an armaments producer, making the city a target of bombing raids which destroyed much of the surviving

Figure 7.8: Meersbrook Park, one of the city's many green spaces, with a view of the city centre

Victorian terraced housing near the city centre, thereby creating an ever greater housing shortage.

By 1951, the city's population had reached 577,000.[65] Planning and housebuilding took off again during the 1950s and 1960s, much of it council-led. The Lower Don Valley was re-zoned for industrial use only, clearing all the existing housing that flanked the factories and steel mills. Large areas of inner-city terraced housing were also demolished and giant modern concrete council estates such as Park Hill were erected in their place (see Figure 7.9). As the manufacturing population began its long decline in the 1970s, there were already significant vacancies in working-class neighbourhoods.[66]

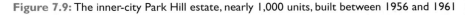

Figure 7.9: The inner-city Park Hill estate, nearly 1,000 units, built between 1956 and 1961

CRISIS

Until the 1970s Sheffield had boasted virtually full employment, with unemployment rates consistently below the national average. The global oil shock of 1973 and the increasing globalisation of trade and manufacturing dealt a major blow to British industry and Sheffield was among the cities hardest hit. Its larger neighbours Manchester and Leeds had more diversified exchange-based economies, providing some measure of protection. Sheffield's large steel firms failed to adapt to the changing economic landscape during the 1970s as the country began to deindustrialise. Meanwhile, corporate restructuring within the steel and heavy engineering industries greatly reduced local control of production, and the number of headquarters in the city fell steadily. Of the 1,000 largest UK firms, those with headquarters in Sheffield fell from 22 in 1976 to just 13 in 1987.67

With the national economy in recession, Margaret Thatcher's Conservative government was elected in 1979. It took swift decisions to privatise key national industries including steel and coal. Factory closures in Sheffield, which had begun in the late 1970s, accelerated through the 1980s, with the local unemployment rate exceeding the national average for the first time in 1981, rising from four per cent in 1978 to 11 per cent in 1981.[68] By 1984 unemployment had soared to 16 per cent, and the manufacturing industry that had employed almost 50 per cent of the city's workforce in 1971 now employed just 24 per cent.[69]

Regenerating Sheffield

Sheffield City Council had been controlled by the left-wing Labour party for an almost unbroken period since 1926, and had a long history of practising a form of municipal socialism based on high expenditure on local services.[70] Like most British local authorities, it had traditionally played a limited role in economic development. It was therefore unprepared for dealing with the economic and social crisis.

With private firms deserting the city, the city council stepped into the breach. It attempted to tackle the deep economic problems of the city through a generous spending regime.[71] The council itself was employing over 21,000 people by the mid-1980s, more than five times the workforce of the largest private firm in the city, with a budget of around £250 million.[72] Meanwhile, the closure of the mines in the city-region sparked two bitter miners' strikes in the mid-1980s headquartered in Sheffield. The council led the defiance of the government's starkly anti-protectionist policies towards the manufacturing industry. Violent police battles with striking miners made national headlines while union and council militancy created a legacy of hostile relations between the public and private sectors in Sheffield.

The council's economic development initiatives

Sheffield City Council's investment and regeneration policies were clearly at odds with the market-oriented policies of the government.[73] The Thatcher government increased its control over local authority spending, cutting off Sheffield's public resources and preventing it from raising more until it changed track. Sheffield's defiant relationship with central government dampened any enthusiasm the private sector may have had for investing in the city.[74]

The council set up its own Department for Employment and Economic Development (DEED) in 1981 (see Box 7.1), to develop local sport, cultural and media industries. DEED supported the formation of worker cooperatives producing 'socially useful' products such as software for the blind. The cultural strategy led to the creation of a Cultural Industries Quarter in a city centre

Box 7.1: Sheffield regeneration timeline, 1981–2007

1981	City council founds its Department for Employment and Economic Development (DEED)
1984–85	National miners' strike headquartered in Sheffield
1986	South Yorkshire Metropolitan County abolished by central government
	City council founds Sheffield Economic Regeneration Council (SERC)
1987	Meadowhall out-of-town shopping centre sanctioned by city council
1988–97	Sheffield Development Corporation (Sheffield's UDC)
1988	Bid to host World Student Games won
1990	Meadowhall out-of-town shopping centre completed
1991	World Student Games hosted
1991	City council's first City Challenge funding bid rejected
1992	City council's second City Challenge funding bid rejected
	City Liaison Group regeneration agency founded
1994–2008	Single Regeneration Budget (SRB) funding
1994	Supertram opens
1995	Core cities lobbying group of eight regional cities founded; Sheffield is lead partner
1997	New Labour national government elected
1997	Appointment of new partnership-oriented council chief executive
1998	City Liaison Group becomes Sheffield First Partnership (SFP)
2000–06	Sheffield's South Yorkshire city-region qualifies for EU Objective 1 funding
2001	Sheffield First for Investment (SFfI) inward investment agency founded
	Sheffield's Burngreave neighbourhood awarded New Deal for Communities funding of £52 million for 10 years
	JOBMatch inward investment programme launched
	JobNet community-based recruitment service founded
2004	Northern Way Growth Strategy for northern regions launched
	Closing the Gap policy for neighbourhood renewal launched
2005	Robin Hood Airport Doncaster Sheffield opens
2007	Sheffield City Region Forum founded
	Creative Sheffield city economic regeneration company founded

neighbourhood of disused metal workshops, to house small-scale businesses such as the Red Tape recording studios.[75] However, the council lacked the resources or know-how to attract major new growth sectors. It continued to promote its locally rooted regeneration policies in the belief that the economy was suffering a temporary set-back and that the burden of financing new expenditure would ease when the 1980s recession ended.[76]

The government employed increasingly draconian tactics to force left-leaning local authorities, of which Sheffield City Council was a leader, to comply with its privatising ethic and cooperate with the private sector in its regeneration efforts. Privatisation, competitive bidding for funds and new single-purpose agencies all reduced council functions and scope for action.[77] Despite its determination to resist the government's market logic, the council's severely constrained finances forced it to abandon funding its home-grown regeneration initiatives.

Central government forces the pace of change

The government had developed urban development corporations (UDCs) during the early 1980s as a way of attracting private investment for the regeneration of the semi-abandoned heartlands of industrial cities. A UDC was a special-purpose government-mandated agency tasked with regenerating core, former industrial zones within cities. Their boards were private sector-dominated, although local authorities and central government were represented on them. Through the allocation of special planning powers and government funds to these new 'quangos' (quasi non-governmental organisations), central government wrested control over infrastructure and economic investment away from local government in these tightly drawn areas.

After initial resistance Sheffield accepted the government-imposed UDC, and in 1988 the Sheffield Development Corporation (SDC) was formed to regenerate the Lower Don Valley. The council had neither the power nor the resources to plan more long-term regeneration initiatives on its own. As a mark of its desperation the council had sanctioned an out-of-town shopping centre, Meadowhall, at the end of the Lower Don Valley.[78] Although Meadowhall did create jobs and return activity to the far end of the Valley, it was a short-sighted decision that poached shoppers from Sheffield's city centre, further reducing the city's long-term economic viability.

The Sheffield Development Corporation was not linked into any city-wide strategy. It had planning powers over 2,000 acres of land and a budget of £50 million (Figure 7.10). It demolished most of the Valley's abandoned steel mills, laid a major road down its length to improve access and created a new low-density landscape of commercial, conference and music venues. It also built a small civic airport, which has since closed. By the time it wound up in 1997, the Sheffield Development Corporation had been 'instrumental to securing the physical regeneration of the valley'.[79]

Figure 7.10: Map of Sheffield city centre and the Lower Don Valley, showing the Sheffield Development Corporation area covering former industrial sites

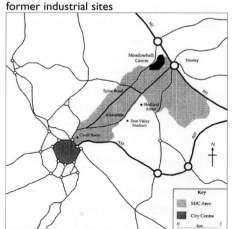

New partnerships

In 1986, running out of options for continuing its economic development work alone, the city council first attempted a form of partnership with the private sector, with the creation of the Sheffield Economic Regeneration Committee (SERC). SERC was essentially a council committee that consulted with, but did not directly involve, the private sector.[80]

SERC submitted a bid to host the World Student Games, which it won in 1988. As a result some high-quality sport-related infrastructure was built in the Lower Don Valley, including a 25,000-seater athletics stadium and a 10,000-seater arena and exhibition centre. However, the council's inability to secure sufficient private finances to pay for the games resulted in a financial crisis that a still hostile central government refused to bail out.[81] The municipality was forced to lay off several hundred workers the following year, and is still paying off the debts incurred by the Games.

Supertram

SERC went on to develop further council-led regeneration projects, in closer collaboration with central government. The most striking example was the project for a new tram system for Sheffield. This received £233 million from the government and £7 million of private funding, most of it from the developers of Meadowhall shopping mall who stood to benefit directly from fast public transport links. The tram's first route was designed to prioritise the regeneration of deprived neighbourhoods in the east and the north, without an accurate assessment of potential usage. As a result, the Supertram failed to attract anything like the predicted passenger numbers and was loss-making from its opening. It was later sold off for £1 million to a private bus company in an attempt to cut its ongoing losses. The disastrous financial impact of the World Student Games, Supertram and other loss-making economic development projects forced drastic budget cuts by the council.

In 1991 central government moved towards a more conciliatory approach that prioritised cooperation with local authorities.[82] New competitive bid-funding schemes such as City Challenge were announced in the early 1990s, with local authority partnership working a key requirement (Box 7.2). However, Sheffield's two bids for City Challenge made through its council-dominated SERC committee were both rejected.

Deeper, wider partnerships

Both central government and the EU, the other potential significant source of funding offering a counterweight to the British government, required all applications to reflect local partnerships rather than to represent single public or

Box 7.2: UK government regeneration initiatives, 1980–2006

1980   UDCs set up: independent fixed-term agencies managed by boards with strong private sector membership, mandated by central government to regenerate specific zones within cities over which they were given planning and land acquisition powers
        Enterprise Zones set up

1991   City Challenge programme: a five-year central government programme aimed at regenerating specific inner-city areas to improve quality of life for residents. Run as competitive-bid scheme, awarded to partnerships that included local authorities

1993   English Partnerships national regeneration agency founded

1994   SRB programme: a repackaging of 20 government regeneration programmes to make regeneration funding simpler. Local authorities and local communities could apply for funds to develop initiatives to improve quality of life in their area. Ran until 2007

1997   Social Exclusion Unit founded

1998   Education Action Zones (+ Health, Work, etc) set up
        New Deal for Communities programme: area-based initiative tackling job prospects, crime, educational under-achievement, poor health and physical environment in cities. Run by a partnership involving residents. Thirty-nine projects in total, each awarded around £50 million

1999   Regional Development Agencies founded for nine regions
        Urban Task Force set up to propose ways of improving the physical quality of cities

2000   Urban regeneration companies (URCs) set up: special-purpose companies dedicated to regenerating a specific zone in a city, in which local authorities play a more central role than in the UDCs. Sole board members are the local authority, the local RDA and English Partnerships (by 2005, there were 21 URCs)
        Community strategy: under the Local Government Act 2000, all local authorities must prepare a strategy for promoting the economic, social and environmental well-being of their area
        Business improvement districts set up
        Neighbourhood Renewal Unit founded

2001   Local strategic partnerships: umbrella partnerships set up by the 88 most disadvantaged local authorities at the request of central government, bringing together public, private, voluntary and community sectors to coordinate the work of specific partnerships
        Neighbourhood Renewal Fund: funding awarded to the 88 most deprived local authorities
        Urban and rural White Papers published

2002   Housing Market Renewal pathfinders set up to regenerate low-demand housing in nine areas

2003   Sustainable Communities Plan

2006   Local government White Paper published

Sources: SDC (2003); Leunig and Swaffield (2007); http://preview.eukn.org/unitedkingdom/urban/index.html

private bodies.[83] In response, desperate for regeneration funding in the face of high unemployment and tight government constraints, Sheffield City Council launched its second partnership coordinating committee in 1992, the more independent City Liaison Group. The City Liaison Group represented wider interests including the private sector, development agencies, higher education and the health services.[84] Its early bids for funding from the national SRB met with success.

The new compliance with the partnership-oriented funding requirements of national and international governments yielded a major increase in funding for Sheffield City Council's regeneration efforts. As a result, the council was able to start developing the scale and variety of projects needed to address the range of economic and social problems the city still faced.

RECOVERY ACTIONS

In 1997 the New Labour government came to power. Its emphasis on combating social inequality spawned a range of new area-based policies targeting deprived neighbourhoods, a boon for cities such as Sheffield.

Centralism and public–private partnerships

Planning for major infrastructure, borrowing and revenue raising still relied heavily on central government. The budgets of local authorities such as Sheffield City Council were largely made up of government grants with tight guidance on how they should be spent (see Figure 7.11). Funding with 'strings attached' prevented the city council from spending its resources in a coordinated way on its own priorities.

The New Labour government focused regeneration initiatives on addressing areas of concentrated multiple deprivation within cities. It continued the tradition of competitive area-based programmes managed by local partnerships, but introduced a stronger emphasis on the involvement of local communities, for example the New Deal for Communities programme (see Box 7.2). The EU also continued to prioritise local community participation and partnership working, in its funding requirements for Objective 1 and Urban programmes.[85]

For these reasons, the appointment of a new council chief executive skilled in partnership working, and the formation of a new partnership management body, the Sheffield First Partnership (SFP) board (the successor to City Liaison Group), became critical to accessing regeneration funding and demonstrating efficiency, coordination and delivery in order to attract more funding. Meanwhile a third critical factor in Sheffield's growing success in attracting regeneration funding was the lobbying activities, led by its council chief executive, which pushed for more city-friendly national policies.

Figure 7.11: Breakdown of Sheffield City Council revenue spending 2007–08

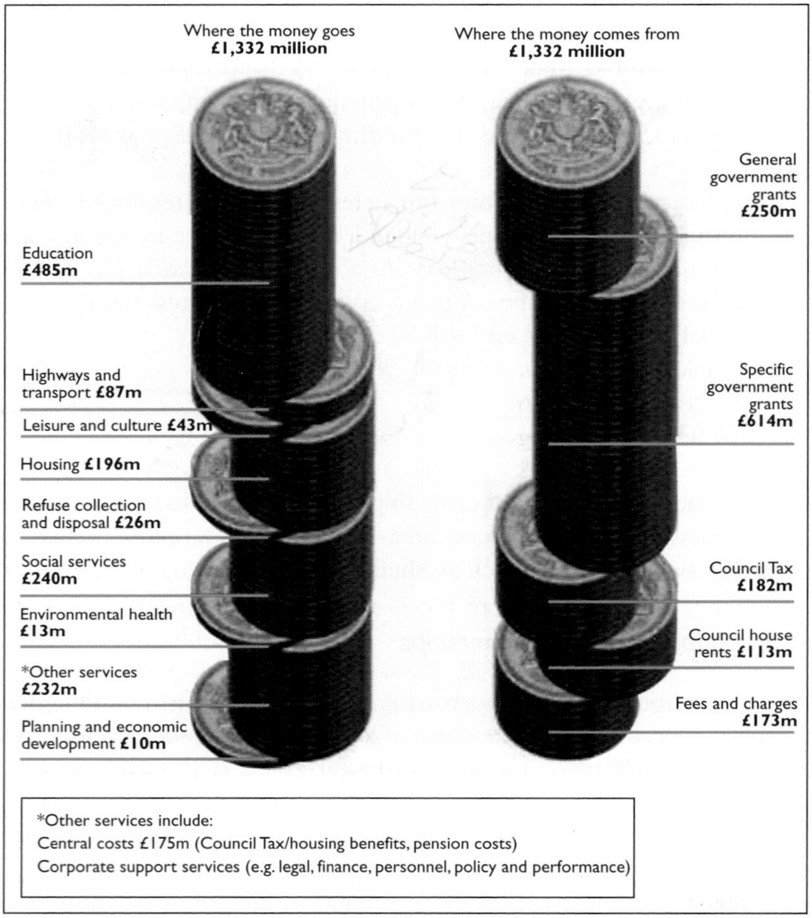

Where the money goes
£1,332 million

Where the money comes from
£1,332 million

General government grants
£250m

Education
£485m

Highways and transport **£87m**

Leisure and culture **£43m**

Housing **£196m**

Refuse collection and disposal **£26m**

Social services
£240m

Environmental health
£13m

*Other services
£232m

Planning and economic development **£10m**

Specific government grants
£614m

Council Tax
£182m

Council house rents **£113m**

Fees and charges
£173m

*Other services include:
Central costs £175m (Council Tax/housing benefits, pension costs)
Corporate support services (e.g. legal, finance, personnel, policy and performance)

Partnerships improve Sheffield's access to funding

The new council chief executive carefully brokered new alliances and persuaded new partners to work with the city council on equal terms. For example, when South Yorkshire gained EU Objective 1 status in 2000 (awarded to regions with GDP below 75 per cent of the EU average), he persuaded the 11 local authorities in the region to recognise Sheffield as the central urban hub of the sub-region, thus ensuring a higher proportion of the funding for the city.

The SFP board coordinated the work of multiple thematic partnerships, set up to manage the different strands of the city's regeneration-related activity (Figure 7.12). The board held regular meetings in public and each thematic partnership included stakeholders from the public, private and voluntary sectors, promoting inclusion and transparent decision making.[86]

In 2002, the Labour government made the partnership board model developed in Sheffield into a requirement for every local authority to formalise the participative decision-making process. These boards were henceforth referred to as local strategic partnerships (LSPs), and SFP became the city's LSP.

Core cities network

Sheffield played a leading role in creating the core cities network in the mid-1990s, including a lobbying group of eight major English cities (Birmingham, Bristol, Leeds, Liverpool, Manchester, Newcastle,

Figure 7.12: Sheffield First Partnership Board

Nottingham and Sheffield) facing serious economic restructuring and regeneration needs. Together they lobbied for more local control over funding.[87] The core cities group pressured national government to recognise struggling cities' needs, helping to develop the Housing Market Renewal (HMR) programme for the regeneration of low-demand housing areas across northern England, more flexible city-level funding arrangements such as the local area agreements (LAAs) and new city-level regeneration agencies such as Creative Sheffield.

New recovery initiatives

City centre strategy

From 1994 the city council had been developing 'Heart of the City', a project to remodel the city centre and create more high-quality office space. In 2001 this work was taken over by the new urban regeneration company (URC), Sheffield One, set up in 2001. It was a government-backed delivery vehicle for regenerating a specific zone of the city. URCs were successors to the 1980s UDCs but established in cooperation with local authorities. The URC worked in partnership with the city council, the RDA and the national regeneration agency English Partnerships (now the Homes and Communities Agency), which holds the necessary land assembly powers.

Sheffield One had responsibility for a tightly bounded zone in the city centre, with four objectives:

- building the centre's economic role;
- creating a centre recognised as a place for learning, culture, retail, leisure and living;
- making the centre more accessible; and
- developing high-quality public spaces in all parts of the centre.

Sheffield One produced a masterplan covering seven areas of its city centre zone. The masterplan's key projects were:

- the Heart of the City project, a group of new public spaces, including the Peace Gardens and the Millennium Galleries (Figure 7.13);
- the new Retail Quarter;
- upgrading Sheffield's main train station;
- City Hall and Barkers Pool, refurbishing the old city hall to create a cultural and conference venue within a mixed-use area;
- Castlegate, mixed-use developments in the city's historic 'gateway';
- user-friendly public and private transport networks in and around the centre; and
- a new e-campus for Sheffield Hallam University.

The masterplan was drawn up to provide a basis for public sector investment in infrastructure to encourage the private sector to commit its own investment (Figure 7.14). For example, Sheffield One used funding from the EU Objective 1 programme to gap-fund the building of private office blocks, and then private developers

Figure 7.13: Millennium Galleries

Figure 7.14: Sheffield One masterplan map of the city centre, showing the seven key project areas

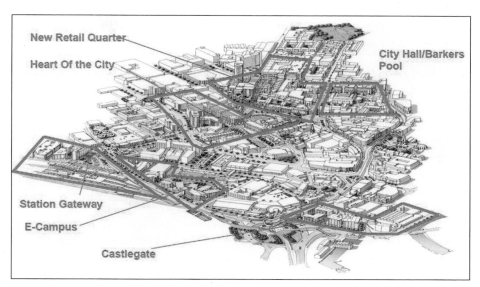

began to build speculatively in the city centre. Other aspects of the masterplan were also implemented by developers, such as the £500 million Retail Quarter.

Neighbourhoods strategy

The sharp inequalities between the city's neighbourhoods led Sheffield City Council to design and lobby for policies focused on deprived neighbourhoods (Figure 7.15). A third of Sheffield's households lived in the 10 per cent most deprived wards in the UK, and over a quarter of these households received Income Support.[88] The city council created its own neighbourhood regeneration strategy in 2004 – Closing the Gap – to integrate the many disparate government initiatives and strategies aimed at neighbourhood renewal in the city's 100 most deprived neighbourhoods. The aim was to close the gap between these and the city average. The SFP board created a new Successful Neighbourhoods Partnership to coordinate all activities linked to this policy.

The council developed a diagnostic tool, the Sheffield Neighbourhood Information System (SNIS), to collect data on 44 key social and economic indicators at neighbourhood level. SNIS tracked change in the 100 Closing the Gap neighbourhoods over time that helped focus resources on the neediest areas, and measure progress toward central government targets. SNIS was also an important tool for providing evidence to support further funding bids to national government, which awarded funding based on evidence of need.

The council then developed area panels to improve resident participation in regeneration decisions, with each panel bringing together representatives from

Figure 7.15: Unemployment figures, by ward, Sheffield compared to the UK average, 2000

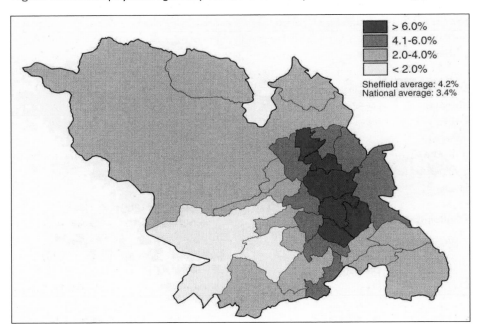

> \> 6.0%
> 4.1-6.0%
> 2.0-4.0%
> < 2.0%
>
> Sheffield average: 4.2%
> National average: 3.4%

the local community headed by the local councillor. The SFP board divided the city into 12 action areas, each with its own area panel. The panel's brief was to improve the quality of council services in the local area, and to get agencies to work together on local priorities, with small amounts of money from the national Neighbourhood Renewal Fund, leading to 140 local projects across the city.

The city council also applied its neighbourhood-based approach to housing regeneration developing masterplans for upgrading housing in nine areas across the city. A substantial amount of the funding for housing improvement in Sheffield came through the HMR programme in 2002. Over one third of Sheffield's housing (63,000 homes) was classed as in need of 'market renewal'. Over a 15-year period, this housing would receive a share of the £2.5 billion of investment designated for South Yorkshire.[89]

Economic strategy

In 1998 responsibility for regional economic development policy in England was transferred to nine regional quangos, the RDAs. Yorkshire Forward, the RDA for Sheffield's region, has since played a dominant role in developing the city's economic strategy. Their economic strategy focused on developing higher education as the main driver of growth and developed its own plans for 'knowledge-based regional clusters' in the creative and digital industries, advanced manufacturing, bioscience and environmental technologies.[90] The central plan of the RDA's strategy for Sheffield was to develop the commercial potential of Sheffield's 'knowledge base', rooted in its history of technological innovation and fuelled by its two major universities (the University of Sheffield and Sheffield Hallam University), and to capitalise on their resources to create new science-related clusters.[91] Over 12 per cent of Sheffield's working population was still employed in the manufacturing sector in 2005. By cooperating with the local universities, the RDA is attempting to address the economy's over-reliance on vulnerable and slow-growth sectors through its promotion of clusters in high-growth sectors.[92]

There is an ongoing debate as to which fields should become the focus of Sheffield's new economy, but four niches are emerging as the main focus:[93]

- advanced manufacturing (linked to the city's steel-making expertise);
- biomedical and healthcare (with a specialisation in surgical blades linked to steel making and knife production);
- creative and digital industries (linked to the Cultural Industries Quarter in the city centre); and
- sports science and technology (linked to the Lower Don Valley sports infrastructure).[94]

These clusters are being promoted through a number of science and skill-based initiatives, supported by the RDA and the city council.

Cluster site creation

The Advanced Manufacturing Park is the result of collaboration between engineers at the University of Sheffield and Boeing, whose £28 million Advanced Manufacturing Research Centre became the anchor for a wider Advanced Manufacturing Park 'cluster site' which opened in 1999. This project was developed and funded by the RDA using Objective 1 funding. It shows how existing industrial expertise and the local universities can generate new economic activity for the city.

The Cultural Industries Quarter, Sheffield's original 'cluster site' founded by the left-wing city council during the 1980s, grew to employ some 3,000 people and constitutes the central plank of the city's creative industries activity.[95] However, it may have reached a plateau.[96] Many of its small firms are highly dependent on grant funding from the SRB or EU Objective 1 programmes, which have now ended and face an uncertain future.

Inward investment initiatives

The city council has shifted away from attempts to attract large firms, recognising that SMEs also offer real benefits to the local economy and have the potential to multiply and expand fast. Nevertheless, the successful attraction of large firms such as Polestar printworks has provided hundreds of low-skilled jobs for local residents, a necessary counterweight to the focus on high-skilled 'knowledge' jobs.

Like many other regenerating cities, Sheffield set up its own inward investment agency to promote the city and attract new businesses. Sheffield First for Investment (SFfI) was founded in 2001. Like the Sheffield One URC, this agency operated at arm's length from the city council. It has received core funding from the council and the EU Objective 1 programme. The Objective 1 funding allowed it to attract inward investors, offering some of the highest public incentives available within the EU, including grant funding for research and development, capital projects, employment and training costs and support for up to 25 per cent of costs for capital projects.

Employment initiatives: JOBMatch (2001) and JobNet (2002)

Recognising the concern of potential employers over whether they would find a local workforce with the right skills, SFfI set up the JOBMatch service in 2001 to link employers to jobseekers in the city, part-funded by the EU Objective 1 programme. JOBMatch liaises with firms already in or coming to Sheffield over their employment needs, and if necessary organises training to provide local jobseekers with the skills employers require. JOBMatch also helps ensure that jobs from public sector-led projects prioritise local residents, especially those in deprived neighbourhoods. It worked closely with Sheffield One to broker voluntary labour agreements with the construction firms involved in its infrastructure projects, for example.

The UK's first community-based recruitment service, JobNet, again part-funded through the Objective 1 programme (with extra funding from the city council and the RDA), was founded in Sheffield to offer a free job brokerage service to local residents and employers. The service operates from around 16 bases in low-income neighbourhoods such as shops and training centres, making it more accessible to hard-to-reach communities where unemployment rates have been persistently high since the decline of the manufacturing industry (Figure 7.16).

Figure 7.16: A JobNet drop-in centre on a high street in the Upperthorpe neighbourhood

Economic masterplan: Creative Sheffield

The latest in the sequence of central government-backed single-purpose agencies to be created in Sheffield is Creative Sheffield, England's first city development company. Established in 2007, it was designed to take over the functions of Sheffield One and SFfI to become the dedicated economic development agency for the city. Its functions include attracting inward investment, strategic marketing, improving the city's physical infrastructure and designing and implanting the city's new economic masterplan.[97]

SIGNS OF RECOVERY

Developing residential appeal and quality-of-life assets

Sheffield's image is being transformed by major investments in infrastructure, particularly in the city centre, combined with ongoing housing and neighbourhood renewal programmes. Its reputation as a city of grime and smoke is giving way to that of a modern urban centre with a burgeoning taste for city living, bolstered by the large numbers of students driving demand for services and new businesses. This, combined with the city's natural assets such as its ample and hilly green spaces, will be critical in attracting 'knowledge workers' to the city, who place a high value on quality-of-life considerations. Meanwhile, rising property prices across the city since 2000 have confirmed its growing residential appeal.

'Innovative producer' role

Sheffield aims to carve out a role as an 'innovative producer' city. The Advanced Manufacturing Park's success in attracting Boeing's research centre is an encouraging breakthrough (see Figure 7.17). The city wants to regain its position as inventor, engineer and producer of some of the world's finest modern equipment. Many more of the highly qualified graduates of Sheffield's universities would stay in the city if they saw such an exciting future. However, it may take decades for the new economy to take root.

Figure 7.17: Advanced Manufacturing Park

Low skills and unemployment

At the other end of the spectrum, skills development requires a sustained effort to break the high levels of long-term economic inactivity. There are worries about intergenerational unemployment impacts among families who have suffered most from deindustrialisation. Intensive outreach programmes and accessible local support will shift this problem, and avoid the spectre of a two-tier city. The local Work and Skills Board has limited resources and too many low-skilled adults are still outside the formal job market, particularly young adults.

Struggling city-region poses challenge

Sheffield's surrounding region was historically highly industrial, and some of South Yorkshire's mines are still active. Its population is also very deprived. This places a constraint on Sheffield's regeneration as it lacks a prosperous region to sustain its growth by providing consumers of its activities, customers at its shops, demand for its professional services and a wider pool of skilled labour. Many struggling former industrial cities in this country and abroad are in declining regions.[98] This makes the city's recovery effort reach across the whole city-region a difficult agenda. Connectivity is a vital and under-resourced challenge in Sheffield. Within the city much more could be done to improve public transport and reduce heavy traffic.

Resources for neighbourhood-level regeneration

Meanwhile, regeneration at neighbourhood level is showing signs of positive pay-back although there are still worrying levels of polarisation, particularly along ethnic lines. Sheffield has encouraged community leadership in parts of the city, fostering some good initiatives. But supportive as the city council is in principle, it prioritises city-wide plans over small-scale, 'piecemeal' initiatives by local communities. Its own administrative structures do not necessarily match the way local communities work. Meanwhile the tail-offs of SRB, EU Objective 1 and neighbourhood renewal funding, which have sustained so many local projects run by the voluntary and community sector, pose a further threat to local communities' own regeneration efforts, leading funding and support shortfalls. Public sector involvement in low-income neighbourhoods is inevitable.

CONCLUSION

Sheffield's image is being transformed by major investments in infrastructure and neighbourhood renewal programmes. This, combined with its growing student population driving demand for new services and business, and its ample green spaces, will be important quality-of-life factors attracting 'knowledge workers' to the city.

The strong partnership arrangements Sheffield has put in place to manage its own regeneration and economic development process are a key way in which the council has coordinated progress. The creation of arm's-length agencies outside the council to manage city centre regeneration, inward investment and now economic regeneration have given a clearer focus to these activities. While some criticise these structures for reducing the role of elected local representatives, others argue that community representatives, businesses, voluntary and civic organisations have gained more say and status than under earlier more bureaucratic structures.

Connectivity is still a decisive factor to link Sheffield to bigger regional centres such as Leeds and Manchester. The future of cities like Sheffield cannot be secure, dependent as they are on the wider economy. Investment decisions made elsewhere and far-reaching social changes are shaping its future. Nonetheless, Sheffield's many initiatives, its powerful drive for change, its natural assets and its historic role as producer, builder, innovator and reformer underpin a future that may weather current storms better than it has in the past.

Figure 7.18: Timeline of important events in Sheffield since the late 1970s

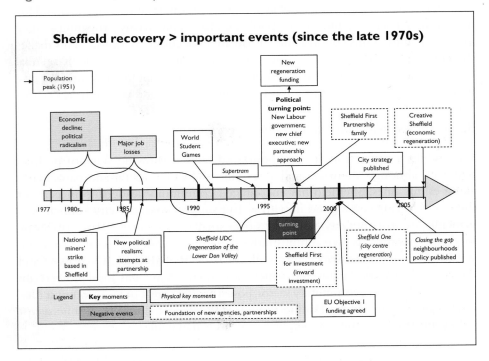

EIGHT

Belfast

CITY CONTEXT

Northern Ireland is a province of the United Kingdom (Figure 8.1). Together with adjacent counties in the Republic of Ireland it comprises the historic Irish region of Ulster. Nowadays, the province consists of six administrative counties and 26 districts (Figure 8.2). The capital, Belfast, with its 269,000 inhabitants, is the dominant city in terms of population, functions and economy. Its metropolitan area has a population of 645,000, more than a third of the Northern Irish population of 1.7 million.[99]

Belfast's name derives from the Gaelic *Béal Feirste*, meaning either 'mouth of the River Farset' or 'approach to the sandbar', the latter referring to a ford on the River Lagan.[100] Early settlements developed along the river and in 1177 the Anglo-Normans invaded the area and built a castle there. More significant settlements emerged only from the 17th century when England tried to gain control over the rebellious region of Ulster. It encouraged the immigration of settlers from the British Isles, mainly Scottish Protestants. Ulster thus became Ireland's most significant Protestant settlement, resulting in severe clashes between the Protestant immigrants and the rural, Catholic indigenous population. In 1801, Britain took control of Ireland

Figure 8.1: United Kingdom regions, location of Belfast

Figure 8.2: Northern Ireland

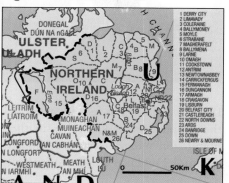

with the Act of Union, which incorporated Ireland into the UK and dissolved the Irish Parliament.

Belfast's economy was traditionally based on exporting wool, grain, butter and salted meat. Industries grew from the opening of the American colonies in the 17th century. Linen weaving was introduced by French Huguenot refugees in the late 17th century. By the early 18th century, Belfast's population had reached 20,000. Over the 1800s Belfast's industries grew in spite of its geographical remoteness and limited supplies of energy and raw materials.[101] When linen production industrialised in the 19th century, Belfast became the world's largest linen producer and expanded its harbour. New sectors such as brewing, rope and sail making emerged and shipbuilding became a key industry. The shipbuilding company Harland & Wolff was founded in 1861. With a workforce of 14,000, it had become the city's largest employer by 1914. The company, famous for building *RMS Titanic*, was the largest shipbuilder in the world then (Figure 8.3). A third important sector, engineering, developed in the early 1900s. In the years before and during the Second World War, aircraft production also became important.

Figure 8.3: Workers leaving Harland & Wolff shipyard after shift, around 1910

Industrialisation was fuelled by cheap labour from poor and rural Ulster, boosting the proportion of Catholics in the 'Protestant city'.[102] Over the 1800s, the population increased from 20,000 to 350,000 (Figure 8.4) and Belfast briefly overtook Dublin as the largest Irish city. Soon after Queen Victoria granted Belfast

Figure 8.4: Population development, Belfast, 1700–1941

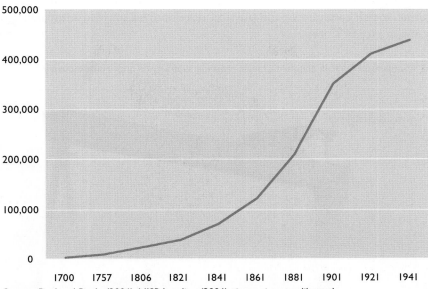

Sources: Boal and Royle (2006); NISRA online (2006); time-axis not calibrated

city status, it became the ninth largest city within the British Isles, 'basically a creation of nineteenth century industrialisation'.[103]

As Belfast grew, tensions around Irish independence increased and paramilitary groups were formed. The Ulster Volunteer Force (UVF), formed in 1912, represented Loyalist or Unionist (mostly Protestant) interests. It supported full integration with the UK by contrast with the Irish Republican Army (IRA), founded in 1914, which represented Irish Republican (mostly Catholic) interests. Conflict over Irish Home Rule led to civil war, which ended in 1921 with the partition of Ireland into the Republic of Ireland and the UK province of Northern Ireland.

CRISIS

The worldwide economic recession of the 1930s badly affected Belfast's export–dependent economy. The shipbuilding and engineering industries were then the target of German air raids during the Second World War, and Belfast experienced decline within its industrial base before most western European industrial cities. The linen industry was among the first to decline.[104] Shipbuilding decreased from the 1960s and by 2001 Harland & Wolff employed only 1,500, down from over 20,000 in the 1950s (Figure 8.5). During the 1960s, 26 per cent of all manufacturing jobs were lost.[105] In addition, industries relocated to industrial estates in suburban locations from the 1950s.[106] From the late 1960s, industrial decline was exacerbated by the increasingly violent civil conflict. Belfast faced 'economic, social, commercial and physical development problems unparalleled in any major city in Europe'.[107]

Figure 8.5: Harland & Wolff shipyard cranes, reminders of a once important industry

In the 1970s, Belfast's employment losses were linked to dramatic global economic restructuring; manufacturing decline could not be offset by service and public sector growth. The proportion of the workforce employed in manufacturing fell by roughly 10 per cent each decade between 1950 and 1990 (see Figure 8.6). Most job losses from 1973 to 1991 came from large industrial companies like Harland & Wolff, Mackie's (engineering) and Shorts Brothers (aircraft manufacturing),[108] despite Northern Ireland's industries receiving far higher subsidies than any other UK region.[109]

Figure 8.6: Percentage of workforce in manufacturing employment, Belfast, 1951–91 (%)

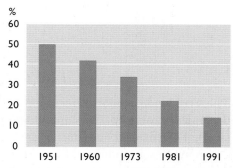

Sources: Gaffikin and Morrissey (1999); Hart (2006)

Figure 8.7: Belfast City Hall

Figure 8.8: Parliament buildings, home of the Northern Ireland Assembly

Figure 8.9: The oft-bombed Europa Hotel and The Crown Bar

Northern Ireland had the UK's highest unemployment rate from the 1970s, peaking in Belfast at 17 per cent in 1987.[110] Yet, unemployment was unequally distributed. While the segregated working-class areas (for example in west Belfast) showed rates as high as 40 per cent, middle-class areas (for example in south Belfast) were far less affected.[111] Many households became dependent on benefits and long-term unemployment reached 50 per cent during the 1980s, almost double the UK average.[112] As a result of this, Northern Ireland was among the poorest EU regions until the early 1990s.[113]

A particular feature of the labour market in Northern Ireland is the high proportion of public sector employment, which was expanded during The Troubles in the 1970s and functioned as a 'safety net', particularly for Catholics, many of whom were excluded from manufacturing employment through discriminatory practices. High-skilled workers, on the other hand, were driven out of the province due to the impact of the conflict on quality of life and the shortage of well-paid jobs.

The violent conflict

Until the late 1960s, religious and political tensions in Northern Ireland were expressed through sporadic violent outbursts. The so-called 'Troubles' began in the late 1960s and only ended with the 1990s peace process. In 1969, the IRA, which had never accepted British rule over Northern Ireland, started a more substantial campaign against the 'British occupation'. The British government responded to the conflict by increasing its military presence. The 1972 'Bloody Sunday' massacre in Londonderry involving the British army and Northern Irish civilians stands out as a turning point. That year, the UK government abolished Northern Ireland's parliament at Stormont and imposed Direct Rule from Westminster in England.[114] During the conflict over 3,600 people were killed and 40,000 injured, two thirds of the victims being civilians. In the 1970s and 1980s much violence focused on Belfast city centre, regarded by the IRA as a legitimate economic target.[115] Many areas in the city thus became insecure 'no-go zones'.

Belfast is a very segregated city with a concentration of social problems in some of its working-class areas. Nine of the 10 most deprived wards in Northern Ireland are in Belfast.[116] Figure 8.10 shows the most segregated areas in west and north Belfast.[117] So-called 'peace lines' were built in many areas where the Protestant and Catholic communities shared borders (Figure 8.11). A total of 17 miles of these physical divides, usually closed at night and on weekends, were erected in the city to prevent hostilities.[118] Areas where the communities share such militarised boundaries are called 'interface areas'. In 2005, there were 25 such interfaces.[119] They became deeply blighted areas, especially in Unionist communities that have experienced steeper population decline due to outmigration to the suburbs.

Access to public housing, like access to jobs, was highly contentious, with widespread discrimination, manipulation and politically vested interests. After Direct Rule was implemented, the Northern Ireland Housing Executive

(NIHE), a unique body in the UK, was set up in 1974 as a province-wide independent body.[120] It has delivered the largest publicly funded housebuilding programme in the UK, receiving substantial central government funding which most local authorities like Sheffield were denied. Throughout the 1980s, social housing was the single most important public spending priority in Northern Ireland.[121]

Population decline

The loss of manufacturing employment and the division of the city provoked a sharp population decline from a late 1940s population peak of 444,000 (see Figure 8.12).

The extent of suburbanisation was exceptional among all the

Figure 8.10: Community segregation, Belfast, 2000

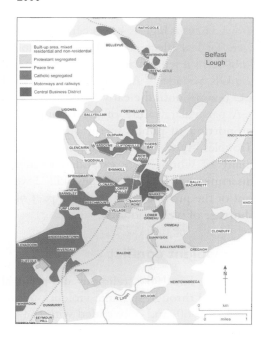

Figure 8.11: Peace line, north Belfast

Figure 8.12: Population decline, Belfast, 1951–90

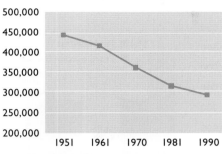

Sources: NISRA (online); Boal and Royle (2006)

seven cities. Between 1951 and 1991 the City of Belfast lost about 205,000 inhabitants, while the adjacent suburban counties grew by about 237,000 (Figure 8.13). Planning policy reinforced suburbanisation through the 1964 regional plan for Northern Ireland, providing for peripheral growth poles and new towns, and new motorways.[122, 123]

Commercial development followed suburbanisation, following the purchasing power of the middle-class residents and offering safer shopping centres. As a result, during the 1970s Belfast showed the highest rates of retail decentralisation in the UK. However, public transport remains poorly organised and in need of modernisation. Belfast is one of the most car-dependent metropolitan areas in the UK and western Europe.[124] Yet 44 per cent of Belfast households do not own a car, so the transport pattern exacerbates existing social inequalities.

Figure 8.13: Population development in city and suburbs, Belfast metropolitan area, 1951–91

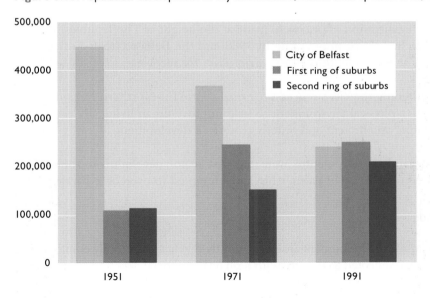

Note: The Belfast metropolitan area consists of the City of Belfast plus the first and second suburban rings. The first suburban ring (or outer suburbs) includes Lisburn, Castlereagh, Newtownabbey and North Down; the second suburban ring (or outer metropolitan area) includes Carrickfergus, Antrim, Comber, Newtownards and Bangor.
Source: Boal (2006, pp 58, 82)

Figure 8.14 shows the growth of commuters into the city and the decline in shorter local journeys.

RECOVERY ACTIONS

The peace process in the 1990s was a key catalyst for change, activating a whole range of recovery projects and initiatives. It is therefore easy to underestimate efforts in the 1980s and early 1990s, but important progress was underway during the violent conflict:

Figure 8.14: Shift in travel patterns to work from within Belfast to commuter areas

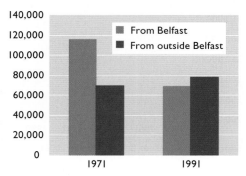

Source: Smyth (2006, p 110) (adapted)

- improvements to public housing by NIHE;
- major infrastructure improvements in roads, railways, energy supplies and telecommunications;
- major regeneration of the Port of Belfast by the Belfast Harbour Commissioners;
- large-scale regeneration on land along the Lagan River; and
- revitalisation of the city centre.[125]

The first regeneration efforts were made at the height of The Troubles with the Making Belfast Work programme in 1988 and the Belfast Urban Area Plan in 1990.[126] The latter identified three major tasks for recovery:

- strengthening the city's role as a regional centre for Northern Ireland;
- creating a physical environment to help improve urban living;
- facilitating an efficient and orderly pattern of development.

Laganside and the city centre were the first major development zones. They introduced new forms of partnership and attempted to overcome barriers.

Laganside

The Laganside redevelopment area was a mostly derelict, industrially contaminated area, poorly connected to the city with high levels of social deprivation and 30 per cent unemployment in adjacent neighbourhoods.[127] The Laganside Corporation, a UDC funded from Westminster, was set up in 1989 to manage the redevelopment. It was a public–private partnership of government departments, statutory agencies such as NIHE, the Belfast Harbour Commission and Belfast City Council. The UDC drew on experiences from the regeneration of waterfront areas in Baltimore, USA and London's Docklands. The objective was to bring social, physical and economic regeneration to the derelict riverside. Most of the land was already under public ownership. The Laganside Corporation had two main tasks: to tackle the environmental problems of disused sites; and to attract residential, civic and commercial uses. Government and EU (Objective 1) money was used as a catalyst to attract private-sector investment.

A key engineering project in the early 1990s was to move Lagan Weir, which protects against floods, downriver. This aimed to increase land values by eliminating tidal mud flats, opening the river for leisure activities and marketing the land for property development. The project included river dredging and aeration to improve water quality. The flagship development from the mid-1990s was Lanyon Place on the riverfront closest to the city centre. Waterfront Hall in Lanyon Place is now a centre for large conferences and cultural events (see Figure 8.15). Private investment here includes the Hilton Hotel and BT's regional headquarters. Another major Laganside development is the Gasworks complex, begun in the mid-1990s on the former city gasworks site and developed into an office park, housing Halifax, Abbey National and Prudential call centres, government offices and other commercial use such as the Radisson Hotel. The Odyssey complex, opened in 2000, was a millennium project on derelict land across the river and now hosts cinemas, a sports arena, a concert venue and shopping centre (Figure 8.16).

Figure 8.15: Lanyon Place with Waterfront Hall

Figure 8.16: Laganside area before redevelopment

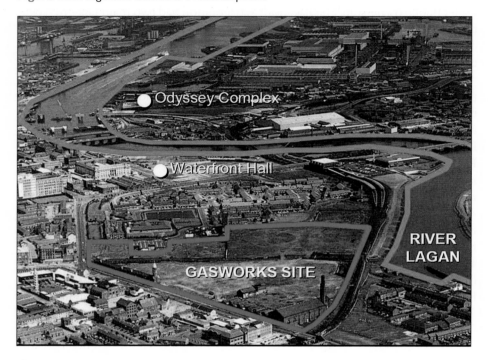

City centre revitalisation

During the mid-1980s, at the height of The Troubles, the city centre's role became very limited. The frequent bombings made it a high-security zone by day and a 'no-go-zone' at night, prompting many shops and businesses to relocate to safer locations. The centre was increasingly characterised by urban blight, derelict buildings and vacant sites. Since the Good Friday Agreement in 1998 the city centre has regained many functions and become a major shopping destination. The first shopping mall opened in the late 1980s, along with bars, restaurants and cultural centres. It became a 'neutral space' where different communities mingled.

The peace process: a catalyst for change

The official end of The Troubles was marked by the signing of the Good Friday Agreement in April 1998. This breakthrough raised hopes for rebuilding the fortunes of this once-wealthy city. The peace process catalysed substantial support for investment and many innovative approaches to urban regeneration.

Regional and local powers

Northern Ireland had lost its directly elected regional government during Direct Rule from 1972. When the peace process was established and security improved, the UK government started ceding powers to regional and municipal authorities in Northern Ireland. In 1999, the Northern Ireland Executive was established with devolved regional powers as part of the Belfast Agreement. Yet, due to continuing political divisions, it was suspended again between 2002 and 2007.

Belfast City Council

Uncertainties over Northern Ireland's status and governance meant that local authorities, including Belfast City Council, enjoyed few powers under Direct Rule. Belfast City Council only gained wider control over service provision and local economic development in 1992. Even now it does not have responsibilities matching those of other European and British cities.[128] However, further devolution is planned.[129] With no elected regional government, the city council had become the major democratic debating forum.[130] In the late 1990s, the council took the initiative in planning Belfast's future, developing a more coherent and strategic approach.

Central government in Westminster

The UK government at Westminster allocated considerable extra resources to Northern Ireland to fund its large, multilayered public sector. This 'complex mosaic' prompted the criticism that Northern Ireland was 'over-governed' and 'over-administered'.[131]

To keep public services outside political and sectarian religious spheres, many key responsibilities were vested in quangos, a patchwork of non-elected agencies granted much of the public budget.[132] NIHE may be the best example. Important urban regeneration efforts included: Making Belfast Work, launched in 1988 by the Department for Social Development (DSD) to target the city's most work-deprived areas; and the Belfast Regeneration Office, to tackle the 36 most deprived areas, predominantly Catholic. The Office manages EU regeneration funding and smaller local government programmes.

European Community (Union)

As the UK's poorest and most peripheral region, Northern Ireland received substantial aid from the European Community through Objective 1 funding between 1994 and 2006 and Objective 2 funding for the new period from 2007 to 2013. EU URBAN funding targets six deprived wards of north Belfast. The EU Programme for Peace and Reconciliation in Northern Ireland and the Border Region of Ireland (Peace III) was formed specifically for Northern Ireland, initially funding projects to overcome community divisions and enhance post-conflict social cohesion. The focus in the second round, 2000–04, was to stimulate economic development through urban regeneration; a third round will run from 2007 to 2013. Belfast Local Strategy Partnership has acted as a trustee for this PEACE funding, supporting over 250 projects. It has two major themes – developing social enterprise and civil society – under its core objective of peace building. The partnership aims to create 'shared places', desegregating the urban landscape, increasing security and reducing inter-communal tensions.

More recent regeneration projects

From the mid-1990s, the peace process restored confidence in Belfast. New projects have since developed around the revitalised city centre, as highlighted below.

Cathedral Quarter

In 1997, the Laganside Corporation took on the regeneration of a warehouse area east of the city centre. With its proximity to the University of Ulster the focus was on culture and creativity (Figure 8.17). New and refurbished housing, converted industrial and commercial buildings attracted higher-income residents. The Merchant Hotel, one of the top of its kind in Europe, opened in 2006 in a former bank (Figure 8.18).

Figure 8.17: 'Cultural incubator': the Black Box entertainment venue and café

Figure 8.18: The Merchant Hotel, Cathedral Quarter

Titanic Quarter

A highly ambitious, large-scale regeneration project is the Titanic Quarter redevelopment of 75 hectares of land on Queen's Island, previously the shipyards of Harland & Wolff. It is planned to create an area of mixed commercial, research and residential uses over the next 15 to 20 years (Figures 8.19 and 8.20). The project is also intended to assist in the regeneration of adjacent working-class neighbourhoods, which have been affected by the closure of the shipyard.[133]

North Foreshore

One major site for future redevelopment is the North Foreshore that has been used as the city's rubbish tip for three decades. The plan is to develop the area with a country park, new housing, an environmental industries park and new waste management facilities.[134]

The Maze

Another major project is the conversion and regeneration of the Maze, a former high-security prison just outside Belfast, which had held para-military prisoners from both sides of the conflict.

Figure 8.19: Advertisement for Titanic Quarter

Figure 8.20: Science Park, Titanic Quarter

The £120 million investment proposal includes a sports stadium, an international centre for conflict resolution, an equestrian centre, a showground and exhibition centre. Some Belfast officials have strongly opposed this large new attraction outside the city, fearing that it will seriously threaten the core.[135]

Neighbourhood renewal and community cohesion

More than anywhere in the UK, neighbourhood renewal in Belfast has to work from the starting point of the strong sectarian divide. Programmes to advance neighbourhood renewal have emerged with support from different sources, including the UK government, the EU and Belfast City Council.

In the early years of the peace process, the aim was to free the city centre of divided spaces. The idea of 'shared spaces' gained ground quickly.[136] Many community initiatives and non-governmental organisations (NGOs) are involved. However, spatial integration and mixed neighbourhoods are long-term processes.[137] Communities elect neighbourhood-based, geographically rooted representatives to local and central government reinforcing territorial 'protectionism'. In north Belfast many Protestant former residents have moved to the suburbs, creating empty homes, but access by the growing Catholic population remains highly sensitive (Figures 8.21 and 8.22).

Figure 8.21: New housing development in a Catholic neighbourhood, north Belfast

Figure 8.22: Abandoned, blighted housing in an interface area, north Belfast

NIHE has delivered high-quality housing in low-income communities. It owns 15 per cent of the housing in Northern Ireland and 19 per cent in Belfast.[138] It has sold many homes to its tenants under the Right to Buy, and is a key actor in neighbourhood renewal. Its vision of a 'shared future' for Northern Ireland involves some integrated housing schemes; however, avoiding violent clashes and improving neighbourhood security has reinforced high levels of segregation between the two communities.

The Equality Commission for Northern Ireland was established following the Good Friday Agreement to monitor equality, to uncover discriminatory practices and to guarantee integrated, fair services to all communities. In a document called *Shared future*, the Northern Ireland government declared:

> The division that perpetuates itself in Northern Ireland is costly both socially and economically. Adapting public policy in Northern Ireland simply to cope with community division holds out no prospect of stability and sustainability in the long run.[139]

Economic development

Economic development in Belfast and Northern Ireland has been driven by a number of factors including special subsidies for inward investment (for example tax concessions for companies); major investment from the US; and the economic boom in the Republic of Ireland to the south.

The Laganside regeneration, especially the Gasworks area, has attracted several new companies, but nearby south and east Belfast has not benefited; 'pockets of deprivation have become more polarised and immune to the associated benefits of inward investment and indigenous business growth'.[140] The Gasworks Employment Matching Service (GEMS), set up in 2002, provided training, support and advice to low-skilled, unemployed residents in these deprived communities. The Gasworks scheme has helped, spreading far out from this area, but economic inactivity is still alarmingly high.

SIGNS OF RECOVERY

Belfast is at an historic turning point combating major social, economic and environmental problems.[141] According to Belfast City Council it has become 'a competitive location for doing business with the world and, increasingly, a great place to live and visit'.[142] The broader region has seen the highest increase in GDP and the highest employment growth in the UK.[143] But Belfast is recovering from a very low point, compared with other former industrial cities. In 2006, among the UK's 60 largest cities, Belfast still performed worst on population losses, employment and earnings.[144]

Economic restructuring

Employment trends in Belfast are still worrying. From 1995 to 2005, overall employment grew following two decades of decline; while manufacturing continued to decline, employment in services grew. One third (over 6,000) of manufacturing jobs were lost in that decade. With only six per cent of the workforce still employed in manufacturing, Belfast has certainly become a 'post-industrial city'.[145] Over a third of manufacturing jobs are concentrated in one company, Bombardier Aerospace, formerly Shorts Brothers, which lost almost 1,000 jobs in April 2009.[146]

Service sector

Belfast's four per cent growth was largely attributable to expansion in the service sector with 23,000 additional jobs (Figure 8.23). Belfast's private investment opportunities include inexpensive land and low office rents, a relatively skilled workforce and tax incentives. Average wages in Northern Ireland were one third lower than the UK average.[147] Two sectors experienced particularly strong growth: hotels and restaurants (39 per cent) and financial services (37 per cent). Many of the latter can be attributed to 'back office' services. Belfast has emerged as a major location for call centres – 6,300 people are employed in 26 call centres.[148]

Figure 8.23 Total change in employment, 1995–2005

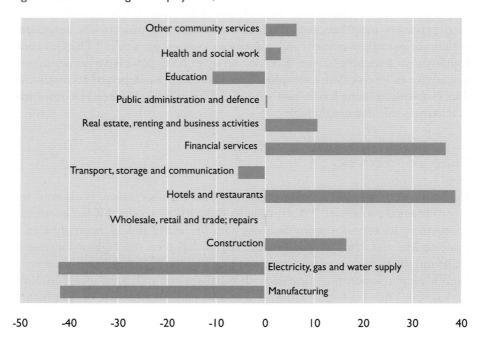

Sources: OECD (2000); Belfast City Council (2007); based on data/censuses from NISRA and DETI

The public sector remained a major employer. While it employs around 30 per cent of working adults in the UK, in Northern Ireland it is around 50 per cent.[149] The current plans to streamline the public administration is partly driven by this.

Tourism has proved to be the most dynamic sector for job creation. In part, Belfast is just catching up on under-investment due to The Troubles, but since the late 1990s Belfast has also unexpectedly emerged as a tourist destination. This is expressed by many low-budget flight connections and an increase in the number of hotels. Around 16,000 full-time jobs derive from tourism.[150] Between 2002 and 2005, visitor numbers increased from 3.6 to 6.4 million, many of them daytrippers from south of the border.[151] Shopping tourists have bolstered Belfast's economy since the recession although many of the jobs in this sector are unstable, temporary or part-time and low-wage.[152]

As businesses operate increasingly on a global scale, company headquarters tend to concentrate in the control centres of the world economy. Belfast is not a prime location for businesses. A recent study of the competitiveness of the UK's 15 largest cities reveals that this is the case in spite of strong recovery and economic growth.[153]

Social exclusion and the labour market

Between 1990 and 2000, the unemployment rate in Northern Ireland dropped from 14 to 4 per cent, below the UK average (see Figure 8.24). Economic inactivity on the other hand is high, with only 59 per cent of the adult working population employed, the lowest in the UK (with an average of 74 per cent).[154] Over 40 per cent of the unemployed are long-term unemployed, the highest proportion in the UK. Twenty-four per cent of the working-age population has no qualifications.[155] Social polarisation is a major concern, particularly as the 1980s and 1990s 'saw the emergence of a twin-speed economy and a dual society',[156] with strong spatial polarisation and 'generations of failure'.[157]

Figure 8.24: Unemployment rate, Northern Ireland and UK, 1990–2005

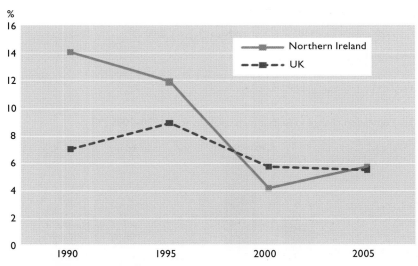

Sources: NISRA online (2006); DENI

Population change

Belfast lost population between 1970 to 2005, declining by almost 150,000, although this decline has gradually slowed (see Figure 8.25).

The surrounding suburban counties all gained population between 1990 and 2005 (Figure 8.26), by 35,000, offsetting Belfast's loss and resulting in a slight increase for the whole metropolitan area. Meanwhile Northern Ireland has the youngest population of the UK, with 22 per cent under 16, due to above-average birth rates. During the past decade Belfast's population has diversified, with immigrants moving into some of the new jobs in hotels, catering, retail and elsewhere. This has changed the atmosphere of the city, giving it a more European ambience.[158]

Figure 8.25: Population decline, 1970–2005

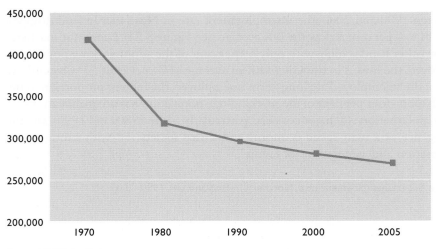

Source: NISRA (online)

Figure 8.26: Population change in Belfast metropolitan area, 1990–2005 (%)

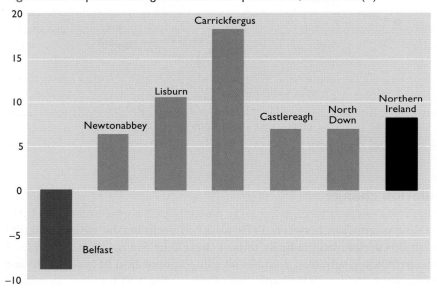

Source: NISRA (online)

Physical regeneration and urban recovery

The public effort to change Belfast's image from a grim, deindustrialised, socially divided and dangerous city into a modern, post-industrial, culturally vibrant and socially cohesive city, has had some impact. Regeneration projects, to entice both businesses and visitors, have transformed the city centre and riverfront into magnets for growth. By 2005, the reclaimed sites along the riverfront and the Lagan River had catalysed £900 million of private and public sector investment[159] and generated over 11,000 jobs.[160]

The 'shared space' approach, free from cultural or religious connotations, has been popular and widely supported. The Victoria Square shopping mall, opened in 2008, offers a major city centre retail centre, rivalling out-of-town developments. The Cathedral Quarter investment converted a decayed central area into a 'Bohemian Quarter', focusing on culture and entertainment. Another recent tourist attraction is the Belfast Wheel which opened in 2007, locally dubbed 'Belfast Aye', linking it with the London Eye.

Transport

Large-scale suburbanisation prompted new road infrastructure, while public transport deteriorated significantly during The Troubles.[161] Bus and rail services are now improving and the main line between Belfast and Dublin only takes two-and-a-half hours. The current aim is to build 70 per cent of new housing on brownfield sites.[162] This could catalyse higher density, combat sprawl and make public transport more attractive.[163]

Belfast's peripheral location on the western edge of the EU makes it rely on air connections. Between 1996 and 2005, the number of passengers using Belfast's two airports almost doubled, from 3.7 to 7.1 million per annum.[164] Belfast has attracted several cheap airlines over recent years. Meanwhile, ferry passengers between Belfast and British ports fell from 2.1 to 1.8 million between 2000 and 2004.

Devolution

From 2002, four years after the Belfast Agreement, the Northern Ireland Assembly was for five years unable to resolve disputes between Republicans and Unionists.[165] In 2007 the Democratic Unionist Party and the Republican Sinn Féin agreed to work together. Their elected leaders became joint heads of the new devolved government based on a power-sharing agreement. Uniting such polarised political views involves compromises, acknowledged as the only way forward. The dual system is costly, cumbersome and bureaucratic.[166] The legacy of Direct Rule makes greater devolution and 'normalisation' crucial. Planning, urban regeneration, some economic development and housing are to be devolved.

The security situation has improved since the end of The Troubles. Tensions prevail between the communities, but attacks on civilians have decreased significantly and although extreme paramilitary groups still occasionally attack there is no sign of a return to the earlier violence (Figure 8.27). Conflict is now mostly limited to anti-social behaviour during the summer 'Marching Season', when religious factions parade in sensitive areas. But mediation, conflict management and multiple community level programmes have contributed to the improved security and cautious reconciliation.

Figure 8.27: Percentage of total deaths attributable to political violence, Northern Ireland, 1972–98

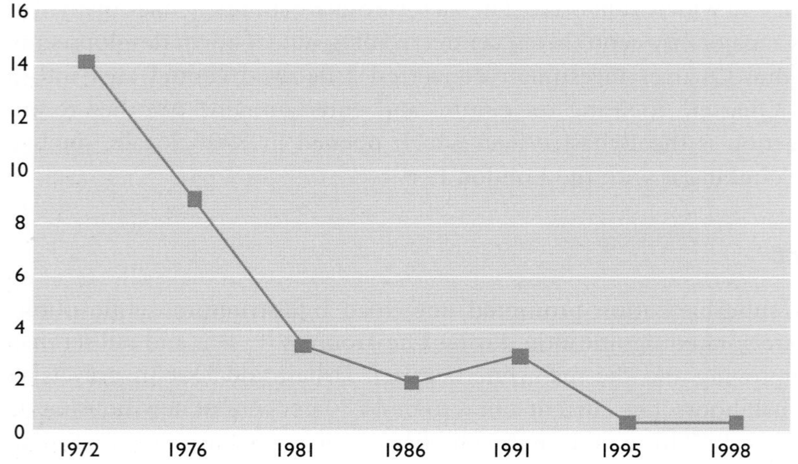

Sources: NISRA, Northern Ireland Police; quoted from Shirlow and Murtagh (2006)

CONCLUSION

Although the regional economy has been growing strongly, Northern Ireland remains poor in comparison with the rest of the UK and western Europe. The economic base was hit hard by economic restructuring, recession and disinvestment. Competitive advantages such as lower wages, a relatively skilled workforce and available space are offset by other factors such as lack of economic diversity and underdeveloped knowledge-based activities. The emergence of a Dublin–Belfast metropolitan corridor offers promise of a closer relationship with the Republic of Ireland, although recession has hit Ireland even harder than the UK.[167]

An 'inheritance' of The Troubles and historic links with Westminster have resulted in an oversized public sector. The Northern Ireland power-sharing Assembly, meeting the imperative of political stability, requires constant compromises between political extremes so more radical solutions to economic, social and political problems are unlikely. But further devolution will force all levels of government to commit to make the public sector more efficient and accountable as government and EU funding will reduce.

The legacy of Direct Rule left local authorities with weak local government structures. Belfast City Council is eager to deliver additional services, as their ambitious guidelines show. Yet an alternative to costly dual services to divided communities is a pre-condition of progress. Local community-based organisations might offer alternative routes.

Although gradual progress is being made in reconciling the communities, segregation along religious and socioeconomic lines continues. Political representation, security, employment, education and housing have a spatial component, and local communities often defend themselves against outside interests. Initiatives to integrate the educational system are limited by deep divisions between Catholic schools and officially non-denominational schools for Protestants. The younger generation growing up with no direct experience of The Troubles may gradually broaden the cultural and religious attitudes of a deeply affected society.

Educational achievements are among the highest in the UK, but some sections of the population have benefited little from job growth since the 1990s, particularly in deprived areas, most affected by the conflict.[168]

Regeneration and reconciliation have so far worked as twin processes in building forward momentum. But political uncertainties and interruptions in the process of devolution have sapped some of the initial energy.

Given the depth of the crisis, Belfast has come a long way, even though much more needs to be done to overcome deep, structural problems. Belfast faces bigger challenges than any other city in our study. Social and political stability within a rapidly changing global economy would help to consolidate Belfast's remarkable progress.

Figure 8.28: Timeline of important events in Belfast since 1980

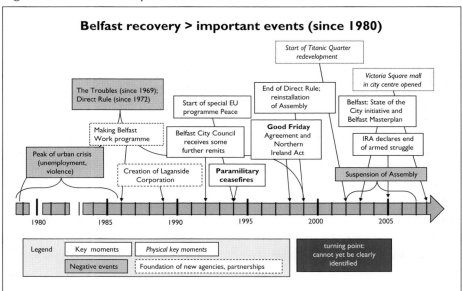

NINE

Bilbao

CITY CONTEXT

The Basque Country (*País Vasco*) is located on the northern edge of the Iberian Peninsula (Figure 9.1) and is one of Spain's 17 autonomous regions. Bilbao is the main city (population 350,000) and capital of the province of *Bizkaia* (in Basque) or *Vizcaya* (in Spanish) (Figure 9.2). The metropolitan area of Bilbao (*Bilbao Metropolitana*) (population 900,000) includes the City of Bilbao and several surrounding municipalities, making it the largest agglomeration on Spain's Atlantic coast and the sixth largest metropolitan area in Spain. Bilbao is located on both sides of the River Nervión which discharges into the Bay of Biscay some 10km from the city centre. The steep slopes of the river valley have confined urbanisation mainly to the lowlands and lower parts of the slopes on both sides of the valley, and this has led to high population density, with 8,733 inhabitants per square kilometre.

Figure 9.1: Map of Spain, main agglomerations, location of Bilbao

Figure 9.2: Map of Basque Country (*País Vasco*) and its three provinces

Bilbao emerged as a small trading and fishing village in medieval times. The Basque Country was incorporated into the Kingdom of Castile in 1200, but a considerable degree of autonomy was granted to the new province (see Box 9.1). The traditional Basque legal system of statutes (*fueros*) gave the region its own laws and institutions that have been preserved to this day. Bilbao was granted city status in 1300 and over subsequent centuries its economy was based on commercial and maritime activities. Benefiting from its favourable position as an

Box 9.1: Timetable of important events influencing Bilbao's development

<1200	Early trading and fishing village
1200	Previously independent Basque province incorporated into Kingdom of Castile
1300	Foundation of Bilbao
1512	Creation of the Consulate of Bilbao (a body regulating trade and shipping)
1452–1841	Enjoying special trading rights
1838	First iron industry
1857	Creation of Tudela-Bilbao Railway Company and Banco de Bilbao

First major phase of industrialisation

1876	Beginning urbanisation of the Ensanche outside the medieval city
1890	Opening of stock exchange
1936–39	Spanish Civil War, Basque fought on Republican side; bombing of Guernica (1937)
1939–75	Spain under Franco's dictatorship; Basque Country stripped of autonomy
1959	Formation of ETA terrorist group
1950s/1960s	Second major phase of industrialisation; high immigration from poorer Spanish regions
1970s	Beginning of economic recession
1978	Spain returns to democracy; new Spanish constitution institutes 17 autonomous regions
1979	Statute of autonomy for Basque Country under new democratic central government
1980	Democratic elections for Basque government and parliament
1981	Economic agreement between central and Basque governments
1983	Flood causes great damage in the old city
1986	Peak of unemployment; accelerating population losses
	Spain becomes member of the European Community
1989	Territorial plan identifies 'opportunity areas'
1991/92	Creation of regeneration agencies Bilbao Metrópoli-30 and Bilbao Ría 2000
1995	Inauguration of new metro system
1997	Inauguration of Guggenheim Museum
2006	ETA agreed on ceasefire

Atlantic sea port and its special trading rights guaranteed by the Spanish King, Bilbao became a rich hub, linking mainland Spain with other parts of western Europe and eventually the Americas.

Until industrialisation, Bilbao was a small city with a population of under 10,000 whose area was confined to the *Casco Viejo* (Old Quarter) (Figure 9.3). However, during the second half of the 1800s, Bilbao rapidly developed into an industrial city, based on the exploitation of nearby iron ore deposits. Coal was transported by sea along the coast from the region of Asturias to fuel the industrial

Figure 9.3: Bilbao's Old Quarter (*Casco Viejo*)

revolution. Iron, steel and shipbuilding industries developed quickly. By the turn of the century, industrial growth was accompanied by the development of major service sector companies, especially in commerce and finance. As elsewhere, industrialisation led to a sharp increase in population. In 1900, the population was over 80,000 (Figure 9.4).

Figure 9.4: Population development, 1842–1980

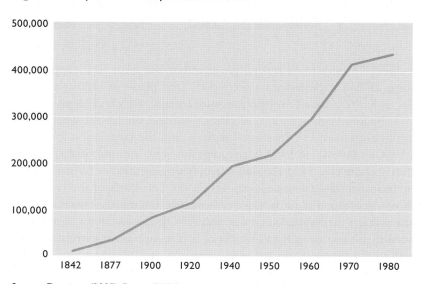

Sources: Domingo (2005); Eustat (2006); time axis not calibrated

Growth and change

New areas were consequently urbanised. Across the river from the medieval *Casco Viejo* the Ensanche became the major urban expansion area, eventually evolving into the modern city centre with the main shopping, office and administrative functions as well as the most favoured residential areas of middle and upper-income households. Mining, industrial and port activities were concentrated along the river, occupying almost the entire Left Bank of the river by the late 1970s (Figure 9.5).

Figure 9.5: Industries and shipyards along the River Nervión

With little direct funding from central government but with tacit support for modernisation, Bilbao experienced a second or 'late' phase of industrialisation in the 1950s and 1960s, based on heavy manufacturing, which strengthened its role as one of Spain's leading industrial cities. Demand for labour was met by massive immigration from less developed regions, and the population rose from 216,000 in 1950 to 410,000 in 1970. Many migrants were accommodated in new working-class housing erected in the outer, steeply sloping areas of Bilbao and the rapidly growing working-class municipalities on the Left Bank of the river. The Right Bank was developed at a slower pace, mostly for the middle classes, and the river became a sharp socioeconomic boundary.[168] Due to a scarcity of available land and the difficult topography, tall blocks of flats were built at extremely high density for all socioeconomic groups, even in prosperous suburban areas. Figure 9.6 shows the different urban municipalities stretching down the river.

Figure 9.6: Aerial map of Greater Bilbao, main municipalities and important areas highlighted

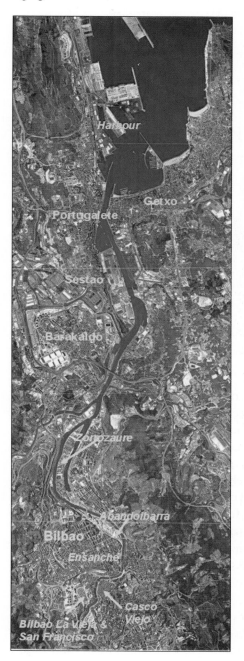

Under the dictatorship of Franco (1939–75), the Basque Country lost most of its special autonomy. During this period, the state suppressed Basque culture, including a ban on the Basque language. The opposition to this found its most extreme expression in the 1959 foundation of the nationalist and separatist armed movement, ETA, which fought for full independence from Spain. ETA's campaign of violence had serious economic and political repercussions, frightening potential investors, dividing opinion and isolating the city and its surroundings from moderating influences for long periods of time. But Bilbao grew despite ongoing political troubles. After the collapse of Franco's regime, Spain returned to democracy in 1978. The new democratic constitution re-instituted regional powers. Through this process, the Basque Country was able to achieve a high degree of autonomy from central government.

CRISIS

The first symptoms of industrial and urban crisis began to show when the world economy went into recession following the 1973 oil shock. However, Spain's limited integration with the international economy under Franco protected the Spanish economy and delayed the impact of the crisis until after the dictatorship collapsed in the mid-1970s. The loss of manufacturing employment and population decline reached their peak towards the mid-1980s. While unemployment was almost non-existent until the early 1970s in Bilbao and across Spain, it reached a record 25 per cent in the first half of the 1980s and was accompanied by severe social problems and intense physical decay (Figure 9.7).

Figure 9.7: Official unemployment rate, 1970–95 (%)

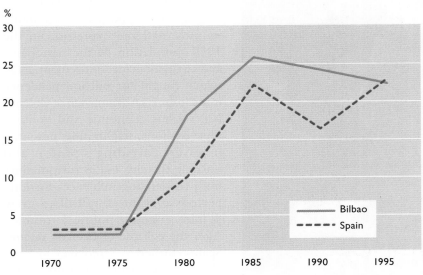

Sources: Gómez (1998); Eustat (2006)

Manufacturing decline

Since Bilbao's industrial structure was dominated by heavy industries, it was particularly hard hit by the crisis.[169] Between 1975 and 1995, 60,000 manufacturing jobs – almost half the existing industrial jobs – were lost in the metropolitan area (Figure 9.8), and the proportion of manufacturing jobs dropped from 46 to 27 per cent.[170] Large industrial companies that had dominated the local economy for a long time, such as the Altos Hornos steelworks in Barakaldo or the Euskalduna shipyard in Bilbao, were modernised and continued production with a fraction of the original workforce or collapsed completely. These structural changes prompted years of industrial action by the unions and outbursts of violent labour conflict in the early 1980s. It was the generation about to enter the labour market that suffered most from deindustrialisation. As a consequence, youth unemployment reached 50 per cent in the 1980s.

Figure 9.8: Number of workers employed in manufacturing, Biscay province, 1970–2000

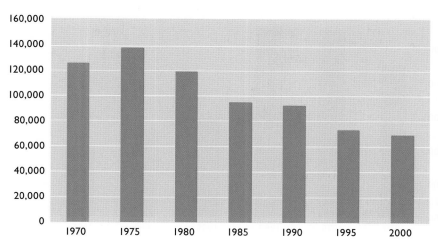

Sources: Gómez (1998); Eustat (2006)

Social consequences

The social consequences of the closure of industries varied. In Barakaldo for example, residents were very dependent on its largest employer, the Altos Hornos steelworks, but the impact of the plant's closure in 1990 was less dramatic than might have been expected because many workers accepted the generous early retirement packages offered by the state-owned company.[171] Many migrant workers returned to their home regions in southern or western Spain and the local proportion of pensioners increased.

In other parts of the city, however, many workers did not receive such generous compensation for the loss of jobs. For hard-hit households this reduction in income meant a rapid deterioration in living conditions. The poverty level of these families was exposed in 1983 when the Nervión flooded large parts of the older inner-city neighbourhoods. Cleaning up after the flood revealed not only the physical decay of the historic neighbourhoods but also the declining living conditions of the working-class population.[172]

Population decline

From the early 1980s Bilbao suffered serious population decline, attributable mainly to migrants returning to their home regions and to the restructuring of administrative boundaries in 1983, when large areas of the City of Bilbao became independent municipalities. As can be observed from Figure 9.9, the city lost more than 70,000 people or 16 per cent of its inhabitants between 1980 and 1995.

Figure 9.9: Population change, Bilbao, 1970–1995

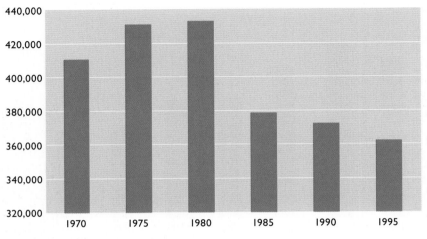

Source: Eustat (2006)

This population decline was not equally distributed, but concentrated in working-class areas such as the Left Bank municipalities of Barakaldo, Sestao and Portugalete, upriver Basauri and Bilbao itself.[173] All of these municipalities lost between 10 and 20 per cent of their population, due mostly to the disappearance of industrial jobs, the poor standard of housing stock and the negative image of these areas.[174] Meanwhile, the metropolitan area grew by some 67,000 inhabitants over the same period[175] and some middle-class municipalities, most of them on the Right Bank, experienced population increase over the same period, suggesting a growing trend of suburbanisation and dispersal. There is some suggestion that the new metro lines are accelerating this process.

Environmental degradation

Bilbao Metropolitana suffered from serious environmental degradation as a result of local industrial activities, leaving the Nervión ecologically dead. Deindustrialisation had also left a total of 340 hectares of obsolete industrial wasteland in metropolitan Bilbao.[176] Many of the sites were covered with derelict industrial buildings and the soil was deeply contaminated by its former industrial uses. In Barakaldo, more than one third of the land was made up of brownfield sites with vacant structures and disused infrastructure.[177] Figure 9.10 shows the scale of the industrial dereliction.

Figure 9.10: Environmental burden and derelict sites

Recovery actions

The return of democracy and the re-instatement of regional power in the Basque Country in the late 1970s occurred just as the industrial crisis was gaining momentum. It is widely accepted among officials, practitioners and scholars that the autonomy of the Basque region was central to facilitating the recovery process in Bilbao. To an extent, local decision makers gained the power to design tailored policies and to allocate resources at the right time. The Basque Country is the only region with full tax collecting powers. Tax is collected through its three provincial governments, although a proportion of the tax (12 per cent in 2000) goes to the central government in Madrid.[178] The City of Bilbao receives half its annual income of €475 million from the provincial government, 37 per cent from its own taxes and the remainder from other sources such as the EU.[179] Most services are placed under the jurisdiction of one of the three administrative levels of the Basque government.

Developing a strategic approach to recovery in the 1980s

In order to deal with the acute urban decline, flexible, integrated interventions were sought. The interaction of political actors from all levels of government, and a cross-party consensus on the need for action, drove the emergence of a strong regeneration strategy. This led to the development of a masterplan embracing a project-based regeneration approach that had proved successful elsewhere in Spain.[180] A key step in the recovery process was the drafting of the strategic plan in the late 1980s. The plan established the regulatory framework for regeneration in Bilbao.[181] The main objective was to arrest decline and re-establish Bilbao as a key competitive node on the European Atlantic axis.[182] Spatially, the territorial plan identified four so-called 'opportunity areas' for regeneration. To create the new forward-looking image, world-famous architects were contracted for all-important projects.[183] In addition, major infrastructure investments were made, particularly in transport and sanitation.

The Strategic Plan for the Revitalisation of Metropolitan Bilbao was agreed in 1991. Bilbao Metrópoli-30 was founded in 1991 to act as a facilitator for the regeneration process and to promote the objectives set by the strategic plan (Box 9.2).[184] This agency is simultaneously a think-tank, lobby organisation and catalyst for investment based on a partnership model with public and private sector shareholders. One of its objectives is to strengthen the interaction between the public and private sectors.

Box 9.2: Bilbao Metrópoli-30

Bilbao Metrópoli-30 could be best described as a think-tank, lobby organisation and catalyst for investment. It is based on a partnership model with public and private sector shareholders. One of its objectives is to strengthen the interaction between public sector plans and interventions and private sector interests. Other tasks include the local and international promotion of Bilbao's new image as a post-industrial city and the funding of research into the metropolitan area. In its founding documents Bilbao Metrópoli-30 identified four fields of action:

- formation of a knowledge-based high-tech sector
- inner-city urban renewal, especially revitalisation of the Old Quarter
- environmental intervention: river cleaning, industrial land recycling, implementation of Agenda 21
- strengthening cultural identity through culture-led regeneration

The agency is currently undertaking a campaign to market the qualities and assets offered by the city-regions population that were identified as key to future progress: innovation, professionalism, identity, community and openness.

Sources: A. Martínez (interview); Rodríguez (2002)

Transport infrastructure

The process of economic and urban recovery received a major boost when Spain joined the European Community in 1986.[185] There followed a focus on changes in land use and the provision of infrastructure. At the same time, social equality and welfare provision rose in importance in the 1980s and were gradually integrated into the city's plans. Substantial investments were also made in the metropolitan transport infrastructure following the aim of improving accessibility for the city's residents and beyond, including internationally. Funding for transport projects came almost entirely from the public sector.

Investment in local public transport was dominated by the inauguration of the new metro system (Line 1) with stations designed by the architect Norman Foster (Figure 9.11). This project was particularly important for Bilbao's regeneration. It was the first major project to be completed and gave residents confidence that recovery was possible.[186] In addition, the two national railway companies RENFE and FEVE, which operate commuter train services in the metropolitan area, modernised their systems. A new addition to the rail-based public transport system is the tramline that connects Bilbao's central areas and runs along the revitalised waterfront. It was opened in 2002 and is run by the Basque transport consortium EuskoTren (Figure 9.12). The bus system was also modernised.

Figure 9.11: The new metro, opened 1995

Another significant investment strand was the modernisation and upgrading of long-distance transport infrastructure. The airport expanded with a new terminal designed by Santiago Calatrava. The port also received a substantial extension. New facilities were built on the open sea, replacing most of the older facilities along the river.

Strategic transport facilities such as international ports and airports, as well as most of the train network, are still under the domain of central government. Many of the investments were enabled by an infrastructure agreement signed between the Basque and Central governments in 1989. Bilbao cannot yet be reached by high-speed trains but a first – still contested – connection to Madrid is planned for 2015.

Figure 9.12: The new tramline, opened 2002

Environmental clean-up

Soil decontamination was essential on many of Bibao's derelict sites. Additionally, the installation of the new water sanitation system, carried out by the province's water provider between 1984 and 2006, had a significant impact on the metropolitan area's environment. The river had been very heavily polluted by industry and untreated household sewage. With a total investment of €1 billion, this project received far more funding than any other project.[187]

Economic restructuring

As early as 1981, the Basque government reacted to global economic restructuring by founding a dedicated business development agency SPRI (*Sociedad para la Promoción y Reconversación Industrial*) to provide assistance to the region's industrial sector.[188] SPRI was equipped with considerable funds, dedicated to developing different funding streams to assist the regional economy in adapting to the new economic requirements. In 2005, almost €50 billion were invested in the province of Bizkaia through the agency's work. A major activity was the development of technology parks.[189] The technology park for Bilbao's metropolitan area was located close to the airport in Zamudio and today employs 6,000 people in 350 businesses.

Another boost came when Spain joined the European Community in 1986 and began benefiting from transfer payments to overcome regional economic differences. Further EU funding was available through programmes targeting regions in industrial decline.[190] The most significant were Resider (1988–97), for restructuring steel-producing regions, and Renaval (1988–92), to assist with restructuring in shipbuilding regions. More important, however, was the Objective 2 funding that the region received through the EU's regional policy from the 1990s.

Social actions

The two most striking social interventions were initiated by the City of Bilbao. Two agencies – Surbisa and Lan Ekintza – were created specifically to tackle social problems resulting from the urban crisis and structural change. Surbisa was set up as a neighbourhood renewal agency to work in the flood-damaged parts of the old city in 1985. Lan Ekintza was set up in 1998 to link fragile parts of the labour force with job opportunities.

Housing

Although Bilbao's population has decreased since the 1970s, housing is a scarce resource due to several factors, including unmet demand resulting from land constraints, insufficient construction during the Franco period, shrinking household sizes and rising aspirations. The government drove owner-occupied housing, which dominated the housing market, through generous subsidised loans.[191] There is thus an undersupply of cheaper, rented housing for low-income groups, who often live in more crowded and lower standard conditions. 'Protected housing' – where a proportion of all new housing must be state-subsidised owner-occupied housing with support from the Basque government – and social housing, offered by the city council, both go some way to responding to this need. *Viviendas*

Municipales, Bilbao's public housing company, is the second largest of its kind in Spain but its stock consists of only 3,542 units.[192] One third of the total is located in Otxarkoaga, by far Bilbao's largest peripheral estate. It has low-standard housing and houses predominantly disadvantaged social groups (Figure 9.13).

Figure 9.13: Otxarkoaga, a low-income outer estate

SIGNS OF RECOVERY

Bilbao's recovery from industrial decline is now one of the best-known success stories in Europe. Physically, Bilbao is a transformed city. This does not imply, however, that all urban problems have disappeared. In this section we give a short evaluation of some of the key issues.

'Opportunity areas'

A development agency, Bilbao Ría 2000, was created in 1992, with authority to deliver regeneration of the 'opportunity areas' through a €560 million investment between 1997 and 2006.[193] Its main aim was to manage the large-scale revitalisation of abandoned land formerly occupied by harbours and industries or by obsolete transport infrastructure. Its remit was later extended to other municipalities in the metropolitan area such as Barakaldo and, more recently, Basauri. Some commentators have described this agency as the most significant urban policy intervention in the regeneration process.[194]

Initially, the territorial plan identified four 'opportunity areas':

- Abandoibarra: brownfield land formerly occupied by harbour and railway infrastructure in central locations on the riverfront. The project involved the creation of Bilbao's new urban heart with a focus on new investment.
- Zorrozaure: a peninsula occupied by mixed – mostly lower-value – harbour and industrial uses as well as some residential buildings and activities. The project, designed by Zaha Hadid, involved restructuring uses and a planned future extension of Abandoibarra.
- Ametzola/Eskurtze: the area south of central Bilbao dominated by dense residential developments. The project involved overcoming the physical divides such as deep railway cuttings (Figure 9.14).
- Miribilla and Morro: abandoned mining areas on the hilly slopes south east of central Bilbao led to a project to reclaim these areas through construction of new housing (Figure 9.15).

The most emblematic and well known of these redevelopment areas is Abandoibarra, located in a prime part of central Bilbao (Figure 9.16), but which had been a physical barrier cutting off much of central Bilbao from the river.

Figure 9.14: Ametzola, overcoming physical divides

Figure 9.15: Miribilla, new housing developments

Figure 9.16: Abandoibarra, before redevelopment – the eventual site of the Guggenheim

In the 1990s, Bilbao Ría 2000 became responsible for the site and invested €184 million up to 2004,[195] reclaiming the derelict site and turning it into a new functional centre capable of attracting local and international investment. Another aim was for the area to serve as a symbol for Bilbao's transformation from a declining industrial city into a revitalised, post–industrial metropolis fit for the 21st century.[196]

The private sector was, however, very cautious about investing in the area and public sector investment was necessary to create confidence in the site itself and Bilbao as a whole.[197] The best-known development on the site is the landmark Guggenheim Museum designed by the architect Frank Gehry. The museum opened in 1997 and immediately became a major tourist attraction, attracting over a million visitors in its first year. The cost of €144 million for this risky but prestigious investment was met entirely through public sector funding, shared by the provincial and regional governments. Other major developments on the Abandoibarra site are the Euskalduna Conference Centre on the former shipyard and a modern shopping mall, the latter being the only significant private sector investment so far.

Economic restructuring

Figure 9.17 clearly shows the economic restructuring in the metropolitan area of Bilbao. There has been a marked shift in employment from the industrial towards the service sector. In 2005, the proportion of the workforce employed in manufacturing was 22 per cent, less than half its 1975 share (46 per cent), although this still represents a significant industrial base. The share of those employed in the service sector has, on the other hand, increased from slightly less than half to over two thirds of the workforce.

Figure 9.17: Employment in manufacturing and service sectors, Bilbao metropolitano, 1975–2005 (%)

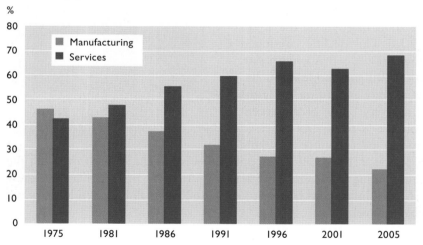

Notes: 2001 and 2005 values for provincial level only, which might vary slightly from the values for *Bilbao Metropolitana*. Manufacturing excludes construction sector.
Source: Eustat (online)

Although manufacturing is shrinking as a share of employment, the actual number of employees in this sector within Greater Bilbao has increased slightly.[198] *Bilbao Metropolitana* has experienced a massive growth in overall employment, rising from 267,000 to 380,000 jobs between 1995 and 2005.[199]

Falling unemployment

The unemployment rate fell from a peak of 25 per cent in the mid–1980s to 9.6 per cent in 2004. Key explanations for the sharp drop in unemployment rates for *Bilbao Metropolitana* are the wide use of early retirement schemes for older industrial workers and the departure of migrants. However, a substantial number of the unemployed might not be registered due to insufficient state support.[200] In addition, young people often leave the region as an estimated 40 per cent of newly created jobs are insecure or semi–informal with no social insurance.[201] However, the creation of the employment agency Lan Ekintza is a signal that the City of Bilbao is committed to its objective of improving the skills and opportunities of those who find it difficult to access the local labour market. Figure 9.18 shows the falling unemployment rate.

Figure 9.18: Unemployment rate, Bilbao, 1995–2005 (%)

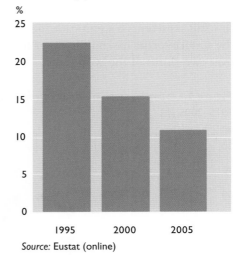

Source: Eustat (online)

Population development

As a consequence of industrial and urban decline, Bilbao lost about 14 per cent of its population between 1970 and 2005, mostly over the 1980s (Figure 9.19). This decline continued during the 1990s, albeit at a lower rate. Since 2000, Bilbao's population has increased slightly, indicating the city's ongoing recovery. Some of this recent population rise is related to increased immigration, especially since the 1990s. In 2006, 5.5 per cent of Bilbao's population was foreign,[202] with over half the immigrants coming from Latin American countries. The metropolitan area grew by some 67,000 inhabitants between 1970 and 2005, mainly driven by increases in suburban municipalities.

Urban regeneration

Despite its initial problems and public sector dominance, the Abandoibarra regeneration with its landmark Guggenheim Museum is widely seen as a success story and Abandoibarra is now attracting private sector investment.[203] The high-profile projects of Bilbao Ría 2000 can be found all over the city and several more are currently in the planning process. Regeneration, based on the financial model of enhancing land values by changing the use of ex-industrial sites, has been very successful. Its financially self-supporting approach enables the agency to finance its own redevelopment strategies.

Figure 9.19: Population development per decade, Bilbao, 1970–2005 (%)

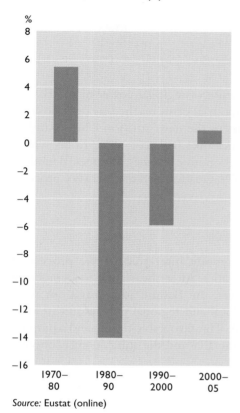

Source: Eustat (online)

A 'Guggenheim effect'?

Several studies attempt to evaluate the effects of the inauguration of the Guggenheim Museum in 1997 on the tourist sector.[204] From one perspective, tourism in Bilbao increased sharply with a growth in airport passengers from 1.4 million in 1994 to 3.8 million in 2005.[205] The Guggenheim has attracted an average of one million visitors per year since it opened.[206] However, large amounts of public money went into building the museum and public subsidies are required to finance its liabilities. Additionally, while employment in the service sector has increased hugely, fewer than a thousand jobs have been created in tourism-related parts of the economy.[207] However, the sheer number of additional tourists seems certain to have created many smaller service outlets, and thus the indirect effects in the city are extremely wide, if immeasurable.[208] The number of conference delegates arriving in the city has also increased tenfold over the last decade, to 178,000 per year, reflecting the effectiveness of projects such as the Euskalduna Conference Centre and the modernisation of the airport.

Transport investments

The metropolitan public transport system is efficient, inexpensive and widely used. A strong commitment by the relevant agencies, together with substantial funding to upgrade and expand the public transport infrastructure of the Bilbao metropolitan area, led to the new metro system carrying 78 million passengers per year.[209] This in turn has led to the densification of areas adjacent to the metro stops.[210]

The municipal bus system won an EU-wide prize in 2005 for its efficiency and accessibility. In the inner city, mobility is enhanced by footbridges across the river and the covering of railway cuttings. Long-distance accessibility and connectivity have been improved considerably by the modernisation and expansion of the airport. However, the international seaport, while ranking among the five largest in Spain, is still underperforming considering the extensive investment into its facilities.

Regional autonomy

The return of democracy and the restoration of regional power in the Basque Country happened shortly before the industrial crisis reached its peak, so local decision makers could tailor their policies to the new situation. The control of revenue-raising powers has allowed provinces like Bizkaia to design a tax system that promotes investment and responds to economic changes. This special funding and political structure, instituted from 1979, greatly aided the recovery process.

CONCLUSION

Bilbao offers some vital lessons for anybody interested in the process of regeneration within Europe's industrial cities. After the return to democracy and the re-instatement of regional power, the Basque administrations were equipped with the power to decide on local and regional policies just in time, before the industrial crisis reached its peak. This favourable timing and a number of intervention factors, such as joining the EU and the subsequent economic

Figure 9.20: Timeline of important events in Bilbao since 1980

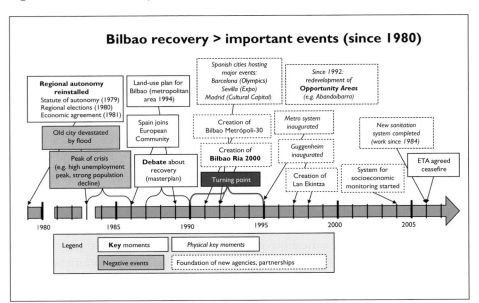

boom, have had a positive impact. The recovery of Bilbao has been facilitated by a combination of determined public sector leadership and an existing entrepreneurial culture. This enabled the design of interventions and special agencies to confront the symptoms of the crisis. Several major investments such as the Guggenheim, the new metro system and the water sanitation project were important components of this strategy. Another beneficial factor is the strong regional and local cultural identity.

TEN

Torino

CITY CONTEXT

Torino is located in Piedmont, northern Italy, on the plain of the River Po, just south of the western Alps. The municipality (*commune*) had 900,608 inhabitants in 2006 making it Italy's fourth largest city. The province surrounding Torino, covering 6,830km² and corresponding roughly to the metropolitan area, consists of 315 municipalities, and had 2,242,775 inhabitants in 2006 (see Figures 10.1 and 10.2).

Figure 10.1: Map of Italy

Figure 10.2: Map of Piedmont region

From Roman garrison to national capital: 25 BC to 1865 AD

Torino boasts a rich history as a military stronghold and trading hub. Its grid network of straight streets in the city centre demonstrates one of its early functions, as a military camp for the Romans in the 1st century AD. Since the 14th century it has been an important political capital, and only later developed into a major industrial city (see Figure 10.3).

The city's strategic geographical position, at the foot of the Alpine passes leading to central and western Europe at a crossing-point over the Po River, helped determine its development. It was a frontier stronghold during the Middle Ages, changing hands between Europe's great military leaders. Captured by the powerful Dukes of Savoy in 1280, it became their capital until the 19th century, playing important political, cultural and economic roles; the magnificent Baroque city core is a testament to the earlier wealth of their dynasty (see Figure 10.4). Political stability and prosperity fuelled demographic growth and economic diversification. By the 18th century, Torino had developed into a centre of artisan manufacturing, chiefly textiles.

Figure 10.3: Map of Torino in 1800

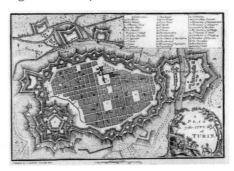

As the 19th century progressed Torino's industries flourished and the value of trade tripled. In the 1830s and 1840s, the Piedmontese government embarked on a major economic stimulus programme to encourage investment in the region. This included public–private joint ventures such as an extensive new railway system, which by 1861 made up 40 per cent of the entire Italian network. The regional government's collaboration with the private sector on economic development projects cultivated a tight-knit oligarchy of civic leaders who would continue to forge the development of the city.

Figure 10.4: Palazzo Madama, Baroque royal palace and Savoy residence

The granting of a Piedmontese constitution in 1848 ushered in a new era of political and economic modernisation that positioned Torino as the springboard for the movement that unified Italy in 1861. In recognition of this role, Torino was crowned the first capital of the new Italy, triggering a demographic boom. Just four years later, however, the capital was transferred to Florence, dealing a severe blow to Torino as political and civic institutions decamped *en masse* to the new capital.

The city had lost its administrative role, and with unemployment reaching 20 per cent, it faced a major identity crisis.

Box 10.1: National political timeline

1861	Unification
1896–1908	Economic boom
1925–43	Mussolini's fascist dictatorship
1946	Christian Democrats take control of national government in power for 40 years
1950/1960s	Italy's 'economic miracle'
1957	Founding member of European Economic Community
1970s	Attempts to devolve power to the regions
1970s–late 1980s	Labour protests and Red Brigade terrorist movement
1990s	Failed attempt to create metropolitan authorities
1992	National political corruption scandal exposed, all four major parties collapse. Successful devolution of power to regions and municipalities
1999	Italy adopts the euro

A new industrial vocation: 1865 to 1945

A coalition of municipal leaders, university professors and local businessmen joined forces to conceive a new direction for their city. Inspired by the popular late 19th-century doctrine of positivism, prizing scientific discovery and technological innovation, these local leaders actively promoted clusters of scientific and industrial activity. During the 1870s and 1880s, public authorities channelled funds into research, constructing a state-of-the-art 'City of Science' campus and founding a university consortium in 1878 to foster links between scientists and industrialists. Great strides were made in the fields of electricity and engineering. Research at the *Politecnico di Torino*, an engineering university, led to a municipal hydroelectric power station providing the region with reliable locally supplied energy for its industrial development. City authorities planned for industrial growth by investing in trade schools to develop skills for industry.

Manufacturing jobs increased by 44 per cent in the decade to 1881. Torino's strong banking sector generated several new banks, consolidating its position as Italy's financial centre and providing the crucial risk capital for new enterprises.

Crises in the agricultural, banking and commercial sectors in the last decade of the 19th century gave a decisive push to Torino's manufacturing. In 1899 30 aristocrats and businessmen, most of them car racing enthusiasts, capitalised on local engineering know-how to found a car industry in the city. They pooled 800,000 Lire of capital to found Fiat, the *Fabbrica Italiana Automobili Torino* (Italian Automobile Factory Torino), whose success became legendary. Meanwhile, other technological developments also flourished, driven by pioneering research at the city's universities. Italy's first cinema industry also developed in the city, and the typewriter manufacturer Olivetti was founded nearby in 1908.

The rise of Fiat

The engineering sector and the car industry in particular, were at the forefront of Torino's industrial boom. By 1911, the car sector employed a third of the city's expanding manufacturing workforce. Fiat led the field. By 1914, the company produced half the cars in Italy as well as components for ships, aeroplanes, trucks and trains. Fiat's chief executive officer Gianni Agnelli expanded the company rapidly, combining local engineering know-how, insights from the new field of scientific management and visits to Henry Ford's factories in Detroit, on which he based his first large-scale factory (see Figure 10.5). The population of the city grew by 43 per cent between 1901 and 1915, but the population of the outer working-class districts grew 500 per cent between 1891 and 1911. As housing shortages worsened, the city became increasingly socially segmented.

The First World War and the rise of fascism

The outbreak of the First World War and increased demand for military equipment fuelled Torino's industrial sector, with Fiat the main beneficiary. Its workforce expanded rapidly, from 3,500 to 40,000, a quarter of all workers in the city.

When Mussolini's fascists took power in 1922, Il Duce's drive for national self-sufficiency encouraged industrial

Figure 10.5: Fiat's Lingotto factory, 1923

growth still further, swelling Torino's workforce with new immigrants. The city grew from 500,000 in 1921 to 700,000 by 1939. Fiat now employed a third of the industrial workforce.

Postwar economic boom

Torino suffered multiple bombing raids in the early years of the Second World War, losing a third of its buildings. Following the fall of Mussolini in 1943, anarchy took hold; extreme food and energy shortages paralysed the city, and violent civil conflict ensued. Torino's civil authorities were ill equipped to manage the new crisis. They relied instead on Fiat and the Catholic Church. These two organisations both worked to fill the social welfare vacuum left by the disintegration of fascism. Fiat developed its own private welfare system.

The Second World War forced many smaller factories out of business, consolidating Fiat's power base in the city. The Italian government singled Fiat out as a key national driver of post-war economic growth, and gave the company over a third of the $58 million of Marshall Plan funding earmarked for Italy's entire engineering sector. This confirmed Fiat's dominant position in the local and national economy.

The 'economic miracle' years

Fiat spearheaded Torino's and Italy's post-war 'economic miracle'. From 1958 to 1963 Italy's industrial output more than doubled while its GDP grew by an annual 6.3 per cent. Fiat concentrated production in its Torino factories. Tens of thousands of new jobs were generated each year, and car manufacturing represented 80 per cent of the city's industrial activity. Economic migrants streamed into the city from Italy's impoverished south. By the late 1960s the industrial giant was producing 95 per cent of Italy's total car output (see Figure 10.6).

Figure 10.6: The Fiat 500 in Torino, 1957

Torino's population peaked at 1.2 million in 1975. By the 1970s Fiat's workforce had reached 115,000. Fiat's production-related decisions determined an estimated 20 per cent or more of all investments in Italy. Meanwhile, as the vehicle industry boomed, the other sectors that had characterised the city-region's economy (textiles, food processing and clothing) declined steadily.

Torino's municipal authorities, overwhelmed and under-resourced, adopted a laissez-faire attitude to the rapidly developing social polarisation. They took little action to remedy the chronic housing, health, transport and education problems in the over-saturated peripheral areas where most immigrants settled. They failed to implement an urban regulatory plan, allowing free rein to property developers. The result was unregulated private construction of sub-standard housing with limited access to basic amenities, exacerbating hostilities between southern immigrants and locals.

Worker protest movement: the 1969 'hot autumn'

Workers' resentment of living conditions and services had been building throughout the 1960s, periodically boiling over into labour militancy, causing regular production stoppages in the factories. The first major strike of the labour movement that beset Fiat in the 1960s, 1970s and 1980s came in 1969. Working-class activism, combined with a growing student protest movement, peaked in 1969 when the 'hot autumn' of strikes paralysed the local production system.

The workers gained a national contract that improved their conditions but the unions were not satisfied. The movement continued into the 1970s and 1980s, and tensions mounted as Fiat's slow decline began (see Figure 10.7).

CRISIS

Fiat had become the 'absolute monarch' of Torino during the post–war period, such that Torino's crisis would inevitably mirror Fiat's. Globalisation and European integration meant Fiat could no longer be protected from global competition. The local economy had become over-concentrated and other sectors had atrophied. The city's traditional economic diversity had been lost, leaving it exposed to the sudden decline of its one dominant industry.

Figure 10.7: Strike at Fiat's Mirafiori factory, 1962

The global oil crisis of 1973 brought Torino's 20-year economic miracle to a halt. The city's population entered a steady decline. Inflation and public debt soared. Fiat in particular was vulnerable because of its low investment in new equipment and research.

The company began to shift production out of Torino in the 1980s amid bitter union protests, largely in order to capitalise on the state's financial incentives to invest in the struggling south of Italy. In the 1980s, Torino's metropolitan area lost roughly 100,000 industrial jobs, mostly from the city itself.[211] Over the 1990s, Fiat's Torino workforce shrank from 92,000 to 47,000.[212] A massive injection of state aid and a programme of restructuring allowed it to continue dominating its largely protected domestic market. But by 2002 less than 30 per cent of Fiat's production took place in Torino.[213] Fiat had once employed 140,000 local workers, but now provided jobs for barely 30,000. The Single European Act of 1992 flooded the Italian market with competition from foreign imports. Fiat's share of its principal domestic market fell steadily, from 52 per cent in 1990 to 34 per cent in 2001, with its European market share also dipping from 11 per cent in 1990 to nine per cent in 2001.[214]

Nevertheless, the slow-burning nature of Fiat's decline gave many local suppliers the necessary warning time to diversify into new international markets, which they did with impressive efficiency.[215] National government also sanctioned generous 'emergency benefits' for laid-off workers. The company's crisis was therefore gentler than feared.

Political and social crisis

The municipal government struggled to cope for a number of reasons:

- Fiat's political dominance, with its high-level political alliances and controlling economic position in the city, had overshadowed a succession of left-wing municipal governments, which had little influence over Fiat's decision making.[216]
- Fiat had provided both housing and social benefits to its workers. The company's decline left a vacuum in many key areas of welfare and service provision, which the municipal authorities were not equipped to deal with.
- Italy's post-war national governments were weakened by continual fiscal crises, instability and lack of cooperation. The major corruption *tangentopoli* scandal in 1992 resulted in the collapse of the traditional national party system.
- Protest and internal terrorist movements further reduced national and local governments' capacity from 1968 to the early 1980s. Anti-capitalist protests began in the factories, spread to the universities and culminated in the violent 'Red Brigades' terror movements delaying reforms.
- The left-wing coalition of communists and socialists that ran Torino from 1975 to 1985 focused on national party politics rather than local necessities. From 1982, the coalition became enveloped in a corruption scandal that eventually led to it being ousted from power, only to be replaced by an unstable, ineffective coalition of centre-left parties without a coherent strategy. Torino then cycled through four mayors during a seven-year period. By 1992, the situation had deteriorated to the extent that the national government dissolved Torino's elected city council, drafting in a government-appointed commissioner to run the city until the 1993 elections. By this time, the city's budget deficit had risen to an unprecedented 121 billion Lire.

Torino's left-wing administrations of the 1970s and 1980s failed to develop the vision and strategies necessary to mitigate the wider economic forces at work and to cushion their social effects. Meanwhile a new wave of immigration from non-EU countries, from the late 1980s, put further pressures on the city's infrastructure and heightened social tensions (see Figure 10.8). The political corruption scandal of 1992, which brought down both local and national governments, paved the way for the new era of collective governance that launched Torino's recovery process.

RECOVERY ACTIONS

Political reforms

With industry no longer at the helm, political renewal was to prove the *sine qua non* of Torino's recovery. The single critical factor that kick-started the new, strategic recovery process was the national reform of 1993 that introduced the direct election of mayors, and gave them increased executive powers and resources.

The 1993 reforms allowed mayors to appoint their own executives, while reducing the power of municipal councils. It also altered the local tax system to increase the financial resources available to mayors. Responsibility for running the city was thus devolved to elected mayors and the executive team they chose. Accountability, trust and transparency suddenly came to characterise a system that had grown out of touch and had long been dominated by insider interests. Legislation throughout the 1990s devolved significant further powers to local executives.

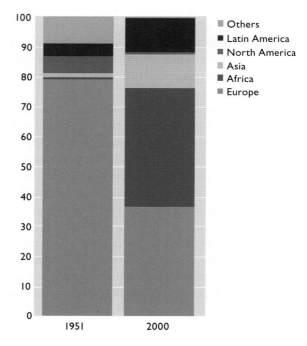

Figure 10.8: Resident foreigners by country of origin, Province of Torino, 1951 and 2000 (%)

Others
Latin America
North America
Asia
Africa
Europe

Sources: ISTAT; IRES Piemonte

New strategies

Torino's first directly elected mayor in 1993 followed a remobilisation of civil society which produced its own centre-left candidate, a university professor, Valentino Castellani. He entered office with 57 per cent of the votes as 'the first mayor elected by the people and not the political parties'.[217]

New collaborative approach to recovery

A non-party-politicised mayor rooted in local priorities gave Torino's administration fresh credibility in the public's eyes.[218] This new atmosphere of trust and cooperation enabled Castellani to mobilise civil society to formulate and execute a recovery strategy.

Torino had a long tradition of civic involvement dating from the medieval era of self-governing northern Italian city-states.[219] With the powers vested in him by the new legislation with his 'clean hands' reputation, Castellani was able to build on this tradition and recruit a group of experts from academic and entrepreneurial spheres to his executive team.[220] Recasting the municipal government's role as a 'forum' and facilitator,[221] he then led a city-wide debate that drew on expertise from civil society to formulate a collective recovery plan: the strategic plan. In doing so, he formed a close-knit and committed network of individuals with the knowledge and resources to implement the plan collectively.

Castellani also resolved to make the municipal government more outward looking, setting out to improve relationships with and gain experience from neighbouring municipalities, the Province of Torino, and particularly the Region of Piemonte. Castellani's new administration also worked to develop strong relations with the EU that proved particularly useful in accessing new learning through their city networking programmes. It also brought resources through their urban renewal, economic and social programmes. The ability to raise funds from non-governmental sources was especially important given the city's budget deficit, and the scarce resources from national government. Torino's two major bank foundations, a legacy from the city's past wealth, now became major sponsors of the city's recovery effort.

Castellani privatised several core municipal services (such as electricity and energy) and transferred some of the city's major museums to foundations including private partners, who were henceforth in charge of managing them. Another important reform involved the introduction of a municipal tax on property, now a significant proportion of the municipal budget.[222]

Three key projects

With its strengthened and slimmed-down executive, the new mayor's administration pressed forward with projects to promote recovery: the urban masterplan, a strategic plan and the creation of a neighbourhoods unit. These projects progressed over 15 years of political continuity from Mayor Castellani and his centre-left successor, Mayor Chiamparino, both of whom won strong second mandates.

Urban masterplan (1995)

Torino's new urban masterplan, ratified in 1995, following 45 years of deferral by previous city administrations, set out a vision for the physical reconfiguration of Torino, transforming it into a better-connected, denser post-industrial metropolis by recycling centrally located brownfields.

The plan built on an existing project, funded by the state-owned railway company, to 'bury' the central railway line that cleaved the city in half and was flanked by deprived neighbourhoods. The urban masterplan proposed transforming the old railway route into a 12km boulevard style arterial road into the city centre, forming Torino's new 'central backbone' (*spina centrale*). This tied in with the redevelopment of four major brownfield zones along its length, totalling over 2.1 million m² of land, to create new mixed-use neighbourhoods. Torino's first metro line, a €700 million 15km route with 21 stations, will connect the deprived ex-industrial areas in the north and south to the main transport network. Together these projects represent €2.45 billion of public and private investment (see Figure 10.9).

Strategic plan (1998–2000)

Torino's strategic plan (*piano strategico*) is possibly the city's most important recovery tool. Inspired by the effectiveness of the strategic planning efforts of other European cities, and galvanised by the severity of the economic and social crisis, in 1998 Mayor Castellani made Torino the first Italian city to debate a strategic economic plan.

The two-year debate that fed into the plan created a strong network of 57 leading individuals from different sectors, all committed to implementing the resulting plan collaboratively.

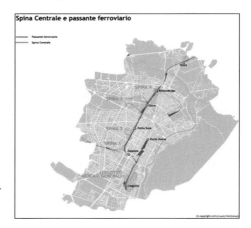

Figure 10.9: Central backbone route (*spina centrale*) and underground railway (*passante ferroviario*)

Hundreds of residents were also involved through dozens of workshops, conventions and seminars. The mayor's administration commissioned candid analysis of the city's strengths, weaknesses, opportunities and threats in an international context, called 'Toward the Plan',[223] to lay the groundwork. The theme of 'internationalisation' was adopted to force the city to look outwards and consider its position in a changing global context.

Two approaches to capitalising on Torino's assets were adopted: one building on the city's industrial history; the other breaking into a new future. In terms of outward-looking efforts, the city founded a metropolitan-level group of public–private agencies, promoting Torino as an attractive destination. Events were seen as a second important tool, attracting visitors, raising the profile of the city and publicising its assets.

One year into the strategic plan debate, the city was awarded the 2006 Winter Olympic Games, a major leap for the once beleaguered city.

In terms of efforts to promote research and industrial innovation, the plan capitalised on Torino's specialised skills and assets based on its industrial expertise, and on its universities (particularly the prestigious Politecnico) whose research fed into its industries. It aimed to develop high-value-added research and innovation activities in sectors in which Torino was already specialised.

The plan itself was organised along six 'lines of action', each broken down into more concrete objectives:

- making Torino an international transport and communications hub;
- constructing a metropolitan government;
- developing training, research and strategic resources;
- promoting enterprise and employment;
- promoting Torino as a city of culture, tourism, commerce and sports;
- improving urban quality by upgrading the local environment to achieve socially and environmentally sensitive regeneration.[224]

Box 10.2: Examples of events

- Torino Book Fair (*Salone del Libro*) (founded 1988, annual)
- Torino Film Festival (founded 1998, every two years)
- Taste Fair (*Salone del Gusto*) (founded 1998, every two years), linked to the Piedmont region's 'slow food' movement
- World Book Capital (2006)
- Winter Olympics (2006)
- Paralympics (2006)
- International Architectural Congress (2007)
- World Design Capital (2008)
- Celebration for 150th anniversary of Italian unification (2011)

Investment promotion agency

An inward investment agency, Invest in Turin and Piedmonte (ITP), was created to promote the region's economic assets internationally, to build relationships with potential investors, to facilitate the location process and to broker the substantial public incentives on offer (including EU Objective 2 funding).

ICT district

The Torino region had a significant competitive advantage in ICT. The Torino Wireless Foundation was created in 2001 to manage the development of a 'district' of ICT enterprises in order to encourage the cross-fertilisation of academic research and enterprise in this sector. It is funded by a mixture of public and private bodies to increase the region's competitiveness in the ICT sector by linking up and promoting its ICT-related activities through a research laboratory and an incubator directly adjacent to the Politecnico University that specialises in ICT research.

The Mario Boella Institute for Higher Research (*Istituto Superiore Mario Boella*, ISMB) is a laboratory for high-tech ICT research, founded by the Politecnico University and the Compagnia di San Paolo bank foundation in 2000. It links over 140 academic researchers with research teams from private companies, such

---

Box 10.3: Examples of new public–private agencies

- *Turismo Torino*, tourism agency for Torino and Piedmont region
- *Invest in Turin and Piedmont (ITP)*, inward investment agency
- *Associazione Torino Internazionale*, association for coordinating and monitoring delivery of the strategic plan, with 120 members from political, economic, cultural and social institutions
- *Convention Bureau*, for promoting convention activity
- *Organising Committee for Winter Olympics (TOROC)*, a non-profit private foundation set up to organise the Games
- *Six territorial pacts* (an initiative to involve multiple levels of government and the private sector in infrastructure and development projects) among neighbouring municipalities
- *Technological parks*, set up to create firms in innovative fields (including the Environment Park and the Virtual Reality Multimedia Park)
- *Torino Wireless Foundation*, to promote the ICT sector

Source: Rosso (2004)

---

as Accent, Motorola and ST Microelectronics. They work together on contracts to develop new technologies that these companies will then commercialise. In partnership with Torino Wireless, ISMB also runs a programme promoting the use of ICT in local SMEs.

I3P is an incubator focused on ICT-related start-up businesses, sponsored by the Politecnico, the provincial and municipal governments, Torino's Chamber of Commerce, Piedmont's regional development agency Finpiemonte and the Torino Wireless Foundation. The Torino Wireless Foundation manages a venture capital fund that provides seed capital to I3P's start-ups (see Box 10.4).

Technology parks

'Green' technologies were also recognised as a sector set to receive increased public funding, and for which private sector demand was fast growing. The Environment Park, a $30,000m^2$ technology park, was set up to develop new environmental technologies that can be commercialised. It houses research laboratories, SMEs and start-ups focused on specific technologies (for example hydrogen energy) to encourage collaboration between research and business. It is sponsored by the regional, provincial and municipal governments, and part-funded by the EU. Many of the new centres are housed in rehabilitated industrial buildings. Torino Wireless Foundation's ICT district occupies some disused train repair workshops and the Environment Park is based in Fiat's old smelting works (see Figure 10.10).

Box 10.4: The I3P incubator

- Professors from the Politecnico University decided to set up an incubator, after visiting other countries (France, Belgium, Finland, UK, US), noticing that business incubators attached to universities were a common feature
- They proposed the idea to the public sector (Chambers of Commerce, region, city)
- In 1999, I3P became Italy's first university-linked incubator
- It was founded as a non-profit joint-stock consortium company (Scpa), with its six joint shareholders as:
  o Politecnico di Torino University
  o Province of Torino
  o Municipality of Torino
  o Chamber of Commerce of Torino
  o Finpiemonte (Regional Financial Agency of the Region of Piedmont)
  o Torino Wireless Foundation (for promoting ICT activity)
Each shareholder contributes €200,000 (totalling €1.2 million)
- I3P focuses on high-tech business ventures in the major engineering sectors

How it works
- I3P provides start-ups with cheap offices in high-tech premises, the consultancy services of business development advisers (for the commercial side) and Politecnico University professors (for the technical side), and help with connecting entrepreneurs to provide start-up capital
- To finance its activities, I3P receives funding from various bodies with which its founding shareholders have strong relationships, for example, the CRT bank foundation part-funded the conversion of old warehouses into I3P's new offices, and the EU and Italian ministries are the main funders of the operating costs

Helping finance entrepreneurialism
- Local banks have agreed to grant low-interest loans of up to €100,000 without a guarantee
- I3P has strong relationships with Piemontech and Innogest, two funds run by the Torino Wireless Foundation. Piemontech is a seed fund, giving grants of up to €200,000; Innogest is a growth fund, giving grants of up to €5 million. These relationships ensure I3P's companies have preferential consideration by these funds
- The Torino Wireless Foundation has also founded an association of 11 venture capitalists (only five of them Italian), called 'Venture Capital Hub', to provide funding for budding enterprises. This will provide up to €1 billion

Promoting entrepreneurialism
- To promote its services and encourage entrepreneurialism, I3P has founded the 'Start Cup' competition for the year's best business idea in the Piedmont region, with a 1st prize of €20,000. This idea spawned many imitations across the Italian regions, and I3P has now launched the 'National Innovation Award' competition for the winners of all the regional competitions, with a 1st prize of €60,000

continued/

Box 10.4: continued

- I3P is a founding partner of a national association of university incubators in Italy, PNI Cube, which shares best practice among 25 university incubators and promotes their work

I3P's ingredients for success

- Strong links to the university and local authorities. "Without the Politecnico and the strong collaboration with local bodies such as the Province and the Chambers of Commerce – we could never have happened," says a project manager at the incubator. These links were critical for finding financial support and giving the project visibility

Results

- As of October 2007, I3P has hosted 88 start-ups, only four of which have failed to develop into businesses (a notably high success rate)
- For the 65 operating start-ups for which data is available, the 'overall value is around €20 million' (Sarti, 2007)
- I3P won a 'Best Science-based Incubator' award in 2004 (Science Alliance, 2004)

Neighbourhoods Unit (1997)

Figure 10.10: The Environment Park under construction

The third major strand of activity linked to the urban and economic strands was neighbourhood regeneration and social inclusion. In 1997, city officials developed an innovative programme called the Plan for Marginal Neighbourhoods (*Progetto Speciale Periferie*, PSP). This was developed into a dedicated neighbourhood renewal department within the council, the Neighbourhoods Unit (*Settore Periferie*). The Plan for Marginal Neighbourhoods, inspired by visits to other European cities experienced in resident participation, proposed a bottom-up model by which residents and their day-to-day experiences of neighbourhood problems were the starting point for designing urban renewal policies for each neighbourhood. The Neighbourhoods Project secured over €580 million of competitive-bid finance for its projects between 1997 and 2007. Boxes 10.5 and 10.6 detail the regeneration projects in Porta Palazzo and Mirafiori Nord.

In each renewal neighbourhood, the Unit opened a dedicated drop-in centre (*laboratorio territoriale*) run by a group of residents, which served as a meeting point for the local community. This encouraged local residents to consult on, develop and deliver aspects of the project in partnership with a neighbourhood forum (*tavolo sociale*), bringing together residents and local organisations with members of the neighbourhood team (see Figures 10.11 and 10.12).

The Neighbourhoods Unit formed an interdepartmental working group consisting of 15 professionals from the departments responsible for delivering services to neighbourhoods, for example police, education, transport, health (the *gruppo di lavoro intersettoriale*). It also formed a neighbourhood–level interdisciplinary

---

Box 10.5: Porta Palazzo neighbourhood regeneration project

Duration: 1998–2001
Residents: 10,000
Funding:
    EU: €2.58 million
    Municipality: €2.58 million
    State Ministry of Public Works: €1 million
    Bank foundation CRT: €260,000
    Bank foundation CSP: €260,000
    Torino Chamber of Commerce: €260,000

- The project area is a decaying inner-city market square that has become a focal point for the city's growing non-EU immigrant population
- The project is managed and implemented by the Porta Palazzo Project Committee, an independent non-profit body featuring decision makers from both public and private sectors
- The project focuses on the social and economic integration of both market vendors and residents. It is piloted by a committee of representatives from the public and private sectors
- Decision making is participatory and local residents are regularly consulted. This neighbourhood project illustrates Torino's commitment to working with and developing the skills of its immigrants
- After its EU funding ended, the project became a local development agency in 2003 and continued its work in the Porta Palazzo neighbourhood

---

Box 10.6: Mirafiori Nord neighbourhood regeneration project

Duration: 2001–06
Residents: 25,000
Funding: €42 million, with €11 million from the EU

- The project aimed to regenerate the area of social housing bordering Fiat's Mirafiori factory, with a focus on environmental sustainability, economic development and social inclusion
- Public spaces redeveloped, new ICT enterprises created, social and cultural services networks supported and social housing upgraded

Figure 10.11: Drop-in centre in the Via Arquata neighbourhood

Figure 10.12: Neighbourhoods Unit staff flanking a local pensioner and ex-Fiat employee who emigrated to Torino from the south in the 1960s

working group for each neighbourhood project, consisting of 15 city employees, for example teachers, planners, social workers. The projects targeted social, environmental and physical problems. They also involved skills development (see Figures 10.13a–b and 10.14).

Torino is the only Italian city to make resident participation a requirement for all its neighbourhood regeneration projects, and has won international recognition for its locally developed, participative approach.

Figures 10.13a–b: Blocks of social housing in the Mirafiori Nord neighbourhood, before the Neighbourhoods Unit rehabilitation project in 2006 (left), and after in 2007 (right)

Figure 10.14: Upgraded housing, new pedestrianised area and new greenery in the previously dilapidated Via Arquata neighbourhood

SIGNS OF RECOVERY

Economically, Torino is in a much better position now than when its first directly elected mayor came to power. Unemployment in the city-region sank to its lowest ever rate, 4.1 per cent, in 2006 with 14,000 new jobs created that year (see Figure 10.15).[225] Activity rates in the Province almost returned to their 1951 levels (see Figure 10.16). However, observers worry that continued reliance on industry leaves Torino exposed to fluctuations in the global car market.[226]

Figure 10.15: Unemployment rate, Province of Torino, 1993–2006 (%)

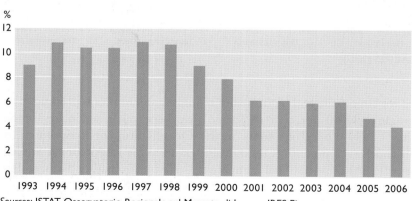

Sources: ISTAT, Osservatorio Regionale sul Mercato di Lavoro, IRES Piemonte

Figure 10.16: Activity rate, Province of Torino, 1951–2002 (%)

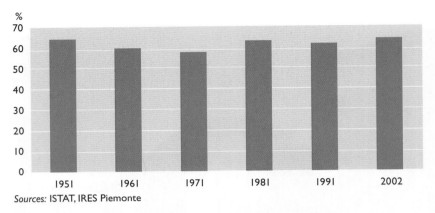

Sources: ISTAT, IRES Piemonte

Meanwhile the population of the municipality of Torino is almost static, while the city's 'first ring' suburbs grew by three per cent and its 'second ring' suburbs swelled by 10 per cent, showing that suburbanisation continues apace.[227] Foreign migrants moving into the city centre compensate for the low birth rate and the outward flow of existing residents.[228] The metropolitan area as a whole gained population slightly, up to 1,715,000 by 2006. Figure 10.17 shows population change in the Torino metropolitan area.

Figure 10.17: Population change, Torino metropolitan area

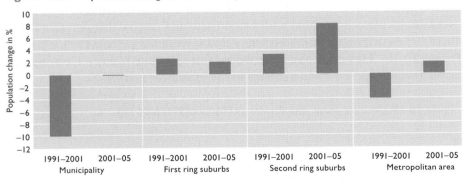

Sources: ISTAT, IRES (2007)

The need for large-scale and high-quality training programmes is pressing given that approximately 60 per cent of Torino's workers lack a secondary school education.[229] Italy comes out badly in the Organisation for Economic Co-operation and Development's (OECD's) Programme for International Student Assessment (PISA) cross-national comparisons of educational standards, and no Italian university now makes it into the world's top 90.[230]

Integrating the metropolitan area into the international system

The introduction of low-cost flights contributed to Torino's growth in visitors,[231] but many airlines cancelled their Torino routes after the 2006 Winter Olympics. On the other hand, by 2009, the high-speed rail link with Milano will promote a new level of cooperation, helping Torino share in Milano's dominant economy. The Torino–Lyon fast rail connection, due for completion by 2011, will reposition Torino within Europe.[232]

Constructing a metropolitan government

National legislation in 1990 aimed to encourage the formation of metropolitan areas, but lacked incentives for municipalities to give up their independence, resulting in little progress.[233] The Metropolitan Conference in 2000 involved 38 municipalities in the Torino area but its lack of formal powers meant it achieved little. However, project- or sector-specific agencies with a metropolitan focus, such as the Torino Internazionale Association and Turismo Torino have proved the most successful attempts at intermunicipal cooperation, although by their nature they only cover certain activities.

Developing training, research and strategic resources

The plan's drive to connect academia and enterprise better has been endorsed by an 'innovation scoreboard' report comparing 12 innovative European regions, which ranks Piedmont as top for its research industry cooperation.[234] International companies such as Motorola, General Motors Powertrains and Jac Anhui, a Chinese car manufacturer, have chosen to locate their research facilities in Torino, all citing the presence of other research centres and universities operating in similar fields as a major reason. The presence of these large private sector centres (Motorola employs over 500 people) is in turn attracting more sector-related activities to the area. The inward investment agency ITP has played an important role in promoting these assets in strategic sectors internationally, despite its restricted budget for these activities.[235]

Promoting enterprise and employment

The economy is now far less reliant on Fiat, with SMEs slowly replacing the behemoth that had previously dominated. The number of businesses in the Torino area has been increasing steadily in recent years, jumping eight per cent between 1999 and 2004, with particular growth in the tourism and construction sectors.[236]

Torino's many SMEs in the car and mechanics sectors are finding new clients abroad, with some help from the Chamber of Commerce's 'From Concept to Car'[237] internationalisation support programme, which aims to connect SMEs to new international customers (thereby reducing their dependency on Fiat).

Components are the city-region's most-exported product, and exports to emerging markets such as Russia (up by 37 per cent) and China (up by 22 per cent) rose substantially during 2006.[238]

The I3P incubator has generated 79 new enterprises with a value of over €20 million in its first seven years of activity, and won an international award for Best Science-based Incubator in 2004.[239] The Environment Park's hydrogen laboratory has designed the first hydrogen-fuelled scooter in Italy. However, the two technology parks' results in terms of innovation have 'fallen below expectations' according to some experts.[240]

ICT has been one of the fastest-growing local sectors, with the number of companies in the Torino area increasing by 47 per cent between 1998 and 2003, albeit from a low base.[241] Overall, the shift from manufacturing to services in Torino is continuing, with the proportion of the Province's labour force employed in the service sector growing from 29 per cent in 1951 to 60 per cent in 2002 (see Figure 10.18). However, the Torino area remains far more industrialised than other metropolitan areas in Italy.

Figure 10.18: Employment by sector, Province of Torino, 1951–2002 (%)

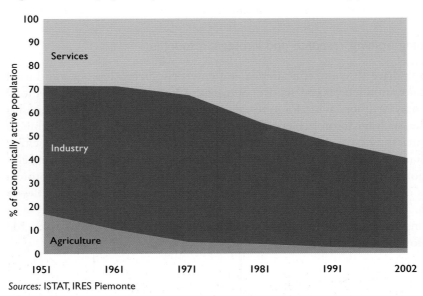

Sources: ISTAT, IRES Piemonte

Promoting Torino as a city of culture, tourism, commerce and sports

Visitor figures for the Province rose from 694,000 in 1997 to 1.15 million in 2004, and 'tourist stay' figures for the city itself increased by 24 per cent during 2005 alone.[242]

Undoubtedly, the city's hosting of the 2006 Winter Olympics was a major contributing factor. It not only stimulated the construction of numerous world-class sporting venues, but also thrust Torino into the global spotlight and provided an exceptional opportunity for the city to advertise itself to a vast international audience. The opening ceremony alone attracted 249 million viewers.[243] The success of the Winter Olympics was also a turning point for Torino's residents, giving them proof of the international appeal of their city that many had doubted, and inspiring a newfound civic pride.

Upgrading urban environments

The Neighbourhoods Unit is held up as a best practice model for the management of area-based urban regeneration projects.[244] However, in 2007 its scope was reduced and its budget cut by the municipality. Meanwhile, the goal of promoting social cohesion in the plan still leaves unresolved the integration of Torino's growing minority ethnic communities (see Figure 10.19). By 2006 there were 80,000 foreigners[245] in the city, almost nine per cent of the total population.[246] However, Torino is a national pioneer in efforts to encourage immigrant participation, instituting new legislation allowing them to vote in local government referenda and creating Italy's first Council for Foreigners in 1995.[247] The second strategic plan seeks to aid immigrant integration with a focus on education.

Figure 10.19: Graffiti in the *Barriera di Milano* area, to the north east of the city

In terms of environmental policy, the fragile mountain environment bordering the city is now recognised as an important resource. The municipality has launched various environmentally friendly initiatives to improve quality of life in the city, including increasing pedestrianisation, the reduction of road-level parking to create cycle lanes and the plan for a metro. The city aims to become a European leader in retro-fitting old buildings to save energy.[248]

CONCLUSION

Torino is fortunate to have some outstanding attributes, extraneous in the industrial era, but now being revalued as historic and environmental assets, on which to build its new post-industrial image and future: a spectacular physical environment at the foot of the Alps; two outstanding universities; attractive historic buildings, squares and urban layout; and the cultural richness and quality of life often associated with Italian cities (see Figure 10.20). Strong local leadership, made possible by the national reform that introduced directly elected mayors in 1993, was critical to the success of Torino's recovery effort. The entrepreneurial do-it-yourself approach to recovery and progress engendered by its new-style mayors has stood Torino in good stead. Entrenched problems such as the integration of immigrants and the reskilling of industrial workers constitute an essential part of the long-term strategy. Fitting more prestigious and 'visible' infrastructure and economic projects with such locally rooted social problems will strengthen the city's recovery. These combined attributes constitute the core of the city's appeal to the tourists, 'knowledge workers', inward investors and innovators on whom the city's future relies.

Figure 10.20: Torino skyline with the Alps in the background

Figure 10.21: Timeline of important events in Torino since the late 1970s

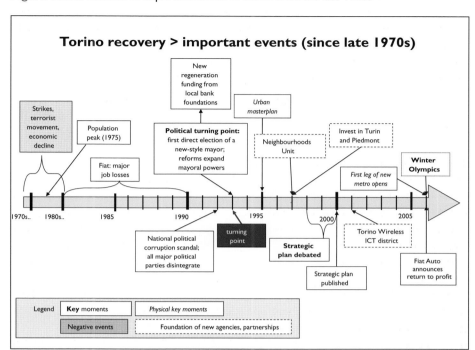

Saint-Étienne

City context

Saint-Étienne is located in central eastern France in the Rhône–Alpes region, 60km southwest of Lyon (see Figures 11.1 and 11.2). The municipality (*commune*) covers an area of 80km and had a population of 180,210 in 1999.[249] The broader Saint-Étienne metropolitan area (*aire urbaine*) comprises 41 municipalities, with 321,703 inhabitants in 1999. It is France's 16th largest urban region in terms of population.

Figure 11.1: Map of France

Figure 11.2: Map of Rhône-Alpes region

There were many geographical obstacles to Saint-Étienne's development given its setting – a hilly, cut-off valley with bitter weather. However, discovery of rich coal and iron resources and its location near Lyon, France's second city, proved decisive in its transformation from a small rural town to prominent centre of industrial production.

By the 1300s, locally mined coal was being used in knife production, fuelling a growing weapons industry. Firearms were being produced *en masse* by local craftsmen as early as the 1570s,[250] and by the 17th century Europe's booming arms industry had given Saint-Étienne national renown. Its Royal Arms Factory was founded in 1764, sponsored by the French royal court, to centralise and expand national arms production, from 3,000 to 20,000 arms per year. During the French Revolution, the city was even briefly renamed *Armeville* (Arms Town).

Saint-Étienne was also famed for its hand-made lace ribbons, and by 1850 ribbon making employed half the city's working population, producing a higher economic turnover than both the coal and metal industries.[251] As the industrial revolution accelerated during the 19th century, the town's mines were deepened and heavy industry expanded. In 1823, continental Europe's first railway was built in Saint-Étienne to facilitate transportation of coal from over 200 mines in and around the city. Saint-Étienne's regional importance grew in step with its industrial expansion; it was made the chief town of the Loire Department in 1855.

State intervention in Saint-Étienne's industrial development

The French state was keen to make France a self-sufficient industrial powerhouse. It therefore subsidised and promoted heavy industry in the region, identifying Saint-Étienne as one of the nation's 'workshops'.[252] In 1868, the state consolidated the multitude of local weapon-producing workshops into a single dedicated factory, the Imperial Arms Factory (*Manufacture Impériale d'Armes*).

By the late 1800s, the city had an industrial fabric of large coal and steel-related factories linked to a dense network of SMEs, providing components and marketing products (Figure 11.3). The highly successful French arms and cycles factory, Manufrance, which pioneered the design and production of modern bicycles and sewing machines and their sale by mail order, soon became the city's chief employer, and Saint-Étienne became famous for producing the country's first bicycle. Although the heavy industries eclipsed ribbon making as they started mass production, it remained one of the city's top four employment sectors (alongside metalwork, arms and cars).

Heavy industries continued to flourish during the early 1900s, profiting from demand for arms prompted by two world wars. Regional inward migration coupled with continuing industrial growth sustained the city's industries. However, France's economy was greatly damaged by near-constant conflict with Germany in the first half of the 20th century, and many cities suffered as resources were diverted to military efforts.

Figure 11.3: A local steel works, late 19th century

Post-Second World War: economic and housing crises

Because of its importance in weapons manufacturing, Saint-Étienne was heavily bombed during the Second World War. The municipal government faced two immediate post-war concerns: reviving its economy and a housing crisis. Housing shortages became more acute from the 1950s with increasing numbers of immigrants, particularly from France's North African colonies. Many were forced to live in squalid conditions in city centre slums.

Under strong central government incentives, the local government responded to the housing crisis during the 1950s and 1960s by sponsoring municipal housing companies to construct large social housing estates, known as *grands ensembles*, on the periphery of the city (see Figure 11.4). These estates added tens of thousands of social housing units but their peripheral location made them socially and economically isolated.

Figure 11.4: 1970s postcard showing the new *grands ensembles* in the peripheral Quartiers Sud-Est neighbourhood, at the south-eastern edge of the city

The decline of the mining sector and gradual closure of local pits began in the 1940s, and cost the city 25,000 jobs over 30 years.[253] The bicycle and ribbon industries were also in decline, while multiple post-war efforts to salvage the city's steel and metalwork firms by restructuring failed to prevent thousands more job losses.[254] Municipal governments relied on the national government to intervene.

The government instigated the further concentration, rationalisation and specialisation of industrial production, and nationalised the coal mines in 1946. The state-mandated reorganisation of Saint-Étienne's economy consolidated its industries into a dozen large companies.[255]

The French government then singled out Saint-Étienne and neighbour cities Lyon and Grenoble as a 'metropolitan growth centre' (*métropole d'équilibre*), a priority development area given grants, tax breaks and low-interest loans to attract investment. This created 9,000 jobs between 1968 and 1975.[256] The related 'regional capital' programme also funded infrastructure projects to increase Saint-Étienne's connectivity, including a new motorway. It subsidised the clean-up of the city's grimy buildings, and construction of the first local university, the *Université Jean Monnet de Saint-Étienne*, in 1969 to complement Saint-Étienne's three existing research institutions (*grandes écoles*).

CRISIS

In 1973, the local economy entered deep crisis. The first global oil shock, followed by a second in 1979, caused rising energy costs, a sharp decline in consumption and a major international recession. Combined with intense competition from emerging overseas manufacturers, this dealt a heavy blow to the local production industries. Over the next two decades, the city's 12 major firms, each of which had employed several thousand workers, shrank dramatically or collapsed. This included the steel and mechanical engineering giant Creusot-Loire, with the loss of 10,000 jobs. While 25,000 of Saint-Étienne's industrial jobs had been lost with the closure of the coal mines in the 1950s and 1960s, a further 25,000 jobs (45 per cent of all jobs in the urban area) were lost between 1975 and 1990, and 9,000 more disappeared by 1994.[257] In all, half the city's industrial jobs disappeared (see Figure 11.5). As conditions and opportunities worsened, population decline set in, with many middle-class households moving out to surrounding suburbs, weakening the municipality's tax base and concentrating lower-income households in the central city (see Figure 11.6)

The 1970s saw several attempts at formulating an urban masterplan to address the city's chronic urban problems, each undermined by disputes between the 40-plus municipalities in the metropolitan area.[258] High unemployment led to social unrest. The local communist party won in the municipal elections of 1977 on a platform of rescuing the city's flagship firm Manufrance, and its 4,000 jobs (see Figure 11.7).[259]

The communist municipality's reaction to the economic crisis was to look to the state to formulate a national economic plan. They adopted a populist, short-term defensive strategy of financial aid to the city's struggling big employers,

Figure 11.7: Contemporary cartoon illustrating the bankruptcy of Manufrance

Figure 11.5: Private sector jobs in the Saint-Étienne region, 1977–2001

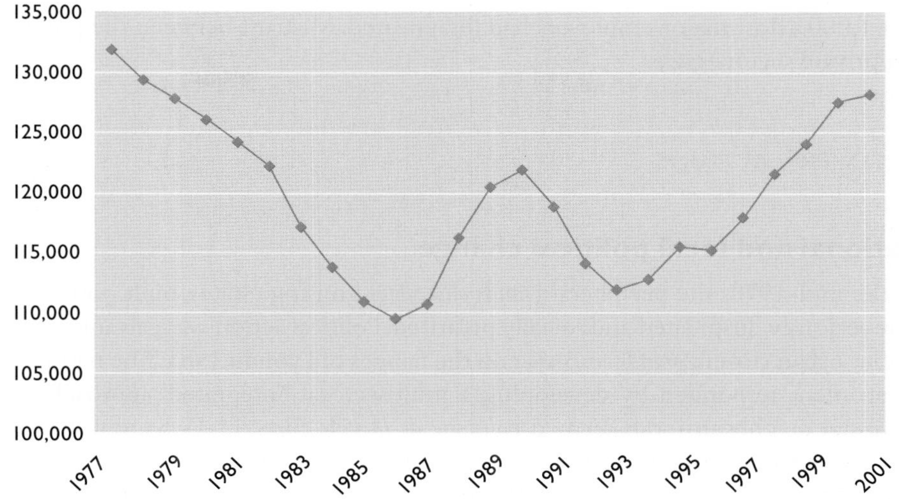

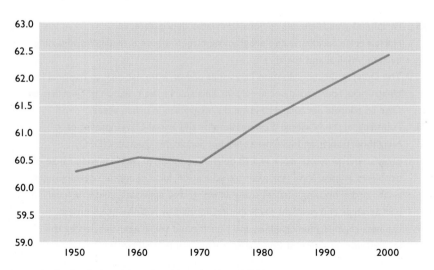

Note: ASSEDIC only records salaried employment, excluding self-employed workers. Saint-Étienne region is defined here in socioeconomic (not administrative) terms, and includes 41 communes.

Sources: ASSEDIC; Saint-Étienne Métropole

Figure 11.6: Percentage of Saint-Étienne's metropolitan area residents living in the suburbs surrounding the core city, 1950–2000

Source: Author's calculation, based on Moriconi-Ebrard (2000)

particularly Manufrance, while failing to create a forward-looking local economic development strategy.[260] By the early 1990s, no local firm had a workforce of over 1,000. Most major employers had disappeared. Mistrust between the public and private sectors grew.

RECOVERY ACTIONS

National and local political change

By the mid-1970s the peripheral *grands ensembles* housing estates, built post-war, were seriously dilapidated and socially polarised. Political action was galvanised by serious urban riots in *grands ensembles* on the fringes of Lyon in 1981. The national government responded by developing a multisectoral 'integrated' approach to distressed neighbourhoods termed *politique de la ville* (Box 11.1). Saint-Étienne became a primary target of these policies.

On the economic front, François Mittérand's socialist government broke with its interventionist *dirigiste* policy and embarked on a programme of liberal reform and decentralisation, beginning with the 'policy of economic rigour' (*politique de rigueur*). This cut aid to declining firms, and focused investment instead on economic restructuring.

Box 11.1: Key dates in France's renewed focus on urban issues (*politique de la ville*)

1970–75	Peripheral *grands ensembles* housing estates depopulate
1977	*Habitat et Vie Sociale*: rescue programme targeting *grands ensembles*, investing in both physical and social
1982	The Deferre Decentralisation Laws shift power from national to regional level
1981	Urban riots spur broad social reform. This sparks the creation of *Quartiers en Crise* to address social and physical disintegration in urban areas
1982–83	Founding of the National Commission for the Social Development of Neighbourhoods, and its *Développement Sociale des Quartiers* (DSQ) programme: projects work in 148 neighbourhoods to tackle a wide range of problems at local level (for example education, local economic development, public order, housing, justice) using an integrated approach involving local partnerships and resident participation, funded by national government, the new regions, municipalities and housing and social agencies, led by the local mayor. Creation of *Zones d'Éducation Prioritaires* (Priority Education Zones), which boost state funding for education in over 7,000 schools in disadvantaged neighbourhoods
1988	Founding of the *Délégation Interministérielle à la Ville* (Interministerial Delegation for Cities) to amalgamate the National Commission (above)

and the 18 ministries involved in tackling urban and social issues, while combining their funding programmes into a single pot. Targets a total of 480 neighbourhoods

1990–99   *Contrats de Ville* (city contracts): five-year 'contracts' between national and municipal government for urban development programmes that integrate social and economic action, now targeting the wider urban agglomeration

1990   Further urban riots erupt across France

1990   The *Ministère de la Ville* (Ministry for Cities) is created to work against 'exclusion' of all kinds, by developing a strategy to target physical, social, economic and educational issues in an integrated way

1990   *Grands Projets Urbains* (GPU) (major urban projects): largely physical projects targeting 14 particularly deprived urban neighbourhoods

1992   The Law for the Territorial Administration of the Republic encourages metropolitan areas to form intermunicipal communities

1996–2001 *Pacte de Relance pour la Ville* (Pact to Relaunch Cities): five-year programme emphasising economic development as part of the city contracts, and creating 'priority zones' in deprived neighbourhoods including 750 low-tax *zones urbaines sensibles* (fragile urban zones), 350 low-tax *zones de redynamisation urbaine* (urban redynamisation zones) and 44 tax-free *zones franches urbaines* (urban-free zones), where businesses benefit from tax exemptions when 30 per cent of their workforce is drawn from the neighbourhood

1999   The Chevènement Law encourages intermunicipal cooperation and devolves responsibility for key policy areas, including *politique de la ville*, to the intermunicipal communities

2000   The Law for Solidarity and Urban Renewal (SRU) develops strategic, integrated local management of urban regeneration; stipulates that every town with over 5,000 residents must provide at least 20 per cent social housing; institutes a 10-year city-region planning document, the *Schéma de Cohérence Térritoriale* (SCoT)

2000–06   *Contrats de Ville* (city contracts) extended for seven years, now covering 1,300 neighbourhoods (6 million residents, 10 per cent of the French population) and focused at metropolitan level. Now the sole envelope for urban policy

2000   *Grands Projets de Ville* (major city projects): now targeting 50 urban neighbourhoods with increased funding, within the *Contrat de Ville* framework

2003   The Borloo Law refocuses *politique de la ville* and aims for a complete restructuring using demolition and mixed-use rebuild to 'wipe out urban ghettos'. Launches a five-year renewal programme in 751 ZUSs which subsumes the *Grand Projets* programme, and creates the *Agence Nationale pour la Rénovation Urbaine* (ANRU) in 530 neighbourhoods

2005   Urban riots erupt again across France

Sources: Power (2003); Mangen (2004); CIC (2007); EUKN (2007)

The year 1983 marked a turning point for local politics in Saint-Étienne, with the election of a centre-right municipal government headed by a mayor, François Dubanchet, who would remain in office until 1994. He ushered in a new era of recovery strategies that have proven more successful than the communist policy of industrial protection. The first period of reform in Saint-Étienne, from 1983 to 1999, focused on employment and economic development; the second, from 2000, focused on increasing the city's residential attractiveness.

Action on employment and economic development: 1983–1999

The new municipal administration's strategy offered support for small businesses in the form of grants and loans for the creation and development of new and existing businesses. It promoted training programmes to develop skills among the unemployed and improve the skills of existing workers. A national programme of investment in research centres enhanced the city's higher education institutions, lending further support to local business.[261]

In spite of a focus on local initiatives and the strong push towards decentralisation by the state, the national government remained heavily involved in Saint-Étienne (largely at the city's own request), effectively limiting opportunities to tackle local problems collectively at ground level. The new local partnership approach was slow to emerge in Saint-Étienne.

A new 'real estate policy' to attract new businesses

New legislation in the 1980s gave municipal authorities more control over local decisions, in a traditionally centralised country. However, they also encouraged fierce competition between the 40-odd municipalities in Saint-Étienne's metropolitan area to attract businesses to locate within their jurisdiction. This was because the laws failed to reform the tax system that allowed municipalities to set their own corporation tax rate (which makes up on average 50 per cent of French municipalities' tax receipts).[262] They also allowed municipalities to sell under-priced municipal real estate to private enterprises. With its oversupply of abandoned industrial sites and its need to compete with neighbouring municipalities to attract enterprises to bolster its weak tax base, Saint-Étienne attracted new businesses by selling them local brownfield sites at discounted prices. The city was still heavily indebted as a result of the previous communist administration's policy of financial aid to major firms, and as a result the policy was implemented using state and EU subsidies.

The short-termist real estate policy attracted a mixture of businesses into a poorly planned low-density landscape of business parks and light industry premises in the former industrial areas of the central city. These soon become the target of fresh regeneration efforts.

Political and institutional changes

The intense competition between municipalities to attract business prevented the formulation of a coherent economic development strategy across Saint-Étienne's metropolitan area, and hampered constructive debate on a strategic approach for the city-region.

Unification of metropolitan municipalities into a single intermunicipal body: 1995

In 1992, the French government introduced a piece of legislation to encourage municipalities in metropolitan areas to consolidate their local plans into intermunicipal cooperative bodies known as communities, using a 20 million franc incentive subsidy.

In 1994, a new centre-right mayor Michel Thiollière came to power. Capitalising on this new legislation, he made it a priority to build a coalition between the municipalities in Saint-Étienne's metropolitan area. He managed to convince 21 of the municipalities to form a community of municipalities (*communauté de communes*), overseen by its own public management body Saint-Étienne Métropole. Saint-Étienne Métropole was able to take charge of certain responsibilities within the remits of economic development and urban planning. However, individual municipalities remained reluctant to pool their local corporation tax for joint projects, and the 1992 law had not given joint decision-making institutions any direct powers.[263]

Intermunicipal body grows and gains fiscal freedoms: 2000

In 1999 the new Chevènement Law encouraged larger intermunicipal bodies by offering fiscal incentives proportional to the number of municipalities uniting, while allowing each intermunicipal body a degree of fiscal autonomy. Importantly, it also set a deadline for federated municipalities to harmonise their corporation tax rates.

In 2000, in response to the new legislation, 43 municipalities in the Saint-Étienne metropolitan area united to form a larger intermunicipal body known as the Agglomeration Community (*Communauté d'Agglomération*), totalling 390,000 residents. The subsidies awarded were what made the unification project worthwhile for each municipality. The mayor of Saint-Étienne became president of this important new body. Further key responsibilities, including economic development, housing and transport, were then devolved to the Agglomeration Community's management body Saint-Étienne Métropole (see Box 11.2). Saint-Étienne Métropole also has increased resources to finance its work, including the harmonised corporation tax from each municipality (see Box 11.3).

The harmonisation of corporation taxes across Saint-Étienne's metropolitan area has created a new atmosphere of cooperation between municipalities in the Agglomeration Community, enabling a more forward-thinking and collective

Box 11.2: Policy competences within which key responsibilities were devolved to the Agglomeration Community's management body, Saint-Étienne Métropole, in 2000

1   Urban planning
2   Economic development
3   Integrated neighbourhood renewal (*politique de la ville*)
4   Housing projects (*équilibre de l'habitat*)
5   Public road system
6   Environment and quality of life
7   Cultural and sporting infrastructure projects
8   Agricultural development
9   Sustainable development
10   Tourism
11   Developing a common identity for the Agglomeration Community around the notion of 'design'
12   Protecting and enhancing the natural environment
13   Developing new higher education policies
14   Support for sporting and cultural events of national and international importance
15   ICT
16   Signing agreements with other intermunicipal bodies or public establishments

Note: The Chevènement Law states that an Agglomeration Community must take on four obligatory competences (see 1—4 above), at least three optional competences (see 5—7), and some additional facultative competences (see 8—16).
For more details, visit www.agglo-st-etienne.fr

Source: Saint-Étienne Métropole (2004)

Box 11.3: Saint-Étienne Métropole's budget and resources, headline figures, 2007

Overall budget: €304.9 million
Spending budget: €211.5 million
Spending budget devolved to municipalities: €111.3 million
Spending budget for Agglomeration Community: €100.2 million
Overall spending resources: €226.8 million
Contributions from communes: €200.7 million (of which the business tax makes up 70 per cent)
Contribution from the state: €10.3 million
Other receipts: €15.8 million

Source: Saint-Étienne Métropole website (www.agglo-st-etienne.fr)

development strategy to emerge. This new strategy focused primarily not on economic development, but on making the city a more attractive place to live.

Action on residential appeal: 2000 to the present

The 1999 Census results revealed that the city had lost 20 per cent of its population (25,000 inhabitants) in just two decades.[264] This statistic shocked local actors into recognising that the employment-oriented recovery strategy was failing to stem population loss. Additionally, the census showed many of the out-movers were highly skilled executives, often with families. Sprawl was becoming a major problem. This left the city with high concentrations of poverty and unemployment, and a diminished tax base.[265] The central plank of the new strategy would be to increase the residential appeal of Saint-Étienne in order to attract middle-class professional families back to the city.

Developing the strategy

The most pressing task was providing attractive housing, in a pleasant urban environment, with well-cared-for public spaces and leisure options. Saint-Étienne was saddled with a reputation as a grey, unfashionable working-class city, so physical regeneration projects would become 'lighthouses' for the city's new image as an avant-garde cultural metropolis, differentiating Saint-Étienne from other similar cities. Internationally renowned architects were invited to design its flagship architectural projects including Norman Foster (Zénith concert stadium), Finn Geipel (Design Village) and Fumihiko Maki (part of the Châteaucreux business district). Saint-Étienne's history of creating products ranging from bicycles and armaments to lace had already given rise to the renowned School of Fine Art and its successful Design Biennale event which brings international designers to the city. The mayor chose 'design' as the theme that would link the various recovery projects and become a byword for the city.

The resources to implement this ambitious strategy were found through the creation of strategic local and national alliances, joining forces with neighbouring municipalities and convincing the state to help the city as compensation for its historic contribution to the country's wealth. The mayor became the key actor in forging these alliances.

The mayor's status on the national stage was boosted by his appointment as senator for the Loire Region. He argued that a burgeoning Saint-Étienne in its orbit would contribute to Lyon's success, while a struggling Saint-Étienne would create a socioeconomic drag that could become Lyon's Achilles heel.[266] The National government responded positively, signing several major new funding agreements (see Box 11.4).

Box 11.4: Recovery timeline

1983	Centre-right mayor Dubanchet takes over from Communist administration
1992	Urban masterplan to regenerate the city centre (coordinated by architect Ricardo Boffil)
1994	Centre-right Thiollière becomes mayor
1995	Community of Communes created; first intermunicipal body
1997	Programme to redesign 100 public spaces with the help of local art and architecture students
1998	Public land recycling agency EPORA founded
	First Design Biennale
	City plays host to several World Cup matches
2000	Community of Communes extended to become Agglomeration Community, containing 43 communes and with more powers; harmonisation of business tax
	Contrat de Ville (city contract) signed, for a six-year period
2001	Major city project (*Grand Projets*) agreement for housing renewal programme in four areas
	Mayor Thiollière re-elected with strong mandate; also elected senator of the Republic and president of the Agglomeration Community
2003	City creates an urban renewal directorate to ensure harmonisation with the housing renewal programme
2004	Start of a series of major renewal projects that will see €1 billion invested over five years
2005	*Agence Nationale pour la Rénovation Urbaine* (National Agency for Urban Renovation) (ANRU) agreement, expanding the *Grands Projets* housing projects into area-based regeneration projects in four areas. Total budget: around €300 million
2006	Second tramline opens
	EPASE city regeneration agency created
	Urban and social cohesion contract (CUCS) signed, for a six-year period

Developing links with Lyon

Saint-Étienne's residential appeal strategy rests largely on its relationship with Lyon, only 60km away, with which Saint-Étienne has traditionally competed. Since 2000 cooperation between the Agglomeration Community and Lyon's much larger Urban Community of 1.3 million inhabitants has been slowly increasing.[267] Closer links with Lyon should encourage more households and businesses to take advantage of Saint-Étienne's much cheaper property and growing attractions.

Improving connectivity between Lyon and Saint-Étienne is a critical component of the residential appeal strategy. Regional and national authorities have cooperated to increase the frequency of inter-city train services to every 20 minutes (current journey time is just under one hour), and to upgrade the stations at both ends of the route. The current motorway link is heavily congested and proposals for a new motorway link (the A45) are hotly debated.

Housing renewal

Upgrading Saint-Étienne's housing is the other main strand of the residential appeal strategy. The city suffers from poor housing, not only in the peripheral *grands ensembles* estates but also in the inner city, where private rents are often lower than social housing rents due to the very poor conditions. The city centre neighbourhood of Tarantaize, for example, had rents as low as €100 per month in 2007 for a small flat with no running water or amenities. By 1999, vacancy rates in the city had risen to over 11 per cent[268] creating a strong case for major investment. The cornerstone of this activity is an ambitious state-funded urban renewal (*rénovation urbaine*) effort involving the comprehensive regeneration of four deprived neighbourhoods, two in the city centre and two on the periphery (see Figures 11.8 and 11.9).

In 2001, the municipality won bids to have these four neighbourhoods included in the *Grands Projets de Ville* national housing regeneration programme, with increased investment. In 2005, this programme was taken over, with significantly increased investment, by the newly formed National Agency for Urban Renovation (*Agence Nationale pour la Rénovation Urbaine*, ANRU). The original investment was tripled to approximately €300 million. By 2011 the ANRU housing renewal programme aims to:

Figure 11.8: Map of the four low-income housing neighbourhoods being regenerated as part of the ANRU programme

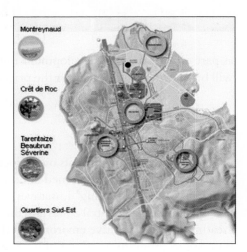

- build or renovate 700 social rented and 450 private dwellings
- demolish 1,070 dwellings (600 social rented, the rest private)
- rehouse 750 households.[269]

The main focus of the programme is on housing, but the extra funding will be spent on upgrading the public realm and improving local infrastructure such as schools and sports facilities in each of the four neighbourhoods. A small amount is reserved for community support and social development programmes.

In addition, the municipality is integrating new housing developments into several of the new business and cluster districts it is creating throughout the city

Figure 11.9: Housing in the central Tarantaize-Beaubrun-Séverine neighbourhood

as part of its economic development initiative (see below). Most new dwellings will be apartments, destined for the private market (see Figures 11.10 and 11.11).

Quality of life

The municipality is running its own programme of large-scale upgrading projects, which have already transformed the city's major central squares. Sensitive re-landscaping and 'greening' initiatives across the city, alongside the increasing pedestrianisation of central zones and the gradual introduction of bicycle lanes, are creating a more attractive environment. The city has also run a widely acclaimed, innovative programme, the Public Spaces Workshop (*l'Atelier Espace Public*), engaging young artists, architects and designers at its Schools of Fine Arts and Architecture to help regenerate and redesign 130 small public spaces across the city, an idea borrowed from Barcelona (Figure 11.12). Each space cost between €30,000 and €250,000.[270]

Figure 11.10: Newly constructed apartment blocks (left) on the Design Village site (right)

Figure 11.11: The new apartments, foreground, and Design Village (architect's impression)

Figure 11.12: Placette Lebon, redesigned by local architecture student Laëtitia Belala

A second tramline, now in operation, is another flagship recovery project. It links the main train station to the town centre, reducing traffic in the city centre. Some of the project's €75 million budget was also spent on upgrading public spaces and facades along its route.

Work is also being done to improve the city's cultural appeal, mainly through the construction of new infrastructure. Two major new music venues, including a new contemporary music centre (*Salle de Musiques Actuelles*) equipped with high-tech studios and performance spaces, are being built on a brownfield site alongside the Guichard sports stadium, home of the local football team, to improve quality of life and to attract new residents.

The Zénith, a 7,000-seat concert stadium designed by Norman Foster, is another of Saint-Étienne's flagship projects, promoting a post-industrial image for the city (see Figure 11.13). Saint-Étienne Métropole has also coordinated a €6 million restoration of Le Corbusier's preserved buildings in nearby Firminy, developing them as a tourist attraction for the metropolitan area.

The city's museums are also part of its cultural package. Its Museum of Modern Art houses France's second largest collection of contemporary art and attracts around 80,000 visitors a year, while the popular Museum of Mining and Museum of Art and Industry attract similar numbers. To promote its new image as a cultural centre, Saint-Étienne has put itself forward as a candidate to become the European Capital of Culture in 2013.

Figure 11.13: The Zénith concert stadium (architect's impression)

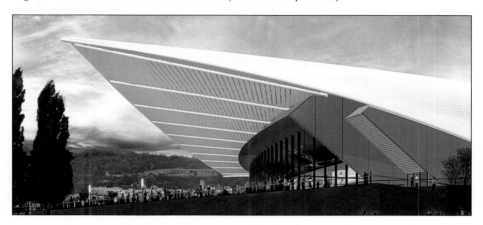

Cluster site creation

The success of the city's residential appeal policy still ultimately rests on the development of new economic activities. The French government operates a national 'cluster policy' which aims to increase collaboration between university, public and private sector researchers and industry in specific internationally competitive sectors. There are 71 such funded clusters in France.[271] Two of Saint-Étienne's sectors have been selected for support and labelled 'clusters': mechanics cluster (which represents around 30 per cent of local businesses and 40 per cent of industrial jobs);[272] and sports and leisure equipment (which involves 10–15,000 employees in the Rhône-Alpes region).[273] Local SMEs in the optics and textiles sectors are also linked into Grenoble's and Lyon's nationally supported clusters for these sectors.

Mayor Thiollière's administration has chosen 'design' as a cross-cutting theme to unite Saint-Étienne's regeneration projects, and to build on the city's historic reputation as a centre of manufacturing design. The city's Design Biennale in 2006, organised by its School of Fine Arts, drew over 170,000 international visitors to the city. A new 'Design Village' cluster site will be located on the site of the famous Imperial Arms Factory, whose restored buildings will house new artist studios and workshops alongside teaching and exhibition spaces (see Figure 11.14). The School of Fine Arts is to move into a rehabilitated building on the site. The Design Village's new housing will bring mixed-use vitality to the 18-hectare brownfield site that had represented Saint-Étienne's industrial decline.

Figure 11.14: Design Village cluster site (architect's impression)

An optics cluster site for research and enterprise was pioneered by the local optics firm Thalès Angénieux, inventor of the zoom lens, in conjunction with the local university and the Loire Department. The new 'Optics/Vision' cluster site is expected to house 120 researchers and engineers – including many from private optics firms – alongside 900 students specialising in optics technology research. The School of Optics (*École Supérieur d'Optique*) in Orsay (near Paris) plans to open a new department on site.

A new business services district adjacent to the central Châteaucreux railway station is being built after the municipality incentivised the supermarket chain Casino, founded in Saint-Étienne a century ago, to relocate their headquarters to the city. The municipality offered Casino an attractive brownfield plot at a discounted rate, opposite the Châteaucreux station with its rail connections to Lyon, and the new tramline to the city centre. The development is one of France's largest office construction projects in recent years and will create office space for over 2,000 employees.

This anchor development should encourage other service sector businesses to cluster on this site. The nearby main station should attract companies from Lyon, where office rents are much higher. The new district will cover 60 hectares, and include 400 new homes, shops, a hotel and offices for several municipal departments. The Loire Department's investment of 500km of fibre-optic cable, allowing high-speed broadband connections across Saint-Étienne's urban region (*Sud Loire*), will be an important support for both the residential appeal and the cluster site strategies.[274]

Agencies delivering the strategy

EPORA land recycling agency

In 1998, the problem of large brownfield sites blighting the city led to the creation of a dedicated 'land recycling agency', the *Établissement Public Foncier de l'Ouest du Rhône-Alpes* or EPORA. Its purpose is to reclaim former industrial and urban brownfield sites across the heavily industrialised western Rhône-Alpes region, including Saint-Étienne. It has played a key role in the recovery process by fast-tracking the physical transformation of the city, which had been riddled with brownfield sites that scarred the local landscape. EPORA has subsidised and accelerated the release of reclaimed sites for new development. These sites are sold on to either local authorities at 40 per cent of cost, or directly to private investors, nominally at cost but with discretionary discounts of up to 40 per cent. EU funding from 1994 has been instrumental in financing EPORA's work.

EPASE city regeneration agency

In 2005, the French government also agreed to help accelerate the delivery of the city's regeneration projects, predicted to take 30 years, by backing a dedicated single-purpose public regeneration agency based in the city, the *Établissement*

Public d'Aménagement de Saint-Étienne or EPASE.[275] The exceptional scale of state investment in the city's physical regeneration – €1 billion over the next five years – justified a powerful local agency to provide expertise alongside an advisory and coordinating role.

EPASE has brought together the directors of seven major institutions linked to the regeneration process to form a group known locally as the 'G7' (see Box 11.5). Those involved describe the monthly G7 meetings as the rare occasions on which public actors take off their institutional hats and share their perspectives on Saint-Étienne's recovery process openly and honestly. They identify the informal nature of these meetings as a major advantage as it allows members to discuss strategy and implementation issues as they arise, in a country where bureaucratic conventions makes this very unusual. The G7 stands out as a rare example of cross-sectoral cooperation in Saint-Étienne.

Box 11.5: Key bodies and projects represented in the G7 working group with EPASE as the central organising agency

1 Epures urban planning agency
2 ANRU/GPV housing renewal programme
3 Agglomeration Community
4 Municipality's Urbanism Directorate
5 Infrastructure Department of the Loire Region
6 EPORA land recycling agency
7 School of Architecture

SIGNS OF RECOVERY

The look and feel of France's archetypal industrial city centre has changed remarkably in the last few years. Beneath the visible changes, certain elements of the strategy are bearing fruit, but other issues hampering its success are yet to be tackled.

Property and house prices

Local house prices rose steeply, from an average of €1,570 per m² in mid-2005, to €1,730 per m² in mid-2007.[276] Prices in Lyon (an average of €3,310 per m² in 2007)[277] are starting to push more businesses and households outwards in search of cheaper alternatives, although some are settling in the valleys between the two cities rather than in Saint-Étienne itself.

There is evidence to suggest the city is successfully attracting back suburban residents. Two thirds of the flats on the Design Village site were sold off in a single weekend, mostly to older couples living in the hills around Saint-Étienne. The flats fetched a far higher price than was expected confirming what city officials had hoped – that high-quality new homes in the city centre would attract buyers. It also reaffirms a wider trend towards city living and away from the strong suburbanisation that has affected Saint-Étienne since the 1970s.[278] Reassured by examples such as this and by the state's long-term commitment to the city, major housebuilders, including Nexity, who built the Design Village apartments, now say they see Saint-Étienne as an exciting investment opportunity.[279]

Inward investment and economic development

Inward investment has begun to trickle back into the city since 2003. The Casino chain's decision to relocate its headquarters to Saint-Étienne and IKEA's decision to open a store on the outskirts of the city in 2005, creating 300 jobs, are oft-quoted examples. The city is also attracting international companies in the vehicle components and optics sectors, alongside call centres and retail (see Table 11.1).

Table 11.1: Recent inward investment and job creation, Saint-Étienne municipality

Company	Origin	Activity	Jobs created
IKEA	Sweden	Home furnishings	300
Cheque emplois service universel (CESU)	Saint-Étienne	Care-related services (*services à la personne*)	300
Carrefour Client Services	Paris	Call centre	214
Carlson Wagonlits Travel	Paris	Call centre	180
SEAC	Japan	Car components	170
AxleTech	USA	Components for off-road vehicles	100
JDSU (ex Acterna)	Canada and USA	Broadband test and measurement solutions and optical products	20

Source: Saint-Étienne Métropole (January 2007)

Saint-Étienne's economic landscape, and indeed that of the whole south Loire urban region (510,000 residents) is still characterised by many SMEs, most of which are individual subcontractors dependent on much larger firms for their orders. Given their importance to the local economy, a strategy to build on their expertise and help them adapt to the changing economic environment could pay off[280] (see Figure 11.15).

Private sector spending on research and development is low in the region; the Loire ranked 37th of 46 Departments in spending terms in 2001. Knowledge workers are under-represented, and there are too few links between local universities, SMEs and business.[281] Saint-Étienne currently has 22,000 students in higher education, and student numbers at its nationally renowned *grandes écoles* are growing rapidly; however, the generalist University of Saint-Étienne lost 15 per cent of its students between 1996 and 2002.[282]

Figure 11.15: A mechanics sub-contractors' workshop in the city centre Crêt de Roc neighbourhood; they are making machine components for major firms including Peugeot

The number of jobs in the city recovered from a drop during the mid-1990s, but has dipped again since 2002 (Figure 11.16). Figure 11.17 shows that while industrial jobs have continued to decline across the urban region, the service sector is growing. However, the growth of service jobs in the city has levelled off since

Figure 11.16: Private sector employment, Saint-Étienne municipality, 1979–2005

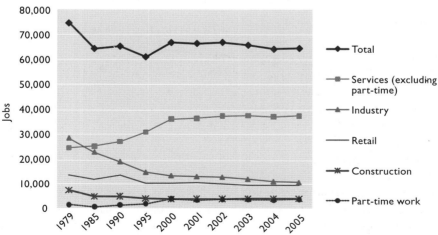

Note: Data intervals are not calibrated.

Sources: ASSEDIC, Saint-Étienne Métropole

Figure 11.17: Sectoral changes in private sector employment, Saint-Étienne urban region

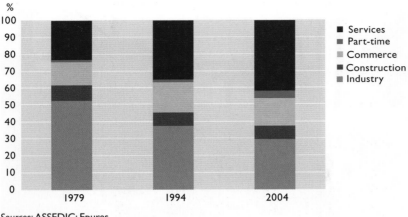

Sources: ASSEDIC; Epures

2001, and most of these jobs are in low-skilled rather than highly skilled services. Meanwhile unemployment in the city's travel-to-work area (96 municipalities, 480,000 residents) is up by one per cent in the five years since 2001, compared to a national increase of just 0.3 per cent over this period, as Figure 11.18 shows. Unemployment worries still dominate local thinking.

Figure 11.18: Unemployment rates, Saint-Étienne travel-to work area and France

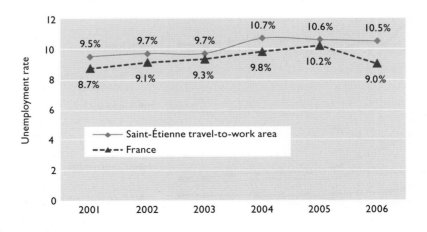

Sources: DRTFEFP, Saint-Étienne Métropole

Population loss and smart growth: the SCoT

Statisticians' estimates indicate that the municipality continues to lose population albeit more slowly, declining from 180,210 in 1999 to 175,700 in 2005 (see Figure 11.19).[283] Between 1990 and 1999, Saint-Étienne's agglomeration had lost 55,000 residents, but gained 31,000 new ones; approximately half of these out-movers bought property in the city's suburban areas.[284]

Figure 11.19: Population and migration rates, Saint-Étienne municipality, 1968–2005

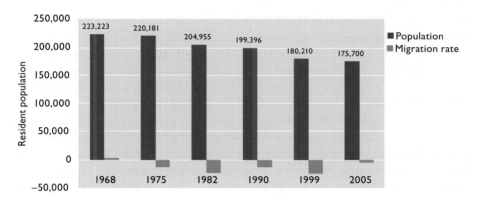

Note: Data intervals are not calibrated; the 2005 figure is an INSEE estimate.
Source: INSEE

To counter the trend toward further suburbanisation a 10-year Framework for Regional Coherence (*Schéma de Cohérence Térritoriale*), known as the SCoT, has been formulated by the city's urban planning agency, encouraged by the national Law for Solidarity and Urban Renewal of 2000.[285] The SCoT is a voluntary agreement covering the whole of Saint-Étienne's urban region, and the city's mayor is particularly proud of the political achievement involved in convincing 117 municipalities (with 510,000 residents) to join the coalition which he hopes will accept the central city's SCoT plan, subject to a vote, and adhere to its ambition of stopping sprawl building. The SCoT 10-year development plan will, if accepted by the mayors of its 117 municipalities, mark a new era of longer-term and more sustainable urban planning which will protect the natural environment surrounding the city, one of its key quality-of-life assets, while concentrating effort in existing communities.

In 2002, Saint-Étienne Agglomeration Community became a member of the Lyon Urban Region (*Région Urbaine de Lyon* or RUL) group, an informal association of municipalities, intermunicipal bodies and Departments that serves as a forum for debate among local politicians, focused on Lyon's metropolitan region.[286]

Social cohesion

Youth unemployment in Saint-Étienne was almost 30 per cent in 1999, and 58 per cent of the registered unemployed have been on benefits long term.[287] The low skill and qualification levels of this former industrial city are possibly its biggest social challenge. Social disadvantage is heavily concentrated in the city's social housing areas, which are home to many of Saint-Étienne's immigrant communities from North Africa.[288] In 1990, 16 per cent of Saint-Étienne's population was classed as foreign, with people of North African descent making up 64 per cent of this total (20,620 people).[289] Inter-ethnic tensions were heightened with the publication of an audit report confirming that the city's main social housing company had intentionally concentrated households of North African origin in specific zones of its housing stock.[290] During France's widespread riots of November 2005, violence erupted in Saint-Étienne's peripheral estates; several cars, nine trucks and two schools were set alight, and the city's transport network was shut down when a Molotov cocktail was lobbed into a bus.[291]

Community-based neighbourhood associations do impressive work at grassroots level, but funding for such community development activities has become tighter in recent years, and the mayor admits that the heavy cost of the physical renewal projects has led to rising debts and less money for other city activities and services.

Some local residents are critical of the city's regeneration projects, which attract middle-class outsiders, saying they create new jobs that are 'not for us'. French urban renewal projects are often criticised because they 'suffer from a lack of consideration concerning [...] social development [and] the involvement of the inhabitants'.[292] The municipality is beginning to see the value of involving residents, but the culture of participation among politicians and civil servants is still in its infancy. Within the ANRU neighbourhoods' regeneration programme, a residents' committee representing all four areas is gradually gaining recognition. However, participation and cohesion, particularly between minority ethnic and traditional French communities, remain extremely sensitive and unresolved issues.

Conclusion

Years of substantial funding and commitment from the state have diversified Saint-Étienne's economy. The city's culture and design-oriented recovery programme involving the promotion of sectors through 'cluster sites' matches the changing global economic landscape, but it remains to be seen whether the chosen sectors, and the strategy of providing physical sites, will actually deliver the depth of transformation required. The future of the local economy, given the concentration of industrial SMEs, is still highly dependent on the fortunes of French industry in the domains of steel, transport, aeronautics, chemicals and medical instruments. Saint-Étienne's regeneration effort is concentrated largely in flagship physical projects, which change the image of the city but are less effective tools for tackling the entrenched economic and social problems that are the inevitable legacy of industrial decline. Turning these problems into an opportunity is a critical challenge. With a new mayor and with the city facing serious funding shortages it is likely that there will be significant changes in the way Saint-Étienne will progress from here.

Figure 11.20: Timeline of important events in Saint-Étienne since 1977

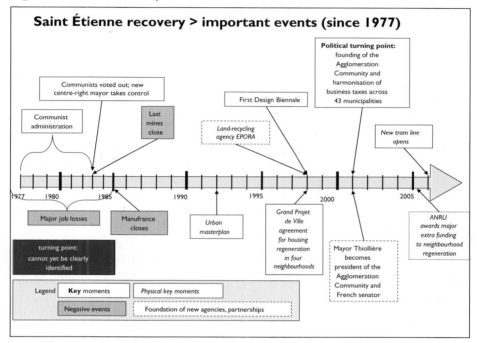

Part Three
Towards a recovery framework

TWELVE

Measuring the recovery of weak market cities

From the 1970s onwards the European cities covered by this study have all suffered from multiple problems caused by profound economic restructuring. The seven cities – Belfast, Bilbao, Bremen, Leipzig, Saint-Étienne, Sheffield and Torino – all showed signs of recovery from decline, although the level of recovery varied considerably between them. The impact of industrial decline and its historic trajectory have been described in detail in the case study chapters of this book in Part Two.

Urban recovery can be defined as progress in overcoming the problems associated with economic restructuring and industrial decline, such as population loss, job losses, urban decay and increasing social deprivation. Urban recovery is the outcome of a complex interaction of different factors. The following changes can be found in cities that are successfully recovering:

- overcoming their structural problems;
- adapting to the requirements of changing political and economic conditions;
- alleviating the worst consequences of the crisis;
- implementing successful regeneration strategies;
- improving the overall quality of life;
- creating a path towards a sustainable future.

A main aim of our research was to establish whether the recovery in selected cities was real and if it could be supported by measurable evidence. Alongside establishing whether recovery is actually taking place and how dynamic it is, a second aim was to understand how it was achieved. By examining the specific responses to the crisis, we gained insight into recovery activities, in the hope that they could be useful to other cities with similar problems. In this chapter we set out to pull together the many strands of evidence collected, both quantitative and qualitative, both observed and documented, to measure as clearly as we can progress under certain leading themes, relating to the performance of cities.[1] The evidence is valid up to the end of 2008, and therefore does not take into account the big financial and economic changes unleashed during 2008. However, most of the indicators, except the economic ones, are rather slow moving and evolve over decades. Therefore we believe that they capture real changes that lay the ground for quite fundamental new directions.

There is already a substantial body of literature dealing with the process of urban regeneration and related issues, but our aim is to provide additional evidence and insight into this complex process of change. In an attempt to measure recovery from the industrial urban crisis with the help of international experts we devised a method for assessing change. This recovery framework enables us to evaluate the performance of each of the seven cities over time, in comparison with its peers. The framework offers other cities a method for approaching their specific problems. It provides some guidance, based on experience, for actions that may help. Ideas about what a successful recovery might look like may differ between different places; the concept of what is understood by recovery must therefore be locally grounded while learning from experience and practice elsewhere. One major limitation on this framework for recovery is the paucity of reliable environmental data at city level. The problem applies across European cities in general.[2] Given the underlying importance of energy, waste, materials, water, biodiversity and other environmental limits facing the cities, we return to environmental sustainability in the concluding section of the book, in order to place the progress of these cities in the context of climate change and resource limits, which pose by far the most serious threats to the future of cities within a constrained planet.[3]

Recovery framework

The framework covers a range of major themes whose prevalence we have established in our research. We briefly explain the significance of each theme as a direct measure of progress or decline or as an underlying factor in recovery.

Measures that quantify changes in city performance:

- *Population:* there is broad consensus that population is an important indicator to measure the development of cities or regions because it usually reflects their economic viability, development of employment and other factors such as quality of life. In addition, regional migration patterns can reveal the significance of suburbanisation in the metropolitan area.
- *Employment linked to social well-being:* employment is another key indicator. It is directly related to economic prosperity alongside population development, social trends and general well-being.[4] Changes in employment help to establish whether a region is successful in keeping and attracting economic activities. The development of the unemployment rate is another useful indicator to measure the strength of the regional/local labour market and related concerns over social well-being.
- *Economic performance:* indicators measuring the economic performance of a city/ region such as levels of employment, types of job, GDP and GVA are widely used to evaluate overall development.[5]

Measures underpinning the recovery potential of ex-industrial cities, using a mix of quantitative and more qualitative evidence

- *Education:* the level of education in a city/region is a key indicator for the assessment of future potential for development because (a) businesses locate and economic activities emerge where they find a sufficiently educated and skilled workforce; and (b) educational levels also influence socioeconomic well-being.
- *Environmental sustainability:* environmental problems have become more widely accepted as determining how forward-looking a city and region are and whether there is a vision for a sustainable future. In many cases local data availability on indicators such as a city's ecological footprint or CO_2 emissions is still limited, making this measure difficult to assess. Transport will be treated as a sub-theme of sustainability, using journeys to work by car, as the cities with the best public transport networks tend to have the lowest percentage of journeys by car.
- *Urban regeneration:* physical regeneration is a visible carrier of messages symbolising change and progress. It applies to city centres, and inner and outer neighbourhoods. It improves the image of a place and creates confidence in the future of a city for investors and inhabitants alike.
- *New-style governance:* in order to work within fiscal constraints and to meet the challenges of increased competition for business, jobs, population, among other things, local government structures often need to remodel their ways of working.
- *Quality of life:* recent studies often try to include some measures of quality of life. The importance of this for a city or region is likely to rise in the future as cities make efforts in this regard to attract people and businesses. However, the lack of adequate data and limitations on the comparability still limit the use of this factor.

Whenever possible, we use quantitative measures, but many aspects of progress towards recovery are observable and demonstrable, but hard to measure precisely. We make clear within the framework the distinction between quantitative and qualitative measures.

Structuring the framework for measuring recovery

We divided the development of the framework into two parts, a quantitative and qualitative set of measures. Using the two sets of measures we hoped to identify common patterns of urban recovery in cities across Europe. The indicators were selected to illustrate and provide evidence for the themes outlined above. The selection of indicators was guided by the experiences of other studies of urban regeneration, by discussions with collaborators within cities and by the availability of data.

Urban experts at our City Reformers Group workshops and during our visits, as well as from our project advisory group, contributed to the development of the framework. Many other indicators were proposed. Although some of them would have added considerable value to the analysis, we were not able to use all of these due to problems in establishing comparable data for a cross–European study over time. This affected particularly the themes *urban regeneration, new-style governance* and *quality of life*.

Part 1: *Quantitive*

This part consists of a set of themes and indicators based on quantitative information and uses statistical data to measure whether a city is recovering from steep industrial decline. We identify key indicators to do this. The information we use came from official city, regional, national and EU statistical offices. Table 12.1 summarises the quantitative indicators used.

Table 12.1: Quantitative indicators used

No	Theme	Indicator
1	Population	Population change (%)[a]
2		Population change (%)[a]
3		Population change (%)[a]
4	Employment	Unemployment change (%)[a]
5	(social)	Unemployment change (%)[a]
6		Employment rate versus national average (=100)[b]
7		Variation of unemployment rates between neighbourhoods within cities (%)[c]
8	Education	Qualified residents (%)[b]
9		Population with tertiary education (%)[c]
10	Economic performance	Change in employment (number of jobs) (%)[d]
11		Change in GDP/capita (PPP) (%)[e]
12		GDP/capita versus national average (=100) (PPP)[d]
13	Environment (sustainability)	Journeys to work by car (%)[c]
14		Variation between city and suburban growth (%)[f]

Sources and notes:
[a] Statistisches Landesamt Bremen (Bremen); Stadt Leipzig, Statistisches Landesamt Sachsen (Leipzig); ONS (Sheffield); NISRA (Belfast); Eustat (Bilbao); ISTAT (Torino); INSEE (Saint-Étienne)
[b] EC (2007)
[c] EC/Directorate-General for Regional Policy (2005); for Bilbao: Lan Ekintza-Bilbao Ayuntamiento (2005), Eustat
[d] See (f); in addition: Industrie- und Handelskammer Leipzig (Leipzig); BAW Institut für regionale Wirtschaftsforschung (Bremen); ONS-Nomis (Sheffield); DETI (Belfast); Plaza 2006 (Bilbao)
[e] Eurostat
[f] Where not available for the exact date, data was used from next best date.

Themes where data was not available or was unclear were not included in Part 1, but are included in Part 2 of the framework (see below). Some indicators that would be helpful could not be included in Part 1 because of inadequate or inconsistent evidence. The following examples show indicators we could not use in Part 1:

- *Export activity:* measuring the economic sectors that are predominantly producing for consumption outside of the city, region or country.
- *Educational levels:* measuring high school achievements is difficult transnationally at a smaller geographical scale.
- *Segregation:* measuring levels of spatial segregation and integration of social and ethnic groups can reveal positive or negative conditions for the development of an inclusive city with low spatial inequalities, but it is hard to capture from available evidence because inequality and minority concentrations are measured very differently. It is also a very contentious issue.
- *Emissions of carbon dioxide and other greenhouse gases:* with rising concerns for the environment, this is becoming a major factor determining quality of life but it is impossible to capture at city level for most cities.

Where possible we used city-level data. Where this was not possible we used regional data, mostly from Eurostat or the Urban Audit, both EU-run data collection research centres collaborating with all member countries. The Urban Audit collects information at city and metropolitan level on over 300 cities. In many cases the metropolitan area or the functional urban region are the most suitable geographic units to compare evidence but their value is often limited by incomplete data. It is therefore complicated to capture the full picture of the city-regional dynamics.

Our work emphasises the importance of a historical perspective for the understanding of European industrial cities throughout the book. In this chapter we use data since 1970 wherever possible. The year 1970 is regularly used as a key reference point, marking the period immediately before the cities entered the phase of decline.

Part 2: Qualitative

National governments and the EU have designed policies specifically aimed at the particular problems faced by post-industrial cities. Funding streams, following on from recovery policies, backed the delivery of many projects. It is not easy to measure the effectiveness of these interventions based only on quantitative data, but nor is it always clear how deep or far reaching the visible but unquantifiable changes are.

In order to understand which particular factors contributed to a turnaround and recovery after decades of decline, it was necessary to explore further sources of information. It became clear that basing the framework exclusively on quantitative data would not explain adequately what was happening. Since the crisis and decline, a whole range of interventions had been tried to support cities in their struggle to overcome decline.

In order to add value to the framework, we decided to include a second part based on qualitative information. The information used for this second set of measures originates from our interviews with urban actors and key experts in the cities, our own observations and a range of secondary sources such as local official publications, independent research and evaluation, recorded statistics, project reports, news coverage and so on.

The first step was to identify policies, actions and tools that were used with the objective of overcoming decline. This created a checklist of recovery actions. The second and more complicated task was to assess the effectiveness of these approaches in the seven cities. The indicators used to measure the strategic responses by the cities, based on more qualitative assessments, were grouped under the main themes already used for the quantitative analysis. Themes not included in Part 1 were added, such as *urban regeneration* and *new governance structures*. Particular attention was given to urban regeneration using seven key indicators. Table 12.2 presents a summary of the indicators used to measure actions under each of the themes in the framework on a more qualitative basis. There is some overlap in

Table 12.2: Indicators of recovery interventions and actions used to make a qualitative assessment of change in the direction of recovery

	Indicators of recovery actions by themes
Population	
1	Strategic response to population losses
Employment (social)	
2	Focus on deprived neighbourhoods
3	Specific skills/qualification initiatives targeting skills mismatches
4	Efforts to integrate ethnic-migrant population
Education	
5	Creating stronger linkages between higher education and local businesses
6	Investment in higher education
Economic performance	
7	Focus on specific economic sectors, e.g. cluster strategy
8	Creation of economic development/inward investment agencies
Urban regeneration (physical)	
9	Investment in high-profile physical projects
10	Investment in/promotion of high-profile events
11	Revitalisation of city centre
12	Regeneration through culture
13	Strengthening of the retail function of the city (centrality)
14	Upgrading of housing
15	Investment in accessibility: long-distance transport infrastructure ('hub functions')
Environment (sustainability)	
16	Investment in public transport
17	Environmental sustainability on the political agenda
18	Actions taken to improve the environment, e.g. land, water, air decontamination
New-style governance	
19	Public administration made more efficient
20	Does the city benefit from devolved powers
21	Coherent strategy guiding the recovery actions (for different tiers of government)
22	Metropolitan-level cooperation

the themes between Part 1 and Part 2. The indicators in Part 2 reflect the policy and practice shifts that underpin the impact of the measures used.

Results

In this section, we look at the results from the quantitative and qualitative assessments.

Part 1: Quantitative assessment

We collected quantitative information for all the indicators shown in Table 12.1. The results between 1970 and 2007 are shown in Table 12.3.

Based on this data, values were attributed to each indicator in each city in order to allow a comparison of their respective performances. This benchmarking approach enables us to rank the cities in relation to their peers. The best and worst results out of the sample were used to establish the range, which was then subdivided into five scores, ranging from 5 as the best or highest to 1 as the lowest or worst. In some cases even a negative performance could receive the highest value if this was still the best performance among the selected cities. An example for this is the indicator, *population development between 1970 and 2007*, which was negative for all cities. This allows us to compare the cities with each other and to identify weaknesses and strengths in their respective performance. Table 12.4 summarises the values we ascribed. Table 12.5 shows the results for each indicator according to this approach in each city.

The overall results of this analysis show the relative ranking of each city in relation to the others in the sample under each main theme. Bilbao is clearly ranked highest on the quantitative measures of recovery, with 56 points. The Basque city is followed by Sheffield (47), Bremen (44) and Torino (43). There is some distance between these four and the remaining three cities: Leipzig and Belfast share fifth position (35) and Saint-Étienne ranks seventh (31).

Figure 12.1 shows the results for each city based on the five quantifiable themes. The vertical axis indicates how many points the cities scored under each of the themes and in total. This helps us to understand particular weaknesses such as the economic performance of Leipzig or population losses in Belfast. It highlights strengths such as economic performance in Bilbao or education in Leipzig within the individual performance of a city.

A detailed analysis of the individual performance of cities can be carried out by theme to gain greater understanding of the measures and their value. We illustrate this using the theme of population. This analysis can be repeated for each of the themes. The first two sections of *Phoenix cities* provide the direct evidence to back our assessment in this chapter.

Table 12.3: Data showing quantitative evidence of change on key indicators

No	Theme	Indicator	Date/period[a]	Cities						
				LEI	BRE	SHE	BEL	BIL	TOR	STE
1	Population	Population change (%)[b]	1970–2007	–14.6	–5.9	–9.1	–35.4	–13.4	–22.9	–20.8
2		Population change (%)[b]	1990–07	–9.0	0.6	–1.5	–8.7	–4.4	–6.4	–11.3
3		Population change (%)[b]	2000–07	2.9	1.3	1.5	–4.0	1.6	0.0	–1.9
4	Employment (social)	Unemployment change (%)[b]	1990–2000	10.1	0.4	–9.5	–7.5	–8.9	–6.2	4.2
5		Unemployment change (%)[b]	2000–2007	1.7	–0.2	–2.8	–0.9	–4.5	–1.8	–4.6
6		Employment rate versus national average (=100)[c]	2001	88.0	95.0	91.0	78.0	n/d[g] (100)	109.0	92.0
7		Variation of unemployment rates between neighbourhoods within cities (%)[d]	2001	10.1	5.7	12.6	15.7	8.1	12.0	20.6
8	Education	Qualified residents (%)[c]	2001	32.3	17.7	20.3	21.6	n/d[g] (20.8)	13.3	19.3
9		Population with tertiary education (%)[d]	2001	24.7	13.4	13.7	13.7	16.9	10.6	13.3
10	Economic performance	Change in employment (number of jobs) (%)[e]	1990–2007	–35.9	–11.0	7.1	9.5	42.4	1.3	4.5
11		Change GDP/capita (PPP) (%)[f]	1995–2004	34.5	38.9	64.9	58.1	69.4	22.6	38
12		GDP/capita versus national average (=100) (PPP)[e]	2001	75	111	76	101	125	121	81
13	Environment (sustainability)	Journeys to work by car (%)[d]	2001	60	51	82	n/d[g] (88)	n/d[g] (56)	58	74
14		Variation between city and suburban growth (%)[a]	1990–2007	2.2	14.9	–0.4	17.7	2.8	12.3	9.7

Sources and notes:
a) Where not available for the exact date, data was used from next-best date.
b) Statistisches Landesamt Bremen (Bremen); Stadt Leipzig, Statistisches Landesamt Sachsen (Leipzig); ONS (Sheffield); NISRA (Belfast); Eustat (Bilbao); ISTAT (Torino); INSEE (Saint-Etienne)
c) EC (2007)
d) EC (2005); for Bilbao: Lan Ekintza-Bilbao Ayuntamiento (2005), Eustat
e) See (a); in addition: Industrie- und Handelskammer Leipzig (Leipzig); BAW Institut für regionale Wirtschaftsforschung (Bremen); ONS-Nomis (Sheffield); DETI (Belfast); Plaza 2006 (Bilbao)
f) Eurostat
g) Where no data was available, the next largest geographical unit was used, e.g. provincial level for Bilbao.

Table 12.4: Values ascribed to each indicator, showing the range from best to worst (based on data in Table 12.3)

No	Theme	Indicator	Date/period	Values				
				5	4	3	2	1
1	Population	Population change (%)	1970–2007	0 to -5	-5 to -10	-10 to -20	-20 to -30	< -30
2		Population change (%)	1990–2007	1 to 5	-1 to 1	-1 to -5	-5 to -10	< -10
3		Population change (%)	2000–07	> 5	1 to 5	-1 to 1	-1 to -5	< -10
4	Employment	Unemployment change (%)	1990–2000	< -5	-1 to -5	-1 to 1	1 to 5	> 5
5		Unemployment change (%)	2000–07	> -5	-1 to -5	-1 to 1	1 to 5	> 5
6		Employment rate versus national average (=100)	2001	> 120	105 to 120	95 to 105	80 to 95	< 80
7		Variation of unemployment (intra-urban) (%)	2001	< 5	5 to 10	10 to 15	15 to 20	> 20
8	Education	Qualified residents (%)	2001	> 30	20 to 30	15 to 20	10 to 15	< 10
9		Population with tertiary education (%)	2001	> 30	20 to 30	15 to 20	10 to 15	< 10
10	Economic performance	Change in employment (number of jobs) (%)	1990–2007	> 15	5 to 15	-5 to 5	-5 to -15	< -15
11		Change in GDP/capita (PPP) (%)	1995–2004	> 60	50 to 60	40 to 50	30 to 40	< 30
12		GDP/capita versus national average (=100) (PPP)	2001	> 120	105 to 120	95 to 105	80 to 95	< 80
13	Environment	Journeys to work by car (%)	2001	< 50	50 to 60	60 to 70	70 to 80	> 80
14		Variation city and suburban growth (%)	1990–2007	< 0	0 to 5	5 to 10	10 to 15	> 15

Table 12.5: Results of the quantitative assessment of recovery (Part 1) where 5 is highest and 1 is lowest value

No	Indicator	Date/period	Cities						
			LEI	BRE	SHE	BEL	BIL	TOR	STE
1	Population change (%)	1970–2007	3	4	4	1	3	2	2
2	Population change (%)	1990–2007	2	4	3	2	3	3	1
3	Population change (%)	2000–07	2	4	4	2	4	3	2
Population (total)			*7*	*12*	*11*	*5*	*10*	*8*	*5*
4	Unemployment change (%)	1990–2000	1	3	5	5	5	5	2
5	Unemployment change (%)	2000–07	2	3	4	3	4	4	4
6	Employment rate versus national average (=100)	2001	2	3	2	1	3	4	2
7	Variation of unemployment rates between neighbourhoods within cities (%)	2001	3	4	3	2	4	3	1
Employment (total)			*8*	*13*	*14*	*11*	*16*	*16*	*9*
8	Qualified residents (%)	2001	5	3	4	4	4	2	3
9	Population with tertiary education (%)	2001	4	2	2	2	3	2	2
Education (total)			*9*	*5*	*6*	*6*	*7*	*4*	*5*
10	Change in employment (number of jobs) (%)	1990–2007	1	2	4	4	5	3	3
11	Change GDP/capita (PPP) (%)	1995–2004	2	2	5	4	5	1	2
12	GDP/capita versus national average (=100)(PPP)	2001	1	4	1	3	5	5	2
Economic performance (total)			*4*	*8*	*10*	*11*	*15*	*9*	*7*
13	Journeys to work by car (%)	2001	3	4	1	1	4	4	2
14	Variation between city and suburban growth (%)	1990–2007	4	2	5	1	4	2	3
Environment/sustainability (total)			*7*	*6*	*6*	*2*	*8*	*6*	*5*
Overall			35	44	47	35	56	43	31

Figure 12.1: Quantitative results for each city based on 5 main themes showing overall performance

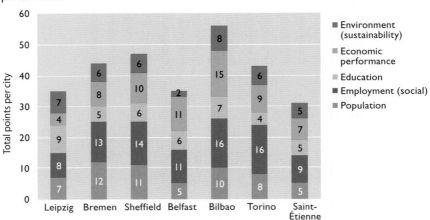

Population indicators as an exemplar of the value of key indicators

Population has been identified as a key indicator in assessing the fortunes of a place. In order to understand its impact and to give it weight, three indicators related to population development were used for this framework: population change overall between 1970 and 2007, population decline since 1990 and population change after 2000.

Many industrial cities in Europe reached their population peak around the 1960s. Cities like Leipzig and Belfast reached their respective peaks by the 1930s. Bilbao, on the other hand, only started to lose population since the 1980s. All of the seven cities experienced significant population losses over the whole period from 1970 to 2007. There are, however, considerable variations between the cities. Bremen lost six per cent of its population. Belfast, which was hit by more dramatic industrial decline and the additional detrimental impact of violent conflict, lost more than one third (35 per cent) of its population. Torino and Saint-Étienne both lost approximately a fifth of their population.

During the period from 1990 to 2007, all cities – apart from Bremen that is now experiencing slight growth – still lost population. Saint-Étienne had the steepest decline during the last 20 years (–11 per cent). In the remaining six cities the decline was considerably lower than in previous decades. Figure 12.2 summarises the population development during the three periods for each the seven cities.

Figure 12.2: Population development in the seven European cities, 1970–2007

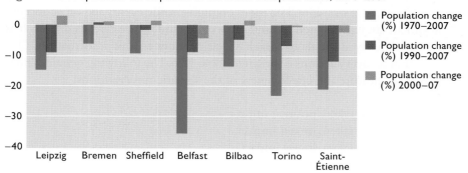

In the most recent period from 2000 to 2007, only two cities, Belfast and Saint-Étienne, continued to lose population while one (Torino) stayed virtually the same. The remaining four cities experienced slight growth. The highest was recorded for Leipzig with three per cent, while Bremen, Sheffield and Bilbao all grew by more than one per cent.

Rather than leaving the metropolitan region, much of the population loss in the cities related to outmigration to the suburbs. While the population of the city declined between 1970 and 2007 it increased in the suburban parts of the metropolitan area. In some of the selected cities suburbanisation was very strong. In Bremen the overall population of the metropolitan area increased by 10 per cent over the period from 1970 to 2007, while the population of the city declined. This is almost entirely explained by the growth in suburban municipalities. In several of the metropolitan areas more people now live in the suburbs than in the city. Belfast, Bremen and Sheffield all experience this phenomenon. Even so, suburbanisation did not reach anything like the same scale as in the US. As a result the strong inner-city decline experienced there was not replicated in Europe.

The overall order of the cities' ranking broadly coincides with our observations from and documentation during the city visits, the views of local actors and the wider set of measures explored in Part 2 below.

Part 2: Qualitative assessment

The qualitative part of the recovery framework is based on interventions that have been widely identified as beneficial for urban recovery. These were grouped under seven themes shown in Table 12.6. *Quality of life* is not used as a separate theme because the indicators for quality of life form an intrinsic part of the qualitative measures overall. We do, however, give an assessment of quality of life at the end based on the general assessment of qualitative indicators.

We ascribe a value to each of these interventions. For each indicator we use an example to illustrate what it means. However, there is considerable debate among urban experts over the effectiveness of some of the interventions that illustrate the selected measures. Some interventions are questioned or are not universally accepted as effective or useful. The focus on high-profile events and on economic development strategies based around enterprise clusters are two examples. It is therefore relatively difficult to attach specific values to this information. Our assessment of recovery actions is shown in Table 12.6. The following general values were used to measure the effectiveness of the specific interventions:

●●●   Action taken, positive impact
●●   Action taken, mixed impact
●   Action taken, lower impact
○   No known action to date

The overall values result from adding up the points for each intervention under each of the themes. The following value system was used: ●●● 3 points; ●● 2 points; ● 1 point; ○ 0 points.

Caution is required with this approach, particularly regarding the distinction between inputs (for example government action) and outcomes (for example the result of those actions). For most of the indicators it is not clear how far government actions have directly or indirectly influenced change, since change

Table 12.6: Checklist of recovery actions and interventions under seven main themes (Part 2)

Recovery actions by themes	Examples	Leipzig	Bremen	Sheffield	Belfast	Bilbao	Torino	Saint-Étienne
Population								
1 Strategic response to population losses	Leipzig: focus on competing with suburbs for population	●●●	●●●	●	●	●	○	●
Employment (social)								
2 Focus on deprived neighbourhoods	Bremen: 10 most deprived areas receive targeted funding through different programmes	●●●	●●●	●●●	●●	●	●●●	●●●
3 Specific skills/ qualification initiatives targeting skills mismatches	Belfast: GEMS; linking population in deprived areas to jobs	●●●	●●	●●●	●●●	●●●	○	●
4 Efforts to integrate ethnic-migrant population	Bremen: creation of integration office, strategic effort	●	●●●	●●●	●	●	●●●	○
Education								
5 Creating stronger linkages between higher education and local businesses	Bremen: innovation strategy; Technology Park in vicinity of university to build collaborative enterprises	●●	●●●	●●●	●	●	●●●	●●
6 Investment in higher education	Bremen: restructuring of scientific profile; investment in natural and high-tech science	●●●	●●●	●●	●●	●	●●●	●
Economic performance								
7 Focus on specific economic sectors, e.g. cluster strategy	Leipzig: focus on five economic clusters, based on economic base and growth sectors	●●●	●●●	●●	●●●	●●	●●●	●
8 Creation of economic development/ inward investment agencies	Bremen: concentrating economic development services in one agency (BIG)	●●	●●●	●●●	●●●	●●	●●●	●●
Urban regeneration (physical)								
Investment in high-profile physical projects	Bilbao: a range of projects by famous architects, including Guggenheim Museum	●●	●●●	●●●	●●●	●●●	●●●	●
Investment in/ promotion of high-profile events	Torino: hosting the 2006 Olympic Winter Games	●●●	●●	●●	●●	●●	●●●	●●●
Revitalisation of city centre	Bremen: historic city centre awarded UNESCO world heritage status; strengthening role	●●●	●●●	●●●	●●●	●●●	●●●	●●●
Regeneration through culture	Leipzig: events related to Bach and Goethe; supporting the New Leipzig School of painting	●●●	●●	●●●	●●●	●●●	●●●	●●●

continued/

Table 12.6: continued

Recovery actions by themes	Examples	Leipzig	Bremen	Sheffield	Belfast	Bilbao	Torino	Saint-Étienne
Strengthening of the retail function of the city (centrality)	Belfast: reinvention as shopping destination; several shopping malls to strengthen city centre versus suburbs	●●●	●●●	●●	●●●	●●	●●●	●●
Upgrading of housing	Leipzig: 'package' of different programmes; aim: solution for vacancies, refurbishment of stock, attracting residents	●●●	●●●	●	●●●	●	●●●	●
Investment in accessibility: long-distance transport infrastructure ('hub functions')	Leipzig: modernisation of airport; refurbishment of large central station; completion of ring highway	●●●	●●	○	●	●●●	●●●	●●
Environment (sustainability)								
Investment in public transport	Bilbao: new metro system; tram line; improved bus services; modernised suburban trains	●	●●	●●	●	●●●	●	●●●
Environmental sustainability on the political agenda	Bilbao: commitment to implementation of Local Agenda 21	●●	●●	●●	●●	●●	○	●●
Actions taken to improve the environment, e.g. land, water, air decontamination	Belfast: land decontamination for Laganside redevelopment	●●	●●●	●	●●●	●●●	●●●	●●●
New government								
Public administration made more efficient	Leipzig: adaptation of West German system, increasing fiscal constraints and need for inward investment required streamlining local government	●●●	●	●●●	●●	○	●●●	●
Benefit from devolved powers	Bremen: as city-state in provided with wide range of remit	●●	●●●	○	●	●●●	●●●	●●●
Coherent strategy guiding the recovery actions (for different tiers of government)	Leipzig: overall strategy as well as thematic strategies, e.g. for housing and urban renewal	●●●	●●	●	●●●	●●●	●●●	●
Metropolitan-level cooperation	Bremen: cooperation with suburban municipalities in metropolitan area, e.g. public transport, planning new development sites	●●	●●●	●	○	●●	●	●●●

occurs through the interaction of many factors. It was not possible to establish the precise interaction of all the variables but the grounded evidence we collected and the contrast with US cities (see Part Four) suggest that government interventions underpinned the process of recovery.

Table 12.7 and Figure 12.3 show the results for each city, giving values under each of the seven qualitative themes. In Figure 12.3 the vertical axis indicates how many points the cities scored in total and under each theme. This assessment also shows how active and/or successful each city was compared with its peers.

According to this qualitative analysis, the cities rank in the following order: Bremen scores highest with 57 points, closely followed by Leipzig (55) and Torino (53). Then

Table 12.7: Results of qualitative assessment of recovery actions under each theme (Part 2)

Indicator	Leipzig	Bremen	Sheffield	Belfast	Bilbao	Torino	Saint-Étienne
Population	3	3	1	1	1	0	1
Employment (social)	7	8	9	6	5	6	4
Education	5	6	5	3	2	6	3
Economic performance	5	6	5	6	4	6	3
Urban regeneration (physical)	20	18	14	18	17	21	15
Environment (sustainability)	5	7	5	6	8	4	8
New governance structure	10	9	5	6	8	10	8
Overall	55	57	44	46	45	53	42

Figure 12.3: Showing results for each city based on the values for the themes outlined in Table 12.7

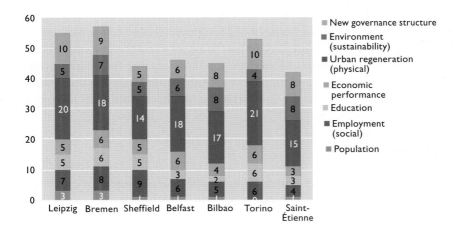

there is a gap between these three and the remaining four cities, which rank in the following order from fourth to seventh: Belfast (46), Bilbao (45), Sheffield (44) and Saint-Étienne (42). This suggests that many interventions generate the potential of the cities for new economic and social development. In the more struggling cities this has not yet played through into big enough quantifiable gains to secure continuing regrowth.

Our framework and measures reflect the overall quality of life theme by capturing a series of interventions that make cities more attractive, and work to eliminate the legacy of industrial blight and neighbourhood decline. Some cities such as Bremen, Leipzig and Torino are indisputably further forward in this progression than others such as Saint-Étienne, Sheffield, Bilbao and Belfast, that started later.

Are the seven cities recovering?

The cities that were most reliant on industry and most damaged by its harsh impact and decline were still struggling the most. This explains Saint-Étienne's continuing problems. Belfast was particularly held back by political troubles until recently, and Sheffield was affected deeply by the dominance of a single industry. All three cities experienced great political turbulence in the 1980s and early 1990s.

Most trends that we measured are moving in the right direction while one or two negative trends have slowed down. There are three hard, quantifiable measures that particularly underline progress:

- *Population:* the majority of the cities in the sample now have growing populations, as shown. Although the growth rates are still relatively low, this is a significant change following several decades of population decline.
- *Unemployment:* since unemployment reached a peak during the mid-1980s in most cities, it has declined significantly. Strikingly, the unemployment rates in these cities are now in most cases below the national average for their country. The only exception is Leipzig, which started a dramatic restructuring process during the 1990s after German reunification.
- *Employment:* employment has been growing in all cities since the 1990s; again Leipzig is the only exception. Some of this progress is related to the increase in less secure, more flexible, temporary or part-time jobs and the growing labour force participation of women. Nonetheless, it indicates that the restructuring process is now in full swing and more new jobs are being created in the service sector than are being lost in the industrial sector. This should help the cities survive the latest recession.[6]

Overall ranking

The differences in performance within cities on different indicators or measures, and also the contrast between quantitative and qualitative measures and performance make any overall or absolute ranking of the cities complicated.

Nonetheless the ranking of the cities on each set of measures does suggest a certain pattern of progress. Most have greatly slowed their decline. Overall Bremen and Bilbao show the best results, followed closely by Torino; then Sheffield and Leipzig; with Belfast and Saint-Étienne some way behind.

Saint-Étienne was the only city that occupied the same – final – position in both parts of the framework. Both Saint-Étienne and Belfast performed badly on quantitative measures. Bilbao and Sheffield showed great variation between the two parts of the framework. Both scored relatively high in the quantitative part of the analysis, but only ranked fifth and sixth in the qualitative part. Leipzig in contrast scored poorly on the quantitative measures, because it was restructuring its economy later and far more radically than others. It ranked second on the qualitative measures, due to its many recovery efforts, and the massive investment incentives provided by the German federal government. Bremen did best on qualitative measures and showed considerable progress on quantitative measures. Table 12.8 shows how the seven cities rank in the two parts of the framework.

Table 12.8: Overall ranking of the seven cities on quantitative and qualitative measures

Framework	1	2	3	4	5	6	7
Part 1 Quantitative measures	Bilbao 56	Sheffield 47	Bremen 44	Torino 43	Leipzig 35	Belfast 35	Saint-Étienne 31
Part 2 Qualitative measures	Bremen 57	Leipzig 55	Torino 53	Belfast 46	Bilbao 45	Sheffield 44	Saint-Étienne 42
Overall ranking of the seven cities with combined scores	Bremen	Bilbao	Torino	Sheffield	Leipzig	Belfast	Saint-Étienne
Combined scores	101	101	96	91	90	81	73

Limitations

There are many ways to use evidence from cities to assess their progress and to draw up a 'score card'. There is little consensus, however, on how to measure, what measures to use or what they signify, particularly how they can be weighted. It is generally agreed that cross-country comparisons and rankings are somewhat uncertain and depend on the quality of the originating data. All cities operate in a constantly changing and evolving political, economic and social environment. External conditions strongly influence local development patterns, and the overall structural conditions have greater force than the individual decisions taken by cities. The ability of cities to influence their own fortunes is restricted by both external forces and local barriers:

- The local economic base may not be robust enough to survive the harsh economic climate of a major downturn in the national or global economy. Cities and regions are part of global systems that expose them to risks such as global capital flows and investment decisions. As government resources shrink, so wider public programmes in favour of weak market cities are likely to shrink too. The overall resource constraints now facing the global economy may influence the recovery trajectories of cities in the future, as we discuss in the final chapter.
- The fortunes of the cities in this sample are often closely related to larger, more dynamic centres in the region. Examples of regional connections from our sample include: Saint-Étienne closely tied to Lyon; Belfast to Dublin; Bremen to Hamburg; Sheffield to Leeds and Manchester; Torino to Milano; Leipzig to Berlin. Often these more dynamic urban centres attract the more educated, more mobile, more youthful and economically more active workforce out of weak market cities. Bilbao is losing some population from these groups to Madrid or Barcelona.
- Higher-level political decisions are important factors in regional and city-level development. Examples include regional development, urban regeneration programmes, transport or higher education funding. We have many illustrations of this but three stand out:
  - the slow process of devolution in Northern Ireland, leaving Belfast without planning powers;
  - the unresolved fiscal problems of Bremen, resulting from the federal system;
  - investment patterns by the public sector with disproportionate impacts.
- Scale, size and agglomeration affect large cities but they do not form part of our recovery framework. The city-region would be a more appropriate geographical scale at which to assess the development and competitiveness of city-regions. However, limitations on data restricted this level of analysis. The structure of the economic base, the type of industries and the city-region dynamism are all-important factors in the analysis of the recovery potential of cities. Our analysis lends support to the idea that larger cities tend to be more diverse and this strengthens their potential for recovery.

Can we identify a model of recovering European cities?

Based on the findings from our study and the ranking of the cities, we have identified three types of post-industrial city in Europe. These broad types of city show that different levels of recovery are possible with different vulnerabilities and strengths:

- *Dominant cities:* larger cities usually with more than 500,000 inhabitants have recovered from industrial shock and entered the new service economy with new vigour. Their larger populations, their agglomeration economies, their more diverse economic base as well as stronger devolved regional powers, have given these cities a recovery potential, unmatched by smaller, more industrially driven cities. Bremen and Torino would be included in this group.

- *Secondary cities:* these medium-sized cities (approximately 300,000 to 500,000) diversify. They are often important centres within their regions. They have therefore demonstrated that they are recovering on many measures. Three cities at the heart of our recovery framework – Bilbao, Leipzig and Sheffield – fit this pattern.

- *Struggling cities:* some smaller, older industrial cities (below 300,000) are still struggling with decline. This applies to several UK and German cities and many US cities. The two cities performing most weakly in our framework, Belfast and Saint-Étienne, show these problems although both may recover more strongly for wider reasons that we discuss in the conclusions.

Scale reflects capacity, resource intensity, population diversity, breadth of economic activity and scope for specialist back-up services. These factors make recovery easier for larger cities. They do not, however, exclude the possibility of recovery in smaller cities, and Bilbao, which ranks top with Bremen, illustrates this.

Are these findings transferable to other cities?

The range of cities chosen for this study all fitted within three key criteria: experience of severe industrial decline, major job and population losses and positive steps taken by the city towards recovery. A recovery framework for ex-industrial towns such as Rotherham near Sheffield or Halle near Leipzig or Bremerhaven near Bremen would need to measure somewhat modified qualitative policy interventions because of their different scale and role, but their core problems and recovery measures would be similar. US cities would also require a distinct perspective and a modified set of measures.

This research and evidence from Brookings suggest that the situation is different in the US. While the process of restructuring itself is similar, it happened earlier, from the 1960s, and with more damaging impacts. Many other characteristics differ considerably from the European experience, such as the much more far-reaching transformation of the metropolitan landscape through suburbanisation, the weakness of policy support and funding from state and federal governments. These differences in comparison with European cities would therefore require a modified framework.

Allowing for these adaptations, we believe that the recovery framework can be applied more widely. It suggests what measures indicate progress and what policy interventions underpin progress. In a resource-constrained planet the recovery framework highlights the capacity of cities to reshape their destinies, reuse their assets and recycle their existing resources. In Part Four we explore the US experience in detail and consider the similarities and differences in approaches to city regeneration.

Part Four
Urban industrial decline and post-industrial recovery initiatives: what can European cities learn from the US?

THIRTEEN

How do US weak market cities compare with Europe?

These next three chapters look at the US experience of urban recovery. Urban regeneration in Europe has long been informed by US approaches and more recently, US cities have also started to observe European approaches. The context in which cities on both sides of the Atlantic operate is of course different. Nevertheless, we can enrich the debate about urban regeneration by examining this juxtaposition.

This part of the book draws mainly on insights gained from research visits to three large old industrial US cities: Pittsburgh, Baltimore and Philadelphia. These three cities are good examples of the struggle of older US cities with industrial decline and urban crisis. It also draws on the large Brookings Institution study of 302 US cities, comparing older industrial cities with a broad cross-section of cities. We draw on evidence from three case studies carried out in Louisville,[1] Chattanooga[2] and Akron,[3] smaller cities that declined but have recently begun to show signs of recovery along the lines of the seven European cities we have looked at so far (see Chapter Fourteen). Figure 13.1 indicates the location of the six US cities.

This chapter gives a general overview of urban development phases in the US, using the three larger, older cities as examples. It explains how these cities developed into industrial giants and how they were subsequently hit by industrial

Figure 13.1: Map of north-eastern US, location of the six cities

decline. Chapter Fourteen describes how the three larger cities responded to the urban crisis, exploring both their assets and ongoing challenges. It then presents evidence of recovery from three smaller cities. Chapter Fifteen gives an overview of the lessons for European cities from the US.

US cities show some unique characteristics, the result of distinctive forms of urban development. The historical evolution of cities highlights the most important characteristics that shape current urban structures and their particular problems. This short overview examines the most important periods of urban development for older industrial cities in the US in four main phases: laying the foundations; industrialisation and rapid growth; urban maturity; urban crisis and suburban growth.

Phase 1: Laying the foundations (until 1870)

Europeans settled on the coastline of North America from the 17th century. From there they gradually penetrated the interior of the vast continent. The American colonies declared their independence from Britain in 1776 and, following their victory in the War of Independence, they became the United States of America. By 1750, Philadelphia was the largest city in British North America. It held this position until after independence when it was overtaken by New York. Philadelphia remained the second largest US city throughout most of the 19th century, although it was briefly overtaken by Baltimore. These two cities had already passed the 100,000 population mark by the mid–19th century. Pittsburgh, on the other hand, which developed as a military settlement and trading town, was not yet growing strongly.

Immigration, mainly from Europe, did not occur on a large scale until the 19th century. The country remained predominantly agricultural until after the Civil War (1861–65) which led to the freeing of slaves and a political union between the booming, urbanising North and the mostly rural, poor and slave-holding South.

Phase 2: Industrialisation and rapid growth (1870–1920)

The period between the Civil War and the First World War was characterised by strong economic and population growth. Like developments in Europe, industrialisation combined with massive immigration dramatically transformed US cities, particularly in the north-east and mid-west regions. Urban growth in the US was fuelled by immigration from abroad while in Europe it was driven mainly by migratory movements from the rural hinterland. Ethnic neighbourhoods emerged in US cities as a result of this, reflecting particular immigration patterns, with, for example, Italians settling in Philadelphia, eastern Europeans in Pittsburgh.[4]

Due to their location at the centre of transport networks, coupled with rapid immigration, the port cities of Philadelphia and Baltimore already had substantial populations by 1870. Nevertheless their populations tripled between 1870 and 1920. Pittsburgh grew even more rapidly, developing from a small city of under

100,000 into one of the 10 largest cities in the US. Interestingly, all three cities reached their highest ranking in the hierarchy of US cities by the 1920s since when they declined in relative importance (Figure 13.2). Philadelphia held its position until the late 19th century, when it lost out to Chicago. Pittsburgh did not have the same advantages of location and commercial tradition. However, it rapidly developed into a typical industrial city during the second half of the 19th century.

Figure 13.2: Rank of the three old industrial cities among all US cities by population, 1790–2007

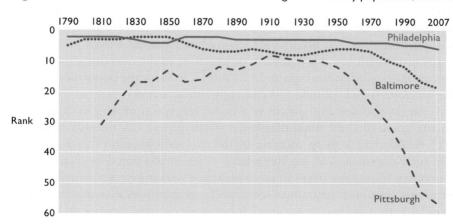

Source: US Census Bureau (www.census.gov/)

It was during this period that the US cities developed their characteristic structures, as identified by scholars of the Chicago School in the 1920s:

- An extreme increase in land values in the downtown area facilitated the formation of a central business district (CBD) with characteristic high-rise office buildings. Other, less profitable, land uses were pushed outwards.
- The adjacent 'zone of transition' was characterised by a heterogeneous mix of uses ranging from temporary lodgings to storage facilities, transport infrastructure, industrial and lower-level office functions.
- This was followed by successive rings of increasingly affluent residential suburbs. Less integrated, more recent immigrants with lower incomes lived closer to the centre, while the middle classes tended to move to peripheral locations, helped by new public transport networks.

The pattern of outward growth explains the so-called 'donut structure' of US cities, with high property values at the centre and towards the periphery and a 'trough' of lower values in the inner zone between.

Phase 3: Urban maturity (1920–50)

For the older US cities of the north-east and mid-west, a third phase can be identified between the two world wars, characterised by a transition from dynamic to slow growth. Cities in other regions showed much higher growth rates, a clear example being Los Angeles.[5] The Great Depression in the 1930s caused a multitude of urban social problems, especially high unemployment rates.[6]

The three cities reached their population peak by around 1950 (Figure 13.3a). While Baltimore and Philadelphia did not lose their positions in the urban hierarchy until later, cities with mono-industrial structures like Pittsburgh started their long decline. It was during this period that suburbanisation started to become a mass phenomenon.[7] As households acquired cars and the federal government directed investment towards highway construction, so the outward growth away from core cities accelerated. Figures 13.3a and 13.3b show the population pattern in the six cities which all followed strikingly similar trends.

This period also saw the growth of a major migration of African-Americans from the rural and still underdeveloped south of the US towards industrial cities,[8] resulting in a sharp increase in the proportion of African-Americans in the total population of the three large cities, as illustrated by Figure 13.4. Exclusionary zoning and deep-set racial prejudice were important contributors to the emergence of clear patterns of residential segregation by race that developed in parallel with suburban expansion.[9] It became common practice to 'red-line' inner-city areas as too risky for investment as they declined, and simultaneously to prevent the integration of black urban dwellers in the wider city by placing restrictive covenants on properties beyond the inner core.[10]

Figure 13.3a: Population development, city level, 1810–2007: three larger cities

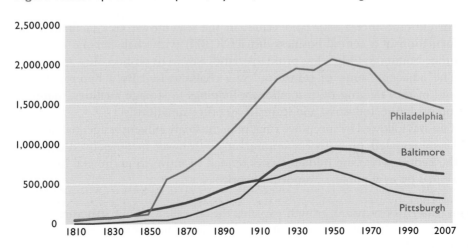

Source: US Census Bureau (www.census.gov/population/www/documentation/twps0076/twps0076.html)

Figure 13.3b: Population development, city level, 1850–1990: three smaller cities

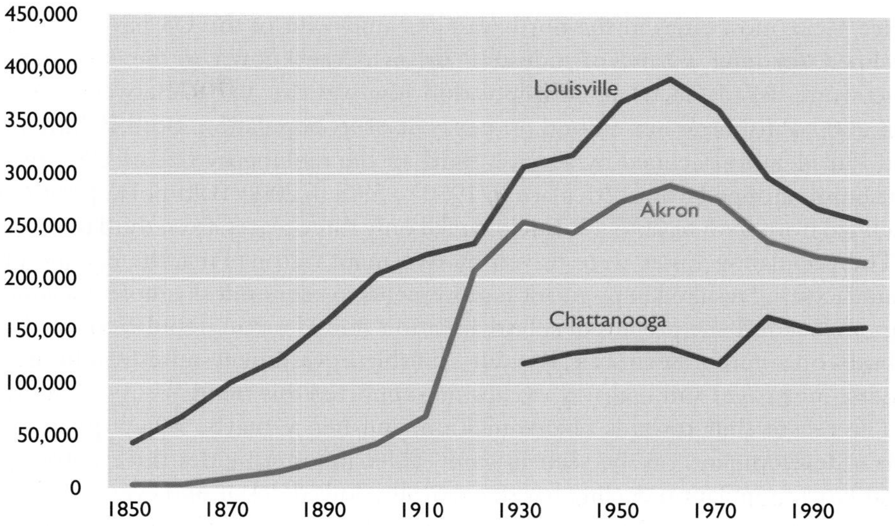

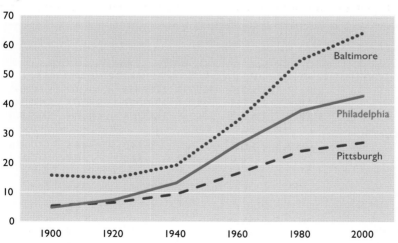

Note: No data for Chattanooga before 1930
Source: US Census Bureau (www.census.gov/population/www/documentation/twps0076/twps0076.html)

Figure 13.4: Rising share of African-Americans in total population, 1900–2000 (%): three larger cities

Sources: US Census Bureau (www.census.gov/population/www/documentation/twps0076/twps0076.html), for 1900–90; US Department of Housing and Urban Development (http://socds.huduser.org/Census/screen3.odb), for 2000

Phase 4: Urban crisis and suburban growth (1950–2000)

Since 1950, most cities in the north-east and mid-west of the US have steadily declined, forming a band of industrial urban decay known as the 'rust belt'. The worst decade in terms of population loss was the 1970s. Between 1950 and 2000, Pittsburgh lost around 50 per cent of its population. Both Baltimore and Philadelphia declined by about a third. In the ranking by size of US cities, Pittsburgh dropped from 12th place in 1950 to 59th in 2000. Baltimore's position declined from sixth to 20th. Philadelphia fell only three places, from third to sixth.

The population losses were driven by two main factors. First, the decline of manufacturing resulted in population movements to economically more dynamic regions. Second, the process of suburbanisation shifted urban populations to the suburbs on an unforeseen scale. Readily available, government-subsidised home-buying mortgages and highway expansion supported this trend.[11]

The recent shift towards re-urbanisation, and hence maybe a new phase of urban development, can be seen in some older industrial cities since 2000. In most cities, population decline has dramatically slowed down, and even reversed in some cases. If the trend continues, cities like Baltimore and Philadelphia may experience population growth for the first time in more than half a century in the near future.

Table 13.1 shows the main population trends for the three large cities: Pittsburgh, Baltimore and Philadelphia. Table 13.2 shows comparable population figures for

Table 13.1: Population in Pittsburgh, Baltimore and Philadelphia (1970–2007)

	Pittsburgh, Pennsylvania		Baltimore, Maryland		Philadelphia, Pennsylvania	
	City	Metro[a]	City	Metro[b]	City	Metro[c]
Population						
1970	520,117	2,556,029	905,759	2,089,438	1,948,609	5,749,093
1990	369,879	2,242,798	736,014	2,382,172	1,585,577	5,899,345
2007	312,819	2,355,712	631,366	2,668,056	1,448,394	5,827,962
Population change (%)						
1970–1990	−28.9	−12.3	−18.7	14.0	−18.6	2.6
1990–2007	−15.4	5.0	−14.2	12.0	−8.7	−1.2
City share of metro (%)						
1970	20.3		43.3		33.9	
1990	16.5		30.9		26.9	
2007	13.3		23.7		24.9	
Rank among all US cities						
1970	24		7		4	
1990	40		12		5	
2007	59	22	20	20	6	5

Notes: [a] Pittsburgh, PA Metropolitan Statistical Area (MSA)
[b] Baltimore–Towson, MD MSA; Baltimore is also part of the larger Washington–Baltimore, DC-MD-VA-WV Consolidated Metropolitan Statistical Area (CMSA)
[c] Philadelphia–Camden–Wilmington–Trenton, PA–NJ–DE–MD CMSA
Source: US Census Bureau (www.census.gov/)

Table 13.2: Main population data for Louisville, Chattanooga and Akron (1970–2007)

	Louisville, Kentucky		Chattanooga, Tennessee		Akron, Ohio	
	City	Metro[a]	City	Metro[c]	City	Metro[e]
Population						
1970	361,472	867,330	119,923	370,857	275,425	679,239
1990	269,063	952,662	152,466[d]	433,210	223,019	657,575
2007	557,789[b]	1,233,725	169,884	514,568	207,934	699,356
Population change (%)						
1970–90	−25.6	9.8	27.1[d]	16.8	−19.0	−3.2
1990–2007	--- [b]	29.5	11.4	18.8	−6.8	6.4
City share of metro (%)						
1970	41.7		32.3		40.5	
1990	28.2		35.2		33.9	
2007	45.2		33.0		29.7	
Rank among all US cities						
1970	39		n/d		52	
1990	58		113		71	
2007	29	42	138	97	95	71

Notes:
[a] Louisville-Jefferson County, KY-IN MSA
[b] Population increase mainly explained by merger of City of Louisville and surrounding Jefferson County in 2006.
[c] Chattanooga, TN-GA MSA
[d] Population increase mainly explained by incorporation of surrounding areas during 1970s
[e] Akron, OH MSA; Akron is also part of the larger Cleveland-Akron-Lorain, OH CMSA
Source: US Census Bureau (www.census.gov/)

the three smaller cities: Louisville, Chattanooga and Akron. The tables highlight the dominance of the wider metropolitan areas over the core cities and the generally declining rank of the cities.

Boom and bust of the 'rust belt' cities

Industrialisation was the main driver behind rapid population growth in older cities like Pittsburgh, Baltimore and Philadelphia. Manufacturing growth was accompanied by service sector activities, building on already existing trade, as in Baltimore, or evolving in tandem with large industrial companies, such as financial services in Pittsburgh. Below we summarise how these cities became 'industrial giants', very much along the lines of their European counterparts.

Pittsburgh was a small city that underwent a transforming process similar to European cities, such as those of the Ruhr area in Germany. The city developed at the confluence of the Allegheny and Monongahela Rivers that come together to form the Ohio River. The region is characterised by a diverse and hilly topography (see Figure 13.5). Its nickname 'Steel City' reflects the industry that dominated

Figure 13.5: Downtown Pittsburgh: the city was founded at the confluence of the Allegheny and Monongahela rivers

the region for most of the 20th century. Many steel mills lined the Monongahela River or 'Mon Valley', while company headquarters were located in the city centre of Pittsburgh. This attracted business services, for example a prominent banking sector, and the foundation of prestigious universities.

A profound restructuring of the economy during the second half of the 20th century led to big population losses as employment shifted from manufacturing to service sector activities, especially the so-called 'eds and meds' (education and medical services). Table 13.3 shows the changes in the ranking of different economic activities in the city by sector in 1950 and 1990.

Table 13.3: Pittsburgh, top-five economic sectors by employment, 1950 and 1990

1950	1990
Primary iron and steel	Education
Construction	Hospitals
Personal services	Construction
Railroads	Eating and drinking
Electrical machinery	Wholesale trade

Source: Deitrick and Beauregard (1995)

Baltimore was founded as a port on the eastern coast. It quickly developed as a centre for commercial activities in the 18th century. Tobacco produced on US plantations was exported to Europe. The port was part of the triangular slave trade and Baltimore became a main port of entry for slaves from Africa. Sugar was imported to Baltimore from the British colonies in the Caribbean.

In addition, Baltimore became the most important entry port for European immigrants after New York. Strong commercial relationships were developed with Bremen, one of our European cities, as Bremen became a major port for European emigration.[12] The development of a good transport infrastructure, using waterways and canals, later followed by railways, connected the city with the expanding hinterland of the fast-growing nation. In the late 19th century the city became a major industrial centre. In addition to shipyards and steelworks, the city hosted important food processing and fertiliser industries.

Philadelphia played an important political role throughout North America's early urban history. Commercial activities emerged around the interface of port and inland transportation networks. While the port of Philadelphia lagged behind New York and Baltimore, Philadelphia secured good inland transport connections by canal and even more importantly by railway. Industrial growth became significant in the late 19th century. While Pittsburgh could be characterised as a mono-industrial city dominated by a few very large companies, Philadelphia's industrial base was characterised by great diversity. The main industries were textiles, metals, machinery, engines, railways and later, chemicals and pharmaceuticals. Rapid population growth during the 19th century meant that the city reached a critical size early on, establishing itself as a second-tier city like Chicago.

Causes and consequences of urban decline

In 2006 the Brookings Institution published a major report, *Restoring Prosperity*, documenting the challenges of old-industrial cities in the US.[13] A follow-up report directed towards policy makers argued for the importance of revitalising older industrial cities in the US,[14] based on a multi-indicator analysis of 1990 and 2000 Census data for the 302 largest US cities by scholars from George Washington University.[15]

Sixty-five of the 302 cities were labelled as economically distressed or weak market cities, among which were the three cities selected as case studies here: Pittsburgh, Baltimore and Philadelphia. These cities had been underperforming on all selected indicators compared with the whole sample during the period from 1990 to 2000. They gradually fell behind more successful cities as their economies showed multiple negative characteristics:

- job losses
- lower than average payroll growth
- lower than average growth of new economic establishments

- lower than average per capita and household incomes
- lower than average labour force participation rate
- higher than average unemployment rate
- higher than average poverty rate.[16]

The three smaller cities, Louisville, Chattanooga and Akron, similarly declined steeply but have recently shown signs of recovery such as rising populations and jobs (see Chapter Fourteen). In many ways, this combination of problems mirrors the European experience, but on every issue the disparities in the US were more extreme, the decline more severe and compensatory support more limited.[17] The global economic crisis of the 1970s brought on the rapid decline of the Fordist mass production system, and the post-Fordist era was characterised by more flexible production modes and the increasing displacement of workers by new technologies. Many manufacturing activities were relocated to less expensive production centres in other regions of the US (mainly the south and west) with lower costs and a less unionised, more flexible workforce. In a further step, many industrial activities completely left the US in search of greater competitiveness and higher profits.

It was the 'rust belt' cities in the north-east and mid-west of the US that were worst hit by industrial losses. The dramatic decline of manufacturing since the 1970s stripped these cities of their main source of employment and economic functions. The three larger cities experienced a sharp and roughly parallel decline in the 1970s and 1980s, slowing somewhat during the 1990s. The other three cities we examined drawing on the Brookings Institution's work show how strong and pervasive the decline in industry was. The steep decline of manufacturing employment in all six cities is illustrated in Figure 13.6.

The older industrial cities were particularly vulnerable because of a series of entrenched weaknesses that were not easy to overcome:

- they were located in weak metropolitan regions, which applied to 47 out of the 65 'weak market cities' identified by the Brookings Institution;
- many had relatively small populations within relatively small agglomerations – this is important for the overall economic viability of cities;
- their levels of human capital and educational attainment were lower and their schools poorer than average;
- conversely, they had higher wages and more unionised labour markets, which acted as a deterrent for new enterprises and were a barrier to competitiveness for existing businesses;
- their crime rates were higher, affecting quality of life;
- a higher proportion of residents were not in the workforce, resulting in low labour market participation rates.[18]

The decline of the cities affected particularly the lower-skilled population and disproportionately African-Americans and other more recently arrived minority

Figure 13.6: Share of employment in manufacturing for the six selected cities, 1970–2000

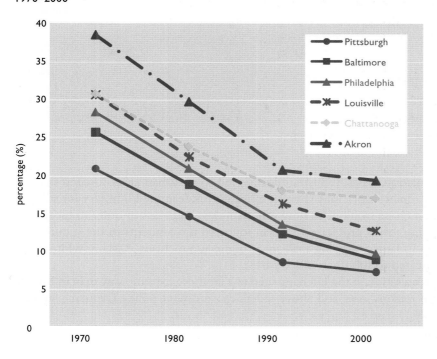

Source: http://socds.huduser.org/Census/screen3.odb

groups, particularly Hispanics. Only a few of the older industrial cities re-emerged in a strong position after the economic restructuring of the 1980s. Success stories emerged around particular strengths, such as financial services in New York or higher education in the Boston metropolitan area.

Table 13.4 illustrates the underperformance of the older industrial cities concentrated in the 'rust belt' on all major indicators compared with the average for the 302 cities studied by the Brookings Institution across the whole of the US.[19] Pittsburgh, Baltimore and Philadelphia lost population throughout each decade between 1950 and 2000. In the 1970s, Pittsburgh lost one in five and Baltimore and Philadelphia one in six inhabitants.[20] The processes of suburbanisation and urban decline were mutually reinforcing, leading eventually to severe fiscal crises in the cities and the fragmentation of suburban jurisdictions, making metropolitan areas difficult to govern.[21]

Before the 1970s, most employment was still located in core cities. However, the relocation of populations to the suburbs gradually undermined the viability of core services alongside industries. Schools, health, policing, public transport and the whole tax base of cities were deeply affected by the dual pressures of job

Table 13.4: Comparison of older industrial cities with other US cities (%)

	Older industrial cities (65)	Other larger cities (237)
Change in employment	–8	+18
Change in annual payroll	+14	+45
Change in establishments	+1	+18
Unemployment rate	10	7
Poverty rate	23	15
Labour force participation rate	59	66

Source: Brookings Institution (2007b, p 15)

and population losses. Industrial decline led to an urban crisis so deep that the role and function of cities were significantly undermined. Those who still had jobs often chose to move to new suburban developments in order to escape the intensifying urban problems.[22] Retail followed the residents to the suburbs and clustered in large shopping malls near highway junctions.[23] Many white-collar jobs relocated to suburban office parks.

Suburbanisation in the US happened in a far more extreme way than in Europe for three reasons, over and above federal government policy favouring suburbs over cities:

- industrial cities received large inflows of southern African–American migr after the Second World War, quickly creating dense, overcrowded ghettos as white urban population began to leave, fuelling further exodus;[24]
- the federal structure of government only weakly supported equalisa programmes and devolved most responsibility to city and state level, mak conditions in cities far more polarised than is common in Europe;[25]
- the free market economy of the US encourages enterprise and wealth creat but has undermined the social solidarity that supports the public interventi we found in Europe.[26]

Baltimore displayed acute urban decline with intense metropolitan growth n graphically. There, the share of the total metropolitan population living in subur areas increased from 57 per cent to 76 per cent between 1970 and 2007. Fig 13.7 shows the changing population distribution between city and suburl Baltimore. Even with strong suburban growth, both the Philadelphia and Pittsbu metropolitan areas experienced overall decline in metropolitan population: some decades as urban population losses were not fully offset by suburban grov

During the 1960s, inner cities underwent a series of powerful changes disrupted earlier patterns of development. Urban renewal programmes fun by the federal government were developed with the main objective of clea inner-city slums and relocating established inhabitants to new, publicly fun housing projects.[27] At the same time, downtown business districts were to

Figure 13.7: Distribution of urban and suburban population, Baltimore metropolitan area, 1970–2007 (%)

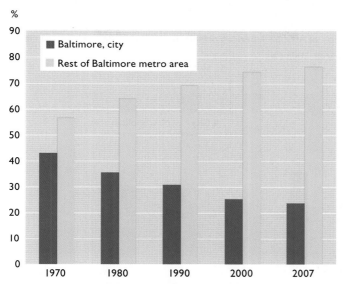

Source: US Census Bureau (www.census.gov/)

linked to the growing suburbs by fast highways to the metropolitan region and beyond, making it possible for business and political leaders literally to drive 'over the ghettos' on elevated freeways.[28] Downtown areas became physically cut off from the rest of the city and themselves lost much of their core rationale as businesses and jobs increasingly moved away. These changes had a devastating effect on low-income inner-city communities, where the proportion of African-American residents rose steeply between 1950 and 1990, driving an accelerating process of 'white flight'.

The 1960s saw the rise of the southern civil rights movement, led by Martin Luther King, as conflict over racial injustice and inequality in US society intensified. In many cities, including Pittsburgh, Baltimore and Philadelphia, racial tensions erupted into severe riots in the late 1960s in the wake of Martin Luther King's assassination. This accelerated the already strong flight of middle-income and predominantly white households from the cities. New suburban housing offered improved lifestyles without the urban pressures and increasing racial animosity of the cities.[29] As a result, lower-income, predominantly minority households were left behind in underinvested, physically decaying inner ghettos, beset by deep social problems.[30] Withdrawal of investment became ever more acute. The great tranches of US inner cities laid waste by the late 1960s riots led to an almost total withdrawal of support.[31] Within five of the six cities, their shares of African-Americans was more than double the share in metropolitan areas as a whole, and in all six cities the concentration was far higher within city than in the suburbs, as Figure 13.8 shows.

Figure 13.8: Concentration of African-American population in the six older, industrial c and in their metropolitan area, 2005 (%)

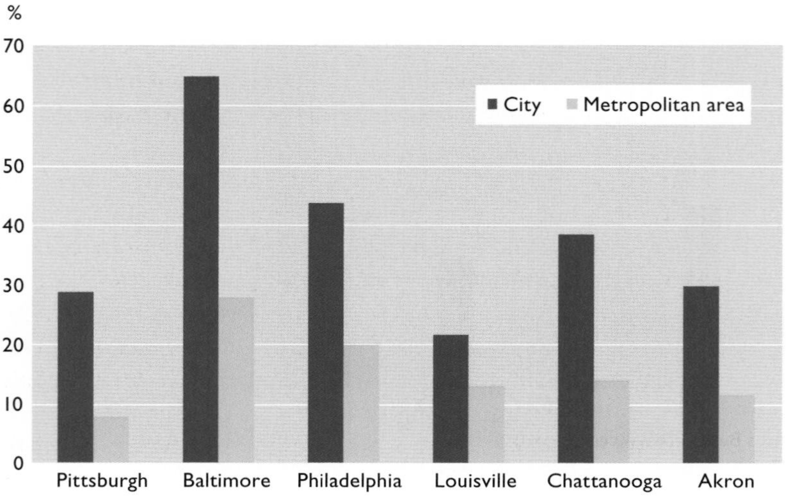

Source: http://socds.huduser.org/Census/screen3.odb

Cities paid a high price for economic restructuring and urban renewal in the 1 and 1970s, but their decline was aggravated by federal government withdr in the 1980s following the election of President Reagan, whose neoliberal market economic agenda and the withdrawal of subsidies further weake the industrial cities. This was parallelled in the UK by the election of Marg Thatcher as Prime Minister in 1979, although her policies were temperei a plethora of compensatory urban initiatives.[32] The state increasingly retre from its redistributional role, and North America's weak social welfare system further constrained. There was considerably less aid for cities from both federal state governments, making the visibility of city governments even more fragil US cities, hit by industrial crisis, in many ways experienced problems somew akin to their European counterparts, but the extent and depth of the proble was far more severe due to several unique American influences:

- the bitter US legacy of slavery divided urban communities far more shar; than in Europe;[34]
- US cities were much more recent and urban traditions were less cultura embedded;
- there was vastly more land per head of population and far more room f expansion into the suburbs;

- public interventions in cities were far more limited and the commitment to equalisation of conditions through public action was far lower;
- the US has been more entrepreneurial, more individualistic and more 'free market' over a much longer period than Europe.

The consequences were extremely serious:

- Fiscal crises resulted from fewer and increasingly poor taxpayers, as revenue bases decreased, while the costs of social services and of maintaining the urban infrastructure increased. Strong labour unions often prevented necessary reforms of the public sector.[35]
- Social stress grew as concentrated unemployment and welfare dependence rose, along with family breakdown, community disintegration, violent crime, anti-social behaviour and substance abuse.[36] The spatial concentration of social deprivation led to intense levels of segregation within a decaying inner-city housing stock. Educational failure through inadequate public schools in inner-city areas caused many households to leave for areas with better schools, while trapping poorer families in a cycle of deprivation. Socioeconomic inequalities were clearly reflected in educational inequalities.[37]
- Suburbanisation in poorly planned new communities greatly expanded the built-up area, making the provision of infrastructure and public services expensive and difficult to manage, and public transport investment unaffordable, with consequent large increases in car traffic. Many metropolitan areas were fragmented into a multitude of small suburban municipalities, each with its own land-use powers, schools and transport. There was little coordinated effort to contain this development. The pattern of sprawl drove high energy use and soaring carbon emissions, which reached double the European average per head by the late 20th century.[38]
- Environmental degradation resulted from obsolete and abandoned former industrial areas of contaminated land and disused buildings. Much of the extensive railroad system was also allowed to fall into disuse. Growing acres of derelict sites overwhelmed policy responses.

As cities lost population, jobs, services and investment, there were fewer and fewer powerful voices in decision-making circles to represent the problems of urban poverty, joblessness and abandonment.[39]

Of the three cities we studied directly, *Pittsburgh* was hit worst by the industrial crisis, particularly by the collapse of the steel industry that vanished almost entirely from the region in the 1980s.[40] The loss of such a dominant industry had serious repercussions. It was driven by high labour costs, competition from cheap imported steel, a record of poor industrial relations, the failure to invest in new technologies and the relocation of production to other regions.[41] Pittsburgh experienced higher than average unemployment, a halving in its population, rising housing vacancies and a declining tax base. It struggled more than other cities because of its location within a steeply declining city-region. The steel towns around Pittsburgh in the 'Mon Valley' were particularly hard hit, since they relied almost entirely on steel. Most of them lost their economic rationale. The decline of the industrial sector had a strongly negative impact on related service sector activities.

Urban decline in *Baltimore* was a consequence of its reliance on post-industrial industry based around its waterfront activities. This led to abandoned warehouses, docks, shipyards and railway facilities alongside defunct industries. Baltimore lost two thirds of its manufacturing employment from 1960, a net loss of around 100,000 jobs,[42] as well as almost a quarter of its population between 1950 and 1990 (–23 per cent). However, these losses were balanced by strong suburban growth, lying as it does in the Washington DC hinterland. Decline was aggravated by acute racial divisions and serious riots in the late 1960s. By the late 20th century, over two thirds of the whole population of the city was black. Large tracts of east and west Baltimore became inner-city slums inhabited by an impoverished, mainly African-American population, experiencing the highest rates of violent crime in the US. The scale of housing abandonment was overwhelming and many neighbourhoods appeared to have lost all recovery potential.

Philadelphia's role as a major industrial centre began to decline as early as the 1920s,[43] but the main decline occurred from the 1970s onwards. In the period between 1967 and 1982, employment in manufacturing more than halved, from 264,000 to 125,000.[44] Philadelphia, like Baltimore, lost a quarter of its population between 1950 and 1990. Suburbanisation was a little slower, but by 2000 three out of four residents of the metropolitan area lived in the suburbs, not in the city. The loss of low-skilled manufacturing jobs had a devastating impact on the working-class population. The problems of unemployment, poverty and crime were concentrated in large disadvantaged neighbourhoods in north, west and south Philadelphia (see Figure 13.9). A combination of political corruption and strong public sector unions hampered progress in the city. As a result, gross mismanagement and negligence took the city to the brink of bankruptcy by 1990.

This gloomy picture was not fixed and rapid changes in new directions were already on the horizon in all the cities we visited. In the next chapter we explore what the cities did to propel their own recovery and to what extent they were helped by regional and national interventions. We highlight the barriers they faced that hampered their progress towards recovery.

Figure 13.9: North Philadelphia contains large areas of social deprivation and urban decay (derelict sites and empty properties abound)

FOURTEEN

Will the US cities recover?

The lack of strong federal support for cities in the US from the 1980s onwards has meant that states and cities themselves have had to react directly to their internal crisis. Efforts to revitalise cities have emerged in the US, just as they have in Europe, albeit with weak support from other tiers of government so that the response has mainly been driven by local leaders. Programmes of renewal evolved in US cities over the long period of urban decline, often driven by extreme racial problems and a gradual recognition that suburban sprawl was itself a problem. Partnerships between the public, private and community sectors have emerged to drive change. In this chapter we summarise the main actions taken by the three larger cities, Pittsburgh, Baltimore and Philadelphia, showing what the prospects are for urban recovery in these cities. We then briefly consider the trajectories of three smaller mid-western 'rust belt' cities that have recovered somewhat.

Stemming decline in Pittsburgh, Baltimore and Philadelphia

Pittsburgh, Pennsylvania

Pittsburgh, one of the first US cities to organise concerted action to combat urban decline, was an early pioneer of urban regeneration. Pittsburgh's Renaissance Programme was launched in 1946 shortly after the Second World War in response to two main problems facing the city in the 1940s:

- steep downtown decline due to the failure to attract new investment and the growing problems of traffic congestion;
- the damage to both air and water quality from polluting industries wreaking environmental damage on an unprecedented scale.

The business community saw these problems as a growing barrier to attracting high-calibre personnel; companies would simply choose other locations.[45] This resulted in the formation of the Allegheny Conference in 1943, a public–private partnership formed by some 150 civic leaders that drove the next two decades of urban regeneration. Local leadership was a key factor in the coordination of a strategic response to the city's problems. Two powerful individuals dominated the coalition: Richard Mellon, heir to a large financial consortium, representing the interests of the local business elite, and David Lawrence, political leader of the city's Democratic Party, representing the interests of the working class. Despite their differences, they cooperated closely in preparing a development plan, which elicited the support of the local population and corporate leaders.

The Renaissance Programme of 1946 aimed to address the deterioration of the downtown area and the degraded urban environment as well as the overspecialisation of the economy and the city's inadequate infrastructure. This strategic response was a turning point in Pittsburgh's history and became a model for subsequent urban regeneration efforts in other cities.[46] The activities were supported by state legislation that allowed Allegheny County and the city of Pittsburgh to undertake urban renewal programmes and to set up authorities such as the Regional Industrial Development Corporation (RIDC) and the Urban Redevelopment Authority (URA) to raise revenues and operate beyond the jurisdiction of a single municipality.[47] Actions under the Renaissance Programme illustrate its focus on economic development:

- continuing support for traditional industrial development helped retain local industries and attract new companies with the objective of diversifying the economy;
- improving air quality by converting from coal to gas reduced air pollution, while water pollution was addressed by creating a sewerage authority and a new treatment plant;
- downtown redevelopment in the 1950s and 1960s prevented further decline of the downtown area, with the city tapping into early federal urban renewal funds;
- investment in two new expressways helped to alleviate the congestion of the downtown area; a new airport built in 1951 improved longer distance connections.

In contrast with these changes, up to the 1960s, attempts at inner-city neighbourhood renewal were not very successful. The renewal of the Lower Hill District, a largely African-American inner-city neighbourhood close to downtown, failed.[48]

The early actions by the city did not alter Pittsburgh's persistent structural problems. Decline looked set to continue unless more targeted actions were taken. Failure to diversify the economy made its industrial base outdated as steel was predicted to disappear from the region within 20 years, along with continuing population decline. Major investment in higher education have boosted the research and development capacity of local companies. Yet the Renaissance Programme continued to focus on physical regeneration projects such as a new all-sports stadium and a rapid transit system.

The dynamics of the situation changed with the election of a new administration in 1970, which capitalised on the civil rights and anti-demolition sentiment of the late 1960s. The Allegheny Conference was labelled elitist and large-scale projects such as plans for the new transit system faded. The focus shifted from downtown urban regeneration to neighbourhood renewal that had been missing from earlier recovery approaches. Unlike many other cities, Pittsburgh avoided wholesale clearance and most neighbourhoods remained remarkably intact. Several factors helped this approach:

- Resident-led initiatives created numerous community-based organisations, many of which evolved into community development corporations (CDCs). CDCs are local asset-based service organisations, often with roots in the labour unions. Their main objective is to alleviate the worst consequences of economic restructuring and reduce government intervention at the local level by providing housing, social welfare, community activities and programmes. As government action declined from the 1970s, they became big local players receiving support from government as a cheaper and more community-oriented alternative to public action. For example, the Manchester neighbourhood is regarded as a model of how to achieve housing preservation without causing displacement of local residents using local community-based organisations in low-income areas.[49]
- The formation of public–private partnerships built on the success of community-based initiatives, attracting involvement from the private sector as well as non-profit organisations.
- The aggressive use of the Community Reinvestment Act, a federal regulation making financial institutions responsible for serving local communities, particularly in distressed areas, brought in considerable additional resources.

In spite of this progress, by the late 1970s, Pittsburgh was increasingly swamped by the problems of deindustrialisation and social stress. In the 1980s, the city reverted to large-scale urban redevelopment programmes focusing again on the downtown area. Neighbourhood renewal funding came under pressure during this period, with the federal government under Reagan cutting almost all its funding streams. Meanwhile manufacturing jobs continued to desert the city.[50]

Unlike its predecessor, 'Renaissance II', as the new drive was called, was less driven by civic leaders and more by the city council itself, which assumed a leading role. The main projects included office skyscrapers, historic preservation and the development of a cultural district in cooperation with the non-profit sector in the downtown area (see Figure 14.1).

In the worst period of deindustrialisation, the focus had shifted to other economic sectors such as education, research, healthcare, advanced technologies and business services. Investors were lured in with tax abatements, land assembly, low-interest loans, street improvements and other infrastructure improvements. In addition, the state invested in the universities and a new airport, the latter with the intention of establishing a logistics hub. The focus on the logistics sector was shared with other US cities such as Louisville and also Leipzig in Germany.

Pittsburgh still showed the typical problems of a declining city, which the economic recession of the late 1980s reinforced. However, in the mid-1990s, project-based urban regeneration again produced ambitious proposals, quickly dubbed 'Renaissance III'. Strong political leadership drove the waterfront revitalisation and the building of a new baseball stadium. The approach to neighbourhood renewal also shifted. Rather than distributing funds equally across all neighbourhoods, Pittsburgh was subdivided into different 'housing markets'

Figure 14.1: Cultural regeneration in downtown Pittsburgh facilitated by foundations and civic engagement

in order to identify the most promising areas for investment. This meant a shift away from rescuing the worst areas to reinvesting in those areas with potential for development and future private sector spin-off investment. The 1980s also saw the demolition of many failed public housing projects built during the 1960s urban renewal period. The recent emphasis has been on improving citizens' quality of life by upgrading public spaces and reducing crime.

Impacts on Pittsburgh

Pittsburgh suffered most among the older industrial cities from decline. But the city's history of ambitious regeneration programmes was driven by strong local leadership, while high levels of community organisation spared the city from the worst social problems. However, Pittsburgh's ongoing struggle to compete with other regions has been accompanied by continuing decline. There has been only slow suburban growth around new businesses and industries to offset urban decline.

The city faces major disadvantages that hold back its recovery:

- It is not located in or near a dynamic agglomeration, too far from other larger cities in the region to form strategic alliances. The lack of a larger catchment area and the weakness of the metropolitan area itself are serious barriers to development.
- The metropolitan area is divided into 130 municipalities in Allegheny County alone. Apart from highways there is little structured cooperation at the

metropolitan level. The management and coordination of the sewer and water systems pose major problems. In an attempt to streamline government structures, the county and city are trying to merge, but this has yet to be approved by the state government and may take several years.

- In spite of the overall population decline, the land under development in the metropolitan area has increased by 40 per cent; in other words, more and more spread out building. New developments have been driven by recent investments in yet more roads. Meanwhile, the lack of adequate job opportunities is driving many young and well-educated people to more competitive places. Racial inequality is an important reality. The African-American population is poor and poorly represented. An increasingly ageing population and low levels of immigration make continuing population decline likely.
- Several major regeneration projects failed to materialise, such as the Skybus public transport system, or to deliver the anticipated benefits, such as the new airport. Coal-fired power plants in the region continue to pollute the air.
- Pittsburgh's CBD is dominated by offices. Considerable efforts have been made, to revitalise the area by establishing a cultural district and by organising events, but it still has a rather empty feel to it.
- The city faced a serious fiscal crisis in 2003, although it has since balanced its budget.

On the other hand, the city has considerable advantages and assets that may help it recover over time:

- Pittsburgh always had a relatively substantial business and financial services sector for a city of its size, and not all of these functions have been lost – four Fortune 500 companies still have their headquarters in the city. Several companies have successfully retooled and re-established themselves in new market niches, while some newly arrived companies have grown on the back of the existing skills base, leading to some industrial recovery around high-tech enterprises.
- Important philanthropic organisations, such as Heinz and Mellon, have reinvested in the city, for example in the fields of higher education and culture. The city is also known for its strong neighbourhood-level organisations.
- Pittsburgh usually ranks high on many quality of life indices, in spite of its problems. House prices in Pittsburgh are among the lowest of larger US cities and far below those in Baltimore and Philadelphia. This may attract younger workers in the future. The city has two outstanding universities, Pittsburgh and Carnegie Mellon, and tertiary education levels are higher than in other cities.

On balance, Pittsburgh has managed to improve greatly its key assets such as the downtown area and its higher education sector, with strong civic leadership and influential community organisations. These signs of progress offer grounds for optimism about future progress towards recovery (see Figure 14.2).

Figure 14.2: 'Cathedral of learning', University of Pittsburgh (higher education is an expanding sector)

Baltimore, Maryland

Baltimore became famous in the 1970s as one of the first declining industrial cities to redevelop its waterfront, influencing dockland revitalisation projects in many other cities, such as Glasgow, Sydney or Bilbao.

Baltimore's history is closely linked with its waterfront, which occupies a central place in the city. During the industrial era, its port facilities, docks and warehouses as well as its vast railway infrastructure, industry and shipyards drove the city's wealth. By the 1960s, many of these activities were dying as industries moved and technological progress displaced older industries. Alarmed by the problems facing key industries and a decreasing property tax base, Baltimore's business elite became increasingly concerned about the future of the city. Following Pittsburgh's lead, the Greater Baltimore Committee was formed, based on the Allegheny Conference.[51] Its main objective was to revitalise the inner city.

The Committee quickly realised that abandoned land along the waterfront offered great potential for development. The 'Inner Harbor Project' emerged in the 1970s, driven by strong political leadership. A public–private partnership was created to renew the downtown and inner harbour areas. The objective was to attract financial services, tourism and hospitality functions to the city centre. Large-scale public funds were provided to kick-start these developments and attract private investment. Among the projects that developed in the inner harbour were hotels, a marine science centre, a national aquarium, sports stadia, high-rise condominium flats as well as retail and entertainment facilities. Since then the redevelopment has triggered a rise in values and the gentrification of many neighbouring areas (see Figures 14.3 and 14.4).

Figure 14.3: Baltimore's inner harbour area at night

Baltimore is located between New York and Washington, within commuting distance of the capital at the heart of the dynamic East Coast corridor. Good transport connections and relatively low house prices make Baltimore an attractive alternative to Washington DC. Since the late 1990s, gentrification has revived some of the well-located older inner neighbourhoods. This revival in urban living has increased the tax base, and attracted more affluent residents, which is now a major policy objective of the city.

Baltimore pioneered ideas such as the homesteading programme, which gives young urban dwellers the right to occupy vacant properties in inner-city areas if they refurbish them. (This is similar to the 'self-user' programme in Leipzig.) Live Baltimore, a local non-profit organisation, is promoting the city as a residential option for middle-class households. Baltimore's 'smart growth' has been shaped by development controls imposed within the state of Maryland, restricting the development of new suburban areas and driving inner-city renewal.[52] As a

Figure 14.4: Gentrification along the waterfront: the inner harbour redevelopment has brought investment to former working-class neighbourhoods such as Fells Point pictured here

result, the population of the city increased for the first time in 50 years in 2005. Employment in the metropolitan area is also growing and expected to continue doing so in the future.

In sharp contrast to this progress and as a consequence of the strong focus on downtown areas, little funding has been directed at poorer areas. Standing out from the revitalised downtown, many inner neighbourhoods have experienced severe decline, and this is particularly true for east and west Baltimore where an impoverished, predominantly African-American, population is concentrated (see Figure 14.5).

Several urban renewal programmes were developed through CDCs from the 1970s onwards. These independent community-based non-profit organisations, supported by government and city funding, operate within cities and can become influential community development organisations within poorer minority areas of cities, helping to change conditons. Under the political influence of CDCs and local politicians, the available funding was dispersed across many neighbourhoods.

During the 1980s, federal and state governments cut back on urban programmes and fewer funds became available. The Enterprise Foundation, created by one of the city's largest developers, launched an ambitious neighbourhood renewal programme in deprived west Baltimore. However, the focus on housing and the attempt to create homeowners did not work from the point of view of city officials. Baltimore was one of a handful of cities that successfully bid for Empowerment Zones in the 1990s, a federal programme implemented by the Clinton administration, ending in 2009.[53] These zones were established in east and west Baltimore. Strong financial incentives and public–private partnerships provided support to highly distressed communities.

One of the biggest failures in urban renewal programmes of the 1950s and 1960s had been the construction of large public housing projects, widely regarded as a failure, helping to create ghettos of concentrated deprivation that blighted urban post-war North America. All the Baltimore public housing estates have been demolished since the mid-1990s.

Eventually, as in Pittsburgh, the 'watering can approach' to poor neighbourhoods was replaced by subdividing the city into different housing markets to focus investment in areas with potential (see Figure 14.6).

Several projects in Baltimore illustrate this approach:

- In an area adjacent to the 'anchor' institution and employer, Johns Hopkins University, a large long-term urban renewal programme is being carried out by east Baltimore Development Inc. (EBDI). This area of east Baltimore has many vacant derelict properties right next to one of the world's most prestigious medical institutions.[54] The programme includes the demolition of nearly all housing alongside new construction. In an attempt to prevent displacement, efforts are being made to encourage the return of the original inhabitants. The programme aims to raise the value of land in this part of the city and to

Figure 14.5: Segregation: residential location of African-American population in Baltimore, 2000

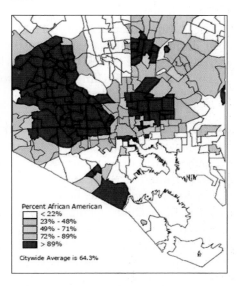

Figure 14.6: 'Housing markets' classifications, Baltimore, 2007

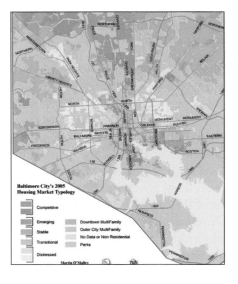

introduce different activities but it also has a social focus offering training and job-related support to local residents.

- The Patterson Park area is a traditional working-class neighbourhood located between gentrified areas along the waterfront to the south and the slums of east Baltimore further north. The local CDC is trying to prevent the process of decline from advancing from the north by 'fighting the ghetto from its fringes'.[55] In the process the CDC has become a major developer by purchasing, rehabilitating and selling strategic properties. This approach is showing some signs of success.

The Healthy Neighbourhoods network, based in several US cities, argues that investment should be concentrated in areas with the potential to build from strength, instead of focusing on the most deprived areas.[56] They insist that the residents should take responsibility for their neighbourhoods. Success is mainly measured by a rise in area house prices. The City of Baltimore has adopted new ways of approaching neighbourhood renewal, relying on carefully monitoring trends in employment, called 'Citistat', in order to target specific areas and problems. In addition a land bank has been founded to organise faster and more efficient acquisition of properties. An affordable housing trust has been created to fund pre-development work to create incentives for developers to come in.

Although the metropolitan area of Baltimore is highly suburbanised, the state of Maryland has recently adopted an anti-sprawl regulation, which will stop further outward growth and concentrate development within the city.

Impacts on Baltimore

Baltimore has experienced strong decline but also has some strategic advantages, such as proximity to the capital. Its bold experiments with innovative investments have begun to turn around an extreme situation. As a result, it has shown recent signs of recovery. Its ambitious regeneration projects, such as the Baltimore Inner Harbor Project, the renewal of older housing through homesteading and gentrification, the limits to sprawl through smart growth policies and the benefits of strong growth in the Washington DC metropolitan area have all benefited the city. Federal government decisions to relocate important public sector agencies out of the capital have generated new local employment.

In contrast with less well-connected cities like Pittsburgh, Baltimore's train links make it far more public transport-oriented than most equivalent US cities. The transportation infrastructure needs modernisation but it compares well with other US cities – almost 20 per cent of workers use public transport, which is the seventh highest rate in the US.[57] Baltimore is also well served by several airports, including the largest domestic and low-fare airport in the US. The port, now highly modernised, has become the largest 'roll-on-roll-off' port in the US, handling mainly cars for export and import.

The metropolitan area of Baltimore will gain an estimated 15,000 direct and 20,000 indirect jobs at the Department of Defence and the National Security Agency over the next few years,[58] due to the Base Realignment and Closure policy (BRAC) moving government jobs out of Washington. The economy of Baltimore has now radically shifted towards post-industrial service and knowledge-based activities. While the city no longer hosts any Fortune 500 headquarters, new and thriving businesses have emerged from within the city or relocated there. The city has two renowned institutions of higher education, Johns Hopkins University and the University of Maryland. Its bio-tech research-based industries and its core medical sciences are of a world-renowned standard. These institutions have helped to fuel the regrowth of the city.

However, Baltimore remains a deeply divided city and faces some very serious difficulties and challenges:

- The persistence of large tracts of concentrated poverty and social dislocation in west and east Baltimore generates a level of social deprivation and exclusion that is unparalleled in the European cities we examined. Any serious inroads into these problems require actions to be expanded, from physical interventions, such as demolition and redevelopment, to programmes that tackle the root causes of disadvantage. The current strategy of investing in areas with more potential is likely to worsen the situation in the most deprived areas, even though it may be a prerequisite for the overall recovery of the city.
- The history of urban renewal in the US is shaped by demolition, large-scale physical interventions and transformation of the landscape, rather than by more incremental organic change. Baltimore's inner city may need this.
- The social indicators for Baltimore speak for themselves. One fifth of the population lives below the US poverty line according to the 2000 Census. The US poverty line is an absolute measure, reflecting much more acute deprivation than European poverty levels. It is fixed by the US government at a level far below equivalent European measures of poverty.[59]
- Educational levels are generally low. Underperforming public schools are a major problem, reinforcing inequalities and driving out families who can afford to move. More importantly, they hamper access to jobs and help entrench patterns of racial separation.
- Violent crime is Baltimore's Achilles heel. In 2007, it had the highest homicide rate of all larger US cities and was the second most dangerous city of more than 500,000 inhabitants. As the homicide rate in the US is approximately five times the level of the UK and Europe, this is a frightening statistic.[60]

On the other hand, the city increased its tax revenues by almost 50 per cent, or an additional US$1.5 billion, between 2001 and 2007, even though property taxes in the city are higher than in the surrounding suburbs. Clearly, the rewards for living within the city now outstrip the lower costs of the suburbs. The growing tax base, if it continues, is a clear sign of progress. Crime has also fallen, albeit from a very high base.[61]

Baltimore currently has an expanding population and enterprise development both in the city and in the wider metropolitan area. It has become an urban tourist destination, which speaks for the success of the inner harbour transformation, the restoration of attractive old streets and the overall dynamism of the city, although the blighted neighbourhoods of the inner city remain a serious threat to its long-term progress.

Philadelphia, Pennsylvania

An urban reform movement evolved in Philadelphia after the Second World War. It was led by business interests and civic groups concerned about the city's future, although the Philadelphia coalition was not formally institutionalised, unlike the 'Allegheny Conference' in Pittsburgh. Strong leadership was an important factor in the urban regeneration efforts that became a priority.

Between the early 1950s and the mid-1970s, this regeneration alliance initiated some large-scale projects in Philadelphia. Among them were many new office buildings, neighbourhood renewal projects such as in Society Hill, some waterfront redevelopment, industrial parks and the expansion of the major universities. Slum clearance also took place with federal urban renewal funding. Although clearance made way for new urban highways to connect to the downtown area, the inner city was generally spared large-scale demolition.

By the 1970s the coalition and its redevelopment efforts had begun to unravel:

> For 20 years the city government had been aggressive in clearing slums and pressing redevelopment. With the demise of federal commitment to urban renewal in the mid-1970s, however, the local coalition of business interests, civic groups and elected officials began to disintegrate. The well-balanced efforts of the redevelopment coalition were thrown off kilter.[62]

From the 1970s onwards, less funding was available for city regeneration due to local fiscal constraints; less funds from federal and state governments; and a more private sector-driven approach to urban regeneration under the Reagan administration in the 1980s. The public sector was overtaken by the private sector as the driving force behind urban regeneration. This was reflected in the shift of focus from urban renewal towards economic development and profit-oriented rebuilding.

Philadelphia, with its diverse economic base, came through the restructuring from the industrial towards the service sector more successfully than other industrial cities.[63] The city started to stabilise and there was much talk of a 're-birth'. The symbols of this were many: new skyscrapers, especially since height restrictions on buildings in the CBD were lifted in 1986; specific projects such as the Gallery shopping mall, the convention centre and sports stadia; as well as the gentrification of several inner-city neighbourhoods (see Figure 14.7).

Figure 14.7: Downtown Philadelphia with the City Hall and the statue of William Penn, founder of the state of Pennsylvania, on top

However, the conditions in many deprived areas in the north, west and south of Philadelphia worsened. The inhabitants of these areas did not seem to benefit from the new growth.

In the late 1980s, the city faced a major financial crisis leading to near bankruptcy. In spite of charging high taxes, the city was no longer able to maintain its public services and infrastructure, nor could it meet its payroll obligations to public sector employees. A new administration under Mayor Rendell in the 1990s set out to consolidate and strengthen the city finances. He cut expenditure and made deals with the powerful labour unions that had previously opposed the restructuring of the public sector. Like Pittsburgh and Baltimore, Philadelphia focused investments on its downtown. The efforts to strengthen the CBD and increase the downtown population have shown impressive results.

In the inner city, Philadelphia had early on in the 1960s switched its focus from slum clearance towards 'blight containment'.[64] Preservation was adopted before it happened in other cities. As in Baltimore and Pittsburgh, however, neighbourhood renewal money had been distributed almost equally throughout the city due to political pressure from neighbourhood organisations and local politicians.

In the 1990s, the focus shifted, and the city identified distinctive housing market types, each requiring particular strategies (see Figure 14.8). A new programme, the Neighbourhood Transformation Initiative, was implemented in 2000, based on data provided by the Reinvestment Fund. The main objective was to fight the blight of urban decay. Derelict buildings were demolished, graffiti was cleared, abandoned cars and dead trees were removed and bare lots of land were cleaned up. Some were planted and turned into community spaces. However, the consensus based on our interviews was that the programme was not totally successful, and the programme ended.

There are still many neighbourhood initiatives linked to neighbourhood CDCs, and progress in upgrading many parts of the inner city continues. However, the challenge is enormous, and the resources have been severely restricted. Future directions are unclear but it is possible that the success of the downtown will flow over into more inner-city areas.

Impacts on Philadelphia

Philadelphia, due to its size, has retained its role as a second-tier city in the US urban system. Economic restructuring has transformed the city, and the economic base is now significantly more diverse. The city seems well placed to maintain the gains it has made and to withstand an economic downturn. Yet some major problems still need to be addressed, including the concentration of poverty and social problems in the city and the legacy of inefficient, sometimes corrupt city government.

Figure 14.8: 'Housing markets' classifications, Philadelphia, 2003

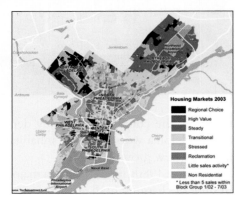

There are three dominant, unresolved issues. First, Philadelphia's reputation for corrupt and inefficient local government has led to inadequate local services, unable 'to provide essential infrastructure and public services at low cost for nearly half a century. Taxes are very high and not off-set by high-quality services'.[65] This is attributed to three main factors: powerful employee unions; weak political leadership tolerating 'parish pump'-style local politics, favouring concessions to particular interest groups and parochial neighbourhood representation based on vested interest; and the burden of welfare responsibilities associated with Philadelphia's status as a county government within a state that has not sufficiently compensated for reduced federal aid to cities.

Second, the quality of the public school system is poor, producing educational levels that do not match national standards. More affluent households either send their children to private schools or to the increasingly popular alternative schools, such as charter schools. Many move to the suburbs where educational standards are higher. This educational system, combining some of the best private schools in the country with some of the worst public schools, reproduces socioeconomic and racial inequalities.

Third, administrative fragmentation has made local governance highly complex. The metropolitan area consists of 353 municipalities covering two states, Pennsylvania and New Jersey. The only significant city-regional government body is the public transport authority, SEPTA. An inadequate level of metropolitan cooperation is further complicated by the sharp political division between the predominantly Republican suburbs and the strongly Democratic city. The overall population of the city has continued to decline, in spite of some recovery in the wider region.

On the other hand, Philadelphia has some significant assets and advantages. It has a dynamic downtown area with a well-developed and imposing CBD housing the third largest and most prosperous downtown population in the country; 62,000 people live there, giving the city centre a vitality and diversity of activities unusual in US city centres. The boom of the downtown area is exerting pressure on real estate prices, forcing some back office activities to the suburbs. This suggests urban regrowth. At the same time, the metropolitan area is relatively dense and successful, with several important suburban centres. So recovery within the city is supported by core strengths in the city-region, in spite of stalled metropolitan growth:

- Public transportation within the city and connections to other cities are better than in many US cities. Philadelphia is an important Amtrak hub. The public transport agency SEPTA is one of the largest in the US.
- Higher education is one of the city's strongest assets. The city has several renowned universities such as Temple University, the University of Pennsylvania and Drexel University, as well as excellent liberal arts colleges in the suburbs.

Economic development has remained strong, as the city has shifted out of manufacturing. Philadelphia still hosts six Fortune 500 companies, although this is down from 13 in 1950. The financial services sector has an important presence in the city and in its suburbs. Growth in the medical and educational sectors provides job opportunities for many lower-skilled people in related services, as well as many knowledge-based job opportunities.

Philadelphia has played a unique historic role as one of the oldest US cities. This offers economic potential around tourism and already attracts many international visitors. With its diversified economy and its transport links, Philadelphia should continue to attract investment in the future, building on its assets in the higher education sector and on its historical role, particularly if it can reduce the high levels of deprivation in some inner-city neighbourhoods (see Figures 14.9 and 14.10).

Table 14.1 summarises the problems and progress in these three cities.

Figure 14.9: Contrasts of the post-industrial landscape: new affordable low-density housing next to abandoned industrial building in north Philadelphia

Figure 14.10: Graduation day at Temple University, the 'anchor' in largely deprived north Philadelphia

Table 14.1: Summary of problems and progress in Pittsburgh, Baltimore and Philadelphia

	Pittsburgh	Baltimore	Philadelphia
Disadvantages	Distance from dynamic regions; weak metropolitan area, uniquely with population decline; fragmentation a barrier for wider planning approaches; decayed inner areas with concentrations of African-Americans	Neighbourhood deprivation: persistence of large tracts of concentrated poverty; extremely high levels of violent crime; very high levels of segregation; public service provision	History of bad government, corruption, political machines; neighbourhood deprivation, persistence of large tracts of concentrated poverty; very high levels of ethnic segregation; low educational levels of population, bad public school system; high taxes, inadequate public services
Advantages	Low cost of living; higher education institutions; quality of life; old industrial skills; strong civic culture	Location in dynamic East Coast corridor, close to booming Washington DC; economic development, new office locations; lower cost of living compared with other cities in East Coast corridor	Location in centre of strong region and metropolitan area; 'critical mass'; booming downtown; attractive amenities: culture
Overview	Pittsburgh is among those old industrial cities, which have suffered most from decline; although social problems are not as dramatic as elsewhere due to relatively intact neighbourhoods and strong civic organisations, new problems of economic decline could fracture the progression towards recovery	Baltimore has also experienced strong decline but seems to show recent signs of recovery, even though the social and physical deprivation of many neighbourhoods in east and west Baltimore remains a major problem	Philadelphia reached a 'critical size' as secondary city, similar to Chicago. Most experts predict a bright future for this city

Urban trajectories

The brief history and progress of three important core cities in the US does not fully explain their trajectories. All three grew fast, declined steeply and now show signs of stemming the decline with significant signs of recovery. The rapid rise in energy costs, the bursting of the house price bubble and the major political shifts under way in the US since January 2009 all point to a greater focus on city restoration, a loss of confidence in sprawl development and a much more robust commitment to tackling climate change, strengthening smart growth policies to prevent further sprawl. There is some positive progress in the cities, in spite of many outstanding and unresolved problems, and it is possible for these major cities to continue this progress, even in the climate of severe economic constraints. A summary of the main evidence on urban trajectories can be found at the end of this chapter in Tables 14.3 to 14.9.

Recovery is possible

Having looked briefly at the experience of three dominant weak market cities undergoing the pains of transformation, a Brookings Institution study identified the emergence of recovering cities, weak market cities that have undergone major economic transformation and survived to show significant positive growth.[66] There were 17 cities that ranked among the economically distressed cities in 1990 but which had moved into the recovery category by 2000.[67] Based on case studies of three of these cities, Louisville,[68] Chattanooga[69] and Akron,[70] it is possible to identify a drive towards recovery following acute decline. These three cities are far smaller than Pittsburgh, Baltimore or Philadelphia, ranking much lower in the hierarchy of US cities. Their population decline was tempered by administrative mergers with surrounding counties and their metropolitan growth was strong. The population trends of these three cities were shown in Table 13.2 in the previous chapter.

All three smaller cities grew again from the 1990s, in spite of the fact that the decline in manufacturing was as steep as in the other three cities. At the same time, African-American populations remained heavily concentrated in the cities rather than suburbs and acute neighbourhood problems remain. We outline the action taken by these three cities to try and reverse often appalling conditions, summarising briefly the long and painful process of decline and recovery, based on the Brookings Institution studies.

Turnaround actions in Louisville, Chattanooga and Akron

Within the restricted urban policy framework of the US, Louisville, Chattanooga and Akron stand out as having begun the process of regrowth and recovery, from a deeply depleted base. This summary does not do justice to the level of effort or the progress achieved but it highlights the potential within urban North America for real change, underlining a strong parallel process with European urban change, in spite of the clear differences in urban and welfare policy, in land use and in social structure.

Louisville, Kentucky

Since its merger with Jefferson County in 2006, Louisville is the largest city in the state of Kentucky with 558,000 inhabitants, located on the Ohio River in a fertile and mineral-rich region (see Figure 14.11).[71] At the crossroads of major navigable river systems, Louisville became a major commercial centre and strategic military location during the American War of Independence in the 18th century and the Civil War in the 19th century. Exploitation of the region's lumber and iron fed major industries. By 1840, it was the 12th largest city in the US. The dominant local industries were whiskey, tobacco, metals, cars, ammunitions and appliances. Major companies, such as Ford Motors, General Electric and Reynolds Tobacco Company, were based there.

Manufacturing employment peaked in the 1970s. The out-migration of middle-class households paralleled intense racial tensions within the city, which was deeply divided by the Civil Rights movement. Between 1970 and 1990, over 100,000 people left and 50,000 manufacturing jobs were lost.

Figure 14.11: Louisville, downtown and waterfront

A coalition of political and corporate leaders in the 1980s proposed ways out of the crisis, becoming the Greater Louisville Economic Development Partnership. It secured finance for ambitious revitalisation investments. Unifying regional jurisdictions became a key driver of recovery. The public–private collaboration led to the turnaround of Louisville through four actions:

- *A 'logistics coup':* the expansion of the local airport in the mid-1980s led to United Parcel Service (UPS) relocating from Chicago, creating an international package-sorting hub, Worldport, for heavy-freight business.[72] UPS now employs 20,000 people, with another 36,000 related jobs, more than compensating for the 50,000 industrial job losses. The logistics sector has benefited from the central location of the city.
- *Manufacturing:* improving community–employer relations helped to anchor two Ford plants, employing 9,300 workers, and the General Electric Appliance Park with 5,200, alongside their suppliers and related industries in the city.
- *Health:* employment doubled in two decades to 72,000 in 2008. Two of Louisville's three Fortune 500 companies are health related.
- *Physical investment:* downtown revitalisation has restored the city's standing through culture and tourism, linked to its history. The central riverfront has been restored with a large urban park.

On the other hand, the concentrated poverty and racial separation within the city, and the very poor educational attainment levels in those areas, still divide the city, in spite of progress. Some neighbourhood renewal is happening, and the city is openly trying to combat sprawl and attract more qualified and more diverse populations.

Chattanooga, Tennessee[73]

Like Kentucky, Tennessee borders on the Deep South, with the Appalachian Mountains to its east. Chattanooga is the fourth largest city in the state of Tennessee with 170,000 inhabitants. The metropolitan area has 515,000 inhabitants, 97th among US metropolitan populations. The settlement of Chattanooga developed on the Tennessee River, following the forced removal of Cherokee Native Americans in the early 19th century.[74] Railroads laid in the mid-19th century connected the city and fostered development.

The city's industrial growth coincided with the period of reconstruction after the Civil War in the 1870s. Industries, based on iron, steel and manufacturing, gave the city the title 'Pittsburgh of the South'. Major factories grew such as bottling plants for Coca-Cola and textile mills powered by electricity from major river dams. Service activities, particularly insurance companies, also grew.

The city began to decline in the 1950s. Suburbanisation followed the common US pattern of white, middle-income flight. The decaying inner city, racial tensions and high levels of pollution encouraged new suburban developments. By 1969, Chattanooga was classed as the most polluted city in the US by the federal government. By the 1980s, the city's dramatic decline was obvious. The share of manufacturing jobs dropped from one third in 1950 to below one fifth in 1990. Downtown became a 'ghost town', a 'rust belt' city, in the southern sun belt.

In the 1980s, strong civic leadership formed the Moccasin Bend Task Force funded by a local philanthropic organisation, aiming to reverse decline and racial polarisation in the city. Appointed by the city and county, it proposed a development plan for a disused land corridor along the Tennessee River.

In 1990, a more representative form of local government was created, led by an elected mayor. Impressive physical regeneration of the city centre was implemented through public–private partnerships, attracting key investments. A new research centre developed, linked to the city's university to support new technologies; the state government was unusually supportive. The strong social disparities in the city generated an initiative to turn around underperforming schools, now a national model, boosting the city's reputation, and performance.

The biggest challenges remain low wages, persistent joblessness, high poverty rates, high crime, low skills and poor educational attainments. African-Americans are two-and-a-half times as likely to be unemployed as white people. But although manufacturing continued to decline throughout the 1990s, strong growth in services, particularly leisure, hospitality, and food, has offset this. Employment has

Figure 14.12: Chattanooga, Walnut Street Bridge at night, the longest pedestrian bridge in the US

increased by 17 per cent since the 1990s, compared with eight per cent in other older industrial cities. The population has increased by two per cent, and seven per cent in the downtown area. Chattanooga has begun to recover based on population growth following consolidation with adjacent urban jurisdictions, a re-expansion of employment, progress in educational reform and physical reclamation.

Akron, Ohio[75]

Akron has 207,000 inhabitants. The metropolitan area has a population of 700,000 and forms part of the larger Cleveland metropolitan area. Its hilly terrain explains its Greek name, meaning 'high place'. The opening of the Ohio and Erie Canal in 1832, a shipping route between the Ohio River and Lake Erie, led to its industrial development, using flowing water as the power source for mills and other industries. By the 1850s, the developing railway network reduced the city's water-born activities.

Akron grew on the back of armaments, becoming an important military base during the Civil War. Flour mills, barrel factories, paper, sewage pipes, matches and farm machinery were all made there. Local coal and steam power provided cheap energy. During the 1890s, many 'dirty industries' collapsed. The only local industry to survive and thrive was the rubber industry. Goodrich, Goodyear, Firestone and General all grew there from the turn of the 20th century, linked to the spectacular growth of the car industry.

Between 1910 and 1920, the population tripled, from 69,000 to 208,000, with many immigrants arriving from southern and eastern Europe. During the Great Depression of the 1930s, industry was hard hit, and employment in the rubber industry declined from 58,000 in 1929 to 33,000 in 1939. After the Second World War, growth was fuelled by the boom of trucking and the invention of synthetic rubber. New migrants, mostly African-Americans from the Deep South, led population to peak in 1960 with 290,000 inhabitants.

Up to 1980, Akron was home to four out of the five largest tyre companies in the US. Akron became the national centre for rubber and tyre production because many older factories were empty and wages were low; good quality coal, good transport and proximity to the industry helped. However, from the 1970s, the decline of the rubber industry drove the decline of the city and the region. By the late 1980s all but one of the large rubber companies was taken over by foreign competitors. Goodyear moved its main production base elsewhere, and the whole metropolitan area lost inhabitants.

Akron took radical action to foster recovery on three fronts:

- The economy has diversified, and manufacturing 'bottomed out'. Rubber and plastics expertise has led to the emergence of the polymer chemical industry. Research facilities have expanded in the city to encourage further innovation. Local universities have connected with local businesses to facilitate this transition. The Goodyear Polymer Science Center at the University of Akron opened in 1990 (see Figure 14.13).

- Strong civic leadership, particularly the mayor, has driven the pace of change. Economic development and research-based higher education, the clean-up of developable land and city-sponsored industrial parks have helped create business incubators. Outside investment has led to new high-tech industries. Collaborative relations with the suburbs and the larger region have underpinned these efforts.
- A new convention centre, a museum of innovation, a baseball stadium and new commercial centres have been developed.

Figure 14.13: The Good Year Polymer Science Center, Akron

The major upgrading of civic infrastructure in the city centre during the 1990s reshaped Akron. US cities echo European efforts to make places more attractive, creating magnets for new investors, leading to additional resources flowing towards innovation and enterprise. While Akron's city population has continued to decline, the metropolitan area has grown, against the trend, and new economic activities are expanding.

Recovery does not happen in a vacuum. Akron, like Chattanooga and Louisville, took multiple actions to turn the city around. Economic progress is visible in employment, economic output, productivity and numbers of people in work.

The metropolitan area now performs better than others in the region. Akron's biggest challenge is to overcome its heavy industrial legacy.

Table 14.2 summarises the process of decline and recovery in the three cities.

Dynamics of recovery

Louisville, Chattanooga and Akron have followed similar trajectories to the three larger cities we looked at, but their recovery process and its impacts have been clearer and stronger. The incorporation of suburban jurisdictions has strengthened the population base and the financial and tax base of Louisville and Chattanooga. This may have influenced the dynamics of recovery, as did their increasingly diversified economies and major reinvestment in city infrastructure. Above all, strong local leadership has transformed the potential of these cities. Tables 14.3–14.9, summarise the evidence from these three cities, in order to synthesise the evidence. In Chapter Fifteen we present an overview of lessons from the US cities for Europe, highlighting contrasts and parallel experiences.

Table 14.2: Summary of decline and recovery in three smaller US cities

	Louisville	Chattanooga	Akron
Core city functions	Commercial activities at major transport hubs, rail and river; industrial concentrations; logistics hub	At crossroads of several transport networks (river, railroad); nicknamed 'Pittsburgh of the South', based on iron and steel; some older service sector functions, especially insurance	Commercial centre along major transport routes (canal, railroad); important army centre; 'rubber city', dominant industry
Main industries as they evolved	Exploitation of resources such as coal, lumber and iron; bottling (whiskey), tobacco (Reynolds); metals, cars (Ford); energy; ammunitions, army equipment; appliances (General Electric Company)	Iron and related industries; bottling (Coca Cola); energy (river dams); textile mills	Energy (water); rubber and tyres; early industries (mills, barrel, paper, sewage pipes, matches, farm machines)
Industrial peak	1970s, in terms of employment	1950s	1970s
Crisis	Loss of manufacturing; lost a quarter of its population between 1970 and 90; suburbanisation and 'white flight'; decay of the inner-city, racial tensions (1960s); fragmented political decision making; anti-urban bias in the mostly rural state of Kentucky	Loss of manufacturing, a 'rust belt' city in fast growing 'sun belt'; suburbanisation and 'white flight'; decay of the inner-city, racial tensions; high levels of pollution	Decline of rubber/tyre industry, relocation, outside competition; suburbanisation and significant outmigration
Turning points	Formation of coalition of political and corporate leaders in 1980s; annexation of neighbouring suburbs	Strong civic leadership in the 1980s recognised need for concerted action; annexation of neighbouring suburbs	Strong civic leadership
Recovery actions and progress	Successful fundraising to finance ambitious revitalisation projects; main drivers of success: logistics (UPS); stabilisation of manufacturing; health care sector, downtown revitalisation	Extensive riverfront redevelopment plan; downtown revitalisation; effort to attract high-tech businesses and investment in higher education; tackling socioeconomic disparities, focus on improving underperforming schools	Economic development with active land management; city suburban cooperation; built on established industrial know-how, e.g. Polymer Science Center; downtown investment, new civic infrastructure
Main challenges	Metropolitan fragmentation; sprawl; deprived inner-city neighbourhoods; job shortages for high skilled, high wage, high-tech employees	Deep social problems, particularly racial disparities; low wages and higher than average poverty rate; low educational levels: demand for new higher-skilled graduates for new jobs; crime	Overcoming problems of being a mono-industrial economic centre; loss of population; being in a 'rust belt' region

Supplementary evidence from Pittsburgh, Baltimore, Philadelphia

In order to capture and synthesise the evidence from the three larger cities, we present an overview of our evidence in Tables 14.3 to 14.9.

Table 14.3: Urban trajectories in Pittsburgh, Baltimore and Philadelphia

Type of industry	Pittsburgh	Baltimore	Philadelphia
Historic development	Steelworks in the Monongahela valley and elsewhere in the region; service sector activities evolved around the industries, especially banking	Shipyards and steelworks; harbour was major port of entry for European migrants; node in colonial transport networks for slaves, sugar, tobacco; commerce with expanding suburban hinterland	Textiles, metals, machinery, trains and railway, and chemicals; however, the city's industrial structure has always been more diverse, with no 'industrial giants'; commerce with expanding suburban hinterland
Roles	Steel, coal, skills, universities	Historic role, downtown, universities, culture	Historic centre, downtown, universities, culture
Pace of growth *Patterns and characteristics*	*Population growth peak:* 676,806 (1950) *Urban hierarchy peak:* 8th (1910)	*Population growth peak:* 949,708 (1950) *Urban hierarchy peak:* 2nd (1830–50)	*Population growth peak:* 2,071,605 (1950) *Urban hierarchy peak:* 2nd (1790–1820) and 2nd (1860–80)
Common characteristics	Strong population growth since mid 19th century; slowdown in growth from 1910; the cities reached their respective peak position in the urban hierarchy early on, suggesting declining relative importance since 1900; all cities experienced population peak around 1950; strong suburbanisation		

Table 14.4: Sudden decline

Sudden decline	Pittsburgh	Baltimore	Philadelphia
Reasons for decline	Sharp decline in steel industry in early 1980s *Population loss:* halved between 1950 and 90 (45%); decreasing share of total metropolitan population from 20% to 14% (1970–2000) as suburbs grew	Loss of major port functions, deindustrialisation *Population loss:* of almost a quarter between 1950 and 90 (23%); strong suburbanisation ('white flight'), decreasing share of total metropolitan population from 43%–26% (1970–2000) as suburbs grew	Since 1920s, loss of industry related to shipbuilding, textiles and apparel *Population loss:* of almost a quarter between 1950 and 90 (24%); decreasing share of total metropolitan population from 34%–27%; *Unionisation:* strong public sector unions versus restructuring
Symptoms of decline	Steel towns along Mon Valley have almost all suffered deeply from industrial decline	Large areas of inner city neighbourhoods virtually boarded up; very high crime rate	Philadelphia was on the brink on bankruptcy; major change after renewed financial crisis of early 1990s; further deterioration of poor inner-city neighbourhoods; Philadelphia was spared the worst excesses of urban renewal
Social conditions	High poverty level	Major race riots in 1968	Race riots in 1964
Common characteristics	Decline or relocation of industries; population shift from cities to suburbs, helped by federal highway construction, subsidised mortgages, etc. after Second World War; suburbanisation particularly strong in Baltimore and Philadelphia; move to suburbs also driven by access to jobs, better schools, lower house prices, lower taxes, etc; urban renewal programmes carried out slum clearance and new built public housing projects for the poor; racial tensions exploded in violent disorders in 1960s; older cities in north-east and mid-west with less space for urban expansion; 'overspill' in independent suburban municipalities; fragmentation became an obstacle for strategic development planning; concentration of poor, predominantly minority ethnic households in very deprived inner-city areas; housing decay and vacancies; deterioration of public services, due to lower tax base and higher social burden; deterioration of inadequate public school system; social problems resulting in rising crime rates and substance misuse		

Table 14.5: Recovery actions

Recovery actions	Pittsburgh	Baltimore	Philadelphia
Turnaround	'Renaissance I' (early 1950s) focus on improving the environment (pollution from 'smoke city'), economic development (creation of RIDC and URA, and some downtown revitalisation 'Renaissance II' (late 1970s) stronger focus on neighbourhood renewal and economic development, such as airport State government investing in universities and new airport (1980s)	Greater Baltimore Committee (1960s) Key project: inner harbour redevelopment (1970s) Selling the city as an overspill city for Washington Encouraging the upgrading of inner neighbourhoods Homesteading	Urban Reform Movement (1950s) less formal than other cities Large-scale public investment (1960–1970s), new office buildings Society Hill neighbourhood renewal, some waterfront revitalisation, slum clearance in North Philadelphia, industrial parks, investment in universities Private reinvestment and stabilisation (1980s) Focus on economic development, rather than urban renewal New skyscrapers Gentrification of inner city neighbourhoods Re-establishing control of city finances and focus investment on city centre (1990s) by Mayor Rendell, now governor of Pennsylvania
Impacts, changes on the ground	Attempts to incubate a new Silicon Valley failed	Population of some inner neighbourhoods becoming more mixed	Downtown repopulated, many inner neighbourhoods upgraded
Ongoing problems	Economic activity; social problems; sprawl	Social problems, spatially concentrated; sprawl of metropolitan area	Social problems, spatially concentrated; legacy of local government problems
Difference between city and metropolitan area	Pittsburgh's metropolitan region is relatively weak, in terms of income and growth, in comparison with other cities	Strong metropolitan area, now additional growth through new office developments in edge cities	Strong, dense metropolitan region

Table 14.6: City and suburbs

Tension between city and suburbs	Pittsburgh	Baltimore	Philadelphia
Downtown	A typical US CBD where office use has almost completely displaced other uses (residential retail) a '9-to-5' city; civic entrepreneurs have enabled the emergence of a 'cultural district' on the northern edge	City centre revitalised through inner harbor redevelopment that now extends along the waterfront	Large, growing and dynamic, resembles Manhattan in some areas
Metropolitan area	Weak, very fragmented (300–500 municipalities); between 1990 and 2000, 40% land use increased without population growth	Will benefit from BRAC restructuring, new office developments in metropolitan edge cities	Relatively strong and very dense metropolitan with several suburban centres; very fragmented (353 municipalities), much of metropolitan area in other state (New Jersey)
Urban population	Almost no downtown population (17,000 in a mile radius of CBD); ageing, shrinking population; 25% African-Americans, many of e astern European background	Growing downtown population (now 37,000) attracting residents from nearby Washington DC; two thirds African-American; changing demographics mean more potential urban dwellers, empty nesters, one-person households, immigrants, gays/lesbians and senior citizens	Has one of the largest growing and wealthy downtown populations of all US cities (now 60,000); 45% African-American; ageing and diversifying population
Public transport	Buses, no regional/metro-level system	Amtrak hub, adequate public transport system	Major Amtrak hub, good public transport system (SEPTA)
Common characteristics	Strong suburbanisation in US metropolitan areas since Second World War, driven by federal highway construction, subsidised mortgages, etc; sprawl problems, inadequate financial and political structures for efficient and affordable public transport systems; municipal fragmentation, metropolitan areas often divided in more than 100 municipalities		

Table 14.7: Deprived areas

Inequality	Pittsburgh	Baltimore	Philadelphia
Area problems	Some isolated enclaves, but also a 'city of neighbourhoods', steel towns in the Mon Valley very detached from economic opportunities	East and west Baltimore have large areas with concentrated urban problems	North and to a lesser degree west and south Philadelphia, as well as Camden in New Jersey are very poor
Crime	Lower than elsewhere	Among the highest rates in larger US cities	High link to deprivation
Neighbourhood renewal	Investment in areas with potential rather than the most dilapidated areas	Focus on areas with potential rather than the worst building institutions around anchor, e.g. John Hopkins University	Focus on areas with potential rather than the worst (Temple University)
Upgrading	Restricted to South Side area and some little enclaves elsewhere	Extending from waterfront area (Fells Point, Canton), now stretching northwards (Patterson Park)	Going on in several nuclei radiating from city centre (South Street, Fish Town)
Common characteristics	Both Philadelphia and Baltimore have large inner-city areas of deprivation (mostly 'black ghettos'); Pittsburgh with its smaller minority ethnic population and complex topography has small isolated enclaves rather than large inner-city 'ghettos'; services in these areas are often sub-standard; communities are often affected by crime, dysfunctional families and social problems		

Table 14.8: Knowledge industries

'Knowledge industries'	Pittsburgh	Baltimore	Philadelphia
Skills and education	*Educational level:* higher than elsewhere in older industrial cities *Higher education:* University of Pittsburgh, Carnegie Mellon University	*Educational level:* very low, damaging to prospects of inner city youth *Higher education:* Johns Hopkins University, University of Maryland	*Educational level:* low in Philadelphia compared with other cities; low quality of public schools (compared with other US cities), already 60 charter schools competing with one of the best private school systems in the US *Higher education:* Temple University, University of Pennsylvania, Drexel University
Economic development	Still three to four top companies including (PNC Bank). *Economic activity:* new economy, 10 largest employers in Pittsburgh are all related to public or civic sector, mainly health and higher education	Most large ones moved away *Economic activity:* 'Meds and eds', public sector; Department of Defence and National Security Agency restructuring (BRAC); some estimated 15,000 direct and further 20,000 indirect jobs expected from this; Port of Baltimore, number one roll-on-roll-off (car export/import).	Six Fortune 500 companies (dropped from 13 in 1950) *Economic activity:* financial services with important presence in suburbs (Vanguard)
Surviving Industries	Some engineering, several managed to retool and establish themselves in market niches	Defence system engineering	Pharmaceutical (often foreign) companies
Common characteristics	'Meds and eds': in all three cities, the higher educational and medical services are now the largest employer; some surviving but revitalised older industries; strong investment in university based research and development		

Table 14.9: Regeneration

Reinvestment regeneration	Pittsburgh	Baltimore	Philadelphia
Urban regeneration projects	Skybus public transport initiative failed; some waterfront developments (Prince Charles mentioned the potential during a visit in the 1980s); baseball stadium	Inner harbour redevelopment; place-making: campaign, tourism, events, attracting mixed population became key objective of urban development strategy	Gallery shopping mall; convention centre; stadia; some waterfront redevelopment; downtown is booming and under real estate pressure, many back office functions have been relocated to suburbs
Quality of life	City ranks highly among older industrial cities	Assets of waterfront, excellent transport links	Historic city, well connected
Common characteristics	Leadership, local decision making, strong local business leadership and civic-minded private sector are more important in US than in Europe, federal government is not a supporter of cities in the US		

FIFTEEN

Lessons for Europe

There are some unique features in the way US cities are run and have evolved that shape many of the particular problems they experience and also their progress. The fiscal autonomy of cities and suburbs with the accompanying power to levy their own taxes allows cities to exercise strong leadership from within, but often leaves struggling cities starved of support. This contrasts strongly with European regions such as the Basque province with its strong devolved power but accompanying responsibility to support cities such as Bilbao. The US model creates serious distributional problems as the greater the urban problems, the higher the need for taxes, but the weaker the tax base, the lower the potential revenues as a result of poorer populations. Poorer declining US cities have far less resources than their European counterparts.

Suburban growth is decoupled from the city in the sense that each new suburban municipality has to raise its own resources for schools, transport and so on. This polarises the city and its suburbs, undermining common interest and focusing suburban wealth on the suburbs rather than the whole city on which they depend. This trend is somewhat countered by the outward movement of poorer households and the suburbanisation of poverty.[76] In European regional and city structures, central governments and the EU play a far greater equalising role. There is far less urban investment and policy direction at federal and state level than in Europe. This makes the private sector far more important, but it also makes urban recovery slower and more difficult, due to the vast infrastructure costs of collective systems, such as public transport, education and welfare.

Over the last decade even the limited federal programmes that supported city recovery have shrunk. The much lower spending on welfare, public heath and social support shows up in high levels of inequality, absolute poverty, child development problems, poor health, poor schooling, high crime, and so on. Many government and Brookings Institution studies show these gaps.[77] Levels of segregation in US cities are extremely high with concentrations of minorities in inner areas, particularly African-Americans, often reaching 80–90 per cent in many poor and segregated neighbourhoods.[78] Such high levels of segregation and exclusion over large areas hold cities back. African-Americans and other minorities, particularly Hispanics, are still disproportionately disadvantaged, usually experiencing lower incomes, lower educational levels and higher levels of poverty. Although race relations are generally improving and achievement among African-Americans and other minorities is rising, there are still major disparities in progress.[79] The condition of inner neighbourhoods often hampers progress and limits opportunity. While neighbourhood problems in European cities increasingly echo these patterns, the intensity of decline, the extent of poverty concentrations along ethnic lines and the sheer scale of dereliction and decay in US cities far exceed what is so far experienced in Europe.

Low-density suburbs have generated a reliance on cars and 'urban freeways' that has pushed up demand for energy, levels of congestion, pollution, unsustainable land use and time lost in travel to double European levels.[80] US urban development is far more energy intensive than that of European counterparts.[81] This has also accelerated the economic decline of cities themselves.

There are major, long-term anchor institutions in US cities, such as their universities, major hospitals, private charities and home-grown companies that play a big role in shaping city progress, growing partnerships, investing in new developments and helping tackle social problems. They have a pervasive, stabilising and independent influence beyond government that is generally benign and aids recovery. These anchor institutions often benefit from large-scale local philanthropy, such as the Penn Foundation in Philadelphia. Important private companies in older industrial cities often invest their profits in family charities that then promote community-based social organisations and major service institutions, such as universities. Carnegie Mellon, the Surdna Foundation, Ford and Goodyear are examples in the cities we visited. However, their large resources are no match for the scale of social and environmental problems the cities face and their spending does not match the scale of public investment in European cities.[82]

The role of community development corporations is recognised, particularly in poorer cities. These neighbourhood-based social enterprises have received government funds, local charitable backing and often local political endorsement. They have generated 'affordable housing', local amenities and social welfare. They play a role in the poorest neighbourhoods, building the capacity of residents, developing social micro-enterprises and community outreach.[83] These corporations have become visible actors in many US cities such as Philadelphia.[84]

Overall, the progress of the six cities is precarious, more so in the aftermath of the financial crisis and recession. The persistence of intense neighbourhood decline in many parts of all the cities, the ongoing high levels of segregation by race and the absence of a wider policy approach to city recovery is hampering progress. In spite of this, some common actions around coalition building and partnerships, physical reinvestment, the expansion of higher education and attempts at school and wider urban reform all point to continuing recovery efforts, and therefore progress. The core lesson from these cities seems to be that by working at problems, adopting a long-term approach and pursuing what works, change is possible.

However, three factors make the recovery of US weak market cities particularly problematic:

- the lack of historic and deeply embedded urban infrastructure and culture, the relatively low overall population density of the US and federal support for the occupation and development of suburban land far beyond cities encouraged sprawl building, low-density land use and heavy reliance on cars and motorways, that made US cities more socially divided than European cities;

- the different cycles of rapid immigration into US cities created many human and social tensions that people sought to escape, fuelling both ghetto segregation and the rapid growth of largely white suburbs, creating much higher levels of decay and inequality than in Europe;[85]
- the fragile systems of social and public support for cities, the greater distance between government policy and ground-level realities, the lack of a pro-urban bias in funding and policy meant that the gaps in incomes, health, education and employment opportunities between older cities and the rest of the country, including surrounding suburbs, widened over the second half of the 20th century without being adequately addressed.[86]

On the other hand, the real costs of sprawl, racial segregation and inequality are increasingly recognised and there is growing acceptance of the role cities can play in the economic prosperity and social betterment of the whole nation.[87]

There are the additional and ever more pressing problems of climate change, energy shortages and wider environmental depletion caused above all by a profligate approach to land use, extraction, consumption, waste, pollution and other environmental abuses. North America stands out as a world leader in energy profligacy and environmental damage, even though Europe also bears a heavy responsibility.[88] This combination of pressures has led to a major reshaping of US perspectives and approaches in favour of more robust policies towards a different kind of city growth.[89] We will return to this shift in thinking in our concluding section.

An important influence on urban development in the US, more particularly older industrial cities of the rust belt, was the intense poverty of the rural Deep South and border states, such as Texas, Tennessee, Kentucky, coupled with a strong legacy of racial discrimination.[90] A great exodus from the rural south to northern inner cities accompanied the Civil Rights era of the 1950s and 1960s.[91] Another influence was later urban expansion of the sun belt and the west, encouraging new investment to flee the worn-out and expensive, already developed cities of the eastern seaboard and the mid-west, leading to the rapid expansion of Florida, California, Arizona, New Mexico and other southern and western states. These continent-wide pressures and opportunities provoked an earlier and more extreme decline in the vast band of 'rust belt' cities in the US, before similar problems hit Europe. Basically the chance to spread industrial growth in the southern and western states drove a more rapid and more widespread urban decline in the US, at least a decade or two before similar problems emerged in Europe.[92]

These unique conditions limit and complicate the comparisons with Europe. Nonetheless, there are many US urban experiences that suggest lessons for Europe. Box 15.1 summarises these points.

5.1: Summary of core lessons from US weak market cities

…ty governments operate in partnership with the private sector. The *private sector* plays a critical role and displays impressive levels of civic-mindedness and interest in local issues. Major support comes from private philanthropic organisations and foundations, aiding cities in real cash terms.

- *Local leadership* has played a strong role in pushing the transformation of US cities, based on partnership with private, philanthropic and community bodies, probably stronger than in Europe, given the highly devolved nature of US urban policy
- *The administrative and fiscal fragmentation* of US metropolitan areas is more extreme than in Europe and an obstacle to regional policy making and planning. *Intermunicipal cooperation* will be a major task in the overarching challenges facing metropolitan city-regions.
- *Suburbanisation* has massively transformed US metropolitan areas and its impact has been much more far-reaching than in Europe. Unsustainable *urban sprawl* is causing exaggerated consumption of land, diversion of funding resources into car-born commuting, expensive services and infrastructure and car-dependent transport. With high petrol and house prices in 2008, growing congestion and less available land, US metropolitan areas became more popular and may become denser in the future.
- *A move back to the city* has begun with cities suffering population decline, with the growth of the downtown populations in cities such as Philadelphia and Baltimore. A more diverse demographic structure supports this trend towards re-urbanisation. The cities offer relatively low-cost housing combined with proximity to jobs, services and amenities. In Baltimore, attracting more affluent people and increasing the tax base have become official policy objectives. In the larger cities, like Baltimore and Philadelphia, several inner-city neighbourhoods have been *gentrified* in recent years. The growth in urban households includes empty nesters, one-person households, immigrants, gays and lesbians and senior citizens.
- Educational and medical services, the *'meds and eds'*, attract high-tech investors into the cities and require low-paid, as well as high-paid workers, making these services more resilient in economic downturns and preventing the outward relocation of such major employers.
- *Neighbourhood renewal approaches* have shifted away from the watering can approach, distributing funds equally across the city, towards a focus on areas with a potential for development, which then might attract further investment. This approach increases inequalities and causes further deterioration of the worst neighbourhoods, whereas European cities tend to focus strongly on *reducing inequalities*.
- *Crime* levels are down from previous peaks but still much higher than in the European countries we studied. Urban safety and reduction in crime are still major tasks.
- *Education* was often mentioned as a key factor in the regeneration of cities. Cities attempt to attract the young and well educated and raise the educational level of the resident population. The failing public school systems remain a major problem in many cities. However, charter schools, state-funded but autonomous schools, freed from normal bureaucratic constraints, have done well.
- The use of *renewable energies* and greater energy efficiency are becoming more important as *environmental concerns* are starting to have an impact. North Americans are adapting to energy pressures by driving less, buying smaller cars and using public transport more. Public transit-oriented developments are increasingly planned, leading to higher densities and encouraging the recovery of older cities.

Urban interventions make a difference

A 'hands-off' and 'hands-on' urban policy has been tested in the very different types of weak market city we have encountered through this work. They are worth remembering. The US urban experience shows that many weak market cities in the US are not yet recovering, or even approaching the point where they might begin to recover.[93] US evidence suggests that urban conditions become much worse when public policy no longer supports the major investment needed to set cities on the road to recovery, following major economic and population shocks. Interestingly, our US case studies show trajectories of local progress and difficulty that support this core argument. As local city leaders with public and private resources redirect their investments in favour of more public, more social, more environmental, renewal, so the private sector becomes a partner in the changing sense of direction of US urban policy.[94] While the entrepreneurialism and innovation of US enterprise is legendary, so too are the extreme inequality and poverty, lack of universal healthcare, failures of public transport infrastructure and heavy carbon emissions.

While 'old Europe' is often seen as staid, overdeveloped and slow to change, it offers maybe some steadier models in the face of the extreme challenges facing older cities, which after all house most of Europe's large and dense population. This experience points us to the final part of our study where we draw together the lessons from seven European cities in comparison with their US counterparts, and debate the prospects for longer-term city recovery in the face of the global environmental threats and resource constraints.

Part Five
Conclusions

SIXTEEN

What have the European cities taught us? Where does the future lie?

Progress out of the ashes of war and industrial collapse

This final part of *Phoenix cities* links the threads of growth, decline and recovery within ex-industrial cities to bigger trends and patterns that underpin their history, progress and future trajectories. First we look at the main strands of progress of the cities. We then consider the lessons from their industrial collapse, subsequent recovery and current constraints. Lastly we assess the future prospects of the cities.

Densely populated European industrial cities, with their long urban roots, gradually took on a new lease of life over the late 20th and early 21st centuries, as they worked their way through political crises, economic meltdown, social disarray and physical degradation. In spite of all their overhanging problems from a disintegrated industrial past and the over-exploitation of the natural and human resources on which they depended, cities were still at the heart of the economic and social systems of the five countries we studied: the UK, Germany, Italy, France and Spain.[1] The seven former industrial cities with so much stacked against them began to make a comeback in the first decade of the 21st century, helped by strong public interventions and a burgeoning European economy, leading to a new climate of confidence.[2] This is now in question at the end of the decade.

The strong actions that all seven cities took to recover built on the urban welfare tradition of European societies dating from the harsh social consequences of the first industrial revolution.[3] There is a broad social consensus that no city, region or nation should be allowed to fall too far behind the average, in order to build the wealth of the whole society on foundations of social equity. Since raw materials, energy, human labour and land had been used collectively to produce vast wealth on which whole nations and eventually the global economy had come to depend, so whole societies became responsible for picking up the pieces in the places that suffered the greatest impacts.[4] The damage left behind by the collapse of older urban industries was so far reaching that it too became a heavier responsibility than the local cities could shoulder.

Two world wars had torn European countries and cities apart over the 20th century. The great industrial cities we studied were at the centre of this conflict, building deadly machines, vehicles, ships and aeroplanes that fed the destruction of war-torn Europe. Their advanced industrial infrastructure and production systems became invaluable in the vast war efforts. The Imperial Arms Factory in Saint-Étienne, founded under Napoleon, was the most spectacular relic of this long history of conflict. Industrial cities became enemy targets as well as lifelines for their national military machines. As dominant producers of weapons, they were subject to constant attack. Their citizens paid a heavy price, and European countries lost their world dominance in the aftermath. But France and Germany, deadly enemies for the first half of the 20th century and for long before, decided to put their differences aside and form what later became the European Community, so that Europe would never again be torn apart by such conflicts.[5] Italy, the UK and Spain, all deeply damaged by the two world wars, soon followed this unifying, resource-pooling path.

Europe's 20th-century wars greatly influenced the fate of the former industrial cities we revisited:

- Industrial cities became immeasurably more powerful as a consequence of their role in armaments, shipbuilding and aircraft manufacture; in the cases of Bremen, Sheffield and Belfast, they still play a role.
- The cities collapsed only a generation after the war, and the debt to them was still a living memory, as the Mayor of Saint-Étienne articulated during our visit, leading to a strong sense of national solidarity that could help them through their industrial crisis.[6]
- The EU was born of the post-war resolve not to let war overshadow Europe again. Much of the national and European support for struggling cities, poorer regions and communities that we have described stemmed from this commitment.[7]
- The strong post-war economic recovery of industrial cities made them the powerhouses of new growth and made their subsequent economic collapse all the more startling and significant for each country.

These four factors drove the efforts, common to all the European countries we visited, to buttress their failing cities against economic collapse and to invest heavily in their recovery.

The seven cities are still struggling to overcome the legacy of economic destruction that they did not expect or plan for. As a result they have a dazzling patchwork of initiatives, programmes and projects, underpinned by not one but several strategies, economic, transport, social, housing and increasingly environmental. Many local actors criticise their governments, regions, councils and partnership bodies for being too multistranded, uncoordinated and insecurely funded. Yet this seems to be in the nature of the cities and of the government-backed programmes that we saw. The efforts offer flexible, responsive and diverse ways of tackling multiple problems, for which no one overarching solution is obvious.[8] This patchwork of solutions offers a strong unifying pattern across different cities, plays to the strength of cities. Cities work and prosper as multifunctional, interacting crossroads of people, goods and networks. A city is more like a jigsaw that is pieced together of many small parts than a grand plan that is delivered on a blank sheet.[9]

The 'hands-on' approach of European urban policy makers, combining local vision, national backing and many stranded multilevel actions, seems to have served weak market cities in Europe well. The more 'hands-off' approach of the US over the past decades of radical economic change has weakened the ability of US weak market cities to round the corner to recovery. In spite of this policy weakness, US cities have adopted many similar approaches that have generally brought the chances of recovery nearer, as our US case studies showed in Part Four.

Ten major strands of action

In attempting to dissect the process of recovery that all cities experienced, we identified 10 dominant strands of action that supported recovery. These emerged at different times and in somewhat different shapes in different cities. But city reformers from all seven cities adopted these approaches as obvious responses to the common problems of economic, social and environmental damage.

New publicly sponsored agencies helping to deliver change

City chief executives and elected mayors rely heavily on central government and the EU for public resources, but they also appeal to the cities' own financial and industrial base, aiming to anchor companies searching out new investment possibilities. Public partnerships with private involvement were the first forms of partnership that emerged. The urban development corporations in Sheffield and Belfast were in this mould. Often, as in the case of Bilbao, Torino, Saint-Étienne and Leipzig, city and regional governments directly set up their own delivery bodies such as Bilbao Ría. These are strongly public bodies, but operate at arm's length from core government administrative functions, attracting private support and operating with many private sector methods, even though they are primarily driven by the public sector. They create innovative structures, programmes and styles of operation, very different from past public structures, creating a new image and economic focus that has attracted inward investment.[10] These bodies invest heavily in renewed infrastructure, a major remodelling and upgrading of the city's physical legacy.

Land reclamation and environmental upgrading

Large port areas, contaminated industrial sites and former mines, disused steel works, gas works, mills and warehouses have all cried out for restoration and reuse. Cities have invented whole new regeneration strategies around their damaged but potentially valuable large-scale industrial assets. Turning polluted, abused and semi-abandoned urban landscapes into useable and attractive spaces requires major public resources, most often directed into partnership bodies dedicated to converting disused city land into an asset from a liability. Leipzig, Bremen, Bilbao, Sheffield, Torino and Saint-Étienne have all led the field in cleaning up large tracts of disused land, poisoned by coal waste, chemicals and other industrial pollution, to allow reuse for housing, new enterprises, cultural facilities and open green spaces. Leipzig in particular has turned many derelict post-demolition sites into community parks. The damaged urban environments in Bilbao, Belfast, Saint-Étienne and Sheffield are being transformed by publicly funded investments.

Physical redesign and restoration of major landmarks

Former industrial era civic buildings such as old town halls, theatres, civic halls, public squares, even old department stores, factories and warehouses have been renovated and given new uses. Whole city centres have been redesigned around the reinstatement of civic buildings and the creation of attractive public spaces. The public realm has restored in even the ugliest and most decayed cities a sense of their intrinsic value and has helped rebuild civic pride, by making city cores attractive places again after decades of blight following industrial overgrowth. Relics of industrial grandeur, such as the giant factories and docks in Saint-Étienne, Belfast and Torino, are being lovingly restored and reused, among them Harland & Wolff's famous Titanic landmark.

The same is true of local landmarks in inner neighbourhoods where disused churches, schools, workshops, vestries, cinemas, banks, public baths and shop fronts, as well as homes, have been revitalised. This reinvestment has attracted new enterprises, including multiple social enterprises, opening up civic spaces to encourage new forms of citizen engagement.[11]

Transport infrastructure

Major upgrading of public transport has aimed to overcome the growing dominance of traffic and the continued expansion of roads which have dissected cities, destroying urban spaces and communities. New and upgraded tramlines in Sheffield and Saint-Étienne, modernised and new metro systems in Bilbao and Torino, restricted car access and car parking in Leipzig and Bremen, and above all the rapid expansion of pedestrian areas in all the cities, particularly noticeable in Belfast, have greatly increased pedestrian street activity and the attractions of city centre living and shopping. Traffic-tamed areas and good public transport have proved to be immensely popular with citizens and visitors, reinstating core cities at their very centres as magnets for regrowth. Only fast public transport connections and tamed traffic prevent cities from becoming congestion hubs; reduced car dependence drives the future viability of these cities.[12]

Accelerated public transport links from the cities to their regions and nearby major urban centres also open up employment opportunities by expanding local labour markets, making it easier to attract inward investment. They also help local housing markets to benefit from the stronger growth of larger, neighbouring cities with their cheaper homes. Lyon and Leeds are striking examples of large second-tier regional centres near Saint-Étienne and Sheffield, but large city neighbours are also important to other cities: Dublin to Belfast, Berlin to Leipzig, Milano to Torino, Hamburg to Bremen.

The expansion of airports to generate international business has connected cities like Bilbao, Leipzig and Belfast to international networks that help their new industries, although already there are tough challenges to face as climate change restrictions affect the real costs of air travel and road traffic, with their almost total reliance on fossil fuels. Cities are now tackling their need for wider connections by prioritising fast rail links, as these are more environmentally benign.[13]

Sprawl containment

All the cities have spread historically far beyond their traditional boundaries and rely on their city-region or metropolitan area for housing and big commercial developments to support a broad-based workforce and modern, growth-oriented economic activity. The aim of recruiting high-skilled labour from a large hinterland around core cities and housing 'knowledge workers' in more affluent suburbs has generated major investment in speeded-up urban and outer urban road networks, which in turn have fuelled more low-density development. The growth in car use outside city centres alongside continuing road investment to carry people to and from suburbs and outlying towns, has generated environmental and congestion problems on an unforeseen scale that locks inner-city populations into dirty, noisy, traffic-bound environments that vex urban planners and environmentalists alike. Bilbao has gone further than any other city in analysing its economic as well as social and environmental costs.[14] The city is extremely dense and strongly favours urban density as a more sustainable model of city development. It has invested heavily in advanced rapid public transport, linking its suburbs to an even denser centre, and it prides itself on the sense of solidarity and shared urban form that the city offers.[15] Sheffield has also remained fairly dense because two thirds of its boundary abuts a protected national park.[16]

Most cities now have containment plans to prevent further sprawl and to strengthen their inner-city recovery, recognising that there are environmental limits to outer building and social consequences from the long-run out-flow of more affluent residents. Leipzig has started to repopulate its almost abandoned core on the back of urban containment and anti-sprawl policies. Saint-Étienne has developed a smart growth agreement with all the communes surrounding it, called the SCoT plan (*Schéma de Cohérence Térritoriale* [Framework for Regional Coherence]), to prevent further sprawl.[17] Northern Ireland now restricts the building of single family houses in an ad hoc fashion due to the associated costs.[18] European cities are openly fighting for repopulation and the reoccupation of city centres with incentives to support this, in order to strengthen their city cores on which urban vitality depends.[19] As a further effort to curtail sprawl building, five of the seven cities – Torino, Saint-Étienne, Sheffield, Belfast and Bilbao – openly promote their hilly or mountainous settings as major environmental assets.

Neighbourhood renewal

The large post-war housing estates and older, decayed inner-city neighbourhoods, often occupied by newer migrants as the indigenous population has dispersed, have been deeply damaged by the deindustrialisation process. Their decayed homes, poor local services and degraded environments have made them deeply unattractive. The double pressure of job losses and influx of newcomers has led to rapid decline and intense social polarisation, distancing these areas from the rest of the city in the quality of their schools, their levels of crime and disorder, their inadequate local shops and street conditions. The cities have prioritised neighbourhood renewal as part of the recovery effort, targeting the most deprived areas with special government funding programmes. A core aim has been to offer support to and improve conditions for vulnerable populations, thereby enhancing their sense of belonging. A majority of cities have used neighbourhood renewal strategically in order to improve the residential appeal of their city with the ambition of attracting new economically active residents into the city itself. Without improving the most extreme social conditions, their ambition to attract new knowledge-based companies into the heart of the city would fail to materialise. Outer estates, which by definition are more segregated, have posed even greater challenges, but a selective mix of limited-scale demolition and multistranded upgrading has made them more attractive.

Neighbourhood renewal has targeted disadvantaged areas, partly in order to attract and retain higher-income, working households, creating a greater social mix. People with more money and more ambition living within the city create a stronger drive for progress and generate more demand for services. Saint-Étienne and Leipzig have openly promoted this approach, but other cities, like Belfast, Bremen and Sheffield, share similar ambitions. Bilbao and Torino, dense cities that have retained strong middle-class residential areas within their core, have worked to retain and enhance these affluent neighbourhoods near the city centre.

Social inclusion and social enterprise

The deindustrialisation process has done so much harm among the less skilled parts of the workforce that urgent programmes have been instituted in all European cities to remedy a new multifaceted form of social exclusion. In six cities, Torino, Bremen, Sheffield, Belfast, Bilbao and Saint-Étienne, community-based projects have grown up in neighbourhoods with working-class, immigrant and minority ethnic populations that had become extremely marginal or had never become fully integrated. In Belfast the most marginal areas were almost always white working-class communities, where a loss of economic rationale and jobs devastated the confidence of communities, made much worse by sectarian conflict. In cities like Sheffield, Saint-Étienne and Torino, with ethnically diverse low-income populations, community-based projects have often been small, involving 10 or fewer workers, a community development approach and an open-door service to people within walking distance. Bilbao and Leipzig have also set up employment agencies and social initiatives aiming to integrate unemployed populations. These projects have attempted to bridge the gap between new economic strategies and the large still declining areas experiencing concentrated poverty among 'left behind', 'left out' people. Only community-focused programmes can reach the most marginal residents, and the cities have responded with support for micro-level programmes. Several neighbourhood-level initiatives became innovative social enterprises, attracting investment and spawning new services and activities, and generating jobs and income as well as facilities and social support. These impressive, if small-scale, social transformations have unlocked new potential of marginal city areas in Torino, Belfast, Bremen, Sheffield, Bilbao, Leipzig and Saint-Étienne.

Jobs and enterprise

The cities are intense 'knowledge hubs' and major industrial cities have supported large specialist universities to fuel their scientific advances and recruit young knowledge workers. All cities want to hold on to their university graduates through the magnet of better conditions and new opportunities, in order to help foster new technologies and new enterprises, particularly in the environmental and new information technology fields. Universities have become anchor institutions in the ferment of change in these cities; they have provided space and skills for new, innovative partnerships that have generated new economic activity.

Cities with universities have actively supported the start-up of new businesses through the provision of 'incubator' spaces, to attract high-tech growth industries employing bright entrepreneurial graduates, often reusing old industrial spaces. Cities have thus generated a new economic climate, favouring the private sector and appealing to young entrepreneurs, using cultural attractions and generating a new kind of 'service city' wealth to foster the knowledge economy. This shift has accounted for many of the new jobs, reflected in the categories of work now dominant in the cities. High-skill enterprises in media, culture, new communication technologies, design and financial services have generated new service demand in retail, entertainment, catering, cleaning, health, childcare and so on, fuelling a cycle of regrowth at a high and low level.[20] Belfast's Cathedral Quarter and Sheffield's revitalised Cultural Industries Quarter have grown through this very targeted clustering of knowledge-based, creative industries.[21]

The cities have also generated a new industrial revolution based on high-tech engineering and off-shoot new industries growing out of their old industrial base. Every city has tried to capitalise on the historic knowledge base of their former giant industries, now adapted to the new economic environment. Small and medium enterprises (SMEs) have become the dominant industrial and entrepreneurial form again, multiplying in the ashes of the collapsed industrial giants of the 20th century. The SMEs have proved more resilient, more flexible and more creative in surviving the economic uncertainties of the current climate than bigger enterprises.[22] Among the small start-up businesses are some innovative companies developing environmental technologies that will potentially build whole new industries. Turbines in Belfast, solar panels in Leipzig, *avant garde* engines in Torino, Bremen and Sheffield point the way to a very different kind of enterprising future.

Building new skills within the population

Changing the skills base of a large underemployed population has been essential to attracting new companies and integrating poorer neighbourhoods and communities. Locally targeted skills-building and support programmes have helped former manufacturing workers and a new generation of marginalised youth into new jobs. Agencies specially set up to match the employment needs of incoming firms with the employment needs of local low-skilled residents have played a key role in attracting new private companies looking for a more skilled and adaptable workforce. Skills development has involved immensely detailed, people-specific, long-term and often relatively small-scale local programmes to achieve this complex skills transition. Cities supported intermediate, semi-subsidised job recruitment and training agreements with private companies in order to help new investors, existing residents and the city's economic base. The potential for linking public commitment, private company involvement and resident support into work contracts with the city was successfully trialled in Sheffield, Belfast, Leipzig and Bilbao. Inward investors have been helped through these channels to bridge the gap with the local workforce.

Higher education institutions have also become involved in economic alliances, through research partnerships, research-based incubators and science parks, often focused on new environmental, biomedical and advanced engineering technologies. Even so, many of the new 'knowledge' jobs have attracted skilled workers from outside the cities. This has helped repopulate cities and diversify their populations, but it limited the direct job benefits for local workers. Former industrial skills have often failed to match the higher-level needs of new job markets. There is much more skill building to do.

Civic leadership and community participation

Civic leaders rely on citizen involvement as they draw up their new plans, recognising that only a whole city effort will make the new approaches to regeneration and renewal work. Citizen participation became a dominant rallying cry in city recovery over the 1990s, although it was often criticised by community activists as tokenism. Nonetheless, city leaders recognise that the dislocation of the post-industrial crisis has meant that they need their citizens to be able to tackle problems and shape consensual ways forward. As big production systems failed, economic prosperity collapsed and public support evaporated. This led to the emergence of more participative local politics. The severity of the economic problems has forced leaders to adopt a more bottom-up approach to tackling city problems. Civic leaders need to reunite their fragmented cities and as a result are focused on making social inclusion a reality, by involving affected citizens directly in finding new solutions. The direct involvement of citizen groups in the future of cities has encouraged local leaders in their bold plans for transformation. Citizens are ready for a new start, while also fighting to protect and build on their urban industrial heritage. All the cities advocate public debate, community participation and carefully brokered planning. This involvement has steadied the hand of leaders and galvanised support for many of the reclamations, restorations and partnerships that have changed the direction of cities. For cities without their citizens are as nothing.

These 10 strands of action together have pulled weak market cities back from the brink of collapse. Doubtless there have been many other less conspicuous factors that will become clearer as the cities evolve. One of the clearest of these is the environmental limits within which such over-exploited cities are now forced to operate.

There was often an implicit tension between economic, social and environmental needs, the three pillars of sustainable action, in the period of intense recovery action, even though the cities broadly applied all three principles in their recovery efforts. Sustainable development, meaning a durable and self-regenerating process of change and progress that does not overstep environmental and resource limits, was poorly understood and only fully recognised in the cities long after their recovery process was under way. The threat of severe resource constraints was largely responsible for the economic and social disintegration that cities underwent in the 1970s and 1980s, following the first major oil crisis. Inspite of this, a return to growth was the overriding priority until 2007–08, when a new high oil price hike and financial crisis undermined confidence in the new economic model.[23]

Over the 1980s and 1990s, fragile urban economies prioritised social and economic imperatives over environmental underpinnings, believing that jobs were the most urgent priority and social need the most legitimate claim on extra resources. These issues were politically popular, whereas climate change was still seen as a far away problem. In spite of this, the framework of sustainable development, involving the interaction of economic, social and environmental needs, underpinned the turnaround of these cities, transforming their conditions in the direction of recovery.

By 2007, climate change had risen to the top of the European agenda and it became clear that the rise in energy demand and the emission of greenhouse gases had to be curbed if dangerous climate change was to be avoided. New industries could be born of the new environmental technologies, and German cities are already leading on this. Other cities like Torino and Sheffield are anxious to catch up. The pressing challenge of climate change and resource constraints may help these cities in the next phase of recovery. This is our core conclusion, which we come to at the end. In the next section we look at the rapid transition now under way into an era of galloping environmental problems.

The three economies of weak market cities

The seven cities went through three major development phases that illuminate their path to the future. The great growth period of the seven cities could be called the *first industrial economy*. The ugly, 'smoke-stack' image, born of their strongest period of industrial expansion, greatly scarred the cities and underlined their biggest future risk, further environmental degradation and more intense social dislocation. The irony is that these manufacturing communities paid the highest environmental and social price for growth during their heyday, when their air, soil and water were poisoned; their 'hovels' were wiped out and replaced by giant mass high-rise housing estates; their workers were valued but mechanised into single-skill machine operators; and their children were born into an industrial society out of which they would be ejected at the point of large-scale industrial failures. There were few immediate or obvious ways out of these problems and their impacts were largely unforeseen.[24]

The epicentres of industrial success were simultaneously symbolic of the short-lived power of plentiful and cheap coal and later oil, highly unionised and specialised industrial workers, social disruption through intense mobility and sheer poverty, resulting from a desperate search for progress by families at the margins of industrial change.[25] Deep tensions accompanied the harsh industrial structures and processes. We can see a similar process now being played out globally in fast developing cities of the South, which have taken over many of our manufacturing roles.[26] The now largely deindustrialised, overdeveloped North is simply trying to clear up the debris left by a disintegrated first industrial economy.[27] The resource impact of the first industrial economy is in the end self-destructive.

The economic conditions of the recent recovery period could be called the *second post-industrial economy*. The seven cities' recovery efforts won wide support. They built a better and arguably more sustainable future on a more diverse, more modest and more tempered approach to their economy, social conditions and environment. Yet now they face an uncertain and precarious future. Europe and the US have undergone the most serious financial crisis since the 1930s, having hit major resource constraints and extraordinary price rises in oil and other commodities, including food. We face global financial and resource uncertainties on an unprecedented scale.[28]

The task of upgrading local environments, remediating damaged land, restoring the stock of older buildings and homes, and transforming the skills base of local populations is far from complete despite progress thus far. Yet, just at the point where the cities are gaining a critical mass of new enterprises, facilities, services and infrastructure, the environmental crunch threatens to limit their progress. The consequences of the 'credit crunch' and volatile energy prices are far-reaching but already these cities, which still rely on manufacturing and its ancillary services to a significant extent, have grown new enterprises on the back of their earlier resource constraints and financial crises. In the face of job shrinkage and vulnerable markets, school leavers and new graduates face poor prospects all over again.[29] These problems affect more vulnerable areas more sharply, so already social inequalities are widening and job losses are hitting poorer families, poorer cities and poorer regions of Europe. Some of the social programmes working to revitalise neighbourhoods and the local employment projects set up to help vulnerable potential workers are being undermined by a shortage of cash and little immediate prospect of renewed funding.[30]

Property values everywhere have fallen, particularly for new commercial property, through which the cities hoped to galvanise new enterprise. The competition between cities to attract new investment has intensified and overdeveloped economies and cities may still lose ground to younger, still developing cities and regions. This uncertainty has caused city development plans to stall and is slowing progress on large developments already under way. The post-industrial economy relies on businesses that are directly or indirectly dependent on media, communications, advanced design, high-tech engineering and 'back office' sectors of the wider financial services industry. They are therefore deeply affected by the wider economic turmoil, although far less so than bigger, more powerful centres. Their relatively cheap and readily available labour, their lower-cost services and reclaimed spaces may help them survive better than more pressured global centres. The new enterprises born of their older industrial roots may build their next round of recovery.

Yet outstanding plans for major infrastructure investment, such as fast rail links to bigger cities or internal tram systems within cities, which would have further enhanced the growth potential and sustainability of cities, are currently in question, and there is a risk that the wider connections needed to prosper in a more interconnected world may not materialise for some time. This second, largely post-industrial, economy has become, if anything, more unstable and unsustainable than the first industrial economy, with even higher consumption of energy and materials, and even more waste.[31]

The *third resource-constrained economy* is only just emerging, driven by finite environmental limits and the urgency of drastically reducing carbon emissions, which have risen rapidly since the outset of the industrial revolution and carried on rising fast, during the post-industrial era. Climate change is in fact largely driven by the first industrial and second post-industrial economies.[32] This makes already used places valuable as local alternatives to the exponential growth of cities in far-off South Asian countries and other parts of the global South.[33] The intense economic, environmental and social constraints facing fast expanding cities of the global South and the growth areas of Europe, such as the London and Paris regions, Bavaria and Frankfurt in Germany, are already far tighter than those that faced European and US cities over the last two centuries. Thus the recurring problems of growth and decline are driven by an unstable wider economy, that is shaken by finite resources, including energy, raw materials and space. These resources are dwindling, hard to access and costly to process.

The ongoing recycling and recovery of the seven cities will happen from now on within far tighter limits than at the turn of the 21st century, when they began to edge back into recovery. This makes the third, resource-constrained economy decisively different from the first two. However, many of the collective investments made over the last two decades have laid the foundations for a more sustainable future. Weak market cities are de facto resource constrained already, and they have learned to make good and mend what they have broken. Figure 16.1 shows the three phases of growth outlined.

We see three future scenarios derived from the past and current patterns, in the light of the global financial crisis and global resource constraints (see Figure 16.2).

Prosperity with a different kind of growth?

Scenarios two and three are already emerging in the seven cities. There is now widespread acceptance of the idea of 'limits to growth', first muted during the first big oil crisis of 1973, which shook the industrial foundation of our cities.[34] Continuing economic growth requires a radical rethink of how we use finite planetary resources, including land, water, air, minerals, natural ecosystems, and above all, energy. The meaning of prosperity in the light of these constraints has to radically change.[35] The world's finite supply of fossil fuels, oil and gas, now underlined by the urgency of limiting their use to prevent over-heating of the planet itself through the greenhouse effect, raises major questions about energy sources and the urgency of energy saving. [36]

Everything the seven cities do relies heavily on energy consumption. They rely on cars and roads, because of their large suburbs. Their homes and buildings are generally highly energy-intensive. Their new office developments invariably use steel, concrete and glass, all energy-intensive and environmentally costly materials that are in ever shorter supply. Air conditioning intensifies the urban 'heat islands', pushing up temperatures even in northern cities. They all seek to expand their airport connections as a way of attracting international investment and recognition. Their economies still rely almost entirely on mostly imported fossil fuels for their growth. Yet they depend on a fundamentally resource-constrained environment.

The cities are thus highly vulnerable to both growing energy and material shortages, and to climate change itself, the 'biggest threat facing humanity'. They are not yet prepared for the 80–90 per cent reduction in carbon emissions that is now agreed as necessary in Europe and the US over the coming 40 years if humanity is to survive this century.[37] It is possible to argue that both the era of industrial giants and the more recent period of post-industrial regrowth based on intense consumerism sowed the seeds of their own eventual destruction. The resource-constrained economy is just emerging and offers a more long-term way forward.

US weak market cities in 2008 responded particularly strongly to the impact of high energy prices on behaviour because they burn almost twice as much energy per head as Europe, and rely far more on energy-intensive cars.[38] House prices fell faster in far-flung suburbs than in inner cities because of the high costs of

Figure 16.1: The three major development phases in weak market cities, based on the experience of the seven European cities

First industrial economy – production and consumption bonanza

Explosive economic growth
Intensive use of resources
Increasing outputs and productivity
Wealth accumulation
Mass goods

Social transformation
Population boom
Dislocated social networks
Overcrowded, insanitary slums
Rising inequality
'Alienation'
Explosion of middle classes

Environmental exploitation
Mass-scale extraction
Massive energy demands
Pollution and land contamination
Loss of biodiversity, greenery
Damaged ecosystems
Rapid resource depletion

Eventual collapse of big heavy industries
Resource depletion, oil price explosion
Major political and social upheaval
Devastating impact on seven cities
Loss of livliehood and wealth
Rapid decay of infrastructure
Damaged urban environments

Second post- industrial economy – struggle to regain ground

Public infrastructure
Reclaim public buildiings and spaces
Place making and local pride
Historic value, embodied energy
Work with universities and other
public institutions

Social integration
Invest in poor communities
Anti-crime measures
Develop new skills for new jobs
Upgrade local environments
Quality of life

New economy
Public generates private investment
Support for local jobs and firms
Some major upcoming companies
New technologies,
e.g. environment, SMEs
Cultural and media growth

Former industrial cities regain population and jobs
More mixed, diverse, 'sober' economies
Significant, tangible but fragile progress towards recovery

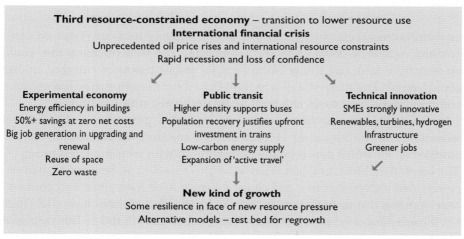

Third resource-constrained economy – transition to lower resource use
International financial crisis
Unprecedented oil price rises and international resource constraints
Rapid recession and loss of confidence

Experimental economy
Energy efficiency in buildings
50%+ savings at zero net costs
Big job generation in upgrading and
renewal
Reuse of space
Zero waste

Public transit
Higher density supports buses
Population recovery justifies upfront
investment in trains
Low-carbon energy supply
Expansion of 'active travel'

Technical innovation
SMEs strongly innovative
Renewables, turbines, hydrogen
Infrastructure
Greener jobs

New kind of growth
Some resilience in face of new resource pressure
Alternative models – test bed for regrowth

Figure 16.2: Scenarios for weak market cities

Hit by further decline – following burst of recovery	Stable low-level survival economy – ticking over	New resource-constrained economy – grows in new more sustainable ways
Based on withdrawal of credit and loss of markets	Based on big investments of past decade	Based on further reuse of existing infrastructure, restoring older buildings, creating a more cared-for collective environment – creating local jobs
Rapid decay of public spaces as public resources shrink under credit crunch	Population accepts lower wages and lower general standards as trade-off for calmer lifestyle, more space and strong sense of belonging	Skills for new alternative economy quickly develop in large populations of former manual workers
Energy costs and new infrastructure needs overwhelm local economy, making it difficult for new enterprises to emerge or survive	Small new enterprises survive with low overheads and energetic efforts of young graduates, entrepreneurs and researchers, often with local roots	New 'green' enterprises emerge around retro-fitting, energy saving and green spaces
Loss of small local services due to general economic shrinkage	Major assets of previously decaying cities help cities and their populations survive	Cities regain population as 'compact living' becomes more attractive
Big job losses at bottom and further skills decline	Cultural and social attractions of city living sustain population growth in city centres	Cities become models of energy-efficient, socially cohesive, culturally and technically innovative economies
City decay and cheap outer building fuels demand for further homes		

car commuting; there was evidence of people moving back into cities to avoid commuting; knock-down prices for 'gas-guzzling' cars were offered as they could no longer be sold; and a new enthusiasm for public transport emerged among commuters.[39] The sharp reaction in the US to dramatic price rises and resource constraints benefited cities, although it also devastated major industries.

In 2009 the US announced a greatly expanded programme of fossil fuel reduction and the House of Representatives approved its first major climate change bill, tempered as it is by the compromises with special interest groups.[40] The combined threats of financial crisis, serious recession and renewed job losses, constrained energy supplies, and climate change itself have generated counter-developments that strongly favour cities, and particularly former industrial cities. On the other hand the pressures to restart economic growth and de facto resource consumption are strong enough to undermine serious attempts at more sustainable growth. Nonetheless, where the US has seemed far behind in the recovery process of its weak market cities, it has now moved rapidly forward in changing thinking on the future of cities within a finite and distressed planetary system. [41]

A new kind of growth

Five factors help ex-industrial cities facing the triple threat of severe economic instability, resource constraints and destabilising climate change:

- their past experience of decline and recovery provides invaluable lessons for dealing with economic turbulence and resource shortages;
- their history of scientific innovation, entrepreneurial, workshop-based inventiveness is linked to their strong university research bases. This is already helping their current phase of development;
- their experience of recycling the physical assets that are in dwindling supply worldwide, all with high embodied energy, helps meet the increase in demand in the resource-constrained environment we face − their land, buildings and dense infrastructure;
- their capacity to conserve energy is based on their concentrated populations, shared spaces and services;[42]
- their history of intense social and political upheaval has thrown up outstanding civic leadership to address acute human needs − rapid population shifts, gross inequality, intense poverty and deep-set worklessness − often provoking civic unrest.

Older industrial cities have already begun to recover under dramatically changed conditions and can exploit their underused assets to build a new kind of resource-constrained economy. Following the disappearance of earlier industrial giants, smaller, more agile companies came to dominate their economies and there is evidence from these cities that these smaller enterprises are in fact showing greater resilience than their giant forebears. [43]

Small companies tend to innovate. They grow on the back of new ideas and can more readily find ways to cut current energy and resource use dramatically. They will quickly find alternatives because they move faster and have more flexibility to change. Energy-saving equipment, alternative energy generation, a new retro-fit industry based on small local builders and local suppliers, alternative food markets and alternative transport which can quarter energy use in buildings are all large potential growth enterprises within cities. [44] It will take a combination of research, invention, enterprise, local capacity, public backing and government regulation to help such new approaches take root.

There are already the seeds of these changes, planted within the cities as outlined in scenario three and shown in Figures 16.3–9.

Figure 16.3: Belfast – first commercial sea turbine being built in Harland & Wolff's historic Titanic dock, 2008

Belfast became the first city in the world to build a commercially viable tidal turbine, now implanted off its coast in Strangford Loch in 2008, to generate electricity from tidal energy. The success of the tidal turbine, outperforming forecast outputs, has reinforced the UK's position as a world leader in marine technology with the prospect of more tidal turbines. The New Science Park in the Titanic Quarter is becoming a production centre for wind and sea turbines.[45] Northern Ireland is almost 100 per cent dependent on imported fossils fuels, and is now seriously debating how to pull itself out of the recession through energy efficiency measures linked to jobs, with a radical civic alliance backing a bold green New Deal.[46]

Figure 16.4: Bremen – huge kite helps container ship across Atlantic in first modern commercial sailing ship

Bremen was the first city in the world to launch a commercial container ship, part-powered by a wind sail in 2008, cutting energy use by 30 per cent. The reconstruction of the old port and the rebuilding of harbour facilities coupled with the strength of the city's scientific and technical skills laid strong foundations for this world first.

Figure 16.5: Torino – incubator workshop in Environmental Park testing hydrogen-based vehicles

Torino's Environment Park has built the first potentially commercial noiseless, pollution-free urban 'Vespa', powered by surplus night-time electricity converted into small hydrogen fuel cells. The city also plans to retro-fit all its old buildings to the highest energy standards, aiming to be a European leader in this most obvious of energy efficiency measures. It, too, wants to lead in environmental innovations.

Figure 16.6: Sheffield – Veolia Environmental Services District Energy Network: state of the art combined heat and power plant, providing electricity and heating for commercial and public buildings across Sheffield

Sheffield heats and lights most of its city centre buildings through a 'state of the art' local combined heat and power plant. The University of Sheffield has developed an advanced manufacturing park based on renewable technologies.

Leipzig has Europe's largest solar power factory on its edge, and has pioneered the reclamation of sulphur-polluted open-cast mining land, converting a large devastated waste land back into a pollution-free 'lake district'.

Figure 16.7: Leipzig – solar factory and generator outside city

Bilbao, the densest city in our study, limits cars through public transport, saving energy and containing sprawl.

Figure 16.8: Bilbao – firmly committed to modern public transport and high-density living

Saint-Étienne is surrounded by a national park, rolling hills and river valleys which are being promoted as 'green tourist' attractions.

Figure 16.9: Saint-Étienne – developing a strong sprawl containment approach to encourage environmental protection and city recovery

A new carbon-capped economy

The cities may be able to halve their energy use within 10 years through tried and tested measures that would pay back the investment in energy saving over the same period. This would reverse the current trends of rising energy use. Some European countries, most notably Germany, are offering big incentives for the crucial task of saving energy to reduce dependence on oil, coal and gas.[47] Car use could be halved with stronger incentives for public transport, dedicating more road space to bus and cycle lanes, widening pavements to encourage pedestrians and severely restricting parking within cities. The cities could apply these policies far beyond the small central core where they have pioneered them, making cities far more liveable and attractive. They have the skill and know-how to spread *avant garde* ideas and can borrow know-how from elsewhere. For example, Belfast is importing know-how from Dublin's light rail designs to transform its currently inadequate public transport.

Transformational approaches to a new phase of city recovery will be driven by stronger government regulation of carbon emissions, a much tighter quota or rationing system for carbon use, driving swift and decisive action by the cities themselves. The attempt to reach a global agreement on carbon reduction and energy saving is designed to prevent polluting places and industries gaining an advantage through short-term lower costs. The necessarily high upfront investments in energy saving and alternative renewable energy generation offer a longer-term payback.[57]

The EU is setting tougher targets than any other major region of the world, which will force all the cities we studied down the road of radical energy shifts and a transformation of their economies. Europe's history since the Second World War of intervening to enforce collective social, economic and environmental benefits makes this proposed regulation of our environment credible. But there are many risks:

- European governments are reliant on the US government and China signing an international agreement on radical carbon reduction in order to reduce the risks of runaway climate change and finite resource depletion.[58]
- Fast-growing Asian, African and Latin American economies now produce most of our goods, rapidly increasing their energy demand and pollution, extracting vastly more resources than are replenishable within the timescale left to avert catastrophe.[59] Limiting their growth is not a current option.
- US cities, states and federal government are rapidly moving into new partnerships on the control of greenhouse gases, the drive for renewable energy and the development of other new green technologies within a context of using double the energy per person of European populations.[60] Their ability to deliver is crucial to our shared future.

There are unmistakable signs that the environmental and social limits that constrained these cities in their first industrial crisis are being replayed around the globe on a vast scale. For these reasons, the seven cities and others like them in the US and throughout Europe are at the forefront of the resource-constrained revolution we are just beginning.

Surviving the new environmental threat

The problem that now most taxes scientists and global leaders is the unknown threat of climate change, linked to environmental limits. Yet our cities are potentially in a stronger position than other, more prosperous places. Their future is precariously balanced between their history of explosive growth, environmental and social damage, and their recent recovery based on a more compact, more socially integrated and more environmentally restorative vision. There are many signs of progress. Ahead of the US government agreeing to international control on energy use, US cities one by one have signed up to the climate change agenda and are beginning to act on it. They can see that it is in their interests to do so, and that they stand to gain from it.[52]

Meanwhile, European cities are being forced through more immediate pressures to act in environmentally helpful ways:

- *short of land*, they have to combat sprawl;
- *short of US-style urban motorways*, they have to rely on public transport;
- *short of space*, they have to maintain high-density and infill building;
- *short of oil*, they use smaller cars and pay more tax on vehicles, road use and cars themselves, making public transport more attractive;
- *short of new resources*, the denser urban forms of European cities create and recreate public squares, building around shared courtyards, maintaining urban parks and providing high-quality public infrastructure and services to unify their dense urban populations.

These more collective, more shared forms of city living are far more energy efficient and more environmentally and socially benign than the more spread-out, suburban-style low-density building that has driven US metropolitan growth. A recent study of New York showed that of itself dense, urban form is at least twice as energy efficient as low-density suburban building, because buildings are joined together in blocks of flats that reduce energy needs through shared walls and floors, and because public transit is a prerequisite for high density as there simply is not the room for cars.[53] Both these characteristics make high-density European cities less resource-intensive than typical US cities, even though they still face the challenge of at least an 80 per cent reduction in current energy use.

The relatively dense urban form of the seven cities and the collective recovery measures taken by the cities have already pushed them in the direction of greater sustainability. Sharing resources is in the nature of cities and it happens more at higher density.[54] The drive for recovery was a common ambition based on collective need. An 80 per cent reduction in energy use could not only generate another round of recovery, but could also demonstrate that city living can work within environmental limits.[55] Socially, there are enormous challenges in proximity between diverse communities, but social progress was born of equalisation, integration and proximity. So it is possible that new, more tolerant forms of sharing resources will emerge in cities, where the imperatives are strongest.

A local approach to environmental care requires vastly more input of human effort but lower inputs of materials and energy.[56] This could address a major unresolved social problem of struggling cities, offering new work opportunities for disaffected youth, particularly minority youth. Opportunities for young people from working-class backgrounds have never fully recovered from the blows to their fathers' and grandfathers' livelihoods. One fifth of school leavers from poor backgrounds were out of work during the strongest recovery period, and double this level in the poorer neighbourhoods of the weaker cities, particularly Saint-Étienne, Sheffield, Leipzig and Belfast.

Currently large numbers of young people are leaving school unprepared for the world of work, poorly educated, low achieving, demotivated and lacking in prospects or role models. This phenomenon across all our cities, common among children of former industrial workers and the children of some immigrant groups in most big European cities, reflects the social Achilles heel of energy-dependent economies – casting labour aside as and when costs dictate, destroying confidence, undermining skills and eventually threatening social stability.

In developing new local enterprises and new skills to combat climate change, there will be many new types of work requiring human inputs and creating new jobs. Cities can develop the pool of small businesses and offer job prospects to the low-skilled, poorly educated, underemployed local labour force: to repair or retro-fit homes and other buildings; to maintain shared spaces; to control traffic and parking; to service public transport, public health, local parks and local social care; vital services to help cities work.[57]

The small-scale community-based skill-building programmes we uncovered in Sheffield, Belfast, Torino, Bilbao and Bremen were far more significant as models than their size suggested because they showed how to break the log-jam of joblessness, unrest and crime on the one hand, and how to find and train fresh, newly skilled workers on the other. If we are to meet our environmental targets, then we will need to employ a newly energised younger generation to do the new, environmentally oriented, skilled but largely manual jobs of the 'third economy', a low-carbon, sustainable economy in transition. The proposed green New Deal in Northern Ireland, the German Energy Agency's *Zukunft Hause* programme, Torino's sustainable old buildings commitment and Kier Construction's building training programme in Sheffield all underpin the significance of this 'new economy'.[58]

The *first* industrial economy played itself out as jobs vanished and was replaced by the *second* post-industrial, knowledge-based, high-tech economy, which still left large parts of the population deskilled and marginalised. Industrial cities have gained costly experience of the limits imposed on human survival by their natural environment, their dependence on finite fossil fuels and their over-concentration on wealth creation to the detriment of social stability and environmental sustainability. This points towards a different kind of future that reconciles resource limits, local economic activity and a new kind of wealth, based on shared, recycled spaces, minimal damage and pollution, people-friendly compact communities. Using the human energy of local populations to achieve this kind of social and environmental transformation will drive the *third*, resource-constrained economy.[59]

The seven cities and their US counterparts have already lived through large-scale economic, social and environmental crises. They have responded with public investment in environmental upgrading, economic development and social support. In the end they found that there were no trade-offs between the three pillars of sustainable development. All were pivotal to recovery and all underpin the new ways now being forged. With today's new triple crises of *economic* uncertainty, *social* polarisation and the *environmental* threat of resource limits and climate change, they are better prepared and in a stronger position to respond than in the previous crisis of 30 years ago.

Will the climate change agenda transform the potential of cities?

Saving energy, reducing damaging emissions and changing behaviour will require strong leadership and regulation, with some form of carbon rationing or taxing that pushes collective rather than individual action and brings society together on a more equal footing. In the same way as the world wars brought European societies closer together in their aftermath, so will the global threat of climate change and the urgency of international agreement on resource distribution push collective action, above all in cities, the large, collective engines of economic and social advance, that are resource hungry and problem prone but that spawn innovation, enterprise and radical change. The costs of not responding to the environmental crisis are unthinkable.[60] But responding involves life-changing reforms. The former industrial cities are already on a more socially and economically tempered pathway towards sustainability. They have been forced to rescue their depleted environments in order to survive.

Urban forms now make up the majority of human settlements. They are the places where it is easiest to undertake collective action since they already have collective structures. Thus the seven European cities and hundreds like them across two continents are good places to start the radical transformations that whole continents will be forced to embrace. They have less to lose than more prosperous cities, having experienced sharp decline and slow, painful regrowth. They are used to the toil of making things that work. They have the technical and industrial know-how that will be needed to develop new solutions. They are big and strong enough to become the seedbeds of new experiments, as indeed they already are. They have learned to recycle their wasted buildings, infrastructure and land. They could become 'zero waste' centres as the imperative of preserving and reusing all possible resources overrides the uncontrolled consumption patterns of the past.

The seven cities have learned over the last 20 years to restore and protect their environments; they could double or triple their tree cover and green spaces, as Curitiba in Brazil has done since 1975, creating shading, cooling, carbon absorption and flood protection.[61] They have struggled to improve their poorest areas and integrate their global migrants into local society, but their efforts show new ways of sharing and cooperating. At the same time, their economic momentum could become more socially and environmentally equitable, as in practice European health, education and welfare systems at least partially demonstrate. These are not far-off dreams, but the stark choices facing human society.[62] How else will the tragedy of the global commons will be averted and the global common weal prevail?[63]

The imaginative power of cities and the infectious nature of new ideas is spreading successful experiments fast. These cities are not as dominated by the higher-level financial services economy as more central, regional and national capitals; they live by the 'stuff of invention' that is closer to the things that people actually use. Tangible, useable goods and services make them more resilient.[64] The uncertain future may give them the chance to show more grounded ways forward. Inventive approaches are more likely to emerge in Belfast or Bilbao, where needs must, than in London or Paris, where extreme wealth has driven intense poverty.

There are overarching links in the cities between social, economic, physical and environmental imperatives. Social problems abound, as a result of economic collapse and the long-run fractures it caused in social structures. Cities respond strongly to this by trying to build new skills, create new jobs and improve neighbourhood conditions. But economic needs create a sense of urgency and city leaders are anxious to attract new investors with a direct benefit to job growth, skill building and investment in the city. A dominant goal is a new kind of economy and 'sustainable' jobs, underpinning a new inventiveness in a resource-constrained environment. Cities have shown that they recover by restoring their urban environments and finding new ways of doing things, thus helping their disadvantaged populations back into work. The two go together in a recycling of used and renewable resources that underpin prosperity with a different kind of growth. These interlocking elements of city recovery together point to a more sustainable future, both for the cities in this study on both sides of the Atlantic, and for the planet. For on the survival of cities, within ever tighter environmental limits, hinges the survival of the planet.

Notes

Part One

Chapter One

[1] ODPM (2004)
[2] Briggs (1968); Power (1993)
[3] Thompson (1990)
[4] Schumacher (1993); Carson (1962)
[5] Cairncross (1991); Rees (1999)
[6] ECOTEC Research and Consulting Ltd/ECORYS (2007); Brookings Institution (2007a, 2007b)
[7] Urban Audit, (2009)
[8] Katz (2004)
[9] Porritt (2005)
[10] DEFRA (2006); WCED (1987)
[11] UN (1992)

Chapter Two

[12] Brookings Institution (2007a)
[13] Ravetz (1974)
[14] Power (1993)
[15] Dunleavy (1981)
[16] JRF (1995); Dorling et al (2007)
[17] ECOTEC Research and Consulting Ltd/ECORYS (2007)
[18] EC/Directorate-General for Regional Policy (2005)
[19] Audit Commission (2008)
[20] Bourdieu et al (1999)

Chapter Three

[21] Young (1990)
[22] The Local Government, Planning and Land Act 1980 (Chapter 65) established urban development corporations (UDCs); DETR (1999)
[23] See CASEreports at http://sticerd.lse.ac.uk/case/_new/publications/series.asp?prog=CR
[24] The Compagnia di San Paolo had assets of €5.7 billion in 2003, making it Europe's fourth biggest foundation in terms of assets (see www.watsonwyatt.com/europe/pubs/globalinvestment/render2.asp?id=14269)
[25] Florida (2002).
[26] Hutton (1995)
[27] Rees (1999)
[28] *The Economist* (2008a)
[29] Power and Mumford (1999)
[30] EC/Directorate-General for Regional Policy (2005)
[31] Power (2007)
[32] ODPM (2004); CURDS (1999a, 1999b)
[33] Shrinking Cities programme: www.shrinkingcities.com/
[34] DETR (1999)
[35] Evidence from the Brookings Institution suggests that US cities are already leading the way in this. See US Conference of Mayors: www.usmayors.org/climateprotection/; Clinton Foundation, International Clinton Climate Initiative: www.c40cities.org/; Gore (2007). Manchester and Newcastle have declared their intention to become 'environmental

leaders' in the field; see www.manchesterismyplanet.com; www.manchester.gov.uk/manchestergreencity

[36] DETR (1999)

[37] The Corrymeela Community exhibition 'Outside in', Waterfront Hall, Belfast, 2007; 'State of the City IV' Conference, Belfast, 19 April 2007

[38] Altar Fresco, the 'City of God', Parish Church of St Thomas and St Edmund, Salisbury.

[39] Newman (2009)

[40] DETR (1999); Power and Houghton (2007); Shrinking Cities programme: www.shrinkingcities.com/

[41] Luxembourg Presidency Conference: Taking Forward the EU Social Inclusion Process, Luxembourg City, 13–14 June 2005

[42] EC/Directorate-General for Regional Policy (2006). This report contains a section entitled 'Cities as engines of regional development' (p 6)

[43] Personal correspondence with Creative Sheffield, with Torino City Council, with Saint-Étienne

[44] Knight Frank LLP (2005)

[45] Belfast City Council (2004)

[46] Parkinson et al (2006); Urban Audit (2009)

[47] Power and Houghton (2007)

Chapter Four

[48] JRF (1995); Power (2009); Marmot (2010); SDC (2010)

[49] Power and Mumford (1999)

[50] Green and White (2007)

[51] Visits to Sheffield, Torino, Bremen and Saint-Étienne, 2006–09

[52] Evidence on costs of upgrading in Saint-Étienne, Sheffield and Bremen

[53] Rogers and Power (2000)

[54] Site visits in Saint-Étienne, Torino, Bremen, Leipzig, Sheffield and Belfast

[55] Döhler-Behzadi (2006); evidence from city visits, 2006–07

[56] Evidence from city visits, 2006–07

[57] Power (1997)

[58] Thiollière (2007)

[59] Visit to Quartiers Sud-Est(Saint-Étienne), Osterholz-Tenever (Bremen)

[60] SCoT plan for Saint-Étienne; Leipzig urban concentration plan

[61] CECODHAS European Social Housing Observatory (2008)

[62] Site visit to Osterholz-Tenever, Bremen, 2007

[63] Jean-François de Ralle, during site visit, May 2006

[64] Richardson (2008)

[65] Visit to Sheffield, 2006

[66] Reported during visits to Sheffield, Belfast, Saint-Étienne and Torino (2006–08); Lupton and Power (2002)

Part Two

Chapter Five

[1] Oswalt (2005)

[2] Heinker (2004)

[3] F. Hahn, interview

[4] M. Schimansky, interview

[5] Heinker (2004)

[6] IHK (2007)

[7] S. Heinig, interview

[8] Nuissl and Rink (2003)

[9] Stadt Leipzig/Department of Urban Development (2005a, 2005b, 2005c, 2005d, 2005e)

[10] Stadt Leipzig/Department of Urban Dvelopment (2006)
[11] Stadt Leipzig (2006)
[12] Heinker (2004)
[13] S. Gabi, interview
[14] Stadt Leipzig/Department of Urban Development (2002)
[15] O. Weigel, interview
[16] Kabisch (2006)
[17] M. Schimansky, interview
[18] A. Kreideweiss, interview
[19] O. Weigel, interview
[20] S. Heinig, interview
[21] Stadt Leipzig/Department of Urban Development (2006)
[22] M. Bernt, interview
[23] J. Schaber, interview
[24] M. Schimansky, interview
[25] Stadt Leipzig/Department of Urban Development (2006)
[26] For example, Stadtforum Leipzig (2006)
[27] Wiest and Zischner (2006)
[28] Stadt Leipzig/Department of Urban Development (2006)
[29] Stadt Leipzig/Department of Urban Development (2006)
[30] M. Döhler–Behzadi, S. Gabi, interviews
[31] M. Schimansky, F. Hahn, interviews

Chapter Six

[32] Bahrenberg (1998)
[33] Taubmann (1999)
[34] Belina (2001)
[35] Lange (2005)
[36] Wauschkuhn (1998)
[37] R. Imholze, interview
[38] Prognos (2002)
[39] G. Warsewa, interview
[40] BAW Institut für regionale Wirtschaftsforschung (2005a, 2005b); Peters (2005, p 69)
[41] Warsewa (2006)
[42] Prognos (2002)
[43] Wauschkuhn (1998)
[44] Visit to Bremen, 2006
[45] Wilms(2003a, 2003b); BAW Institut für regionale Wirtschaftsforschung (2005a)
[46] Prognos (2002)
[47] D. Kuhling, interview
[48] Meurer (2005)
[49] R. Imholze, M. Grewe–Wacker, interviews
[50] D. Haubold, interview
[51] Freie Hansestadt Bremen, Der Senator für Bau und Umwelt (2003)
[52] K. Stadler, interview
[53] R. Schumann and Mr Schweser, interviews
[54] R. Schmidt, interview
[55] Lange (2005)
[56] S. Bussenschutt, interview

Chapter Seven

[57] ONS (2005)
[58] Lawless (1990)
[59] Lawless (1986)

[60] Watts (2004)
[61] Vision of Britain (2007)
[62] Fawcett (2000)
[63] Moggridge (1998)
[64] Watts (2004)
[65] Vision of Britain (2007)
[66] Watts (2004)
[67] Lawless (1990)
[68] Digaetano and Lawless (1999)
[69] Sheffield City Council (1993)
[70] Seyd (1990)
[71] Booth (2005)
[72] Crouch and Hill (2004)
[73] Leunig and Swaffield (2007)
[74] Digaetano and Lawless (1999)
[75] Dabinett (2004)
[76] Strange (1993)
[77] Elcock (2006)
[78] Booth (2005, p 265)
[79] Booth (2005)
[80] Lawless (1990)
[81] Middleton (1991)
[82] Booth (2005)
[83] Crouch and Hill (2004)
[84] Booth (2005)
[85] Fothergill and Grieve Smith (2005)
[86] Watts (2004); Audit Commission (2004)
[87] Core Cities (2006)
[88] Sheffield City Council (2004)
[89] Sheffield City Council (2004, p 19)
[90] Yorkshire Forward (2006, pp 10–11)
[91] Regional Development Agencies Act 1998
[92] Crouch and Hill (2004)
[93] Creative Sheffield (2005)
[94] Creative Sheffield (2005)
[95] Dabinett (2004)
[96] Dabinett (2004)
[97] Kerslake and Wilson (2007)
[98] See Brookings Institution (2007b); Plöger (2007a, 2007b, 2007c, 2008); Winkler (2007a, 2007b, 2007c)

Chapter Eight

[99] Northern Ireland Statistics and Research Agency (NISRA): www.nisra.gov.uk/
[100] Royle (2006, p 12)
[101] Royle (2006, p 19)
[102] Boal (2006, p 71)
[103] Hanna (1999, p197)
[104] Hart (2006)
[105] Hart (2006, p 89)
[106] Hart (2006, p 88)
[107] DENI, quoted in Hanna (1999, p 198)
[108] Hanna (1999)
[109] OECD (2000, p 23)
[110] Borooah (1998, p 273)
[111] Hart (2006); OECD (2000, p 20); Leonard (1998)
[112] Gaffikin and Morrissey (1999)

[113] OECD (2000)

[114] Knox and Carmichael (2006)

[115] OECD (2000)

[116] Northern Ireland Statistics and Research Agency (NISRA): www.nisra.gov.uk/

[117] Graham and Nash (2006, p 267)

[118] Murtagh (2002, p 46)

[119] Shirlow and Murtagh (2006, p 61)

[120] Murtagh (2002)

[121] Murtagh (2002)

[122] Morrison (2006)

[123] Smyth (2006)

[124] McEldowney et al (2003); Smyth (2006, p 100)

[125] Hanna (1999, p 199)

[126] OECD (2000, p 28)

[127] OECD (2000)

[128] S. McCay, interview

[129] Belfast City Council (2006)

[130] Hanna (1999, p 198)

[131] Knox and Carmichael (2006, p 942)

[132] Knox and Carmichael (2006, p 946)

[133] Branson (2007)

[134] S. McCay, interview; Belfast City Council: www.belfastcity.gov.uk/

[135] Branson (2007)

[136] P. Elliott, interview

[137] B. Murtagh, interview

[138] J. Frey, interview

[139] OFMDFMNI (2005)

[140] Hemphill et al (2006)

[141] OECD (2000)

[142] Belfast City Council (2007, p 3)

[143] OECD (2000, p 18)

[144] Centre for Cities (2007)

[145] Hart (2006)

[146] Institute of Directors, Northern Ireland Division (2009)

[147] OECD (2000)

[148] Invest Northern Ireland: www.investni.com

[149] Livesey et al (2006)

[150] Belfast City Council (2007)

[151] Belfast City Council (2007)

[152] S. Russam, interview

[153] Cushman and Wakefield (2007)

[154] Cushman and Wakefield (2007)

[155] Parkinson (2007)

[156] Shirlow and Murtagh (2006)

[157] S. Russam, interview

[158] Parkinson (2007)

[159] Laganside Corporation, online

[160] Sterrett et al (2005)

[161] Smyth (2006)

[162] Northern Ireland Planning Service: www.planningni.gov.uk

[163] B. Murtagh, interview

[164] DRDNI (2006)

[165] Branson (2007)

[166] J. Dennison, interview; Parkinson (2007)

[167] Yarwood (2006)

[168] B. Murtagh, interview

Chapter Nine

[169] Beascoechea (2003)
[170] Goméz (1998, p 108); Meyer (2001, p 297); Rodríguez (2002, p 74); González (2005, p 97)
[171] Eustat (2006)
[172] N. Tejerina, interview
[173] J. Urriolabeitia, interview
[174] Rodríguez et al (2001)
[175] Rodríguez et al (2001)
[176] Eustat (2006)
[177] M. Valdevielso and J. Alayo, interview
[178] N. Tejerina, interview
[179] Zubiri (2000)
[180] Bilbao Ayuntamiento (2007)
[181] Rodríguez et al (200, p 167)
[182] Rodriguez (2002, p 81)
[183] González (2006)
[184] M. Valdevielso, interview
[185] González (2006, p 843)
[186] Mangen (2004)
[187] P. Emparanza, interview
[188] Barreiro and Aguirre (2005)
[189] B. Plaza, J. Aurtenetxe, interviews
[190] Plaza (2000, p 203)
[191] Rodríguez et al (2001)
[192] Donner (2000)
[193] *Viviendas Municipales*: www.bilbao.net/viviendas/
[194] Bilbao Ría (2000)
[195] Rodríguez et al (2001)
[196] Bilbao Ría 2000
[197] Rodríguez (2002)
[198] J. Alayo, interview
[199] Plaza (2007)
[200] Plaza (2007)
[201] Lan Ekintza (2007).
[202] M. Baelo, L. Vicario, interviews
[203] Lan Ekintza (2007).
[204] M. Valdevielso, J. Alayo, M. Candida, interviews
[205] For example, Rodríguez et al (2001); González (2006); Plaza (2007)
[206] Bilbao Ayuntamiento (2007); Lan Ekintza (2007)
[207] Plaza (2007)
[208] Plaza (2007)
[209] J. Alayo, interview
[210] Siemiatycki (2005)
[211] P. Emparanza, interview

Chapter Ten

[212] Maggi and Piperno (1999)
[213] Rosso (2004)
[214] Whitford and Enrietti (2005)
[215] ANFIA (2006)
[216] Whitford and Enrietti (2005)
[217] Pinson (2002)
[218] Chiaberge (1993, p 5)
[219] Dente et al (2005)
[220] Putnam (1993)

[221] Dente et al (2005)

[222] Pinson (2002)

[223] Rosso (2004)

[224] Torino Internazionale (1998)

[225] Torino Internazionale (2000)

[226] IRES (2007)

[227] IRES (2007)

[228] IRES (2007)

[229] IRES (2006)

[230] Kresl (2007)

[231] *The Economist* (2005)

[232] IRES (2006)

[233] Scenari Immobiliari (2007)

[234] Borrelli and Santangelo (2004)

[235] ITP (2007)

[236] ADIT (2005)

[237] L'Eau Vive & Comitato Rota (2005)

[238] There are two other internationalisation support programmes, for the aerospace and ICT sectors, which are too recent to evaluate

[239] IRES (2007)

[240] Science Alliance (2004)

[241] NUTEK (2007)

[242] L'Eau Vive & Comitato Rota (2005)

[243] IRES (2006)

[244] ISF (2007)

[245] Buoni Esempi (2003)

[246] A foreigner is defined as any resident not holding Italian citizenship

[247] Scenari Immobiliari (2007)

[248] Torino Internazionale (2006)

[249] Scenari Immobiliari (2007)

Chapter Eleven

[250] INSEE (2006). The latest confirmed population data available is from the 1999 Census, conducted decennially by France's statistics institute, INSEE. A population estimate for the municipality of 175,700 was released by INSEE for 2005.

[251] Merley (1990)

[252] Verney-Carron (1999)

[253] Frerot (2005)

[254] Cretin (1986, p 915)

[255] Levy (1999, p 102)

[256] Levy (1999)

[257] Le Galès (2003, p 32)

[258] Le Galès (2003)

[259] Tomas (1978)

[260] Ardagh (1995, p 62)

[261] Béal et al (2007)

[262] Levy (1999)

[263] Le Galès (2003)

[264] Levy (1999)

[265] INSEE (2006)

[266] Ville de Saint-Étienne (2005)

[267] Ville de Saint-Étienne (2005, pp 5–6)

[268] UJM (2007)

[269] INSEE (2006)

[270] Mairie de Saint-Étienne (2006)

[271] Masboungi and de Gravelaine (2006, p 30)

[272] DIACT (2006)
[273] *Le Point* (2005, p 403)
[274] *Les Echos* (2005)
[275] Epures (2006a)
[276] DATAR (2005)
[277] Se Loger (2007)
[278] Se Loger (2007)
[279] Epures (2006b)
[280] *L'Express* (2007)
[281] UJM (2006a)
[282] Chalaye (2006)
[283] INSEE Rhône-Alpes (2006)
[284] INSEE Rhône-Alpes (2007)
[285] Epures (2006b)
[286] Epures (2006b)
[287] UJM (2006b)
[288] INSEE (2006)
[289] INSEE (2006)
[290] INSEE Rhône-Alpes (2007)
[291] MIILOS (2005)
[292] Mairie Info (2005)
[293] Dormois et al (2005, p 245)

Part Three

Chapter Twelve

[1] Brookings Institution (2007a)
[2] Urban Audit (2009)
[3] Jackson (2009); Porritt (2009)
[4] Parkinson et al (2006)
[5] Layard (2006)
[6] *The Economist* (2010)

Part Four

Chapter Thirteen

[1] Bennett and Gatz (2008)
[2] Eichenthal and Windeknecht (2008)
[3] Ledebur and Taylor (2008)
[4] Massey and Denton (1993)
[5] Fogelson (1967)
[6] Teaford (1990)
[7] Jackson (1985)
[8] Lemann (1991)
[9] Massey and Denton (1993)
[10] King (1968)
[11] Jackson (1985)
[12] Olson (1981)
[13] Brookings Institution (2007b)
[14] Brookings Institution (2007a, 2007b)
[15] Wolman et al (2007)
[16] Wolman et al (2007)
[17] Katz (2008)
[18] Wolman et al (2007)

[19] Wolman et al (2007)
[20] US Bureau of Census
[21] Brookings Institution (2007a, 2007b)
[22] Wilson (1987)
[23] Brandes Gratz (1994)
[24] Lemann (1991)
[25] Wilson (1987)
[26] Jencks (1993)
[27] Pluntz (1990); Kotlowitz (1992)
[28] Massey and Denton (1993)
[29] Massey and Denton (1993)
[30] Jargowsky (1997)
[31] Kerner Commission (1968)
[32] Power (1993)
[33] Teaford (1990); Clark et al (1965)
[34] Silberman (1965)
[35] McGahey and Vey (2008)
[36] Wilson (2009)
[37] Katz (2008)
[38] Giddens (2009)
[39] Wilson (1996)
[40] Muller (2006a, 2006b)
[41] E. Muller, interview, 2008
[42] Harvey (2000)
[43] Gyourko (2005)
[44] Teaford (1990)

Chapter Fourteen

[45] Muller (2006a, 2006b)
[46] Teaford (1990)
[47] Lubove (1996)
[48] Muller (2006a, 2006b)
[49] Bright (2000)
[50] Deitrick and Beauregard (1995)
[51] Teaford (1990)
[52] S. Iyer, interview, 2008
[53] Roberts and Sykes (2000)
[54] J. Shannon, interview, 2008
[55] E. Rutkowski, interview, 2008
[56] M. Sissman, interview, 2008
[57] EAGB (2007)
[58] B. McDearman, interview, 2008
[59] Wilkinson and Pickett (2009)
[60] UN Data http://data.un.org/Data.aspx?d=UNODC&f=tableCode%3a1
[61] Personal correspondence with Brad McDearman
[62] Beauregard (1989)
[63] Beauregard (1989)
[64] Teaford (1990)
[65] Gyourko (2005)
[66] Brookings Institution (2007a)
[67] Brookings Institution (2007a); Wolman et al(2007)
[68] Bennett and Gatz (2008)
[69] Eichenthal and Windeknecht (2008)
[70] Ledebur and Taylor (2008)
[71] Bennett and Gatz (2008)
[72] Friedman (2007)

[73] Eichenthal and Windeknecht (2008)
[74] Brown (2001)
[75] Ledebur and Taylor (2008)

Chapter Fifteen

[76] Berube and Kneebone (2006)
[77] Brookings Institution (2007a); OECD (2007)
[78] Jargowsky (1997)
[79] Wilson (2009)
[80] Simon (2008)
[81] UN Environment Programme (2006); Bulkin (2009)
[82] Burnett (2007)
[83] The American Assembly (2007); McGahey and Vey (2008)
[84] Sirianni and Friedland (2001); Burnett (2007)
[85] Nivola (1999)
[86] Brookings Institution (2007a)
[87] Brookings Institution (2007a); Obama (2008)
[88] Diamond (2006)
[89] The American Assembly (2007)
[90] Myrdal (1944); King (1958); Dollard (1989)
[91] Lemann (1991)
[92] Berube and Katz (2006)
[93] Brookings Institution (2007b)
[94] Brown et al (2008)

Part Five

Chapter Sixteen

[1] Reader (2005)
[2] ODPM (2004)
[3] Luxembourg Presidency Conference (2005)
[4] Briggs (1968)
[5] Treaty of Rome, 1957; Committee on Climate Change (2008); Trans-European Transport Network Executive Agency priority projects: (http://tentea.ec.europa.eu/en/ten-t_projects/30_priority_projects/30_priority_projects.htm)
[6] Saint-Étienne visit, meeting with Mayor Thiolliere, 2007
[7] Titmuss (1958)
[8] Power (1997)
[9] Power and Houghton (2007)
[10] Visit to Sheffield by American City Reformers, September 2006
[11] Development Trust Association Scotland Annual Conference and Awards, March 2006, Glasgow
[12] DETR (1999); Power and Houghton (2007)
[13] Epures (2006b); Northern Way (2006); inter-European fast railway network
[14] Emparanza (2006)
[15] Alayo (2008)
[16] Power (2006)
[17] Epures (2006a)
[18] Sustainable Development Commission visit to Northern Ireland, 2008
[19] Davoudi et al (2008)
[20] D. Dorling, informal communication on Sheffield's economic recovery, 2007
[21] Florida (2002)
[22] Visit to Saint-Étienne, 2007; *The Economist* (2009c, 2009d)
[23] Krugman (2009)
[24] Power (1993)

[25] Social documentary films portrayed these three facets of industrial growth and collapse, in 'I'm All Right Jack', 'The Full Monty' and 'Raining Stones'

[26] UN Habitat (2004)

[27] Davis (2007); McGahey and Vey (2008)

[28] Jackson (2009)

[29] *The Economist* (2009a)

[30] City visits and exchanges with Torino, Saint-Étienne and Sheffield, 2009

[31] Giddens (2009)

[32] Rees (2003)

[33] UN Habitat (2008)

[34] Meadows (1972)

[35] Jackson (2009)

[36] McKay (2008)

[37] Rees (2003); Committee on Climate Change (2008)

[38] American Clean Energy and Security Act, June 2009

[39] Brown et al (2008); visit to Washington DC, July 2009

[40] US Global Change Research Program (2009)

[41] Arrow et al (2003); WWF (2010)

[42] Girardet (2004)

[43] *The Economist* (2008a); visits to Saint-Étienne, May 2007; Torino, May 2008; Belfast, May 2009

[44] Beddington (2009)

[45] Committee on Climate Change (2008); visits to Edinburgh University Marine Technology Centre, 2007; Belfast, 2009

[46] Power (2008)

[47] HM Government, (2009); *The Guardian* (2009); Simmons (2010)

[48] Stern (2007)

[49] Climate Change Congress Copenhagen (2009); UN (2009)

[50] Giddens (2009); International Scientific Congress (2009)

[51] American Clean Energy and Security Act, June 2009; *The Economist* (2009b)

[52] Brown et al (2008)

[53] Knoflacher and Rode (2005)

[54] DETR (1999); Rogers and Power (2000)

[55] English Heritage (2006); RCEP (2006); Power (2008); Beddington (2009)

[56] Power (2008)

[57] LSE Housing (2008)

[58] Visits to Torino, May 2008; Berlin, November 2008; Belfast, June 2009; meeting with Kier Construction, March 2009

[59] Miliband (2009)

[60] Stern (2009)

[61] Rabinovitch (1992)

[62] Diamond (2005)

[63] Arrow et al (2003); WWF (2010)

[64] Creative Sheffield, March 2009, personal communication

References

ADIT (Agence pour la Diffusion de l'Information Technologique) (2005) *Le Management Stratégique des Régions en Europe: Une étude comparative. Tome II: Les pratiques régionales*, www.adit.fr/images/pdf/Strat_region_II.pdf

Alayo, J. (2008) 'Is the Basque region a special case?' Response, City Reformers Group meeting, London School of Economics and Political Science, 21–22 October

American Assembly, The (2007) 'Retooling for growth: building a 21st century economy in America's older industrial areas', The 106th American Assembly, 8–11 November, The Hotel Hershey, PA, New York: The American Assembly

ANFIA (Associazione Nazionale Filiera Industria Automobilistica) www.anfia.it/

Ardagh, J. (1995) *France today* (2nd edn), London: Penguin

Arrow, K., Dasgupta, P., Goulder, L. et al (2003) 'Are we consuming too much?', Stanford, CA: Stanford University

Audit Commission (2004) *People, places and prosperity: A possible framework for the local delivery chain*, www.audit-commission.gov.uk/nationalstudies/localgov/Pages/peopleplacesandprosperity.aspx

Audit Commission (2008) *A mine of opportunities: Local authorities and the regeneration of the English coalfields*, Swindon: Audit Commission, www.audit-commission.gov.uk/nationalstudies/localgov/Pages/amineofopportunities.aspx

Bahrenberg, G. (1998) 'Der Stadtstaat Bremen: zu klein und leistungsschwach für die Selbstständigkeit?', *Informationen zur Raumentwicklung*, vol 10, pp 687–94

Barreiro, P. and Aguirre, J. (2005) '25 años del plan integral de saneamiento de la Ría de Bilbao', *DYNA* (enero-febrero), pp 25–30

BAW (Bremen Economic Research Institute) Institut für regionale Wirtschaftsforschung (BAW Institute for Regional Economic Research) (2005a) 'europaregion-nordwest.de', *Konzeptstudie im Auftrag der Industrie- und Handelskammern*

BAW Institut für regionale Wirtschaftsforschung (2005b) *Hafenareale als urbane Investitionsstandorte*, Regionalwirtschaftliche Studien 21, Berlin

Béal, V., Dormois, R. and Pinson, G. (2007) 'Redeveloping Saint-Étienne: The weight of the inherited structure of social and political relationships in a French industrial city', in H.-J. Bürkner, (ed) *Urban trajectories under conditions of decline: Economic crises and demographic change as a trigger for new concepts of regeneration*, Leipzig: LIT-Verlag

Beascoechea, J. (2003) 'Jerarquización social del espacio urbano en el Bilbao de la industrialización', *Scripta Nova: Revista Electrónica de Geografía y Ciencias Sociales*, vol VII, no 146, www.ub.es/geocrit/sn/sn-146(022).htm

Beauregard, R. (1989) 'City profile: Philadelphia', *Cities*, November, pp 300–8

Beddington, J. (2009) 'Getting our houses in order', *Prospect Magazine*, issue 154

Belfast City Council (2004) *Belfast: State of the city report*, www.belfastcity.gov.uk/stateofthecity/docs/ConferenceReport2004.pdf

Belfast City Council (2006) *Belfast: Capital city 2006–2010*, Belfast: Belfast City Council

Belfast City Council (2007) *Belfast: A profile of the city 2007/08*, Belfast: Belfast City Council

Belina, B. (2001) *Die Bremischen Häfen im Jahr 2050. Zur Zukunft der Häfen in der Stadt Bremen*, Institut für Geographie, Materialien und Manuskripte, Universität Bremen, no 23

Bennett, E. and Gatz, C. (2008) *Louisville, Kentucky – A restoring prosperity case study*, Washington DC: Brookings Institution

Berube, A. and Katz, B. (2006) *State of the English Cities: The state of American cities*, London: Department for Communities and Local Government

Berube, A. and Kneebone, E. (2006) *Two steps back: City and suburban poverty trends, 1999–2005*, Washington DC: Brookings Institution

Bilbao Ayuntamiento (2007) *La metamorfosis de la metropolis industrial de Bilbao*, Bilbao Ayuntamiento

Bilbao Ría (2000) www.bilbaoria2000.org/ria2000/index.htm

Boal, F. (2006) 'Big process and little people: The population of Metropolitan Belfast 1901–2001', in F. Boal and S. Royle (eds) *Enduring city, Belfast in the twentieth century*, Belfast: Blackstaff

Boal, F. and Royle, S. (eds) (2006) *Enduring city, Belfast in the twentieth century*, Belfast: Blackstaff

Booth, P. (2005) 'Partnerships and networks: the governance of urban regeneration in Britain', *Journal of Housing and the Built Environment*, vol 20, no 3, pp 257–69

Borooah, V. (1998) 'Growth and political violence in Northern Ireland, 1920–96', in S. Borner and M. Paldam (eds) *The political dimension of economic growth*, London: Macmillan

Borrelli, N. and Santangelo, M. (2004) 'Turin: where territorial governance and politics of scale become keystones for the city development strategy', Paper presented at 'City Futures: An international conference on globalism and urban change', Chicago, 8–10 July

Bourdieu, P. et al (1999) *The weight of the world: Social suffering in contemporary society*, Cambridge: Polity Press

Brandes Gratz, Roberta (1994) *The living city: How America's cities are being revitalized by thinking small in a big way*, New York: John Wiley and Sons

Branson, A. (2007) 'Together but not united', *Regeneration & Renewal*, 1 June

Briggs, A. (1968) *Victorian cities*, Harmondsworth: Penguin Books

Bright, E. (2000) *Reviving America's forgotten neighbourhoods: An investigation of inner city revitalization efforts*, New York/London: Garland Publishing

Brookings Institution (2007a) *Metro nation: How US metropolitan areas fuel American prosperity*, Washington, DC: Brookings Institution, www.brookings.edu/~/media/Files/rc/reports/2007/1106_metronation_berube/MetroNationbp.pdf

Brookings Institution (2007b) *Restoring prosperity: The state role in revitalizing America's older industrial cities*, Washington, DC: Brookings Institution

Brown, D.E. (2001) *Bury my heart at Wounded Knee: An Indian history of the American West*, New York, NY: H. Holt

Brown, M., Southworth, F. and Sarzynski, A. (2008) *Shrinking the carbon footprint of metropolitan America*, Brookings Institution Metropolitan Policy Program, Washington, DC: Brookings Institution

Bulkin, B. (2009) 'Rethinking travel – and systems thinking', Environment on the Edge lecture series, 18 August, www.modavox.com/voiceamerica/vshow.aspx?sid=1545

Buoni Esempi (2003) *L'Esperienza in Evidenza: Il 'Settore Periferie' del Comune di Torino*, Intervista con l'Arch Giovanni Magnano, dirigente del Settore Periferie, www.buoniesempi.it/scheda.aspx?protocollo=535

Burnett, K. (2007) 'Restoring prosperity in weak market cities: How NGOs help to shape cities in the US', Presentation at City Reformers Group Meeting, 20 September, London School of Economics and Political Science

Cairncross, F. (1991) *Costing the earth*, London: Business Books

Carson, R. (1962) *Silent spring*, New York, NY: Fawcett Crest

Casey, L. (2008) *Engaging communities in fighting crime*, London: Cabinet Office

CECODHAS European Social Housing Observatory (2008) *Affordability of Housing in the European Union*. Research Briefing, Year 1, Issue 1: March 2008

Centre for Cities (2007) *Cities outlook 2008*, www.centreforcities.org/assets/files/pdfs/CitiesOutlook.pdf

Chalaye, S. (2006) *Observatoire de l'Innovation: Indicateurs de positionnement pour la Loire et le Sud Loire*, Rapport d'étude Epures/CREUSET, Saint-Étienne: Epures

Chiaberge, R. (1993) 'La notta magica di Castellani', *La Republica*, 22 June, p 5

CIC (Commission on Integration and Cohesion) (2007) *French Lessons: A cross-channel look at regeneration, cohesion and integration*, London: HMSO.

Clark, K.B., Wilson, W.J. and Myrdal, G. (1965) *Dark ghetto: Dilemmas of social power*. Middletown, Connecticut: Wesleyan Press

Climate Change Congress Copenhagen (2009) Climate Change: Global Risks, Challenges and Decisions, Copenhagen 10-12 March

Committee on Climate Change (2008) *Building a low-carbon economy –the UK's contribution to tackling climate change.* Norwich: TSO

Core Cities (2006) *London and the core cities: Shared platform,* Manchester@ Core Cities, www. corecities.com/dev07/Summits/2006/CC%20&%20London%20Shared%20Platform.pdf

Creative Sheffield (2005) *Creative Sheffield business plan,* http://creativesheffield.co.uk/creative_sheffield_business_plan.pdf

Cretin, C. (1986) *L'Expansion Stéphanoise dans la Plaine Forézienne: Étude méthodologique d'un milieu urbain,* Doctoral thesis, University of Lyon II

Crouch, C. and Hill, M. (2004) 'Regeneration in Sheffield: from council dominance to partnership', in C. Crouch et al (eds) *Changing governance of local economies,* Oxford: Oxford University Press

CURDS (Centre for Urban and Regional Development Studies) (1999a) *Core cities: Key centres for regeneration,* Synthesis Report, Newcastle upon Tyne: CURDS

CURDS (1999b) *Core cities: Key centres for regeneration,* Final Report, Newcastle upon Tyne: CURDS

Cushman and Wakefield (2007) *UK cities monitor, 2007,* London: Cushman and Wakefield

Dabinett, G. (2004) 'Creative Sheffield: creating value and changing values?', *Local Economy,* vol 19, no 4, pp 414–19

Dabinett, G. and Ramsden, P. (1993) 'An urban policy for people: lessons from Sheffield', in R.F. Imrie and H.Thomas (eds) *British urban policy and the urban development corporations,* London: Paul Chapman

DATAR (2005) 'Mise en place de l'Etablissement Public d'Aménagement (EPA) Saint-Étienne 2015', Lettre de mission de François Wellhoff (dirécteur), www.loire.equipement.gouv.fr/IMG/pdf/lettre_mission_FW_cle2414b3.pdf

Davis, M. (2007) *Planet of slums,* London: Verso

Davoudi, S., Hall, P. and Power, A. (2008) 'Key issues for planning futures and the way forward', *21st Century Society: Journal of the Academy of Social Sciences,* vol 3, no 3, pp 227–45

DEFRA (Department for Environment, Food and Rural Affairs) (2006) *Securing the future – UK government sustainable development strategy,* London: DEFRA

Deitrick, S. and Beauregard, R. (1995) 'From front-runner to also-ran – the transformation of a once-dominant industrial region: Pennsylvania, USA' in P. Cooke (ed) *The rise of the rustbelt,* London: UCL Press

Dente, B., Bobbio, L. and Spada, A. (2005) 'Government or governance of urban innovation? A tale of two cities', *DisP,* vol 41, no 162, pp 41–52, Zürich: Netzwerk Stadt und Landschaft NSL, www.nsl.ethz.ch/index.php/content/download/1182/7163/file/

DETR (Department of the Environment, Transport and the Regions) (1999) *Towards an urban renaissance,* Final Report of the Urban Task Force, London: The Stationery Office

DIACT (Délégation interministérielle à l'aménagement et à la compétitivité des territoires) (2006) *Les Pôles de Compétitivité. Entreprises, centres de formation, unités de recherche: S'unir pour promouvoir des projets innovants,* www.diact.gouv.fr/datar_site/datar_framedef.nsf/webmaster/dossiers_framedef_vf?OpenDocument

Diamond, J. (2006) *Collapse : how societies choose to fail or survive,* London: Penguin

Digaetano, A. and Lawless, P. (1999) 'Urban governance and industrial decline: governing structures and the policy agenda', *Urban Affairs Review,* vol 34, no 4, pp 546–77

Döhler-Behzadi, M. (2006) 'Urbanität ohne Dichte [Urbanity without density]', Presentation, Urban Age German Cities Summit, Halle, 10 May

Dollard, J. (1989) *Class and caste in a Southern town,* Madison, WI: University of Wisconsin Press

Domingo, M. (2005) 'Vivienda obrera en Bilbao y el bajo Nervión: Las casas baratas, una nueva forma de alojamiento (1911-1936)', Doctoral thesis, Universitat de Girona

Donner, C. (2000) *Housing policies in the European Union. Theory and Practice.* Vienna

Dorling, D., Rigby, J., Wheeler, B., Ballas, D., Thomas, B., Fahmy, E., Gordon, D. and Lupton, R. (2007) *Poverty and wealth across Britain 1968–2005,* York: JRF, www.jrf.org.uk/publications/poverty-and-wealth-across-britain-1968–2005

Dormois, R., Pinson, G. and Reignier, H. (2005) 'Path-dependency in public–private partnership in French urban renewal', *Journal of Housing and the Built Environment*, vol 20, p 245

DRDNI (Department for Regional Development Northern Ireland) (2006) *Northern Ireland transport statistics, 2005–2006*, Belfast: NISRA

Dunleavy, P. (1981) *Politics of mass housing in Britain 1945–1975: A study of corporate power and professional influence in the welfare state*, New York, NY: Oxford University Press

EAGB (Economic Alliance of Greater Baltimore) (2007) *Economic progress for Greater Baltimore, 2000–2007*, Baltimore, MD: EAGB

EC (European Commission) (2007) *State of the European Cities report: Adding value to the European urban audit*, Brussels: EU

EC/Directorate-General for Regional Policy (2005) *Urban audit 2005: Key indicators on living conditions in European Cities*, Brussels: EU

EC/Directorate-General for Regional Policy (2006) *Cities and the Lisbon Agenda: Assessing the performance of cities*, Brussels: EU

Economist, The (2005) 'A survey of Italy', 26 November

Economist, The (2008a) 'When fortune frowned', Special Report on the World Economy, 9 October

Economist, The (2008b) 'Briefing: America's suburbs: an age of transformation', 1 May

Economist, The (2009a) 'No way to start out in life: the plight of the young jobless calls into question Labour's record', 16 July

Economist, The (2009b) 'The other kind of solar power', *Technology Quarterly*, Solar-thermal technology, 4 June, www.economist.com/sciencetechnology/tq/displayStory.cfm?story_id=13725855

Economist, The (2009c) 'Back in the driving seat', 12 March

Economist, The (2009d) 'The lives of others', 6 August

Economist, The (2010) 'The spectre that haunts Europe', 11 February

ECOTEC Research and Consulting Ltd/ECORYS (2007) *State of European cities report: Adding value to the European Urban Audit*, http://ec.europa.eu/regional_policy/sources/docgener/studies/pdf/urban/stateofcities_2007.pdf

Eichenthal, D. and Windeknecht, T. (2008) *Chattanooga, Tennessee: A restoring prosperity case study*, Washington, DC: Brookings Institution

Elcock, H. (2006) 'Local political leadership in Britain: Rake's progress or search for the Holy Grail?', *Public Policy and Administration*, vol 21, no 2, summer

Emparanza, P. (2006) Presentation at City Reformers Group Meeting, LSE, September 21/22

English Heritage (2006) *Heritage counts: The state of England's historic environment*, London: English Heritage

Epures (2006a) *Schéma de Cohérence Territoriale (SCoT) Sud Loire*, Rapport de Présentation: Annexes, www.scot-sudloire.fr/

Epures (2006b) *Schéma de Cohérence Territoriale (SCoT), Sud Loire*, Rapport de Présentation: Synthèse, Saint-Étienne: Epures

EUKN (European Urban Knowledge Network) (2007) *National Urban Policy of France*, www.eukn.org/eukn/themes/Urban_Policy/French-Urban-Policy_1050.html

Eustat (Regional Statistics Agency) (2006) 'The Basque statistics system', www.eustat.es/about/sist_estad_vasco_i.html

Fawcett, A.P. (2000) 'A tale of two cities: Sheffield and Nottingham – architecture and the provincial city in inter-war Britain', *Planning Perspectives*, vol 15, no 1, pp 25–54

Florida, R. (2002) *The rise of the creative class: And how it's transforming work, leisure, community and everyday life*, New York, NY: Basic Books

Fogelson, R. (1967) *The fragmented metropolis: Los Angeles, 1850–1930*, Cambridge, MA: Harvard University Press

Fothergill, S. and Grieve Smith, J. (2005) *Mobilising Britain's missing workforce: Unemployment, incapacity benefit and the regions*, London: Catalyst

Freie Hansestadt Bremen, Der Senator für Bau und Umwelt (2003) *Technologiegebiete in Bremen – ein Standortvergleich*, Map

Frerot, O. (2005) *Intervention d'Olivier Frerot*, DDE de la Loire, CCI de Saint-Étienne Montbrison, 6 September

Friedman, T. (2007) *The world is flat: The globalized world in the twenty-first century*, London: Penguin

Gaffikin, F. and Morrissey, M (1999) 'The urban economy and social exclusion: the case of Belfast', in F. Gaffikin and M. Morrissey (eds) *City visions: Imagining place, enfranchising people*, London: Pluto Press, pp 34–57

Giddens, A. (2009) *The politics of climate change*, Cambridge and Malden, MA: Polity

Girardet, H. (2004) *Cities people planet: Liveable cities for a sustainable world*, New York, NY: John Wiley & Sons

Goméz, M. (1998) 'Reflective images: the case of urban regeneration in Glasgow and Bilbao', *International Journal of Urban and Regional Research*, vol 22, no 1, p 108

González, S. (2005) 'The politics of the economic crisis and restructuring in the Basque Country and Spain during the 1980s', *Space and Polity*, vol 9, no 2, p 97

González, S (2006) 'Scalar narratives in Bilbao: a cultural politics of scales approach to the study of urban policy', in *International Journal of Urban and Regional Research*, vol 30, no 4, pp 836–57

Gore, A. (2007) *The assault on reason: How the politics of blind faith subvert wise decision-making*, London: Bloomsbury Publishing PLC

Graham, B. and Nash, C. (2006) 'A shared future: territoriality, pluralism and public policy in Northern Ireland', *Political Geography*, vol 25, p 267

Green, A.E. and White, R.J. (2007) *Attachment to place, social networks, mobility and prospects of young people*, York: Joseph Rowntree Foundation, www.jrf.org.uk/publications/attachment-place-social-networks-mobility-and-prospects-young-people

Gyourko, J. (2005) *Looking back to look forward: Learning from Philadelphia's 350 years of urban development*, www.brookings.edu/press/Journals/2005/brookingswhartonpapersonurbanaffairs2005.aspx

Guardian, The (2009) 'Key oil figures were distorted by US pressure, says whistleblower', 9 November

Hanna, B. (1999) 'Belfast: a partnership approach to local governance', in F. Gaffikin and M. Morrissey (eds) *City visions: Imagining place, enfranchising people*, London: Pluto Press

Hart, M. (2006) 'From smokestacks to service economy: foundations for a competitive city?', in F. Boal and S. Royle (eds) *Enduring city, Belfast in the twentieth century*, Belfast: Blackstaff, pp 84–98

Harvey, D. (2000) *Spaces of hope*, Berkeley, CA: University of California Press

Heinker, H.-H. (2004) *Boomtown Leipzig, Anspruch und Wirklichkeit* [*Claim and reality*], Leipzig: Faber & Faber.

Hemphill, L. et al (2006) 'Leadership, power and multisector urban regeneration partnerships', *Urban Studies*, vol 43, no 1, pp 59–80

HM Government (2009) *The UK Low Carbon Transition Plan: National strategy for climate and energy*, London: The Stationery Office

Home Office (2009) *Crime in England and Wales 2008/09, Volume 1: Findings from the British Crime Survey and police recorded crime*, London: Home Office

Hutton, W. (1995) *The state we're in*, London : Jonathan Cape

IAW (2003) 'Entwicklungspotential und -optionen der bremischen Wissenschaftslandschaft', *Beitrag zum Gutachten Technologiestadtteil Bremen*, March

IfS (Institut für Stadtforschung und Strukturpolitik) und ForStaR (Forschungsinstitut Stadt und Region) (2004) *Evaluation der Programme 'Wohnen in Nachbarschaften – WiN' und 'Stadtteile mit besonderem Entwicklungsbedarf – die Soziale Stadt' in Bremen*, Juni

IHK (Industrie- und Handelskammer zu Leipzig) (2007) *Statistischer Bericht* [*Statistical report*], Leipzig: IHK

INSEE (*Inst. National de la Statistique et des Études Économiques*) (2006) *Les résultats du recensement de 1999: Saint-Étienne*, www.recensement-1999.insee.fr/RP99/rp99/page_accueil.paccueil

INSEE Rhône-Alpes (2006) 'Rhône-Alpes: une région attractive pour les étudiants', *La lettre analyses*, no 55, www.insee.fr/fr/insee_regions/rhone-alpes/rfc/docs/LA55.pdf

INSEE Rhône-Alpes (2007) 'La hausse des créations d'entreprises reprend en 2006', La lettre résultats, no 75, www.insee.fr/fr/insee_regions/rhone-alpes/rfc/docs/LR75.pdf

Institute of Directors, Northern Ireland Division (2009) Transcript of online discussion with Sir Reg Empey, Minister for Employment and Learning, 30 April, www.delni.gov.uk/sirregempeytranscript30thapril2009.pdf

International Scientific Congress (2009) 'Climate change: global risks, challenges and decisions', Copenhagen, 10–12 March

IRES (Istituto Regionale Economico Sociale, Regione Piemonte) (2006) *Piemonte Economico e Sociale 2005: I dati e i commenti sulla regione.* Torino: IRES, http://213.254.4.222/cataloghi/pdfires/665.pdf

IRES (2007) *Piemonte Economico e Sociale 2006: I dati e i commenti sulla regione,*, www.regiotrend. piemonte.it/

ISF (Initiative Sports Future) (2007) *World's most watched TV sports events: 2006 rank and trends report*, www.initiative.com/english/homepage.html and www.futuressport.com/index.html

ITP (2007) 'Regional news', www.centroestero.org/invest/index.php?lang=eng

Jackson, K. (1985) *Crabgrass frontier: The suburbanization of the United States*, New York, NY: Oxford University Press

Jackson, T. (2009) *Prosperity without growth: The transition to a sustainable economy*, London: Sustainable Development Commission

Jargowsky, P. (1997) *Poverty and place: Ghettos, barrios, and the American city*, New York, NY: Russell Sage Foundation

Jencks, C. (1993) *Rethinking social policy: Race, poverty, and the underclas,* New York: Harper Perennial

Josvig, H. (1968) *Sheffield-Rotherham*, Freiburg: Geographischen Institute der Albert-Ludwigs Universität

JRF (Joseph Rowntree Foundation) (1995) *Inquiry into income and wealth*, York: JRF

Kabisch, S. (2006) Presentation at City Reformers Group meeting, London School of Economics and Political Science, September

Katz, B. (2004) *Brookings Institution – Supporting papers for WMC proposal to the Joseph Rowntree Foundation*, December, London: London School of Economics and Political Science

Katz, B. (2008) 'The Restoring Prosperity Initiative', Presentation at the City Reformers Group meeting, London School of Economics and Political Science, 21 October

Kerner, O. (Kerner Commission) (1969) *Report of the National Advisory Commission on Civil Disorders*, New York, NY: Bantam Books

Kerslake, R. and Wilson, J. (2007) 'How Sheffield's transformation was built on respect, partnership and devolution', in C. Murray (ed) *Working together: Transformational leadership for city growth*, London: Smith Institute, pp 66–74

King, M.L. (1958) *Strive toward freedom: The Montgomery story*, New York, NY: Harper and Brothers

King, M.L (1968) '*Where do we go from here: Chaos or community?*', Uckfield: Beacon Press

Knight Frank LLP (2005) *Sheffield central area activity report*, autum, http://resources.knightfrank.com/GetResearchResource.ashx?id=10740

Knoflacher, H. and Rode, P. (2005) 'Mobility and transport: travelling less, living better, who pays?', Urban Age Programme, February

Knox, C. and Carmichael, P. (2006) 'Bureau shuffling? The review of public administration in Northern Ireland', *Public Administration*, vol 84, no 4, p 945

Kotlowitz, Alex (1992) *There are no children here: The story of two boys growing up in the other America*, New York, NY: First Anchor Books

Kresl, P.K. (2007) *Planning cities for the future: The successes and failures of urban economic strategies in Europe*, Cheltenham: Edward Elgar Publishing

Krugman, P. (2009) 'A continent adrift', *The New York Times*, 16 March

Lan Ekintza-Bilbao Ayuntamiento (2005) *Anuario Socioeconómico de Bilbao 2004*

Lan Ekintza-Bilbao Ayuntamiento (2007) *Anuario Socioeconómico de Bilbao 2006*

Lange, H. (2005) 'Die Entwicklung Bremens von der Handelsstadt zur Industriestadt und zum Dienstleistungsstandort', *Statistische Hefte*, vol 1, no 2 (September), pp 53–61

Lawless, P. (1986) *Severe economic recession and local government intervention: A case study of Sheffield*, Sheffield: School of Regional and Urban Studies, Sheffield City Polytechnic

Lawless, P. (1990) *Urban regeneration in Sheffield: From radical intervention to partnership, 1979–1989*, Working Paper, Sheffield: Centre for Regional Economic and Social Research, Sheffield Hallam University

Layard, R. (2006) *Happiness: Lessons from a new science*. London: Penguin

L'Eau Vive & Comitato Rota (2005) *L'Immagine del Cambiamento: Sesto rapporto annuale su Torino*, Milano: Edizioni Angelo Guerini e Associati

Ledebur, L. and Taylor, J. (2008) *Akron, Ohio: A restoring prosperity case study*, Washington, DC: Brookings Institution

Le Galès, P. (2003) *The governance of local economies: A French case study*, Seminar Paper 5, Los Angeles, CA: Department of Sociology, UCLA, http://repositories.cdlib.org/cgi/viewcontent.cgi?article=1010&context=uclasoc

Lemann, N. (1991) *The promised land: The great Black migration and how it changed America*, New York, NY: Alfred A. Knopf

Leonard, M. (1998) 'The long-term unemployed, informal economic activity and the "underclass", in Belfast: rejecting or reinstating the work ethic', *International Journal of Urban and Regional Research*, vol 22, no 1, March, pp 42–59

Le Point (2005) 'Saint-Étienne: L'industrie à l'épreuve de la mécanique des pôles', 29 September, no 1724, p 403

Les Echos (2005) 'Sports et Loisirs/Rhône-Alpes/Projet à vocation nationale et régionale', 12 July, www.lesechos.fr/poles/articles/200058489.htm

Leunig, T. and Swaffield, J. (2007) *Cities limited*, London: Policy Exchange

Levy, J. (1999) *Tocqueville's revenge: State, society and economy in contemporary France*, Cambridge, MA: Harvard University Press

L'Express (2007) 'Thiollière peut-il relancer Saint-Étienne?', 7 February, www.lexpress.fr/info/region/dossier/saintetienne/dossier.asp?ida=431620&p=1

Livesey, D. et al (2006) 'Public sector employment 2006: seasonally adjusted series and recent trends', *ONS Labour Market Trends*, vol 114, no 12, pp 419–38

LSE Housing (2008) Special Event: 'Can existing homes and communities halve their CO_2 emissions? Learning from Germany's experience', 10 December, London School of Economics and Political Science

Lubove, R. (1996) *Twentieth-century Pittsburgh, Vol 2: The post-steel era*, Pittsburgh, PA: University of Pittsburgh Press

Lupton, R. and Power, A. (2002) 'Social exclusion and neighbourhoods', in J. Hills, J. Le Grand and D. Piachaud (eds) *Understanding social exclusion*, Oxford: Oxford University Press, Chapter Eight.

Luxembourg Presidency Conference (2005) Taking Forward the EU Social Inclusion Process, Luxembourg City, 13–14 June

McEldowney, M., Scott, M. and Smyth, A. (2003) 'Integrating land-use planning and transportation – policy formulation in the Belfast Metropolitan Area', *Irish Geography*, vol 36, no 2, pp 112–26

McGahey, R. and Vey, J. (2008) *Retooling for growth: Building a 21st century economy in America's older industrial areas*, Washington DC: Brookings Institution

McKay, D. (2008) *Sustainable energy – without the hot air*, Cambridge: UIT

Maggi, M. and Piperno, S. (1999) *Turin: The vain search for gargantua*, Working Paper No 124, Torino: IRES Piemonte

Mairie de Saint-Étienne (2006) *Le Renouveau Stéphanois: Quartiers ANRU/Rénovation urbaine*, www.saint-etienne.fr/

Mairie Info (2005) 'Après 11 nuits de violences, 3.500 véhicules brûlés et 800 arrestations effectuées', 7 November, www.maire-info.com/article.asp?param=6280&PARAM2=PLUS

Mangen, S.P. (2004) *Social exclusion and inner city Europe: Regulating urban regeneration*, Houndsmills/New York, NY: Palgrave Macmillan

Marmot, M. (2010) *Strategic review of health inequalities in England post 2010*, 'the Marmot Review', www.ucl.ac.uk/gheg/marmotreview

Masboungi, A. and de Gravelaine, F. (2006) *Construire un Projet de Ville: Saint-Étienne 'in progress'*, Paris: Éditions Le Moniteur

Massey, D. and Denton, N. (1993) *American apartheid: Segregation and the making of the underclass*, Cambridge, MA: Harvard University Press

Meadows, D.H. (1972) *The limits to growth*, New York, NY: Signet

Merley, J. (1990) *Histoire de Saint-Étienne*, Toulouse: Privat

Meurer, P. (2005) 'Überseestadt und Hafenkante – Gesamtstädtische Positionierung', in BAW Institut für regionale Wirtschaftsforschung, *Hafenareale als urbane Investitionsstandorte*, Regionalwirtschaftliche Studien 21, Berlin

Meyer, K. (2001) 'El Guggi und Los Fosteritos, Die Revitalisierung von Hafen- und Industriebrachen im Großraum Bilbao', in D. Schubert (ed) *Hafen- und Uferzonen im Wandel: Analysen und Planungen zur Revitalisierung der Waterfront in Hafenstädten*, Berlin: Edition Stadt und Region, no 3

Middleton, P. (1991) *Cities in transition*, London: Michael Joseph

MIILOS (Mission Interministérielle d'Inspection du Logement Social) (2005) *Rapport définitif no 2004–121, Juillet*, Office Public d'Aménagement et de Construction de Saint-Étienne, Paris: Ministère de L'Emploi, de la Cohésion Sociale et du Logement

Miliband, E. (2009) 'One giant leap for a greener Britain', *The Guardian*, 20 July 2009

Moggridge, H. (1998) 'Gardens and landscapes 1930–2000', Conference paper presented to the Garden History Society and Twentieth Century Society, London, September

Moriconi-Ebrard, F. (2000) *De Babylone à Tokyo: Les grandes agglomérations du Monde*, Paris: Ophrys

Morrison, B. (2006) 'Planning the city; planning the region', in F. Boal and S. Royle (eds) *Enduring city: Belfast in the twentieth century*, Belfast: Blackstaff, pp 141–54

Muller, E. (2006a) 'Downtown Pittsburgh: renaissance and renewal', in J. Scarpaci and K. Patrick (eds) *Pittsburgh and the Appalachians: Cultural and natural resources in a postindustrial age*, Pittsburgh, PA: University of Pittsburgh Press

Muller, E. (2006b) 'The Steel Valley', in J. Scarpaci and K. Patrick (eds) *Pittsburgh and the Appalachians: Cultural and natural resources in a postindustrial age*, Pittsburgh, PA: University of Pittsburgh Press

Murtagh, B. (2002) *The politics of territory: Policy and segregation in Northern Ireland*, Ethnic and Intercommunity Conflict Series, Houndsmill: Palgrave

Myrdal, G. (1944) *An American dilemma: The Negro problem and modern democracy*, New York, NY: Harper & Row

Newman, K.S. (2009) *No shame in my game: The working poor in the inner city*, London: Vintage

Nivola, P. S. (1999) *Laws of the Landscape: How Policies Shape Cities in Europe and America*. Washington DC: Brookings Institution

NOMIS (2007) *Labour market profile: Sheffield*, www.nomisweb.co.uk/reports/1/2038432027/pdf.aspx

Northern Way (2006) *Sheffield City region development programme*, www.thenorthernway.co.uk/downloaddoc.asp?id=277

Nuissl, H. and Rink, D. (2003) *Urban sprawl and post-socialist transformation: The case of Leipzig (Germany)*, UFZ Report 4/2003, Leipzig: UFZ Centre for Environmental Research, www.ufz.de/data/ufzbericht4-03547.pdf

NUTEK (2007) *Globalisation and regional economies: Case studies in the automotive sector*, www.eiir.org/index.php?option=com_content&task=section&id=102&Itemid=147

Obama, B. (2008) 'A more perfect union', speech, Philadelphia, 18 March

ODPM (Office of the Deputy Prime Minister) (2004) *Competitive European cities: Where do the core cities stand?* (Parkinson Report), London: ODPM

OECD (Organisation for Economic Co-operation and Development) (2000) *Urban renaissance, Belfast's lessons for policy and partnership*, Paris: OECD

OECD, OECD Factbook 2007 (Paris, 2007)

OFMDFMNI (Office of the First Minister and Deputy First Minister) (2005) *A shared future: Policy and strategic framework for good relations in Northern Ireland*, Belfast: OFMDFMNI

Olson, S. (1981) *Baltimore: The building of an American city*, Baltimore, MD: Johns Hopkins University

ONS (Office for National Statistics) (2001) *2001 Census: Census area statistics, Sheffield (local authority)*, http://neighbourhood.statistics.gov.uk/dissemination/LeadKeyFigures.do?a=3&b=276794&c=sheffield&d=13&e=16&g=365736&i=1001x1003x1004&m=0&enc=1

ONS (2005) *Regional profile: Yorkshire and The Humber 2005*, www.statistics.gov.uk/cci/nugget.asp?id=1128

Oswalt, P. (ed) (2005) *Shrinking cities, vol 1, International research*, Ostfildern–Ruit: Hatje Crantz

Parkinson, M. (2007) *Where is Belfast going?* Liverpool: European Institute for Urban Affairs, Liverpool John Moores University.

Parkinson, M. et al (2006) *State of the English cities: A research study*, London: ODPM

Peters, J. (2005) 'Strukturwandel und Beschäftigungsentwicklung des Landes Bremen 1994 bis 2004', *Statistische Hefte*, vol 1, no 2 (September), p 69

Pinson, G. (2002) 'Political government and governance: strategic planning and the reshaping of political capacity in Turin', *International Journal of Urban and Regional Research*, vol 26, no 3, pp 477–93, Oxford: Blackwell

Plaza, B. (2000) 'Política industrial de la comunidad autónoma del País Vasco: 1981–2000', *Economía Industrial*, no 335/336, p 203

Plaza, B (2006) 'The return on investment of the Guggenheim Museum in Bilbao', *International Journal of Urban and Regional Research*, 30, 2, pp 452-67

Plaza, B. (2007) 'Museums as economic re-activators: challenges and conditions for their effectiveness', Paper presented at EURA Conference, Glasgow, 12–14 September

Plöger, J. (2007a) *Belfast City report*, CASEreport 44, London: London School of Economics and Political Science

Plöger, J. (2007b) *Leipzig City report*, CASEreport 42, London: London School of Economics and Political Science

Plöger, J. (2007c) *Bremen City report*, CASEreport 39, London: London School of Economics and Political Science

Plöger, J. (2008) *Bilbao City report*, CASEreport 43, London: London School of Economics and Political Science

Pluntz, R. (1990) *A history of housing in New York*, NY: Columbia University Press.

Porritt, J. (2005) *Capitalism as if the world matters*, London: Sterling

Porritt, J. (2009) *Living within our means: Avoiding the ultimate recession*, London: Forum for the Future

Power, A. (1993) *Hovels to high rise: State housing in Europe since 1850*, London: Routledge

Power, A. (1997) *Estates on the edge: The social consequences of mass housing in Northern Europe*, New York, NY: St Martin's Press

Power, A. (2006) 'Investing in communities: landscapes, local people and jobs', Presentation to Sheffield Civic Trust, 20 September

Power, A. (2007) *City survivors: Bringing up children in disadvantaged neighbourhoods*, Bristol: The Policy Press

Power, A. (2008) 'Does demolition or refurbishment of old and inefficient homes help to increase our environmental, social and economic viability?' *Energy Policy*, vol 36, no 12, December, pp 4487–501

Power, A. (2009) *Strategic Review of Health Inequalities in England post-2010. Task Group 4: The built environment and health inequalities final report*, 12 June 2009, www.ucl.ac.uk/gheg/marmotreview/consultation/Built_environment_report

Power, A. and Houghton, J. (2007) *Jigsaw cities: Big places, small spaces*, Bristol: The Policy Press

Power, A. and Mumford, K. (1999) *The slow death of great cities? Urban abandonment or urban renaissance*, York: York Publishing Services for the Joseph Rowntree Foundation

Power, A. Plöger, J. and Winkler, A. (2008) *Transforming cities across Europe: An interim report on problems and progress*, CASEreport 49, London: London School of Economics and Political Science

Prange, M. and Warsewa, G. (2000) *Arbeit und nachhaltige Stadtentwicklugn – das Handlungsfeld lokale Ökonomie*, Berlin: Social Science Research Center Berlin

Prognos (2002) *Wirkungsanalyse des Investitionssonderprogramms (ISP) des Landes Bremen*, Bremen: Evaluierungsgutachten, July

Putnam, R.D. (1993) *Making democracy work*, Princeton, NJ: Princeton University Press

Rabinovitch, J. (1992) 'Curitiba: towards sustainable urban development', *Environment and Urbanization*, October, vol. 4, pp 62–73

Ravetz, A. (1974) *Model estate: Planned housing at Quarry Hill*, Leeds: Croom Helm

RCEP (Royal Commission on Environmental Pollution) (2006) *The urban environment: Summary of the Royal Commission on Environmental Pollution's report*, London: RCEP

Reader, J. (2005) *Cities*, London: Vintage

Rees, W. (1999) 'Achieving sustainability: reform or transformation?', in D. Satterthwaite (ed) *The Earthscan reader in sustainable cities*, London: Earthscan

Rees, M. (2003) *Our final hour: A scientist's warning: How terror, error, and environmental disaster threaten humankind's future in this century – On earth and beyond*, London: Heinemann

Richardson, L. (2008) *DIY community action: Neighbourhood problems and community self-help*, Bristol: The Policy Press.

Roberts, P. and Sykes, H. (2000) *Urban regeneration: A handbook*, London: Sage Publications

Rodríguez, A. (2002) *Reinventar la ciudad: Milagros y espejismos de la revitalización urbana en Bilbao*, Lan Harremanak 6, pp 69–108

Rodríguez, A., Martínez, E. and Guenaga, G. (2001) 'Uneven redevelopment: new urban policies and socio-spatial fragmentation in Metropolitan Bilbao', *European Urban and Regional Studies*, vol 8, no 2, pp 161–78

Rogers, R. and Power, A. (2000) *Cities for a small country*, London: Faber & Faber.

Rosso, E. (2004) 'Torino: policies and actions at a metropolitan level', Paper given at the Conference 'La Gouvernance Metropolitaine: Recherche de coherence dans la compléxité', Montréal, 7–8 October, http://ejc.inrs-ucs.uquebec.ca/Torino.pdf

Royle, S. (2006) 'Belfast: foundations of the twentieth century', in F. Boal and S. Royle (eds) *Enduring city, Belfast in the twentieth century*, Belfast: Blackstaff

Saint-Étienne Métropole (2004) *Status Modifiés de la Communauté d'Agglomeration Saint-Étienne Métropole: Adoptés par le Conseil de Communauté du 12 juillet 2004, compte-tenu des amendements proposés en séance*, www.agglo-st-etienne.fr/

Sarti, F. (2007) Interview notes, 29 June, Astrid Winkler

Scenari Immobiliari (2007) *Il Mercato Immobiliari di Torino*, http://repository.demaniore.com/galleries/mercati_immobiliari/07_01-Ag_Demanio-St_TORINO-Gen07.pdf

Schumacher, E.F. (1993) *Small is beautiful: A study of economics as if people mattered*, London: Vintage

Science Alliance (2004) 'I3P Turin incubator wins best science incubator award', http://cordis.europa.eu/wire/index.cfm?fuseaction=article.Detail&DCtmpl=BI&RCN=2839

SDC (Sustainable Development Commission) (2003) *Mainstreaming sustainable regeneration: A call to action*. London: SDC

SDC (2010) *Sustainable development: The key to tackling health inequalities*, London: SDC

Se Loger (2007) 'Immobilier Saint-Étienne', www.seloger.com/prix-immobilier.htm

Seyd, P. (1990) 'Radical Sheffield: from socialism to entrepreneurialism', *Political Studies*, vol 38, no 2, pp 335–44

Sheffield City Council (1993) *Poverty and the poor in Sheffield 1993: The review of areas of poverty*, Sheffield: Sheffield Directorate of Planning and Economic Development, Sheffield City Council

Sheffield City Council (2004) *Closing the Gap: A framework for neighbourhood renewal*, www. sheffield.gov.uk/your-city-council/neighbourhood-renewal-and-partnership/closing-the-gap

Sheffield City Region (2007) *City Region Development Programme*, Sheffield: Sheffield City Region

Shirlow, P. and Murtagh, B. (2006) *Belfast: Segregation, violence and the city*, Contemporary Irish Studies Series, London: Pluto Press

Siemiatycki, M. (2005) 'Beyond moving people: excavating the motivations for investing in urban public transit infrastructure in Bilbao, Spain', *European Planning Studies Journal*, vol 13, no 1, pp 23–44

Silberman, C. (1965) *Crisis in black and white*, New York, NY: Random House; London: Jonathan Cape

Simmons, M. (2010) 'At risk: the sustainability of oil and gas', Presentation to AON Annual Energy Insurance Symposium, 14 January

Simon, D. (2008) 'There are two Americas', *Guardian Weekend* 6 September

Sirianni, C. and Friedland, L. (2001) *Civic innovation in America: Community empowerment, public policy and the movement for civic renewal*, Berkeley and Los Angeles, CA: University of California Press

Smyth, A. (2006) 'Belfast: return to Motown', in F. Boal and S. Royle (eds) *Enduring city: Belfast in the twentieth century*, Belfast: Blackstaff, pp 99–121

Stadt Leipzig/Office for Economic Development (2005) *Leipzig means business, 2005*

Stadt Leipzig/Department of Urban Development (2002) *Stadtentwicklungsplan Wohungsbau und Stadterneuerung*, Beiträge zur Stadtentwicklung 34

Stadt Leipzig/Department of Urban Development (2005a) *Monitoringbericht 2005: Kleinräumiges Monitoring des Stadtumbaus*

Stadt Leipzig/Department of Urban Development (2005b) *Stadterneuerung – Neue Freiräume im Leipziger Osten, Das Neue Leipzig*

Stadt Leipzig/Department of Urban Development (2005c) *Stadterneuerung – Wohnen im Eigentum selbstnutzer.de. Das Neue Leipzig*

Stadt Leipzig/Department of Urban Development (2005d) *Stadterneuerung und Stadtumbau in Leipzig – gestern-heute-morgen*, Beiträge zur Stadtentwicklung 43

Stadt Leipzig/Department of Urban Development (2005e) *The Olympic idea: Planning for Olympic Games in Leipzig 2012*, Beiträge zur Stadtentwicklung 45

Stadt Leipzig/Department of Urban Dvelopment (2006) *Monitoringbericht 2006: Kleinräumiges Monitoring des Stadtumbaus*

Stadtforum Leipzig (2006) *Aktuelle Fragen und Probleme der Leipziger*, Stadtentwicklung, no 01 (October)

Stenke, G. and Wilms, W. (2006) *Innovationsbericht 2006. Benchmarkanalysen zu FuE-Potenzialen und Innovation im Land Bremen*, BAW Studie, July

Stern, N. (2007) *The economics of climate change: The Stern review*, Cambridge: Cambridge University Press

Stern, N. (2009) *A blueprint for a safer planet: How to manage climate change and create a new era of progress and prosperity*, London: Bodley Head

Sterrett, K., Murtagh, B. and Millar, G. (2005) 'The social turn and urban development corporations', *Planning, Practice & Research*, vol 20, no 4 (November), pp 373–90

Strange, I. (1993) 'Public–private partnership and the politics of economic regeneration policy in Sheffield c 1985–1991', Unpublished doctoral thesis, Sheffield: University of Sheffield

Taubmann, W. (1999) 'Die Entwicklung der Bremischen Häfen unter dem globalen Wettbewerbsdruck', *Berichte zur deutschen Landeskunde*, vol 73, no 2–3, pp 291–314

Teaford, J. (1990) *The rough road to renaissance. Urban revitalization in America, 1940–1985*, Baltimore, MD: Johns Hopkins University Press

Thiollière, M. (2007) *Quelle ville voulons-nous?*, Paris: Autrement, coll. Acteurs de la société

Thompson, F.M.L. (ed) (1990) *The Cambridge social history of Britain, 1750–1950, vol 2: People and their environment*, Cambridge: Cambridge University Press

Titmuss, R.M. (1958) *Essays on 'The welfare state'*, London: George Allen & Unwin

Tomas, F. (1978) 'De l'Urbanisme sous la Veme République', in *Mélange en l'Honneur d'Étienne Fournial*, Saint-Étienne: Université Jean Monnet de Saint-Étienne

Torino Internazionale (1998) *Verso il Piano: Informazioni di base e primi indirizzi strategici*, Torino: Torino Internazionale

Torino Internazionale (2000) *Il Piano Strategico della Città*, Torino: Torino Internazionale

Torino Internazionale (2006) *Second strategic plan for Torino's Metropolitan Area: A brochure*, Torino: Torino Internazionale

Trans-European Network Executive Agency, http://tentea.ec.europa.eu/en/ten-t_projects/30_priority_projects/30_priority_projects.htm

UJM (Université Jean Monnet de Saint-Étienne) (2006a) *Compte rendu du 2e séminaire d'échange entres chercheurs et acteurs du projet urbain stéphanois: De la grande industrie au territoire de PME – le cas de l'agglomération stéphanoise*, Saint-Étienne: UJM

UJM (2006b) *Compte rendu du 3e séminaire d'échange entres chercheurs et acteurs du projet urbain stéphanois: L'intégration de l'agglomération stéphanoise dans l'aire métropolitaine lyonnaise*, Saint-Étienne: UJM

UJM (2007) Séminaire organisé dans le cadre de l'atelier de recherche 'Travail de mémoire, mémoires partagées', 12 January

UN (United Nations) (1992) *Rio declaration on environment and development*, www.un-documents.net/rio-dec.htm

UN (2009) Copenhagen Accord, http://unfccc.int/resource/docs/2009/cop15/eng/l07.pdf

UN Environment Programme (2006) World Conservation Monitoring Centre (UNEP-WCMC) 'Environment on the Edge 2005–06 lecture series', New Hall, Saint Edmunds College, Cambridge, UK

UN Habitat (2004) State of the World's Cities: Globalization and Urban Culture, www.unhabitat.org/content.asp?cid=3389&catid=7&typeid=46&subMenuId=0

UN Habitat (2008) *State of the world's cities: Harmonious cities*, www.unhabitat.org/content.asp?cid=5964&catid=7&typeid=46&subMenuId=0

Urban Audit (2009) *Urban Audit Analysis II: Issues, approach, results, May 2009*, RWI Essen, Difu, NEA, Policy Research and Consultancy

US Census Bureau, www.census.gov/

US Global Change Research Program (2009) *Global Climate Change Impacts in the United States: A State of Knowledge Report from the U.S. Global Change Research Program*. New York, NY: Cambridge University Press

Verney-Carron, N. (1999) *Le Ruban et L'Acier: Les élites économiques de la région stéphanoise au XIXème siècle (1815–1914)*, Saint-Étienne: Université de Saint-Étienne

Ville de Saint-Étienne (2005) *Convention ANRU Saint-Étienne*, http://i.ville.gouv.fr/divbib/doc/gpvstetienne.pdf

Vision of Britain (2007) 'Sheffield district: total population', www.visionofbritain.org.uk/data_theme_page.jsp?u_id=10076882&c_id=10001043&data_theme=T_POP

Warsewa, G. (2006) *The transformation of European Port Cities: Final report on the new EPOC Port City Audit*, IAW Forschungsbericht 11

Watts, H.D. (2004) *Discovering cities: Sheffield*, Sheffield: Geographical Association

Wauschkuhn, M. (1998) 'Strukturwandel und standortpolitscher Handlungsbedarf im Land Bremen', Materialien des Universitätsschwerpunktes *Internationale Wirtschaftsbeziehungen und Internationales Management*, vol 15, April

WCED (World Commission on Environment and Development) (1987) *Our common future* (Brundtland Report), Oxford: Oxford University Press

Whitford, J. and Enrietti, A. (2005) 'Surviving the fall of a king: the regional institutional implications of crisis at Fiat Auto', *International Journal of Urban and Regional Research*, vol 29, no 4, pp 771–95

Wiest, K. and Zischner, R. (2006) 'Upgrading old housing areas in East German inner cities: processes and development paths in Leipzig', *Deutsche Zeitschrift für Kommunalwissenschaften* (DfK), vol 45, no 1 (pdf version)

Wilkinson, R. and Pickett, K. (2009) *The spirit level: Why more equal societies almost always do better*, London: Allen Lane.

Wilms, W. (2003a) 'Technologiepark Universität Bremen. Ergebnisse der Unternehmensbefragung 2002', *BAW Monatsbericht*, no 8

Wilms, W. (2003b) *Technologiestadtteil Bremen. Stadtentwicklungsgutachten für einen qualitative durchstrukturierten Technologiestadtteil in der Freien Hansestadt Bremen*, BAW Institut für Wirtschaftsförderung, May

Wilson, W.J. (1987) *The truly disadvantaged: The inner city, the underclass, and public policy*, Chicago, IL: University of Chicago Press

Wilson, W.J. (1996) *When work disappears: The world of the new urban poor*, New York, NY: Alfred A. Knopf.

Wilson, W.J. (2009) *More than just race*, London: W.W. Norton & Co

Winkler, A. (2007a) *Sheffield City report*, CASEreport 45, London: London School of Economics and Political Science

Winkler, A. (2007b) *Torino City report*, CASEreport 41, London: London School of Economics and Political Science

Winkler, A. (2007c) *Saint-Étienne City report*, CASEreport 40, London: London School of Economics and Political Science

Wolman, H., Hill, E., Atkins, P., Blumenthal, P., Furdell, K. and Weiss, E. (2007) 'Explaining changes in central city population, income and housing affordability: a multi-method examination of the role of state and local public policy', Unpublished paper

WWF (2010) One Planet Living, www.oneplanetliving.org/index.html

Yarwood, J. (ed) (2006) *The Dublin–Belfast development corridor: Ireland's mega-city region?*, Aldershot: Ashgate

Yorkshire Forward (2006) *The regional economic strategy for Yorkshire and Humber 2006–2015*, www.yorkshire-forward.com/sites/default/files/documents/Regional%20Economic%20Strategy%202006-2015%20progress%20update.pdf

Young, H. (1990) *The Iron Lady: A biography of Margaret Thatcher*, New York, NY: Noonday Pr

Zubiri, I. (2000) *El sistema de concierto económico en el contexto de la Unión Europea*, Círculo de Empresarios Vascos

Index

Page references for figures are in *italics*; those for notes are followed by n and the note number, e.g. 375–6n35